SOMETHING ABOUT THE AUTHOR

SOMETHING ABOUT THE AUTHOR

Facts and Pictures about Authors
and Illustrators of Books for Young People

ANNE COMMIRE

VOLUME 21

GALE RESEARCH COMPANY
BOOK TOWER
DETROIT, MICHIGAN
48226

Editor: Anne Commire

Associate Editors: Agnes Garrett, Helga P. McCue

Assistant Editors: Dianne H. Anderson, Kathryn T. Floch, Mary F. Glahn,
D. Jayne Higo, Linda Shedd, Susan L. Stetler

Consultant: Adele Sarkissian

Sketchwriters: Rosemary DeAngelis Bridges, Mark Eisman, Barbara G. Farnan

Research Assistant: Kathleen Betsko

Editorial Assistants: Lisa Bryon, Susan Pfanner, Elisa Ann Sawchuk

Production Supervisor: Nancy Nagy

Cover Design: Arthur Chartow

Special acknowledgment is due to the members of the *Contemporary Authors* staff
who assisted in the preparation of this volume.

Also Published by Gale

CONTEMPORARY AUTHORS

*A Bio-Bibliographical Guide to Current Writers in
Fiction, General Nonfiction, Poetry, Journalism,
Drama, Motion Pictures, Television,
and Other Fields*

(Now Covers More Than 60,000 Authors)

Library of Congress Catalog Card Number 72-27107

ISBN 0-8103-0093-1

Table of Contents

Introduction vii   Acknowledgments xi
Forthcoming Authors ix   Illustrations Index 215
Author Index 227

v

Introduction

Beginning with Volume 15, the time span covered by *Something about the Author* was broadened to include major children's writers who died before 1961, which was the former cut-off point for writers covered in this series. This change will make *SATA* even more helpful to its many thousands of student and professional users.

Authors who did not come within the scope of *SATA* have formerly been included in *Yesterday's Authors of Books for Children,* of which Gale has published two volumes.

It has been pointed out by users, however, that it is inconvenient to have a body of related materials broken up by an arbitrary criterion such as the date of a person's death. Also, some libraries are not able to afford both series, and are therefore denied access to material on some of the most important writers in the juvenile field.

It has been decided, therefore, to discontinue the *YABC* series, and to include in *SATA* at least the most outstanding among the older writers who had been selected for listing in *YABC*. Volumes 1 and 2 of *YABC* will be kept in print, and the listings in those two volumes will be included in the cumulative *SATA* index.

A Partial List of Authors and Illustrators
Who Will Appear in Forthcoming Volumes of
Something about the Author

Adrian, Mary
Ahlberg, Allan
Ahlberg, Janet
Ainsworth, William H.
Allard, Harry
Allen, Agnes B.
Allen, Jack
Ames, Mildred
Ashley, Bernard
Atwater, Richard
Ault, Phil
Ayme, Marcel
Bach, Alice H.
Baldwin, James
Ballantyne, Robert M.
Baskin, Leonard
Becker, May Lamberton
Bennett, Jay
Beim, Jerrold
Beim, Lorraine
Bell, Robert S. W.
Bernheim, Evelyne
Bice, Clare
Binzen, Bill
Blyton, Enid
Blos, Joan W.
Boegehold, Betty
Bolognese, Don
Boning, Richard A.
Bonsall, Crosby Barbara
Bowden, Joan C.
Bowman, James C.
Boylston, Helen
Branscum, Robbie
Brewton, Sara W.
Bridgers, Sue Ellen
Briggs, Raymond
Bright, Robert
Brisley, Joyce Lankester
Broger, Achim
Bronin, Andrew
Bronson, Wilfrid
Brookins, Dana
Brooks, Charlotte K.
Bruna, Dick
Brunhoff, Jean de
Brunhoff, Laurent de
Burchard, Marshall

Burchard, S. H.
Burgess, Gelett
Burkert, Nancy Ekholm
Burstein, Chaya
Butler, Hal
Carey, M. V.
Carigiet, Alois
Carrick, Malcolm
Carroll, Ruth R.
Chandler, Caroline Augusta
Chesterton, G. K.
Christopher, John
Clarke, Joan B.
Cleaver, Bill
Cleaver, Elizabeth
Cleaver, Vera
Clements, Bruce
Cohen, Joel H.
Cohen, Miriam
Colby, Jean Poindexter
Cole, Joanna
Collodi, Carlo
Cooper, Elizabeth Keyser
Cox, Palmer
Craik, Dinah M.
Crews, Donald
Dabcovich, Lydia
Danziger, Paula
Dasent, Sir George Webbe
Dauer, Rosamund
D'Aulnoy, Marie-Catherine
DeGoscinny, Rene
Delessert, Etienne
Disney, Walt
Ditmars, Raymond
Donovan, John
Doty, Jean Slaughter
Dumas, Philippe
Eaton, Jeanette
Eckert, Allan W.
Elwood, Roger
Erickson, Russell E.
Ernst, Kathryn F.
Erwin, Betty K.
Etter, Les
Everett-Green, Evelyn
Fabre, Jean Henri
Falkner, John Meade

Falls, C. B.
Farber, Norma
Farmer, Penelope
Fischer, Hans Erich
Flory, Jane Trescott
Forest, Antonia
Foster, Marian Curtis
Freeman, Barbara C.
Freschet, Berniece
Fujikawa, Gyo
Gackenbach, Dick
Gans, Roma
Gardam, Jane
Gardner, John C.
Gatty, Margaret
Gauch, Patricia L.
Gault, Clare
Gault, Frank
Gelman, Rita G.
Gemme, Leila Boyle
Giovanni, Nikki
Goble, Dorothy
Goble, Paul
Gorey, Edward St. John
Gould, Chester
Grabianski, Janusz
Greene, Ellin
Gregor, Arthur S.
Gridley, Marion E.
Grimm, Jacob
Grimm, Wilhelm
Gross, Ruth B.
Gruelle, Johnny
Gutman, Bill
Gwynne, Fred
Halacy, Daniel S., Jr.
Haley, Gail E.
Hale, Lucretia P.
Hayes, Geoffrey R.
Hazen, Barbara S.
Heide, Florence Parry
Hentoff, Nat
Henty, George Alfred
Hicks, Clifford B.
Highwater, Jamake
Hirshberg, Albert S.
Hoban, Lillian
Hoban, Tana

Hood, Thomas
Housman, Laurence
Hughes, Ted
Hunt, Clara Whitehill
Ingelow, Jean
Isadora, Rachel
Jacobs, Joseph
Jacques, Robin
Jameson, Cynthia
Jeschke, Susan
Jewell, Nancy
Johnston, Norma
Jones, Hettie
Judson, Clara Ingram
Kahl, Virginia
Kahn, Joan
Kalan, Robert
Kantrowitz, Mildred
Keith, Eros
Kemp, Gene
Kennedy, Richard
Kent, Jack
Kerr, Judith
Kessler, Ethel
Ketcham, Hank
Klein, Aaron E.
Knotts, Howard
Koehn, Ilse
Kotzwinkle, William
Kraske, Robert
Leach, Maria
Leckie, Robert
Levoy, Myron
Levy, Elizabeth
Lewis, Naomi
Lines, Kathleen
Livermore, Elaine
Lowry, Lois
Lubin, Leonard
Macaulay, David
MacDonald, George
MacGregor, Ellen
MacKinstry, Elizabeth A.
Mark, Jan
Marryat, Frederick
Mazer, Norma Fox
McKee, David
McKillip, Patricia A.
McNaught, Harry
McPhail, David
Mendoza, George
Milgrom, Harry
Miller, Edna
Molesworth, Maria L.
Molly, Anne S.
Momaday, N. Scott
Moore, Lilian
Moore, Patrick

Morgenroth, Barbara
Moskin, Marietta
Murphy, Shirley Rousseau
Myers, Elisabeth P.
Myers, Walter Dean
Nordhoff, Charles
Oakley, Graham
O'Brien, Robert C.
O'Hanlon, Jacklyn
Orr, Frank
Orton, Helen Fuller
Overbeck, Cynthia
Packard, Edward
Paulsen, Gary
Peake, Mervyn
Pearson, Susan
Perkins, Lucy Fitch
Perrault, Charles
Plotz, Helen
Pogany, Willy
Pope, Elizabeth M.
Porter, Eleanor Hodgman
Poulsson, Emilie
Prather, Ray
Prelutsky, Jack
Pursell, Margaret S.
Pursell, Thomas F.
Pyle, Katharine
Rae, Gwynedd
Ransome, Arthur
Raphael, Elaine
Rawls, Wilson
Rayner, Mary
Rawls, Wilson
Rees, David
Reid, Mayne
Reynolds, Marjorie
Ribbons, Ian
Richler, Mordecai
Roberts, Elizabeth Madox
Rock, Gail
Rockwell, Anne
Rockwell, Harlow
Rockwell, Norman
Rose, Elizabeth
Rose, Gerald
Ross, Diana
Ross, Frank, Jr.
Ross, Wilda
Roy, Cal
Ruskin, John
Sabin, Francene
Sabin, Louis
Salten, Felix
Schick, Alice
Schneider, Leo
Schoonover, Frank
Schulman, Janet

Seaman, Augusta
Sendak, Jack
Sewall, Marcia
Sewell, Anna
Sewell, Helen
Shapiro, Milton J.
Shearer, John
Silverstein, Shel
Simon, Hilda
Smith, Doris Buchanan
Steiner, Charlotte
Stevens, Leonard A.
Stevenson, James
Stong, Phil
Sutton, Felix
Svend, Otto S.
Tallon, Robert
Taylor, Ann
Taylor, Jane
Taylor, Mark
Tenniel, Sir John
Todd, Ruthven
Tomalin, Ruth
Tomes, Margot
Tripp, Wallace
Tunis, John R.
Turska, Krystyna
Van Iterson, S. R.
Varga, Judy
Villiard, Paul
Waber, Bernard
Wagner, Jenny
Walters, Hugh
Watson, Nancy D.
Watts, Franklin
Welber, Robert
Welles, Winifred
Wellman, Alice
Westall, Robert
Wild, Jocelyn
Wild, Robin
Wilde, Oscar
Willard, Nancy
William-Ellis, Amabel
Wilson, Gahan
Windsor, Patricia
Winn, Marie
Winterfeld, Henry
Wolde, Gunilla
Wolf, Bernard
Wolitzer, Hilma
Wong, Herbert H.
Wood, Phyllis Anderson
Wyss, Johann David
Yeoman, John
Yonge, Charlotte M.
Zei, Alki
Zollinger, Gulielma

In the interest of making *Something about the Author* as responsive as possible to the needs of its readers, the editor welcomes your suggestions for additional authors and illustrators to be included in the series.

GRATEFUL ACKNOWLEDGMENT

is made to the following publishers, authors, and artists,
for their kind permission to reproduce copyrighted material.

ABELARD-SCHUMAN. Illustration by Lili Cassel from *Riddles of Many Lands* by Carl Withers and Sula Benet. Copyright 1956 by Carl Withers and Sula Benet. Reprinted by permission of Abelard-Schuman, a division of Harper & Row, Publishers.

HARRY N. ABRAMS, INC. Sidelight excerpts from *America's Great Illustrators* by Susan E. Meyer. Copyright © 1978 by Harry N. Abrams. Reprinted by permission of Harry N. Abrams, Inc.

ADDISON-WESLEY PUBLISHING CO., INC. Illustration by Will Winslow from *Benvenuto* by Seymour Reit. Text copyright © 1974 by Seymour Reit. Illustrations copyright © 1974 by Will Winslow./ Sidelight excerpts and illustration by Margot Zemach from *Self-Portrait: Margot Zemach* by Margot Zemach. Text and illustrations copyright © 1978 by Margot Zemach. All reprinted by permission of Addison-Wesley Publishing Co., Inc.

ATHENEUM PUBLISHERS. Illustration by A. Delaney from *The Secret of the Strawbridge Place* by Helen Pierce Jacob. Copyright © 1976 by Helen Pierce Jacob./ Drawing by Gabriele Margules from *Out of the Ark: An Anthology of Animal Verse,* compiled by Gwendolyn Reed. Copyright © 1968 by Gwendolyn Reed./ Photograph from *I Saw You from Afar* by Carol Morse Perkins and Marlin Perkins. Copyright © 1965 by Carol Morse Perkins and Marlin Perkins./ Illustration by Ruth Sanderson from *Don't Hurt Laurie* by Willo Davis Roberts. Copyright © 1977 by Willo Davis Roberts./ Illustration by Joan Sandin from *A Trainful of Strangers* by Eleanor Hull. Copyright © 1968 by Eleanor Hull. All reprinted by permission of Atheneum Publishers.

BARRIE & JENKINS LTD. Sidelight excerpts and photographs from *Jules Verne* by Kenneth Allott. Copyright © 1973 by Miriam Allott. Reprinted by permission of Barrie & Jenkins Ltd.

BILLBOARD PUBLICATIONS, INC. Photo by Robert F. Conneen from "Howard Chandler Christy" by Susan E. Meyer, May, 1978 in *American Artist.* Reprinted by Billboard Publications, Inc.

THE BOBBS-MERRILL CO., INC. Illustration by Howard Chandler Christy from *The Courtship of Miles Standish* by Henry Wadsworth Longfellow. Copyright 1858 by Henry Wadsworth Longfellow. Copyright 1886 by Ernest W. Longfellow. Copyright 1883 and 1888 by Houghton Mifflin Co. Copyright 1903 by The Bobbs-Merrill Co./ Illustrations by Howard Chandler Christy from *James Whitcomb Riley's Complete Works.* Copyright 1883, 1885, 1887, 1888, 1890, 1891, 1892, 1893, 1894, 1896, 1897, 1898, 1899, 1900, 1901, 1902, 1903, 1904, 1905, 1906, 1907, 1908, 1909, 1910, 1911, 1912, 1913, 1916 by James Whitcomb Riley./ Illustration by Howard Chandler Christy from *Out to Old Aunt Mary's* by James Whitcomb Riley. Copyright 1887, 1898, 1904 by James Whitcomb Riley. Copyright 1904 by The Bobbs-Merrill Co. All reprinted by permission of The Bobbs-Merrill Co., Inc.

BRADBURY PRESS, INC. Jacket illustration by Bernard Colonna from *All the Children Were Sent Away* by Sheila Garrigue. Reprinted by permission of Bradbury Press, Inc.

CHAPMAN & HALL LTD. Illustration by Phiz from *Barnaby Rudge: A Tale of the Riots of Eighty* by Charles Dickens./ Sidelight excerpts from *Life and Labours of Hablot Knight Browne "Phiz"* by David C. Thomson./ Illustration by Phiz from *The Old Curiosity Shop* by Charles Dickens./ Illustration by Phiz from *The Posthumous Papers of the Pickwick Club* by Charles Dickens./ Illustration by Phiz from *A Tale of Two Cities* by Charles Dickens. All reprinted by permission of Chapman & Hall Ltd.

CHATTO & WINDUS LTD. Illustration by Quentin Blake from *Around the World in Eighty*

Days by Jules Verne. Translation and abridgment copyright © 1966 by John Webber. Reprinted by permission of Chatto & Windus Ltd.

CHILDRENS PRESS. Illustration by Charles Payzant from *Children of Hong Kong* by Terry Shannon. Copyright © 1975 by Terry Shannon. Reprinted by permission of Childrens Press.

COLLIER-MACMILLAN PUBLISHERS LTD. Illustration by Charles Mikolaycak from *The Cobbler's Reward* by Barbara Reid and Ewa Reid. Copyright © 1978 by Barbara Reid and Ewa Reid. Copyright © 1978 by Charles Mikolaycak. Reprinted by permission of Collier-Macmillan Publishers, a division of Cassell & Collier Macmillan Publishers Ltd.

WILLIAM COLLINS PUBLISHERS, INC. Illustration by Ruth Orbach from *Please Send a Panda* by Ruth Orbach. Copyright © 1978 by Ruth Orbach. Reprinted by permission of William Collins Publishers, Inc.

CONSTABLE & CO. LTD. Sidelight excerpts from *Flora Shaw* by C. Moberly Bell. Reprinted by permission of Constable & Co. Ltd.

COWARD, McCANN & GEOGHEGAN, INC. Sidelight excerpts from *Jules Verne* by Marguerite Allotte de la Fuÿe (translated from the French by Erik de Mauny). Copyright 1956 by La Librairie Hachette. Reprinted by permission of Coward, McCann & Geoghegan, Inc.

THE CROSSING PRESS. Illustration by Robert Katona from *Walk When the Moon Is Full* by Frances Hamerstrom. Copyright © 1975 by Frances Hamerstrom. Reprinted by permission of The Crossing Press.

CROWN PUBLISHERS, INC. Sidelight excerpts from *Everett Shinn, 1876-1953: A Figure in His Time* by Edith De Shazo. Reprinted by permission of Crown Publishers, Inc.

ANDRÉ DEUTSCH LTD. Illustration by Faith Jaques from *The King's Birthday Cake* by John Cunliffe. Copyright © 1973 by John Cunliffe and Faith Jaques. Reprinted by permission of André Deutsch Ltd.

DODD, MEAD & CO. Illustration by William Moyers from *Horace Higby and the Scientific Pitch* by William Heuman. Copyright © 1968 by William Heuman./ Photograph from *Wonders of the World of Shells* by Morris K. Jacobson and William K. Emerson. Copyright © 1971 by Morris K. Jacobson and William K. Emerson./ Illustration by Jessie Willcox Smith from *Dream Blocks* by Aileen C. Higgins./ Illustration by Jessie Willcox Smith from *The Now-A-Days Fairy Book* by Anna Alice Chapin./ Illustration by Jessie Willcox Smith from *The Little Mother Goose* by Jessie Willcox Smith./ Illustration by Mead Schaeffer from *Moby Dick; or, The White Whale* by Herman Melville. Copyright 1923 by Dodd, Mead & Co. All reprinted by permission of Dodd, Mead & Co.

DOUBLEDAY & CO., INC. Sidelight excerpts from *This Is Where I Came In: The Impromptu Confessions of Edward Anthony* by Edward Anthony. Copyright © 1960 by Edward Anthony./ Sidelight excerpts from *Hans Brinker* by Mary Mapes Dodge./ Illustration by Carroll Lane Fenton and Mildred Adams Fenton from *The Fossil Book* by Carroll Lane Fenton and Mildred Adams Fenton. Copyright © 1958 by Carroll Lane Fenton and Mildred Adams Fenton./ Sidelight excerpts from *Writing Books for Boys and Girls*, edited by Helen Ferris./ Illustration by W. H. D. Koerner from *The Leopard Woman* by Stewart Edward White. Copyright 1916 by Doubleday, Page & Co./ Illustration by Everett Shinn from *Rip Van Winkle* by Washington Irving. Copyright 1939 by Garden City Publishing Co., Inc./ Photograph by Dare Wright from *Edith and Midnight* by Dare Wright. Copyright © 1978 by Dare Wright. All reprinted by permission of Doubleday & Co., Inc.

DOVER PUBLICATIONS, INC. Picture by Valery Carrick from *Nursery Rhymes from Many Lands,* translated by Rose Fyleman. Reprinted by permission of Dover Publications, Inc.

WM. B. EERDMANS PUBLISHING CO. Illustration by Reynold H. Weidenear from *Bird Life in Wington* by J. Calvin Reid. Copyright 1948 by Wm. B. Eerdmans Publishing Co. Copyright renewed © 1976 by John Calvin Reid. Reprinted by permission of Wm. B. Eerdmans Publishing Co.

ELSEVIER-DUTTON PUBLISHING CO., INC. Illustration by Jessie Willcox Smith from *Bugs and Wings and Other Things* by Annie W. Franchot. Copyright 1918 by E. P. Dutton & Co./ Sidelight excerpts from *You, Your Children, and War* by Dorothy W. Baruch. Copyright 1942, 1970 by Dorothy W. Baruch. Both reprinted by permission of Elsevier-Dutton Publishing Co., Inc., division of the American Elsevier Publishers, Inc.

EXPOSITION PRESS, INC. Sidelight excerpts from *The Immortal Eight* by Bernard B. Perlman. Reprinted by permission of Exposition Press, Inc.

EYRE & SPOTTISWOODE (PUBLISHER) LTD. Picture by Jean de Bosschère from *The Fairies Up to Date,* verses by Edward and Joseph Anthony. Reprinted by permission of Eyre & Spottiswoode (Publisher) Ltd.

FARRAR, STRAUS & GIROUX, INC. Illustration by Richard Cuffari from *The Lion and the Rose* by Rosemary Weir. Copyright © 1970 by Rosemary Weir./ Illustration by William Geldart from *The Fox at Drummers' Darkness* by Joyce Stranger. Text copyright © 1976 by Joyce Stranger Ltd. Illustrations copyright © by J. M. Dent & Sons Ltd. Both reprinted by permission of Farrar, Straus & Giroux, Inc.

FOUR WINDS PRESS. Illustration by Rosalind Fry from *Three Giant Stories,* as told by Lesley Conger. Text copyright © 1968 by Lesley Conger. Illustrations copyright © 1968 by Scholastic Magazines, Inc./ Illustration by Imero Gobbato from *Tops and Bottoms,* adapted from *A Folk Tale* by Lesley Conger. Text copyright © 1970 by Lesley Conger. Illustrations copyright © 1970 by Imero Gobbato. Both reprinted by permission of Four Winds Press, a division of Scholastic Book Services.

FRANK BOOK CORP. Illustration by Alex Brychta from *Numbers 1 to 10 and Back Again* by Alex Brychta. Copyright © 1977 by Alex Brychta. Reprinted by permission of Frank Book Corp.

FRANKLIN PUBLISHING CO. Illustration by Carol A. Hoover from *Freddie* by Charlotte Isham. Copyright © 1975 by Charlotte H. Isham. Reprinted by permission of Franklin Publishing Co.

THE FRASER GALLERY LTD. Illustration by Phiz from *The Personal History of David Copperfield* by Charles Dickens. Reprinted by permission of The Fraser Gallery Ltd.

FUNK & WAGNALLS, INC. Illustration by Eric Sloane from *Mr. Daniels and the Grange* by Eric Sloane and Edward Anthony. Copyright © 1968 by Eric Sloane and Edward Anthony. Reprinted by permission of Funk & Wagnalls, Inc.

GARRARD PUBLISHING CO. Illustration by Cary from *Isaac Newton: Scientific Genius* by Pearle and Harry Schultz. Copyright © 1972 by Pearle Henriksen Schultz and Harry P. Schultz. Reprinted by permission of Garrard Publishing Co.

GOLDEN PRESS. Illustration by Roberto Innocenti from *Sails, Rails and Wings* by Seymour Reit. Copyright © 1978 by Western Publishing Co., Inc./ Illustration by Su Zan Noguchi Swain from *The Rocky Mountains* by Herbert S. Zim. Copyright © 1964 by Western Publishing Co., Inc. Both reprinted by permission of Golden Press, a division of Western Publishing Co., Inc.

G. K. HALL & CO. Illustration by Charles Shaw from *Footsy* by Ernie Rydberg. Text copyright © 1973 by Ernie Rydberg. Illustrations copyright © 1973 by Charles Shaw. Reprinted by permission of G. K. Hall & Co.

HARCOURT BRACE JOVANOVICH, INC. Illustration by Feodor Rojankovsky from *Frog Went A-Courtin'* by John Langstaff. Copyright 1955 by John M. Langstaff and Feodor Rojankovsky./ Illustrations by Richard Bennett from *It's Perfectly True and Other Stories* by Hans Christian Andersen. Copyright © 1966 by Mary Rehan. All reprinted by permission of Harcourt Brace Jovanovich, Inc.

HARPER & ROW, PUBLISHERS, INC. Illustration by W. H. D. Koerner from *Keeping Up with Lizzie* by Irving Bacheller. Copyright 1910, 1911 by Harper & Bros./ Picture by Robert Lopshire from *Big Max* by Kin Platt. Pictures copyright © 1965 by Robert Lopshire./ Illustration by Geraldine Spence from *The Nothing Place* by Eleanor Spence. Copyright © 1972, 1973 by Eleanor Spence. All reprinted by permission of Harper & Row, Publishers, Inc.

HARVEY HOUSE, PUBLISHERS. Illustration by Ray Abel from *Cabeza de Vaca, Defender of the Indians* by Gertrude Kerman. Text copyright © 1974 by Gertrude Lerner Kerman. Illustrations copyright © 1974 by Harvey House, Inc. Reprinted by permission of Harvey House, Publishers.

WILLIAM HEINEMANN, LTD. Illustration by Faith Jaques from *The Magical Cockatoo* by Margery Sharp. Text copyright © 1974 by Vigocrafts Ltd. Illustrations copyright © by William Heinemann, Ltd. Reprinted by permission of William Heinemann, Ltd.

THE HERITAGE PRESS. Illustration by John Groth from "The Last Leaf," in *The Stories of O. Henry.* Copyright 1907, 1908, 1909, 1910 by Doubleday & Co., Inc. Reprinted by permission of The Heritage Press.

HODDER & STOUGHTON LTD. Illustration by W. H. D. Koerner from *The Leopard Woman* by Stewart Edward White. Copyright 1916 by Doubleday, Page & Co. Reprinted by permission of Hodder & Stoughton Ltd.

HOLT, RINEHART & WINSTON. Illustration by William Bock from *The Vinlander's Saga* by Barbara Schiller. Text copyright © 1966 by Barbara Schiller. Illustrations copyright © 1966 by Holt, Rinehart & Winston, Inc./ Illustration by Everett Shinn from *The Happy Prince and Other Tales* by Oscar Wilde. Copyright 1940 by John C. Winston Co./ Illustration by Everett

Shinn from *The Night Before Christmas* by Clement Clarke Moore. Copyright 1942 by The John C. Winston Co. All reprinted by permission of Holt, Rinehart & Winston.

THE HORN BOOK, INC. Sidelight excerpts from an article, "You'll Find It in Ireland" by Richard Bennett, March, 1941 in the *Horn Book* Magazine. Copyright 1941 by The Horn Book, Inc./ Sidelight excerpts from *Caldecott Medal Books: 1938-1957,* edited by Bertha M. Miller and Elinor W. Field. Copyright © 1957 by The Horn Book, Inc./ Sidelight excerpts from *Illustrators of Children's Books: 1957-1966,* compiled by Lee Kingman and others. Copyright © 1968 by The Horn Book, Inc./ Sidelight excerpts from an article, "Margot Zemach" by A. L. Lloyd, August, 1974 in *Horn Book* Magazine. Copyright © 1974 by The Horn Book, Inc./ All reprinted by permission of The Horn Book, Inc.

HOUGHTON MIFFLIN CO. Picture by Marjorie Flack from *The Country Bunny and the Little Gold Shoes* by Du Bose Heyward. Copyright 1939 by Du Bose Heyward and Marjorie Flack./ Picture by John Vernon Lord from *The Giant Jam Sandwich,* story by John Vernon Lord, verses by Janet Burroway. Copyright © 1972 by John Vernon Lord./ Illustration by Jessie Willcox Smith from *'Twas the Night Before Christmas* by Clement C. Moore. Copyright 1912 by Houghton Mifflin Co./ Illustration by Alister Macdonald from *The Tale of a Shipwreck* by James Norman Hall. Copyright 1934 by James Norman Hall. All reprinted by permission of Houghton Mifflin Co.

ALFRED A. KNOPF, INC. Woodcut by Richard Bennett from *The Saginaw Paul Bunyan* by James Stevens. Copyright 1932 by Alfred A. Knopf, Inc./ Illustration by Ted Lewin from *Hub* by Robert Newton Peck. Text copyright © 1979 by Robert Newton Peck. Illustrations copyright © 1979 by Alfred A. Knopf, Inc./ Illustration by Ted Lewin from *Soup for President* by Robert Newton Peck. Text copyright © 1978 by Robert Newton Peck. Illustrations copyright © 1978 by Alfred A. Knopf, Inc. All reprinted by permission of Alfred A. Knopf, Inc., a division of Random House, Inc.

LERNER PUBLICATIONS CO. Illustration by Joanne Isaac from *Amanda* by Joanne Isaac. Copyright © 1968 by Lerner Publications Co. Reprinted by permission of Lerner Publications Co.

J. B. LIPPINCOTT CO. Illustration by Jessie Willcox Smith from *The Book of the Child* by Mabel Humphrey./ Illustration by Allan Eitzen from *The Luck of the Golden Cross* by Kathryn Vinson. Copyright © 1960 by Kathryn Vinson. Both reprinted by permission of J. B. Lippincott Co.

LIPPINCOTT & CROWELL, PUBLISHERS. Illustration by Rosalind Fry from *A Baby Starts to Grow* by Paul Showers. Copyright © 1969 by Paul Showers./ Illustration by Paul Galdone from *Follow Your Nose* by Paul Showers. Text copyright © 1963 by Paul Showers. Illustrations copyright © 1963 by Paul Galdone./ Etching by John Ross and Clare Romano Ross from *Poems of Henry Wadsworth Longfellow,* selected by Edmund Fuller. Copyright © 1967 by Edmund Fuller. Illustrations copyright © 1967 by John Ross and Clare Romano Ross./ Sidelight excerpts and photograph from *Jessie Willcox Smith* by S. Michael Schnessel. All reprinted by permission of Lippincott & Crowell, Publishers, a division of J. B. Lippincott Co.

LITTLE, BROWN & CO. Illustration by N. C. Wyeth from *The Bounty Trilogy* by Charles Nordhoff and James Norman Hall. Copyright 1932, 1933, 1934, 1936 by Charles Nordhoff and James Norman Hall. Copyright 1940 by Little, Brown & Co. Copyright renewed 1960, 1961, 1962./ Sidelight excerpts from *My Island Home* by James Hall. Copyright 1952 by James Norman Hall./ Illustration by Jessie Willcox Smith from *Little Women* by Louisa M. Alcott. Copyright 1896, 1910, 1911 by J. S. P. Alcott. Copyright 1915 by Little, Brown & Co./ Illustration by Warren Chappell from *Doctor Dogbody's Leg* by James Norman Hall. Copyright 1937, 1938, 1939, 1940 by James Norman Hall. All reprinted by permission of Little, Brown & Co.

LOTHROP, LEE & SHEPARD CO. Illustration by Rita Flodén Leydon from *Slapdash Sewing* by Carol Barkin and Elizabeth James. Copyright © 1975 by Carol Barkin and Elizabeth James./ Illustration from *In Other Words: A Beginning Thesaurus* by Andrew Schiller. Copyright © 1977, 1968 by Scott Foresman and Co. Both reprinted by permission of Lothrop, Lee & Shepard Co., a division of William Morrow & Co., Inc.

MACMILLAN, INC. Illustration by Richard Bennett from *Where the Winds Never Blew and the Cocks Never Crew* by Padraic Colum. Copyright 1940 by Padraic Colum./ Illustration by Howard Chandler Christy from *Dorothy Vernon of Haddon Hall* by Charles Major. Copyright 1902 by Macmillan Co./ Illustration by Chris Hammond from *The Parent's Assistant or Stories for Children* by Maria Edgeworth. Copyright 1897 by Macmillan Co., Ltd./ Illustration by John Groth from *A Christmas Carol* by Charles Dickens. Illustrations copyright © 1963 by Macmillan Co./ Illustration by Lisl Weil from *What Makes Me Feel This Way?* by Eda LeShan. Copyright © 1972 by Eda LeShan. Copyright © 1972 by Macmillan Publishing Co., Inc./ Illustration by Charles Mikolaycak from *The Cobbler's Reward* by Barbara Reid and Ewa

Reid. Copyright © 1978 by Barbara Reid and Ewa Reid. Copyright © 1978 by Charles Mikolaycak./ Illustration by Erick Ingraham from *Harry and Shellburt* by Dorothy O. Van Woerkom. Copyright © 1977 by Erick Ingraham. All reprinted by permission of Macmillan, Inc.

McGRAW-HILL, INC. Illustration by Lois Fisher from *How to Live with Your Teen-Ager* by Dr. Dorothy W. Baruch. Copyright 1953 by Dorothy W. Baruch./ Illustration by Linda Strauss Edwards from *The Sneaky Machine* by Marguerita Rudolph. Text copyright © 1974 by Marguerita Rudolph. Illustrations copyright © 1974 by Linda Strauss Edwards. Both reprinted by permission of McGraw-Hill, Inc.

DAVID McKAY CO., INC. Illustration by Donna R. Sabaka from *Big Fun to Grow Book* by Allan A. Swenson. Copyright © 1977 by Allan A. Swenson. Reprinted by permission of David McKay Co., Inc.

JULIAN MESSNER. Photograph by William M. Stephens from *Come with Me to the Edge of the Sea* by William M. Stephens. Copyright © 1972 by William M. Stephens. Reprinted by permission of Julian Messner, a division of Simon & Schuster, Inc.

HUMPHREY MILFORD LTD. Illustration by Phiz from *A Tale of Two Cities* by Charles Dickens. Reprinted by permission of Humphrey Milford Ltd.

WILLIAM MORROW & CO., INC. Illustration by Robert Hofsinde from *Indian Costumes* by Robert Hofsinde. Copyright © 1968 by Robert Hofsinde./ Illustration by Lydia Rosier from *Peacocks* by Lynne Martin. Text copyright © 1975 by Lynne Martin. Illustrations copyright © 1975 by Lydia Rosier./ Illustration by Terrence Fehr from *Underground Furnaces: The Story of Geothermal Energy* by Irene Kiefer. Text copyright © 1976 by Irene Kiefer. Illustrations copyright © 1976 by Terrence Fehr. All reprinted by permission of William Morrow & Co., Inc.

NORD-SÜD VERLAG. Illustration by David McKee from *Joseph, the Border Guard* by Kurt Baumann. Copyright © 1971 by Nord-Süd Verlag. Reprinted by permission of Nord-Süd Verlag.

OXFORD UNIVERSITY PRESS, INC. Illustration by Phiz from *A Tale of Two Cities* by Charles Dickens. Reprinted by permission of Oxford University Press, Inc.

PARENTS' MAGAZINE PRESS. Illustration by David McKee from *Joseph, the Border Guard* by Kurt Baumann. Copyright © 1971 by Nord-Süd Verlag. Reprinted by permission of Parents' Magazine Press.

PRAEGER PUBLISHERS, INC. Illustration from *India: A World in Transition* by Beatrice P. Lamb./ Photograph from *Babe Ruth: His Life and Legend* by Kal Wagenheim. Copyright © 1974 by Praeger Publishers, Inc. Both reprinted by permission of Praeger Publishers, Inc.

PRENTICE-HALL, INC. Illustration by Steve O'Neill from *Dinosaur Dos and Don'ts* by Jean Burt Polhamus. Copyright © 1975 by Jean Burt Polhamus and Steven O'Neill. Reprinted by permission of Prentice-Hall, Inc.

G. P. PUTNAM'S SONS. Illustration by Paul Frame from *Let's Go to a Stock Car Race* by Robert Hood. Copyright © 1974 by Robert E. Hood./ Illustration by Tom Huffman from *Ink, Ark., and All That* by Vernon Pizer. Copyright © 1976 by Vernon Pizer./ Jacket illustration by Barbara Higgins Bond from *Bob Gibson: Pitching Ace* by David Lipman and Ed Wilkes. Copyright © 1975 by David Lipman and Ed Wilkes. All reprinted by permission of G. P. Putnam's Sons.

RAND McNALLY & CO. Illustration by Milo Winter from *A Christmas Carol* by Charles Dickens. Copyright 1913 by Rand McNally & Co./ Illustration by Milo Winter from *Treasure Island* by Robert Louis Stevenson. Copyright 1915 by Rand McNally & Co./ Illustrations by Milo Winter from *Twenty Thousand Leagues Under the Sea* by Jules Verne. Copyright 1922 by Rand McNally & Co./ Illustration by Milo Winter from *A Wonder Book for Girls and Boys* by Nathaniel Hawthorne. Copyright 1913 by Rand McNally & Co./ Illustration by Mead Schaeffer from *The Adventures of Remi,* translated and arranged by Philip Schuyler Allen. Copyright 1925 by Rand McNally & Co. All reprinted by permission of Rand McNally & Co.

RANDOM HOUSE, INC. Illustration by John Polgreen from *The Look It Up Book of Space* by Ira M. Freeman. Copyright © 1969 by Random House, Inc./ Illustration by Mead Schaeffer from *The Man Without a Country* by Edward Everett Hale. Copyright 1940 by Random House, Inc. Both reprinted by permission of Random House, Inc.

CHARLES SCRIBNER'S SONS. Illustrations by Feodor Rojankovsky from *Cricket in a Thicket* by Aileen Fisher. Text copyright © 1963 by Aileen Fisher. Illustrations copyright © 1963 by Feodor Rojankovsky./ Illustration by Arnold Roth from *A Comick Book of Sports* by Arnold Roth. Copyright © 1974 by Arnold Roth./ Illustration by Francoise from *Chouchou* by Francoise. Copyright © 1958 by Charles Scribner's Sons./ Illustration by Francoise from

Jeanne-Marie at the Fair by Francoise. Copyright © 1959 by Charles Scribner's Sons./ Illustration by Jessie Willcox Smith from "North-West Passage," in *A Child's Garden of Verses* by Robert Louis Stevenson. Copyright 1905 by Charles Scribner's Sons./ Illustration by Stephen Walker from *The Drac* by Felice Holman and Nanine Valen. Copyright © 1975 by Felice Holman and Nanine Valen./ Illustration by N. C. Wyeth from *The Mysterious Island* by Jules Verne. Copyright 1920 by Charles Scribner's Sons./ Illustration by Donna Diamond from *The Boy Who Sang the Birds* by John Weston. Copyright © 1976 by John Weston. All reprinted by permission of Charles Scribner's Sons.

SIMON & SCHUSTER, INC. Sidelight excerpts from *Mary Mapes Dodge of St. Nicholas* by Alice Howard. Copyright 1943, © 1970 by Alice Barrett Howard. Reprinted by permission of Simon & Schuster, Inc.

STERLING PUBLISHING CO., INC. Illustration by Joyce Behr from *Biggest Riddle Book in the World* by Joseph Rosenbloom. Copyright © 1976 by Joseph Rosenbloom. Reprinted by permission of Sterling Publishing Co., Inc.

TAPLINGER PUBLISHING CO., INC. Sidelight excerpts from *Jules Verne* by Jean Jules Verne (translated from the French by Roger Greaves). English translation copyright © 1976 by Taplinger Co., Inc. Reprinted by permission of Taplinger Publishing Co., Inc.

TYNDALE HOUSE PUBLISHERS. Illustration by Joseph E. DeVelasco from *Ivan and the Secret in the Suitcase* by Myrna Grant. Copyright © 1975 by Tyndale House. Reprinted by permission of Tyndale House Publishers.

UNIVERSITY OF OKLAHOMA PRESS. Sidelight excerpts and photographs from *The World, the Work and the West of W. H. D. Koerner* by W. H. Hutchinson. Copyright © 1978 by University of Oklahoma Press. Reprinted by permission of University of Oklahoma Press.

THE VIKING PRESS. Illustration by Leo Politi from *Angelo the Naughty One* by Helen Garrett. Copyright © 1972 by Helen Garrett and Leo Politi./ Illustration by Richard Doyle from *In Fairy Land* by William Allingham. Both reprinted by permission of The Viking Press.

WALKER & CO. Illustration by Laura Lydecker from *Bee Tree and Other Stuff* by Robert Newton Peck. Text copyright © 1975 by Robert Newton Peck. Illustrations copyright © 1975 by Laura Lydecker. Reprinted by permission of Walker & Co.

FREDERICK WARNE & CO., INC. Photograph by William Vandivert from *Understanding Animals as Pets* by Rita Vandivert. Text copyright © 1975 by Rita Vandivert. Photographs copyright © 1975 by William Vandivert. Reprinted by permission of Frederick Warne & Co., Inc.

FRANKLIN WATTS, INC. Illustration by Yvette Santiago Banik from *Quick and Easy Housekeeping* by Rubie Saunders. Copyright © 1977 by Franklin Watts, Inc. Reprinted by permission of Franklin Watts, Inc.

WAVELAND PRESS. Illustration by Keo Felker Lazarus from *A Totem for Ti-Jacques* by Keo Felker Lazarus. Reprinted by permission of Waveland Press.

ALBERT WHITMAN & CO. Illustration by John and Lucy Hawkinson from *Little Boy Who Lives Up High* by John and Lucy Hawkinson. Copyright © 1967 by Albert Whitman & Co./ Illustration by George Armstrong from *The Pelican Mystery* by Ruth Hooker and Carole Smith. Text copyright © 1977 by Ruth Hooker and Carole Smith. Illustrations copyright © 1977 by Albert Whitman & Co. Both reprinted by permission of Albert Whitman & Co.

WORLD'S WORK LTD. Picture by Robert Lopshire from *Big Max* by Kin Platt. Pictures copyright © 1965 by Robert Lopshire./ Illustration by Feodor Rojankovsky from *Frog Went A-Courtin'* by John M. Langstaff. Copyright 1955 by John M. Langstaff and Feodor Rojankovsky./ Illustration by Erick Ingraham from *Harry and Shellburt* by Dorothy O. Van Woerkom. Copyright © 1977 by Erick Ingraham. All reprinted by permission of World's Work Ltd.

THE WRITER, INC. Sidelight excerpts from an article, "Dialect Does It," June, 1956 in *The Writer*. Reprinted by permission of The Writer, Inc.

YEARLING BOOKS. Illustration by Unada from *Ali Baba and the Forty Thieves and Nine Other Tales from the Arabian Nights,* retold by Ned Hoopes. Copyright © 1968 by Ned Hoopes. Copyright © 1968 by Dell Publishing Co., Inc. Reprinted by permission of Yearling Books.

Illustration by Paul Frame from *Let's Go to a Stock Car Race* by Robert Hood. Copyright © 1974 by Robert E. Hood. Reprinted by permission of Florence Alexander./ Sidelight excerpts from A Personal Collection from The Archives of Pennsylvania Academy of The Fine Arts. Reprinted by permission of The Archives of Pennsylvania Academy of The Fine Arts./

Photograph by Dare Wright from *Edith and Midnight* by Dare Wright. Copyright © 1978 by Dare Wright. Reprinted by permission of Bill Berger Associates, Inc./ Sidelight excerpts from *In Search of Paradise* by Paul Briand, Jr. Copyright © by Paul Briand, Jr. Reprinted by permission of Paul Briand, Jr./ Photograph by Brown Brothers from *The American Heritage History of the American People* by Bernard A. Weisberger. Copyright © 1970, 1971 by American Heritage Publishing Co., Inc. Reprinted by permission of Brown Brothers./ Sidelight excerpts from *Books Are by People* by Lee Bennett Hopkins. Copyright © 1969 by Scholastic Magazines, Inc. Reprinted by permission of Curtis Brown Ltd./ Sidelight excerpts from an article, "Every Picture Tells a Story" by Faith Jaques in *Federation of Children's Book Groups Yearbook, 1973-1974*. Copyright © by Faith Jaques. Reprinted by permission of Faith Jaques./ Sidelight excerpts from *The World, the Work and the West of W. H. D. Koerner* by W. H. Hutchinson. Copyright © 1978 by University of Oklahoma Press. Reprinted by permission of W. H. D. Koerner./ Sidelight excerpts from *This Is Where I Came In: The Impromptu Confessions of Edward Anthony* by Edward Anthony. Copyright © 1960 by Edward Anthony. Reprinted by permission of Paul R. Reynolds, Inc./ Sidelight excerpts from an article, "Who's Who—And Why," August 22, 1925 in the *Saturday Evening Post*. Reprinted by permission of the *Saturday Evening Post*./ Sidelight excerpts from an article, "Off the Cuff" by Lesley Conger in *The Writer*. Copyright © 1977 by Shirley Suttles. Reprinted by permission of Shirley Suttles./ Sidelight excerpts from *Introduction to Favorite Poems, Old and New*, edited by Helen Ferris. Copyright © 1957 by Helen Ferris Tibbets. Reprinted by permission of Anne Ferris Tenney./ Illustration by Vera Bock from "The Blind Beggar's Daughter of Bednall-Green," in *Loves Enchantment*, collected by Helen Ferris. Copyright 1944 by Doubleday, Doran & Co., Inc. Reprinted by permission of Anne Ferris Tenney./ Illustration by Leonard Weisgard from *Favorite Poems, Old and New*, edited by Helen Ferris. Copyright © 1957 by Helen Ferris Tibbets. Reprinted by permission of Leonard Weisgard.

PHOTOGRAPH CREDITS

Rose Fyleman: Howard and Joan Coster; Ned Hoopes: Steve Friedman; Vernon Pizer: Harris and Ewing; Kin Platt: Jerry Eisenberg; Jean Burt Polhamus: Portrait World; James Norman Schmidt: Peter Olwiler; Dorothy Van Woerkom: Bel Air Photo.

SOMETHING ABOUT THE AUTHOR

ANTHONY, Edward 1895-1971

PERSONAL: Born August 4, 1895, in New York City; died August 16, 1971 in Gloucester, Mass.

CAREER: Author, newspaperman, and publisher. Member of the staff of the *Bridgeport Herald* and the *New York Herald;* became publisher of *Woman's Home Companion,* 1943, and *Collier's,* 1949. In 1928, he was publicity director of Herbert Hoover's presidential campaign.

WRITINGS; Merry-Go-Roundelays, Century, 1921; (for children) *The Pussycat Princess,* Century, 1922; (with Joseph Anthony) *The Fairies Up-to-Date* (illustrated by Jean de Bosschere), Little, Brown, 1923; *"Razzberry!",* Holt, 1924; (editor) *How to Get Rid of a Woman* (illustrated by George de Zayas), Bobbs-Merrill, 1928; (with Frank Buck) *Bring 'Em Back Alive,* Simon & Schuster, 1930; (with F. Buck) *Wild Cargo,* Simon & Schuster, 1932; (with Clyde Beatty) *The Big Cage,* Century, 1933; (with Gordon B. Enders) *Nowhere Else in the World,* Farrar, Straus, 1935; (with Abel A. Schecter) *I Live on Air,* F. A. Stokes, 1941; *The Sex Refresher* (illustrated by George Price), Howell, Soskin, 1943; *Every Dog Has His Say* (poems; illustrated by Morgan Dennis), Watson-Guptill, 1947; (for children) *Oddity Land* (illustrated by Erik Blegvad), Doubleday, 1957; *This Is Where I Came in: The Impromptu Confessions of Edward Anthony* (autobiography), Doubleday, 1960; *O Rare Don Marquis: A Biography,* Doubleday, 1962; (with C. Beatty) *Facing the Big Cats,* Doubleday, 1965; (with Henry Trefflich) *Jungle for Sale,* Hawthorn Books, 1967; (with Eric Sloane) *Mr. Daniels and The Grange,* Funk & Wagnalls, 1968; *Astrology and Sexual Compatibility,* Essandess, 1971.

SIDELIGHTS: **August 4, 1895.** Born in New York City, Anthony's childhood was spent in a lower class Jewish-Irish section of New York City in a tenement building. "My father's favorite theme was that he was lucky to be in the United States. He had come to this country from a small Hungarian town outside of Budapest as a youngster—I never could learn the exact age but I imagine it was ten or twelve—and he was full of stories about oppression in Austria-Hungary, which was then the name of his homeland. He had been brought over by an uncle who had told him countless tales about the lack of any future for him in his native land. No, his uncle did not think America's streets were paved with gold, but he did think it was the land of opportunity.

"In this country he met and married my mother whose parents had brought her as a tot to New York from a small town in Austria. Both were Jewish.

"My father was in the pleating business. Just how he got into it I don't know. . . . My father was known as Anthony the Pleater. He had concentrated on his first name which is so common among Hungarians—Anthony. Not many years afterward he sought and secured court permission to adopt Anthony as his official last name. He said it was merely a matter of convenience. He was tired of having people misspell and mispronounce his name. . . . [Edward Anthony, *This Is Where I Came In: The Impromptu Confessions of Edward Anthony,* Doubleday, 1960.[1]]

1905. After an encounter with a lady customer who refused to pay her bill, Anthony's father was sued. The gossip surrounding this incident became so malicious that the family moved to Harlem in New York City. The new neighborhood

EDWARD ANTHONY

proved no better than the old; Anthony soon became a member of one of the many neighborhood "gangs" common to this section of the city. "We moved to 120th Street and Madison. We had a ground-floor flat in a building that wasn't the worst kind of tenement although it didn't miss by much. . . .

"At that time the neighborhood was predominately Jewish and Irish. Some blocks were a mixture of each but in the main a street in that neighborhood would be either one or the other."[1]

1911. "At the conclusion of my junior year in high school, I took a summer job selling business-school courses to high-school students who did not plan to go to college. The sale— or attempted sale—was made through the parents.

"I found selling a lot of fun. It was a great thrill—almost indescribable as I look back upon it now—to make a sale, and I took the disappointments in stride. . . .

"On the whole I was pretty lucky as a business-course salesman. I sold enough courses to earn several hundred dollars that summer. (I received a small salary and what seemed a generous commission for each sale I made.)"[1]

Anthony decided to take the night school courses in his senior year of high school. "I took the shorthand and typewriting course, figuring that it would be helpful in connection with my secret ambition to become a newspaper reporter. But on graduation from high school I could find no one in the newspaper world who was interested in my services. I figured that if I could get any kind of job around a newspaper office— say, as copy boy—I'd get to know some newspaper people

who might eventually let me try my hand at some minor phase of news writing.

"I knew a copy boy on a New York newspaper and when he told me about his duties I felt I too was qualified. I was a pretty good sprinter and could be counted upon to get to the desk of the man yelling 'Co-peeee!' as fast as the next kid. I had other talents too, including a reasonably good memory, which meant that when one of the editors or reporters sent me out for a pack of Sweet Caps I would not return with Melachrinos or Murads. But I could not get a job on a newspaper despite these qualifications."[1]

The aspiring newspaper man had to content himself with various jobs outside of a newspaper office. At one time Anthony became a ghost writer for a party-giving bachelor, and later a secretary for a large company stenographic pool. "Life wasn't all work though. I had various ways of having fun. A friend who knew his way around at the Polo Grounds and served as turnstile attendant in exchange for admittance to the ball game showed me how to work out a similar deal and I saw the great New York Giants of John J. McGraw several times on that basis.

"I also haunted the New York Public Library and did a lot of miscellaneous reading there in the second-floor reading room which has always seemed to me one of the most fascinating places in the world.

"I also found it fun to 'supe' at the Metropolitan Opera House in New York. A supernumerary earned fifty cents and the right to hear the opera. There was no such luxury as a seat, of course; you were expected to find a place to stand or perch where you would not be in the way. Once I found myself roosting high up on some scaffolding in the wings. Below me I could see a friend in a similar vantage point and I couldn't help thinking how much excitement there would be if one of us happened to fall during the performance. I'm told that today's 'supes' are not permitted to practice this kind of monkey-roosting and I must admit that makes sense."[1]

1916-1918. During World War I, Anthony wrote the book and lyrics for a soldier show with the help of George M. Cohen and Victor Hugo. "During World War I, I had about as dull and unglamorous an assignment as anyone in the service. Unable to get into a fighting unit because of nearsightedness and flat feet—they were pretty fussy in those days—I kept trying until I wound up as a private in the Quartermaster Corps."[1]

1919. "My first job when I got my discharge from the Army after World War I was with L. Bamberger & Company, the Newark department store. I became assistant to Felix Fuld who was a full partner in the enterprise. He and Louis Bamberger and vice-president Michael Schaap, who later became head of Bloomingdale's in New York, were among the ablest and more likable men I've ever known."[1]

After Newark, Anthony tried his hand as a publicity man for book publishers in New York City. This enterprise was short lived.

Early 1920's. ". . . After I'd quit book publicity, I had part-time jobs with three different publications: the New York *Herald, Farm & Fireside,* and *Judge,* the comic weekly. This triple operation kept me pretty busy but it was a lot of fun despite the inevitable headaches."[1]

1922. An early book for children published. Became a member of the New York Newspaper Club. "The Century Company published a juvenile of mine called *The Pussycat Princess*.

"The reviews were favorable but I imagine no better or worse than the average children's book gets.

"Although I was a minor figure in the newspaper game, in 1922 or thereabouts a friend had put me up for membership in the now extinct New York Newspaper Club that once held forth in the Bush Terminal Building, and I was admitted."[1]

1925. Sent to a sanitarium as a suspected tubercular patient for a few months. At thirty, Anthony had held a variety of writing jobs and had written four books. "In June . . . I was sent to a nursing home for the tubercular in Saranac, New York, after a severe pneumonia that left me weak and many pounds underweight. A well-known and highly regarded specialist in respiratory ailments had been called in, and, after he had completed his examination, declared that I had t.b. He suggested a few weeks in the just mentioned nursing home, followed by a 'long rest' in a t.b. sanitarium.

"Pronounced non-tubercular, I was discharged from the Trudeau Sanitarium in the fall of 1925. Broke but cheerful I returned to New York to make a new start. I was thirty years old, had worked hard and sometimes intelligently but had so scattered my energies that little stood out and I had accomplished nothing recognizable."[1]

1928. Publicity director for Herbert Hoover's presidential campaign in New York. "One of our principal jobs was supplying speech material. After a while we developed a formula for translating into the simplest journalese the planks in the Republican platform, with quotes from Mr. Hoover's speeches, and a few timely touches of our own.

"The question was frequently asked 'Who wrote Mr. Hoover's speeches?' The answer is 'Mr. Hoover.' In fact he wrote and rewrote them. Occasionally he would ask those close to him for suggestions but the finished product was always his own. If he used a suggestion he couched it in his own language. It is safe to say that the addresses of Herbert Hoover, before, during, and after the presidency, have been 99.9 Hoover.

"Some years later I heard Mr. Hoover make a few salty comments on ghost written presidential speeches. He declared with a laugh that there ought to be a law requiring presidential candidates who used ghost writers to announce the name of the author of each ghosted speech so that, as he put it, 'we'd know whom to elect.'"[1]

December, 1928. Married Esther Howard, his secretary at the political publicity office. "Esther and I decided to get married soon and to keep it quiet, that is, not to send out an announcement. We had become acquainted with so many new people as a result of our political activities that we figured we'd get involved in too much correspondence if we sent one out. . . ."[1]

1930. Collaborated with Frank Buck, famous wild animal trapper, on his book *Bring 'Em Back Alive*. "Writing a book in collaboration was as new an experience to me as it was to Buck. We both had a lot to learn about this 'as told to' business.

The upper porch railing was gone and six posts of the lower porch balustrade had been used to patch a gaping hole in the lattice underneath. ■ (From *Mr. Daniels and the Grange* by Eric Sloane and Edward Anthony. Illustrated by Eric Sloane.)

"I previously had had four books published but they were all solo sins and in entirely different fields. . . .

"Eventually we finished the book and then our only problem was that Buck wanted to call it *Claws and Fangs*. He had strong convictions about his suggestion and I only made matters worse by calling the title conventional. I had written dozens of titles but only one I thought any good—*Bring 'Em Back Alive*."[1]

1932. *Wild Cargo,* another book by Anthony and Frank Buck, was published. Later the book was made into a motion picture. "I broke with Buck not long after the publication of *Wild Cargo,* which was a success both as a book and a motion picture. The opening night of the movie at the Radio City Music Hall in New York was a spectacular event. Buck, the toast of the town, was all over the place autographing programs, meeting well-known people, shaking hands, bowing his acknowledgment of the compliments of handsomely groomed women.

"When I first met Frank and he was broke, discouraged and thirsting for recognition, he said to me . . . 'Some day I want to know how it feels to be a celebrity.' Now he knew. It seemed that everyone in the Music Hall wanted to meet him and wish him well."[1]

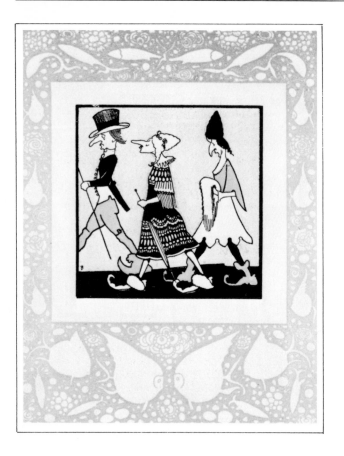

On the way they sing a ditty:
We have nice, enormous feet!
We are lovely, we are pretty,
Aren't crooked noses sweet!
■ (From *The Fairies Up to Date,* verses by Edward
and Joseph Anthony. Pictures by Jean de Bosschère.)

Summer, 1932. Collaborated with Clyde Beatty, the famous circus trainer, on a successfull book, *The Big Cage,* which was also made into a motion picture. "The success of *Bring 'Em Back Alive* resulted in a number of people turning up who allegedly had had exciting experiences involving wild animals. Would I write their stories? I decided to try my hand at one more animal book and when Clyde Beatty, the country's top animal trainer, asked me to do his life story, I readily agreed. Clyde was a great showman and was liked by practically everyone, including the press, because of his daring, modesty, and dry sense of humor. I recall that when I inquired about him of people who knew him or had dealt with him, the emphasis was always on the man's genuiness." [1]

January 1, 1943. Became publisher of *Woman's Home Companion.* Prior to this appointment, Anthony had been head of the publicity department for Collier's and simultaneously had written three successful books and a syndicated comic strip. As publisher of *Companion,* Anthony believed that women were ready for good fiction and contemporary articles. "In the next few years we were able to prove that, in addition to the more familiar type of woman's magazine fiction, you could publish John Steinbeck's *The Pearl,* which ignored the traditional happy-ending formula and managed to draw a better reader response than so-called 'safer' fiction. All the evidence we could gather through reader mail, re-

search, etc., indicated that the Steinbeck story was popular with our readers. We were able to make an equally convincing case for the acceptance by our readers of a dramatic but unorthodox novelette by Stefan Zweig, and for stories by Dorothy Parker and others whose work was of a higher quality than that of the authors of sugary romance. Since we had a definite responsibility to the management of the company, to a board of directors and a long list of stockholders, we did not attempt to make a literary magazine out of the *Companion* but we did seek what we considered a better type of popular fiction to mix with the more conventional kind of story. But even in the latter category we encouraged our editors to get it across to the fictioneers that there was no law against letting people talk and act like human beings in the pages of the *Companion,* that perhaps the incidence of overangelic characters had been a bit too high in the past." [1]

1949. Became publisher of *Collier's Magazine.* "The trail leads everywhere when you're involved in publishing national magazines. No two days are alike and not many are dull because of the colorful people you are thrown in with and the bizarre and arresting things involving them that have a way of happening." [1]

1951. After almost ten years Anthony relinquished his publishership of *Women's Home Companion.*

1954. Relinquished his position at *Collier's.* For over thirty years Anthony had worked for the Crowell-Collier Company in various capacities.

1956. Became public relations chief for the Seventh Co., Inc., a statistical-research organization in New York. That same year saw the suspension of his former magazines, *Collier's* and *Woman's Home Companion.* Anthony was stunned and understandably upset over the termination of his former company. "On December 15, 1956, I read in the newspapers that *Collier's* and the *Woman's Home Companion* were about to suspend publication. For over thirty years I had been an employee of the company that published them. So it is understandable that this news should have set in motion a train of memories, beginning with the days when the company published a farm magazine called *Farm & Fireside.* I had been out of the company two and a half years but the news was a wrench just the same." [1]

August 16, 1971. Died in Gloucester, Massachusetts of a heart attack at the age of seventy-six. "In *Doctor Zhivago* Boris Pasternak deplores the point of view that finds writers dispensing finalities on the meaning of this and the meaning of that. One naturally ponders the significance of the things that happen to one in a lifetime, Pasternak concedes, but since he classifies many of them as 'riddles' he believes that to publish the fruits of such speculations is 'pretentious and presumptuous.'

"Who am I to rush in where Pasternak fears to tread?" [1]

Oddity Land, a book of nonsense verse, was reviewed by a *New York Herald Tribune* critic who wrote, "This is nonsense that will be enjoyed beyond the nursery. The antic rhymes, smooth and clever or mischieviously odd, the artfully crazy images that seem to be created because a rhyme is necessary, are strung together in groups with brief rhyming introductions. It is just plain fooling and good fooling." *Horn Book* called it, "New nonsense verse built of ridiculous ideas and pure fun with words and rhyme—sometimes in the vein enjoyed by Ogden Nash. Erik Blegvad's witty sketches on every page capture the madness of the poet's animals, birds, fish, and other creatures described as living in *Oddity Land. . . .*"

Universal Pictures adapted Anthony's and Clyde Beatty's work, *The Big Cage,* into a motion picture of the same name in 1933. The Van Beuren Corp. adapted *Wild Cargo* by Anthony and Frank Buck into a motion picture of the same name in 1934.

FOR MORE INFORMATION SEE: This is Where I Came In: The Impromptu Confessions of Edward Anthony, Doubleday, 1960; *Horn Book,* February, 1968. Obituaries—*New York Times,* August 18, 1971; *Washington Post,* August 20, 1971; *Publishers Weekly,* September 13, 1971.

APPEL, Benjamin   1907-1977

OBITUARY NOTICE: Born September 13, 1907, in New York, N.Y.; died April 3, 1977, in Princeton, N.J. Author of some thirty works of fiction and nonfiction. Appel's career as a writer was interspersed with stints as a farmer, bank clerk, and factory worker, among other occupations. Soon after World War II he went to the Philippines as a special assistant to the United States High Commissioner. This experience produced the book, *Fortress in the Rice,* which was later adapted for the screen. For children, Appel wrote several series of books entitled "We Were There . . ." and "Why the [Russians, Chinese, etc.] Are the Way They Are." *Brain Guy,* his first novel and perhaps his best-known, is one of his many books that detailed life in New York's Hell's Kitchen. His last books, published shortly after his death, were *Hell's Kitchen,* a young adult novel, and *Heart of Ice,* based on an 18th century French fairy tale. *For More Information See: Oxford Companion to American Literature,* 4th edition, Oxford University Press, 1965; *Who's Who in America,* 38th edition, Marquis, 1974; *Contemporary Authors,* Volume 13-16, revised, Gale, 1975. *Obituaries: New York Times,* April 4, 1977; *AB Bookman's Weekly,* June 27, 1977; *Contemporary Authors,* Volume 69-72, Gale, 1978.

ARDIZZONE, Edward (Jeffrey Irving) 1900-1979

OBITUARY NOTICE—See sketch in *SATA* Volume 1: Born October 16, 1900, in Haiphong, French Indochina (now Vietnam); died November 8, 1979, in London, England. Painter, illustrator, and author. Ardizzone is best known as the author or illustrator of more than 120 books for children. He wrote and illustrated his first children's book, *Little Tim and the Brave Sea Captain,* in 1935. The story developed from an impromptu tale told to his own children and was followed by a series of "Little Tim" seafaring adventures. *Tim All Alone* (1956) was awarded the first Kate Greenaway Medal of the Library Associaton of Great Britain. Ardizzone also illustrated many adult books, including the works of Shakespeare, Dickens, Bunyan, Thackeray, and Trollope. As an official war artist during World War II, Ardizzone completed more than 300 paintings of combat scenes and often accompanied Allied troops into battle in France, North Africa, Sicily, Italy, and Germany. Among his works exhibited in

the Imperial War Museum are paintings of the fall of France, the bombing of London, and the Normandy and Anzio offensives. One of his best known works exhibited in the Imperial War Museum are paintings of the fall of France, the bombing of London, and the Normandy and Anzio offensives. One of his best-known paintings, "Magic Carpet," depicts several turbanned Indian children on a flying carpet. It was reproduced by UNICEF for one of its collections of international Christmas cards. Ardizzone's work is exhibited at the Tate Gallery, Liverpool Gallery, and in private collections. *For More Information See: Current Biography,* Wilson, 1964; *Contemporary Authors,* Volume 5-8, revised, Gale, 1969; *Who's Who in the World,* 4th edition, Marquis, 1978; *International Who's Who,* Europa, 1979; *Who's Who,* 131st edition, St. Martin's, 1979. *Obituaries: New York Times,* November 9, 1979; *Time,* November 19, 1979; *School Library Journal,* January, 1980; *Contemporary Authors,* Volume 89-92, Gale, 1980.

AUNG, (Maung) Htin   1910- (The Fourth Brother, U. Htin Aung)

PERSONAL: Born May 18, 1910, in Pegu, Burma; son of U Pein and Daw Mi Mi; married Daw Tin Hla (now an advocate), April 3, 1942. *Education:* University of Rangoon, B.A. (honors), M.A., 1928; University of London, LL.B. (honors), LL.M.; Cambridge University, LL.B. (honors); Lincoln's Inn, London, barrister-at-law, 1932; Trinity College Dublin, M.Litt., Ph.D., LL.D., 1933; St. Antony's College, Oxford, B.C.L., 1969. *Home:* 107 University Ave., Rangoon, Burma.

CAREER: University of Rangoon, Rangoon, Burma, senior lecturer, 1933-36, professor of English, 1936-48, professor

HTIN AUNG

of anthropology, 1948-60, rector, 1946-60, vice-chancellor (honorary post), 1959-60; Burma Council of National Education, secretary, 1936-46; UNESCO National Commission, vice-chairman, 1949-54; Fulbright professor at various American universities, 1949; International Universities Association, member of administration board, 1950-60; leader of Burmese delegation to UNESCO General Conference, 1950 and 1951; Inter-University Board of India, president, 1954; Rangoon-Hopkins Center, University of Rangoon, Burma, co-director, 1954-58; Fulbright board of Burma and Thailand, chairman, 1954-58; Government of Burma, ambassador to Ceylon, 1959-63; Columbia University, School of International Affairs, New York, N.Y., visiting professor, 1963-65; State University (New York), Indiana University, and Wake Forest University, visiting professor, 1965-68; St. Antony's College, Oxford, associate senior fellow, 1968—.

MILITARY SERVICE: British Army, 1939-45; captain, honorary colonel, and aide-de-camp to Presidents of Burma, 1952-62. *Member:* South East Asian Universities Association (president, 1955), Burma Research Society (president, 1956), Rotary Club of Rangoon (president, 1955), Rangoon Chess Club (founder-member). *Awards, honors:* Order of Yugoslav Army; Order of Sithu (Burma); Order of White Elephant (Thailand); honorary LL.D. from Johns Hopkins University, 1951, University of Rangoon, 1952, Trinity College, Dublin, 1956, and Vidyodaya University, Ceylon, 1961; honorary D.H.L. from Wake Forest University, 1970.

WRITINGS: Burmese Drama, Oxford University Press, 1937; (editor) *Book of English Verse,* Oxford University Press, 1938; *Burmese Folk Tales,* Oxford University Press, 1948; *English Verse Selections: First Series* (poems), E. M. Bailey, 1950; *Thirty Burmese Tales,* Oxford University Press, 1952; *Burmese Law Tales,* Oxford University Press, 1962; *Folk Elements in Burmese Buddhism,* Oxford University Press, 1962; *The Stricken Peacock: Anglo-Burmese Relations, 1752-1948,* Martinus Nijhoff [The Hague], 1965; (editor and translator) Thingazar Sayadaw, *Burmese Monk's Tales,* Columbia University Press, 1966; *Epistles Written on the Eve of Anglo-Burmese War,* Martinus Nijhoff, 1967; *A History of Burma,* Columbia University Press, 1968; (with Helen G. Trager) *Kingdom Lost for a Drop of Honey, and Other Burmese Folktales,* Parents Magazine Press, 1968; *Burmese History Before 1287: A Defence of the Chronicles,* Asoka Society [Oxford], 1970; *Folk Tales From Burma,* Sterling, 1976. Chairman of editorial committee, Burmese supplement of *Atlantic Monthly;* editor, *Journal of Burma Research Society.*

WORK IN PROGRESS: Lord Randolf Churchill and the Dancing Peacock: British Conquest of Burma 1852-1855.

SIDELIGHTS: Aung's mother died while he was quite young. His father, a Burmese administrator, was away from home a great deal of the time, leaving young Aung to spend most of his time with the people of the jungle, sharing their lives, rituals, and beliefs. He attended schools in Rangoon. In 1928 he received his B.A. and M.A. degrees from the University of Rangoon.

Aung earned a doctorate degree in English literature from Trinity College in Dublin. He found great similarity between the Elizabethan and Burmese drama and wrote a book on the subject—*Burmese Drama,* now considered a classic and the only handbook on the subject. While pursuing his doctorate, he obtained his Barrister degree, and studied geog-

raphy, history, anthropology, political science and Law at Leiden in Holland, the Sorbonne in Paris, the London School of Economics, and Cambridge.

In 1933 Aung returned to Burma, where he became professor in English at the University of Rangoon. In 1946 he became president (rector) of the university, but continued to teach English, anthropology, geography, and law several hours a week. He also wrote books and articles for papers and journals. During his leaves of absence from the university he continued his education in England.

In 1958 Aung was elected vice-chancellor of the University of Rangoon and appointed Burmese ambassador to Ceylon, where he remained until 1962. After leaving the foreign service, Aung joined the faculty of Columbia University in New York as a visiting professor in international relations. He later was a visiting professor in Southeast Asian studies, anthropology, and English literature at Wake Forest University in North Carolina. He also served as director of the Folk-Lore Institute at Indiana University. In 1968 he returned to England and was elected a senior fellow and life member of St. Antony's College, Oxford.

During his university years Aung wrote prolifically, scribbling on college pads or class workbooks. His material was derived from anything he saw, heard, or read—and he read widely.

FOR MORE INFORMATION SEE: Guardian (Rangoon), August, 1958.

BARUCH, Dorothy W(alter) 1899-1962

PERSONAL: Born August 5, 1899, in San Francisco, California; died September 4, 1962 in Los Angeles, California; daughter of Clarence and Rosalie (Neustadter) Walter; married Herbert Baruch, April 23, 1919; married Hyman Miller (a physician), June 20, 1946; children: (first marriage) Herbert, Nancy (Mrs. Cecil Vesey). *Education:* Bryn Mawr, student, 1917-19; University of Southern California, student, 1919-20; Whittier College, Broadoaks School of Education, B.E., 1930; M.E., 1931; Claremont College, Ph.D., 1937. *Home:* California. *Office:* 201 Lasky Dr., Beverly Hills, California.

CAREER: Author, educator, psychologist. Organized and directed the Gramercy Cooperative Nursery School, 1924-27; involved in the formation and direction of various organizations related to education and community action, from 1928; Whittier College, Whittier, California, professor of education in the Broadoaks School of Education, 1930-40; taught in-service teacher training courses, Burbank City and Los Angeles City Schools, 1940-41; University of Southern California, lecturer, 1941; Claremont College, special lecturer in inter-racial relations, 1944-45; consulting psychologist, private practice, from 1946; author of several books, for children and for adults, the first published 1927. Contributor of short stories to children's magazines as well as articles on education, child psychology, and related subjects to many periodicals; distinguished lecturer before public and professional conferences on these subjects. *Wartime service:* Worked with War Manpower Commission during World War II. *Member:* American Group Therapy Association; American Psychosomatic Society.

WRITINGS—Fiction for children: *A Day with Betty Anne,* Harper & Brothers, 1927; *In and Out with Betty Anne* (illustrated by Winifred Bromhall), Harper & Brothers, 1928; *Big Fellow: The Story of a Road-Making Machine* (illustrated by Jay Van Everen), Harper & Brothers, 1929.

The Two Bobbies (illustrated by Phyllis I. Britcher), John Day, 1930; *Big Fellow at Work* (illustrated by Berta and Elmer Hader), Harper & Brothers, 1930; *I Like Automobiles* (illustrated by Gyo Fujikawa), John Day, 1931; *Blimps and Such* (illustrated by Elizabeth Tyler Wolcott), Harper & Brothers, 1932; *I Like Animals* (illustrated by Corinne P. Waterall), Harper & Brothers, 1933; *I Like Machinery* (illustrated by C. P. Waterall), Harper & Brothers, 1933; *Bobby Goes Riding* (illustrated by Esther Braun), Lothrop, 1934; *I Know a Surprise* (illustrated by George and Doris Hauman), Lothrop, 1935; *The Funny Little Boy* (illustrated by Lietta), Lothrop, 1936.

(With Elizabeth R. Montgomery) *Sally Does It* (illustrated by Robb Beebe), D. Appleton-Century, 1940; *Dumbo of the Circus* (based on the Walt Disney Production), D. C. Heath, 1948; *I Would Like to Be a Pony, and Other Wishes* (illustrated by Mary Chalmers), Harper, 1959; *Kappa,s Tug-of-War with Big Brown Horse: The Story of a Japanese Water Imp* (illustrated by Sanryo Sakai), Tuttle, 1962; *Kobo and the Wishing Pictures: A Story from Japan* (illustrated by Yoshie Noguchi), Tuttle, 1964.

Non-fiction for children: (With Oscar Reiss) *My Body and How It Works: A First Physiology* (illustrated by Syd Browne), Harper & Brothers, 1934; (with Elizabeth R. Montgomery and William S. Gray) *Good Times with Our Friends* (health primer; illustrated by Eleanor Campbell), Scott, Foresman, 1941, teacher's edition, 1949; (with E. R. Montgomery) *The Girl Next Door* (health and personal development text), Scott, Foresman, 1947, teacher's edition, 1948; (with E. R. Montgomery) *Three Friends* (health and personal development text), Scott, Foresman, 1944, teacher's edition, 1954; (with E. R. Montgomery) *Five in the Family* (health and personal development text), Scott, Foresman, 1946, teacher's edition, 1947; (with E. R. Montgomery and W. W. Hauer) *You* (illustrated by Clara Ernst and Felix Traugott), Scott, Foresman, 1948, teacher's edition, 1948.

DOROTHY W. BARUCH

Non-fiction for adults: *Parents and Children Go to School: Adventuring in Nursery School and Kindergarten,* Scott, Foresman, 1939; *You, Your Children, and War,* D. Appleton-Century, 1942; *A Primer for and about Parents: Parents Can Be People,* D. Appleton-Century, 1944; *Glass House of Prejudice,* Morrow, 1946; (with Lee Edward Travis) *You're Out of the Service Now: The Veteran's Guide to Civilian Life,* D. Appleton-Century, 1946; *New Ways in Discipline: You and Your Child Today,* Whittlesey House, 1949; (with Hyman Miller) *One Little Boy,* Julian Press, 1952; *How to Live with Your Teen-Ager* (illustrated by Lois Fisher), McGraw, 1953; (with H. Miller) *The Practice of Psychosomatic Medicine as Illustrated in Allergy,* McGraw, 1956; *New Ways in Sex Education: A Guide for Parents and Teachers* (illustrated by L. Fisher and Robert Demarest), McGraw, 1959; (with H. Miller) *Sex in Marriage: New Understandings,* Harper, 1962.

SIDELIGHTS: Born in San Francisco, California and educated at Bryn Mawr, Whittier, Claremont colleges and at the University of Southern California. Her career as an educator began when Baruch organized a local cooperative nursery school for her two children and other neighborhood children. Later, she became professor of education and director of the pre-school department at Whittier College in California. "A child's first contacts with society lie within the walls of his home. His relationships with people there, what he does, how he feels, how he thinks, all enter into the formation of his attitudes toward society. If he lives in a home where he sees totalitarianism in action, where a dictator holds sway, he will be unlikely to form sound concepts concerning the democratic way of life. If he lives in a home where he has

Junior's drive to beat the cop
Hides the wish to beat his pop.
■ (From *How to Live with Your Teen-Ager* by Dr. Dorothy W. Baruch. Illustrated by Lois Fisher.)

day-by-day experiences with democratic living, then he undoubtedly will form deeply within him the essence of that which will enable him to carry democracy on.

"A child's next contacts with society lie within the walls of his school. His relationships with people there, what he does, how he feels, how he thinks, again enter into the formation of his attitude toward a larger society. In school he may experience autocracy in action. Or he may experience democracy in fluid continuity, day upon day." [Dorothy W. Baruch, *You, Your Children, and War,* D. Appleton-Century, 1942.[1]]

In 1946 Baruch began a private practice as a consulting psychologist. She wrote several books for parents as well as books for children. One of her books for parents was *One Little Boy.* "This book was written for those who want to know what children are like underneath the usually-spoken thoughts. . . . It could be about any child.

"The thoughts and feelings of childhood are deep and dark. If they creep out inadvertently and we meet them with the shock of believing them abnormal, we do one kind of thing to a child. If we meet them with the embracing sympathy born of having already encountered them and seen them as natural, we do another." [Barbara Bader, editor, *American Picture Books from Noah's Ark to the Beast Within,* Macmillan, 1976.[2]]

Baruch died at the age of sixty-three on September 4, 1962 in Los Angeles, California. Her children's book, *Kobo and the Wishing Pictures: A Story from Japan* was published, posthumously, in 1964.

During her lifetime Baruch strove to bring about greater understanding between parent and child, and to enhance the child's understanding of himself. One of her books, *New Ways in Sex Education,* has elicited this comment from *Kirkus Reviews,* "This will probably do as much for the field of sex education as Dr. Baruch's *New Ways in Discipline* did to revolutionize that area. And it will probably arouse professionally as much controversy—and among laymen create even more sense of shock, for once again she approaches sensitive fields of emotion with a completely realistic viewpoint. . . . This will prove to be immensely valuable in making for better understanding, sounder emotional life, and happier, better adjusted maturity. It may help parents solve some of their own problems as well." With similar candor, Dorothy Baruch attempted to provide young readers with extensive yet comprehensible information on physiology, personal hygiene, and personal development in her non-fiction for children.

In her fiction for children, Dr. Baruch unobtrusively applied her knowledge and experience as a child psychologist to teach while entertaining. Using rhyme, rhythm, and onomatopoeia, Dr. Baruch's style encourages children to read and learn new words and to enjoy themselves at the same time. *I Know a Surprise,* a representative example of her children's books, drew this comment from the *New York Herald Tribune:* "Its usefulness is in leading a very young reader on from page to page and thus inducing confidence in his new powers of reading."

FOR MORE INFORMATION SEE: New York Herald Tribune, September 15, 1935; *Kirkus Reviews,* February 1, 1959; *Horn Book,* April, 1964; Barbara Bader, *American Picturebooks from Noah's Ark to the Beast Within,* Macmillan, 1976.

KURT BAUMANN

BAUMANN, Kurt 1935-

PERSONAL: Born August 19, 1935, Oberhallau, Switzerland; son of Hermann (a farmer) and Verena (Bachmann) Baumann; married Iren Zweifel (a teacher), February 2, 1963; children: Mischa Clemens, Liv Tullia. *Education:* Attended Institut Minerva Zurich, 1959-62, and University of Zurich, 1962-69. *Religion:* Protestant. *Home:* Arosastrasse 6, 8008 Zurich, Switzerland.

CAREER: Goldsmith in Schaffhausen, Switzerland, 1952-56; farm worker in Ytteroey Island, Norway, 1956; goldsmith in Uppsala, Sweden, 1956-57, and Schaffhausen, 1958; writer, 1972—; Institut Minerva, Zurich, Switzerland, history and literature teacher, 1973—. *Military service:* Entered Swiss Army in 1955. *Member:* Schweizerischer Schriftstellerverband (Swiss Writers Association).

WRITINGS—For children: *Ein Weihnachtsmärchen* (title means "A Christmas Tale"), Dr. Peters-Verlag [Hanau], 1971; *Joachim der Zöllner,* Nord-Süd, 1971, translation by Margaret Baker, published as *Joseph the Border Guard,* Parents' Magazine Press, 1971; *Joachim der Strassenkehrer,* Nord-Süd, 1972, translation by Margaret Baker, published as *Joachim the Dustman,* A. & C. Black, 1974; *Der Regenbogen* (title means "The Rainbow"), Nord-Süd, 1972; *Der*

Schlafhund und der Wachhund, Nord-Süd, published as *Dozy and Hawkeye,* Hutchinson, 1974; *Drei Könige* (title means "The Three Kings"), Nord-Süd, 1972; *Joachim der Polizist,* Nord-Süd, 1975, published as *Joachim the Policeman,* A. & C. Black, 1975; *Der rote Vogel Felix,* Nord-Süd, 1976, published as *Beyond the Clouds,* Macdonald & Jane's, 1976; *Küchengeschichten,* Nord-Süd, 1977, published as *Mickey's Kitchen Contest,* Andersen Press, 1978; *Der Rattenfänger von Hameln,* Nord-Süd, 1977, published as *The Pied Piper of Hamelin,* Methuen, 1978; *Der Prinz und die Laute,* Nord-Süd, 1979, published as *The Prince and the Lute,* Gollancz, 1980; *Jonas Dreschflegel,* Bohem Press [Zurich], 1979; *Waldkonzert* (title means "Concert in the Forest"), Bohem Press, 1980; *Aesop'sche Fabeln* (title means "Aesop's Fables"), Nord-Süd, 1980; *Der Vogel und das Eichhörnchen* (title means "The Bird and the Squirrel"), Nord-Süd, 1980; *Eine Reise in die Stadt* (title means "A Trip into the City"), Nord-Süd, 1981; *Joachim der Hotelier* (title means "Joseph the Hotel Keeper"), Nord-Süd, 1982.

Plays—For children: *Der Vogel Felix oder Die Streithähne* (title means "Felix the Bird or The Fighting Cocks"), Sauerländer [Aarau], 1978; *Nanai Joachim,* Sauerländer, 1979.

Play—For television: "Nicht Einschüchtern Lassen," Fernsehspiel, ZDF Rappelkiste [Mainz], 1976.

WORK IN PROGRESS: A musical play, dealing with ecology; poetry.

SIDELIGHTS: Baumann was born in a small village on the Swiss side of the Rhine. Growing up in a "land-locked" country, he had hoped to become a sailor, but ended up as a goldsmith's apprentice. Although he has worked at many jobs over the years, he always falls back on his skill as a goldsmith to help finance his continuing study. He is now a college history and literature teacher and lives in Zurich, Switzerland with his wife and young son, for whom he wrote the story of Joachim.

The cat raised the violin to his chin and began playing so beautifully that Joseph's heart was melted. ■ (From *Joseph, the Border Guard* by Kurt Baumann. Illustrated by David McKee.)

BEGLEY, Kathleen A(nne)   1948-

PERSONAL: Born March 28, 1948, in Philadelphia, Pa.; daughter of Thomas and Catherine (Harvey) Begley; married Wiley Lamar Brooks, Jr. (an executive editor), April 19, 1977. *Education:* Temple University, B.A., 1970; Villanova University, M.A., 1974; graduate study at University of San Francisco and University of California, Berkeley, 1976. *Home:* 135 Irving Rd., York, Pa. 17403.

CAREER: Delaware County Daily Times, Primos, Pa., general assignment reporter and author of youth column, "Coed," 1966-70; *Camden Courier Post,* Camden, N.J., urban affairs reporter and author of weekly column, "Wednesday," 1970-71; *Philadelphia Inquirer,* Philadelphia, Pa., special assignment reporter, 1971-76; *Chicago Daily News,* Chicago, Ill., feature writer for "Insight" column, 1977-78; *US* (magazine), New York, N.Y., Chicago correspondent, 1978—; Roosevelt University, Chicago, director of journalism department, 1978-79; WITF-TV, Hershey, Pa., producer of "360" show, 1979—; *York Daily Record,* York, Pa., daily columnist, 1979—. Instructor at Temple University, 1973-75, St. Joseph's College, Philadelphia, autumn, 1975, Community College of Philadelphia, autumn, 1975, and University of California, Berkeley, autumn, 1976.

WRITINGS: Deadline (autobiography; Junior Literary Guild selection), Putnam, 1977; *Getting on the Air,* Putnam, 1981.

SIDELIGHTS: "When I began working on the manuscript for *Deadline,* I set up a highly organized, extremely quiet, nicely decorated office in which to write. After several days, I realized that my approach was all wrong. For ten years, I had worked in a succession of noisy, rowdy, crowded city rooms—and I had become accustomed, even dependent, on a lot of activity in my milieu. Why should I stop when it came time to write about my journalistic experiences for G. P. Putnam's young adult readers? As a result, I never worked in the office again. Instead, I did my best to simulate a newspaper office right in my dining room—brimming trash cans and all. And I never wrote a page without both the radio and the television booming into my ears."

HOBBIES AND OTHER INTERESTS: Travel in Europe, Great Britain, Morocco, and Brazil, needlepoint, tap dancing, gourmet cooking, embroidery.

BENARY-ISBERT, Margot   1889-1979
(Margot Benary)

OBITUARY NOTICE—See sketch in *SATA* Volume 2: Born December 2, 1889, in Saarbruecken, Germany; died May 27, 1979, in Santa Barbara, Calif. Translator and author of books for young people. Following World War II, Benary-Isbert and her family emigrated from Germany and made their home in the United States. Her first novel, *Die Arche Noah,* was published in Germany in 1948 and appeared in English translation as *The Ark* in 1953. She wrote more than ten novels for young people, including *Blue Mystery, The Wicked Enchantment,* and *Dangerous Spring.* Benary-Isbert also wrote the German translations of the works of Julia Cunningham. *For More Information See: More Junior Authors,* Wilson, 1963; *Contemporary Authors,* Volume 5-8, revised, Gale, 1969. *Obituaries: Publishers Weekly,* June 25, 1979; *Horn Book,* August, 1979; *School Library Journal,* September, 1979; *Contemporary Authors,* Volume 89-92, Gale, 1980.

SULA BENET

BENET, Sula   1903-

PERSONAL: Born September 24, 1903, in Poland; daughter of Moris and Sophia Benet; married Waldemar Syrkus. *Education:* Graduated from the University of Warsaw, 1935; Columbia University, Ph.D., 1944. *Home:* 315 Central Park W., New York, N.Y. 10025.

CAREER: Author, anthropologist. Has been on the faculty at Pratt Institute, Brooklyn, New York; professor of anthropology, Hunter College, New York City, 1944—. Visiting lecturer, Quaker International Conference and Seminar, Hungary, summer, 1964. Has been the recipient of several grants and fellowships, including Buell Quain Fund and the Institute of Intercultural Studies travel grant, Columbia University, summer, 1949, and a City University of New York faculty research award, USSR, summers, 1971 and 1972; currently a fellow and senior research associate of the Research Institute for the Study of Man. *Member:* New York Academy of Science; American Anthropological Association (fellow); American Ethnological Society; Polish Institute of Science.

WRITINGS—For children: (Compiler; with Carl Withers) *The American Riddle Book* (illustrated by Marc Simont), Abelard, 1954; (compiler; with Withers) *Riddles of Many Lands* (Junior Literary Guild selection; illustrated by Lili Cassel), Abelard, 1956.

Other: *Konopie w Wierzeniach i Zwyczajach Ludowych,* Warsaw Society of Science, 1936; *Song, Dance, and Customs of Peasant Poland* (preface by Margaret Mead), Roy, 1951, reprinted, AMS Press, 1977; *Patterns of Thought and Be-*

havior in the Culture of Poland, Columbia University Press, 1952; *Festival Menus 'Round the World,* Abelard, reissued as *Festive Recipes and Festival Menus,* 1970; (editor, translator) *The Village of Viriatino,* Anchor Books, 1970; *Abkhasians: The Long-Living People of the Caucasus,* Holt, 1974; *How to Live to Be 100: The Life-Style of the People of the Caucasus,* Dial, 1976.

Contributor of articles to journals in her field, including "The Paleolithic Period in Poland," *American Anthropologist,* July, September, and October, 1944.

SIDELIGHTS: Benet and Carl Withers have compiled two riddle books with their field of anthropology in mind, and according to a *Saturday Review* critic, to good effect. "Among the 1,000 items [in *The American Riddle Book*] are included every type of interesting riddle the compilers could discover, old ones, new ones, and some from foreign countries to contrast with those more familiar to us. . . . Children of all ages will have a hilarious time sharing this book at home with their friends."

Concerning *Riddles of Many Lands, Booklist* had this critique: "[The authors] present an anthology of more than 700 folk riddles from many countries, regions, and tribal or ethnic

(From *Riddles of Many Lands* by Carl Withers and Sula Benet. Illustrated by Lili Cassel.)

groups. For each group represented an attempt has been made to include something familiar, humorous, beautiful and particularly appropriate to the scene of culture. Although of special significance to the folklorist, and despite the fact that many of the riddles may seem pointless because of unfamiliar terms or concepts, the book will be useful with and fun for children.''

FOR MORE INFORMATION SEE: Saturday Review, August 21, 1954; *Booklist,* May 15, 1956; Martha E. Ward and Dorothy A. Marquardt, *Authors of Books for Young People,* second edition, Scarecrow, 1971; *American Men and Women of Science: The Social and Behavioral Sciences,* edited by the Jaques Cattell Press, 12th edition, Bowker, 1973.

BENNETT, Richard 1899-

PERSONAL: Born July 22, 1899, in Ireland; came to the United States, about 1903. *Education:* Attended University of Washington, Seattle, and Columbia University.

CAREER: Author and illustrator. Art teacher for twelve years in various sections of the United States; decided to devote his complete attention to book illustrating, 1934.

WRITINGS—All self-illustrated; all published by Doubleday, except as noted: *Shookum and Sandy,* 1935; *Shawneen and the Gander,* 1937, reissued, 1961; *Hannah Marie,* 1939; *Mister Ole,* 1940; *Mick and Mack and Mary Jane,* 1948; *Little Dermot and the Thirsty Stones, and Other Irish Folk Tales,* Coward-McCann, 1953; *Not a Teeny Weeny Wink,* 1959.

"Oh, dear, oh, dear!" sighed Little Claus in the sack. He twisted and turned about, but he couldn't manage to loosen the cord. ■ (From *It's Perfectly True and Other Stories* by Hans Christian Andersen. Illustrated by Richard Bennett.)

(From "The Emperor's New Clothes," in *It's Perfectly True and Other Stories* by Hans Christian Andersen. Illustrated by Richard Bennett.)

Illustrator: *Puget Sound: Twelve Woodcuts by Richard Bennett,* University of Washington Book Store, 1931; Alan Michael Buck, *My Saint Patrick,* Lothrop, 1937; Mary Gould Davis, editor, *With Cap and Bells,* Harcourt, 1937; Hans Christian Andersen, *It's Perfectly True, and Other Stories* (translated from the Danish by Paul Leysac), Harcourt, 1938; A.M. Buck, *Hound of Culain,* Lothrop, 1938; Jeannette (Covert) Nolan, *Red Hugh of Ireland,* Harper, 1938; A.M. Buck, *Dermont of the Bright Weapons,* Oxford University Press, 1939; Seumas MacManus, *Well o' the World's End,* Macmillan, 1939; Olive Kennon (Beaupre) Miller, *Heroes, Outlaws, and Funny Fellows,* Doubleday, 1939; A.M. Buck, *Harper's Daughter,* Oxford University Press, 1940; Padraic Colum, *Where the Wind Never Blew and the Cocks Never Crew,* Macmillan, 1940; Harold W. Felton, editor, *Legends of Paul Bunyan,* Knopf, 1947; Corinne Running, *When Coyote Walked the Earth,* Holt, 1949.

Bryan MacMahon, *Jack O'Moora and the King of Ireland's Son,* Dutton, 1950; Evelyn (Sibley) Lampman, *Witch Doctor's Son,* Doubleday, 1954; Anna B. and Hjalmar J. Loken, *When the Sun Danced,* Lothrop, 1954; William L. Brown and Rosalie Moore, *Whistle Punk,* Coward McCann, 1956; Edmund Gilligan, *Shoe the Wild Mare,* Knopf, 1956; Ellis Credle, *Tall Tales from the High Hills,* Thomas Nelson, 1957; William MacKellar, *Ghost in the Castle,* McKay, 1960.

SIDELIGHTS: Bennett was born in Ireland and, although he immigrated to the United States when he was only four years old, he made frequent return trips to his homeland. Indeed, Ireland became a major influence in his children's writings and illustrations. "One of the major requirements for any one who wants to write original stories for children with an Irish background is, I think, to have an aunt that keeps a shop. If the shop is the 'corner house,' with roads stretching to the four winds from the space before the door, so much the better. High and low, rich and poor, will sooner or later drop in and if you keep quiet in the little parlor above the shop and your ears have become 'tuned,' so to speak, to the new inflections, you can sit back and thoroughly enjoy the 'richness' that drifts up the back stairs. There will be a good amount of shrewd comments on the growing tension of the foreign situation, the latest angles on the Dublin murder of last week, and of course a bit of polite curiosity in reference to Mrs. McCarthy's 'Yank,' whom they know very well is sitting in the little parlor just above their heads. I really think my aunt's business improved fifty per cent during the first week on my first trip to Ireland. All sorts of trifling purchases would be made—a candle, a bag of sweets, a grain of sugar— all just an excuse to get a glimpse of Mrs. McCarthy's 'Yank.'

"During these first trips to Ireland, however, in the late 1920's, I was chiefly interested in the lovely landscape of the coastal regions of County Cork. The ancient 'bohereens' and crumbling ditches, ivy-covered ruins and the irregular coastline that stretched itself in long headlands far out into the Atlantic all lent themselves so well to the medium of the woodcut which I was particularly interested in during those years.

"I tramped the countryside for miles around photographing and sketching everything that interested me. 'Ye are mad for walking, Mr. Bennett,' an old man said to me one day. 'I heard ye were over the mountain. Is there anything at the other side of it worth seeing at all?' Indeed I am sure I saw more nooks and crannies of that charming landscape than

a great number of the old people who had spent their whole life in that region.

"During the latter 1930's, after the publication of my first juvenile, the 'richness' that drifted up the back stairs to my aunt's parlor from the shop below took on a new importance.

"It was on a 'fine soft afternoon' in the summer of 1938 that I chanced to overhear the conversation between two women in the shop below that gave me the idea for *Hannah Marie* [1939]. It seemed a near neighbor of one of the women was 'hounded by bad fortune,' as she put it, and things were going from bad to worse. No one could find a solution for the poor man's troubles until some one happened to notice he had had the nerve to plant a patch of potatoes on the side of a fairy fort that stood in one corner of his field. That, I needn't tell you, was the cause of all his troubles and if you happen to be an Irishman there is no need for an explanation.

"It was during my visits to relatives who had little farms 'up the country,' however, that I found the richest source of story material.

"It was on these visits, too, that I first became aware of the tremendously important part the domestic animal plays in the life of the average Irish farmer. Any member of the family will tell you in all seriousness of the peculiarities of some animal or bird with such fidelity he may just as well be describing a member of the immediate family. Indeed, the donkey and the goat and the goose take on a new importance and dignity and it is with this idea in mind I wrote *Shawneen and the Gander* [1937].

Once on a time there was an Old Woman who made brooms (only she called them besoms) out of the heather that grew on the mountain. ■(From *Where the Winds Never Blew and the Cocks Never Crew* by Padraic Colum. Illustrated by Richard Bennett.)

In their tales Paul is a bearded and mackinawed Hercules who moves mountains, tames rivers, subdues hurricanes, slays fearsome beasts, and, above all, rules men with incomparable humanity. ▪ (From *The Saginaw Paul Bunyan* by James Stevens. Woodcuts by Richard Bennett.)

"Oh yes, indeed, if it's an idea you're after, you'll find it in Ireland." [Richard Bennett, "You'll Find it in Ireland," *Horn Book*, March, 1941.[1]]

Bennett's works are included in the Kerlan Collection at the University of Minnesota.

FOR MORE INFORMATION SEE: Horn Book, March, 1941; Kunitz & Haycraft, editors, *Junior Book of Authors*, second edition, H.W. Wilson, 1951; Bertha Mahony Miller, editor, *Illustrators of Children's Books, 1946-1956*, Horn Book, 1958.

My castle has a lot of doors;
Each one is numbered too.
No matter which you open first,
Two pages wait on you.

—L.J. Bridgman

BIEMILLER, Carl Ludwig   1912-1979

OBITUARY NOTICE: Born in 1912 in Haddonfield, N.J.; died October 2, 1979, in Monmouth, N.J. Editor and writer. Biemiller was a founding editor of *Holiday* magazine and served as its executive editor from 1945 to 1957. He had previously been an assistant publisher of the *Philadelphia Daily News*. He wrote more than one thousand articles for newspapers and magazines, three novels for adults, and ten novels for teenagers. Among his books for young people is a science-fiction trilogy, *The Hydronauts, Follow the Whales,* and *Escape from the Crater. Obituaries: New York Times,* October 3, 1979.

BOWEN, Robert Sidney   1900(?)-1977

OBITUARY NOTICE: Born about 1900, in Boston, Mass.; died April 11, 1977, in Honolulu, Hawaii. Author, editor, and journalist. Serving with the U.S. Aviation Service during the First World War, Robert Sidney Bowen qualified as an ace fighter pilot by shooting down eight enemy aircraft. His interest in aviation never waned, and he served as editor-in-chief of *Aviation Magazine*, editor of *Flying News*, and publicity director of the American Society for Promotion of Aviation. A free-lance writer of fiction for more than forty years, Bowen wrote dozens of adventure novels including *Hot Rod Rodeo, They Flew to Glory, Infield Flash,* and the "Dave Dawson" series. *For More Information See: Authors of Books for Young People,* 2nd edition, Scarecrow, 1971; *Contemporary Authors,* Volume 73-76, Gale, 1978. *Obituaries: New York Times,* April 14, 1977; *Contemporary Authors,* Volume 69-72, Gale, 1978.

BROWNE, Hablot Knight   1815-1882 (Phiz)

PERSONAL: First name is pronounced *Hab*-lo; born July 12, 1815, in Kennington, Surrey, England (some sources cite June 15, 1815, in Lambeth); died July 8, 1882, in West Brighton, England; son of William Loder Browne; mother's maiden name, Hunter; married Miss Reynolds, 1840; children: Gordon, Edgar, Walter, and six other children. *Education:* Attended school at Botesdale in Suffolk; became an apprentice to the engraver, William Finden, around 1830; attended St. Martin's School of Art.

CAREER: Illustrator. With Robert Young, set up engraving and etching business, Number 3 Furnivall's Inn, London, 1834; began work as full-time illustrator when he took over work on the serialization of Charles Dickens' *The Posthumous Papers of the Pickwick Club,* 1836; went on to illustrate the original editions of many of Dickens' works, the best-known novels of Charles Lever and William H. Ainsworth in their original editions, along with such classics as *Gulliver's Travels* and *Robinson Crusoe.* As house illustrator, provided designs for woodcut illustrations for the periodical, *The Library of Fiction;* resident artist, *Ainsworth's Magazine,* 1844; contributor of illustrations to various periodicals of the time, including *Union Magazine, The Illuminated Magazine, London Magazine,* and *New Sporting Magazine.* Most of the novels for which Browne provided illustration first appeared in serial form in such periodicals as the *Monthly Magazine, Evening Chronicle,* and *Bell's Life of London. Awards, honors:* Isis Medal, Society of Arts, 1833, for engraving of John Gilpin's ride.

HABLOT KNIGHT BROWNE

ILLUSTRATOR—Under pseudonym Phiz: *Dombey and Son: The Four Portraits*, Chapman & Hall, 1848; *Dombey and Son: Full-length Portraits*, Chapman & Hall, 1848; *Four Plates to Illustrate the Cheap Edition of "The Old Curiosity Shop,"* Chapman & Hall, 1848; *Four Plates to Illustrate the Cheap Edition of "Barnaby Rudge,"* Chapman & Hall, 1849; *Home Pictures*, Cundall & Addey, 1851; *Illustrations of the Five Senses*, Grant & Griffith, 1852; *Six Illustrations of "The Posthumous Papers of the Pickwick Club,"* [London], 1854; *Merry Pictures by the Comic Hands of H. K. Browne, Crowquill, Doyle, Leech, Meadows, Hine, and Others*, W. Kent, 1857; *Hunting Bits*, [London], 1862; *Racing and Chasing: The Road, the River, and the Hunt*, Ward, Lock, & Tyler, 1868; *Sketches of the Seaside and the Country*, [London], 1869; *Phiz's Baby Sweethearts*, Routledge, 1883; *Phiz's Funny Alphabet*, Routledge, 1883; *Phiz's Funny Stories*, Routledge, 1883; *Phiz's Merry Hours*, Routledge, 1883.

Book illustration: Henry Winkles, *Cathedral Churches of England and Wales*, (illustrated with others), [London], Volume I, 1836, Volume II, 1838; Charles Dickens, *Sunday under Three Heads*, Chapman & Hall, 1836; C. Dickens, *The Posthumous Papers of the Pickwick Club* (illustrated with Robert Seymour), Chapman & Hall, 1837, reissued, Penguin, 1972; Edward Caswall (under pseudonym Quiz), *Sketches of Young Ladies*, Chapman & Hall, 1837; Robert Surtees, *Jorrocks' Jaunts and Jollities; or, The Exploits of That Renowned Sporting Citizen, John Jorrocks*, Walter Spiers, 1838; C. Dickens, *The Life and Adventures of Nicholas Nickleby*, Chapman & Hall, 1838-39, facsimile reprint, Scolar Press, 1972-73; E. Caswell (under pseudonym E. C.), *Morals from*

the Churchyard, Chapman & Hall, 1838; William Chatto (under pseudonym Stephen Oliver; music by D. Blake), *The Old English Squire: A Song*, [London], 1838; James Grant, *Sketches in London*, [London], 1838, a portion reissued as *Penny Theatres*, Society for Theatre Research, 1952; C. Dickens, *Sketches of Young Gentlemen*, Chapman & Hall, 1838; Charles Lever (under pseudonym Harry Lorrequer), *The Confessions of Harry Lorrequer*, William Curry, 1839; William Jerrold (under pseudonym Captain Barabbas Whitefeather), *The Hand-book of Swindling*, [London], 1839; W. Chatto (under pseudonym Joseph Fume), *A Paper: Of Tobacco*, [London], 1839; John Robertson, *Solomon Seesaw*, 3 volumes, [London], 1839.

Henry Fielding, *The History of the Life of Jonathan Wild, the Great*, Charles Daly, 1840; *A Legend of Cloth Fair, and Other Tales*, J. W. Southgate, 1840; *The London Magazine, Charivari, [and] Courrier des Dames* (illustrated with John Leech and Gilbray the Younger), Simpkin, Marshall, 1840; Theodore Hook, *Precepts and Practice*, 3 volumes, [London], 1840; George Reynolds, *Robert Macaire in England*, 3 volumes, [London], 1840; C. Dickens, *Sketches of Young Couples*, Chapman & Hall, 1840; C. Dickens, *Barnaby Rudge: A Tale of the Riots of 'Eighty* (illustrated with George Cattermole), Chapman & Hall, 1841, reprinted, Penguin, 1973; C. Lever (under pseudonym Harry Lorrequer), *Charles O'Malley, the Irish Dragoon*, 2 volumes, [Dublin], 1841; Frances Trollope, *Charles Chesterfield; or, The Adventures of a Youth of Genius*, 3 volumes, [London], 1841; Camden Pelham, *The Chronicles of Crime; or, The New Newgate Calendar*, 2 volumes, [London], 1841; C. Dickens, *The Old*

(From *Mervyn Clitheroe* by William Harrison Ainsworth. Illustrated by Phiz.)

Curiosity Shop (illustrated with Cattermole), Chapman & Hall, 1841, reissued, Penguin, 1872; C. Dickens *Master Humphrey's Clock* (derived in part from *Barnaby Rudge* and *The Old Curiosity Shop;* illustrated with Cattermole), Chapman & Hall, 1841; William Neale, *Paul Periwinkle; or, The Pressgang,* W. Tegg, 1841; Joseph Hewlett, *Peter Priggins,* Baudry's European Library, 1841; C. Dickens, editor and co-author, *The Pic-Nic Papers* (illustrated with George Cruikshank), Ward, Lock, 1841.

Cornelius Mathews, *The Career of Puffer Hopkins,* D. Appleton, 1842; Thomas Miller, *Godfrey Malvern; or, The Life of an Author,* 2 volumes, T. Miller, 1842-43; William Maxwell, *Rambling Recollections of a Soldier of Fortune,* [Dublin], 1842; Sir Walter Scott, *Waverly Novels* (Abbotsford edition; illustrated with others), Robert Cadell, Volume I, 1842, Volume X, 1846; George James (under pseudonym F. DeLunatico), *The Commissioner; or, DeLunatico Inquirendo,* William Curry, 1843; C. Dickens, *The Life and Adventures of Martin Chuzzlewit,* Chapman & Hall, 1843-44, reissued, Penguin, 1975; C. Lever, *Our Mess,* [Dublin], Volume I: *Jack Hinton the Guardsman,* Volumes II and III: *Tom Burke of Ours,* 1843, both published separately, [London], 1857; William Carleton, *Traits and Stories of the Irish Peasantry,* new edition, 2 volumes (illustrated with others), W. S. Orr, 1843-44, another edition illustrated solely by Browne, Routledge, 1853.

George Raymond, *Memoirs of R. W. Elliston, Comedian, 1744-1810,* 2 volumes (illustrated with G. Cruikshank), [London], 1844-45; *Fiddle Faddle's Sentimental Tour,* [London], 1845; George Rodwell, *Memoirs of an Umbrella,* [London], 1845; C. Lever, *The O'Donoghue: A Tale of Ireland Fifty Years Ago,* [Dublin], 1845; C. Lever, *St. Patrick's Eve,* [London], 1845; Samuel Sowerby, *Samuel Sowerby; or, Doings at Ravensdale Priory* (illustrated with twenty plates

(From *Paul Periwinkle; or, The Pressgang* by William Neale. Illustrated by Phiz.)

from *The Commissioner*), [London], 1845; Charles Rowcroft, *Fanny the Little Milliner; or, The Rich and the Poor,* [London], 1846; Henry Glasford Potter (under pseudonym Democritus), *A Medical, Moral, and Christian Dissection of Teetotalism,* 11th edition, Sherwood, Gilbert & Piper, 1846; W. Carleton, *Valentine McClutchy, the Irish Agent,* James Duffy, 1846.

J. S. LeFanu, *The Fortunes of Colonel Torlogh O'Brien,* [Dublin], 1847; R. Surtees, *Hawbuck Grange; or, The Sporting Adventures of Thomas Scott, Esq.,* Longmans, 1847, reissued, Folio Society, 1955; F. W. N. Bayley, *The Illustrated Musical Almanack, Visiting Table-book, and Drawing-room Annual for 1847* (illustrated with others), H. Hurst, 1847; John Smith, *Irish Diamonds; or, A Theory of Irish Wit and Blunders,* [London], 1847; C. Lever, *The Knight of Gwynne: A Tale of the Time of the Union,* [London], 1847; *The Long Lost Found,* parts 1-3, [Edinburgh], 1847; William H. Ainsworth, *Old Saint Paul's,* new edition (illustrated with John Franklin), Parry, Blenkarn, 1847; C. Dickens, *Dealings with the Firm of Dombey and Son, Wholesale, Retail, and for Exportation,* Bradbury & Evans, 1848, reissued as *Dombey and Son,* Penguin, 1970; William Jerrold, *The Disgrace to the Family,* [London], 1848; Henry and Augustus Mayhew, *The Image of His Father; or, One Boy Is More Trouble than a Dozen Girls,* [London], 1848; Daniel Defoe, *The Life and Adventures of Robinson Crusoe,* Routledge, 1848; Angus Reach, *A Romance of a Mince Pie,* Kent, 1848.

(From *The Waverley Novels* by Sir Walter Scott. Illustrated by Phiz.)

C. Lever, *Confessions of Con Cregan*, 2 volumes, William S. Orr, 1849; W. H. Ainsworth, *Crichton*, 1849; George James, *The Fight of the Fiddlers*, [London], 1849; James Hannay, *Hearts Are Trumps*, [London], 1849, another edition published as *Christmas Cheer in Three Courses* (illustrated with Henning and Hyne), Ward & Lock, 1858; Albert Smith, *The Pottleton Legacy*, [London], 1849; Samuel Lover, *Metrical Tales* (illustrated with others), 1850; C. Dickens, *The Personal History of David Copperfield*, Bradbury & Evans, 1850, reprinted, Fraser Press, 1970; C. Lever, *Roland Cashel*, [London], 1850; W. H. Ainsworth, *Mervyn Clitheroe*, Routledge, 1851-58; J. S. LeFanu, *Ghost Stories and Tales of Mystery*, William S. Orr, 1851; Mrs. Hawkshaw, *Aunt Effie's Rhymes for Little Children*, [London], 1852; C. Lever, *The Daltons; or, Three Roads in Life*, 2 volumes, [London], 1852; Julia Maitland, *The Doll and Her Friends; or, Memoirs of the Lady Seraphina*, [London], 1852; Francis Smedley, *Lewis Arundel; or, The Railroad of Life*, [London], 1852.

C. Dickens, *Bleak House*, Bradbury & Evans, 1853, reissued, Macmillan (London), 1963; F. Smedley, *The Fortunes of the Colville Family*, [London], 1853; Lady Pamela Campbell, *The Cabin by the Wayside: A Tale for the Young*, Routledge, 1854; W. J. Sorel (under pseudonym Christian LeRos), *Christmas Day*, [London] 1854; C. Lever, *The Dodd Family Abroad*, [London], 1854; F. Smedley, *Harry Coverdale's Courtship, and All that Came of It*, [London], 1854-55; Lord George Byron, *The Illustrated Byron* (illustrated with Birket Foster, Gustave Janet, and others), Henry Vizetelly, 1854-55; Horace Mayhew, *Letters Left at the Pastrycook's*, 9th edition, Nathaniel Cooke, 1854; Anna Stothard, *A Peep at the Pixies; or, Legends of the West*, [London], 1854; Mary and Elizabeth Kirby, *The Discontented Children and How They Were Cured*, [London], 1855.

C. Lever, *The Martins of Cro-Martin*, [London], 1856; Henry Fielding, *The Adventures of Joseph Andrews*, Routledge, 1857; Tobias Smollett, *The Adventures of Peregrine Pickle*, Routledge, 1857; H. Fielding, *Amelia*, Routledge, 1857; C. Lever, *Davenport Dunn; or The Man of the Day*, [London], 1857-59; T. Smollett, *Humphry Clinker*, Routledge, 1857; C. Dickens, *Little Dorrit*, Bradbury & Evans, 1857, reissued, Oxford University Press, 1966; C. Lever, *Nuts and Nutcrackers*, 3rd edition, [London], 1857; Augustus Mayhew, *Paved with Gold; or, The Romance and Reality of the London Streets*, Chapman & Hall, 1857-58, reprinted, Cass, 1971; George Halse, *Queen Loeta and the Mistletoe*, [London], 1857; W. H. Ainsworth, *The Spendthrift*, Routledge, 1857; *Aunt Mavor's Third Book of Nursery Rhymes*, [London],

"Permit me to introduce my friends—Mr. Tupman—Mr. Winkle—Mr. Snodgrass." ■ (From *The Posthumous Papers of the Pickwick Club* by Charles Dickens. Illustrated by Phiz.)

"I am hospitably received by Mr. Peggotty." ■ (From *The Personal History of David Copperfield* by Charles Dickens. Illustrated by Phiz.)

1858; George Thornbury, *The Buccaneers; or, The Monarchs of the Main,* [London], 1858; Margaret Gatty, *Legendary Tales,* [London], 1858; Harriet Beecher Stowe, *The Minister's Wooing,* [London], 1859; C. Dickens, *A Tale of Two Cities,* Chapman & Hall, 1859, reissued, Macdonald & Co., 1975; Robert Brough, *Ulf the Minstrel; or, The Princess Diamonducks and the Hazel Fairy,* Houlston & Wright, 1859, reissued in *The Little Red Man and Other Tales* (illustrated with others), [London], 1870.

Halwin Caldwell, *The Art of Doing Our Best* (illustrated with John Absolon and others), J. Hogg & Sons, 1860; James Ware, *The Fortunes of the House of Pennyl,* Blackwood's London Library, 1860; W. H. Ainsworth, *Ovingdean Grange: A Tale of the South Downs,* Routledge, Warne, & Routledge, 1860; Grace and Philip Wharton, *The Wits and Beaux of Society,* 2 volumes (illustrated with J. Godwin), [London], 1860; G. Halse, *Agatha: A Fanciful Flight for a Gusty Night,* [London], 1861; *The Confessions of a Page; or, Revelations of the Times of George the Fourth,* [London], 1861; Jacob and Wilhelm Grimm, *Grimm's Goblins,* G. Vickers, 1861; Jonathan Swift, *Gulliver's Travels in Lilliput and Brobdingnag,* G. Vickers, 1861; *The New Mysteries of London,* J. A. Berger, 1861; C. Lever, *One of Them,* [London], 1861; Harry Pennell, *Puck and Pegasus* (illustrated with Leech and Portch), [London], 1861; C. Lever, *Barrington,* [London],

1862; Matilda Edwards, *Snowflakes and the Stories They Told the Children,* [London], 1862.

Anthony Trollope, *Can You Forgive Her?,* 2 volumes (illustrated with others), Chapman & Hall, 1864; Maria Edgeworth, *The Parent's Assistant,* new edition, Routledge, Warne, & Routledge, 1864; G. Halse (under pseudonym Rattlebrain), *Sir Guy de Guy,* Routledge, 1864; Charles Ross, *The Strange Adventures of Two Single Gentlemen,* [London], 1864; Mark Lemon, *Tom Moody's Tales,* [London], 1864; C. Lever, *Luttrell of Arran,* Chapman & Hall, 1865; R. Surtees, *Mr. Facey Romford's Hounds* (illustrated with J. Leech), Bradbury & Evans, 1865, reprinted, Folio Society, 1952; Thomas Hood, *Cassell's Penny Readings* (illustrated with B. Bradley and W. Brunton), [London], 1866-68; Charles Greatrex (under pseudonym Lindon Meadows), *Dame Perkins and Her Grey Mare; or, The Mount for Market,* [London], 1866; *Ghost Wives* (illustrated with P. Gray and others), [London], 1867.

S. O. Beeton, editor, *London's Great Outing,* [London], 1868, reissued as *The Derby Carnival,* [London], 1869; Captain L. Benson, *The Book of Remarkable Trials and Notorious Characters* (illustrated with a selection of plates from *The Chronicles of Crime*), J. C. Hotten, 1871; James Rice (under pseudonym Martin Legrand), *The Cambridge Fresh-*

(From *The Old Curiosity Shop* by Charles Dickens. Illustrated by Phiz.)

man; or, Memoirs of Mr. Golightly, [London], 1871; Hablot Knight Browne (under pseudonym Damocles), *All About Kisses,* C. H. Clarke, 1875; C. Lever, *Novels* (Harry Lorrequer edition), Routledge, Volumes I-X, 1876, Volumes XI-XXI, 1877, Volumes XXII-XXXI, 1878; W. H. Ainsworth, *The Star-Chamber: An Historical Romance,* Routledge, 1879; William Shakespeare, *The Complete Works of Shakespeare* (illustrated with others), Ward, Lock, 1882-84; G. Halse, *A Salad of Stray Leaves,* Longmans & Co., 1882; *Follow My Leader; or, Lionel Wilful's Schooldays,* 3 volumes, Hogarth House, c. 1885; *A Frog He Would A-wooing Go, and Other Nursery Rhymes* (a reissue of 1850's illustration), Routledge, 1890.

Illustrations in collected works of Dickens: *The Standard Library Edition of the Writings of Charles Dickens,* 32 volumes, Houghton, 1894; *The Complete Works of Charles Dickens,* 30 volumes, edited by Richard Garnett, Chapman & Hall, 1900; *The Oxford India Paper Dickens,* 17 volumes, Henry Frowde, 1901-02, reissued as *The Fireside Dickens,* 23 volumes, Henry Frowde, 1903-07, reissued as *The Eighteen Penny Illustrated Edition of the Works of Charles Dick-*

ens, 20 volumes, Henry Frowde, 1908; *The Biographical Edition of the Works of Charles Dickens,* 19 volumes, edited by Arthur Waugh, Chapman & Hall, 1902-03; *The Authentic Edition of the Works of Charles Dickens,* 21 volumes, Scribner, 1901-05; *The Nonesuch Dickens,* 23 volumes, edited by Arthur Waugh, Hugh Walpole, and others, Nonesuch Press, 1937-38; *The New Oxford Illustrated Dickens,* 21 volumes, Oxford University Press, 1951-59.

SIDELIGHTS: **July 12, 1815.** Born the thirteenth of fourteen children into an economically depressed family.

1823. Father died, plunging the family into desperate financial straits.

1833. Awarded Isis Medal of the Society of Arts.

1834. Set up engraving and etching business; received first book commission as illustrator.

1836. Illustrated *Pickwick Papers.* "I signed myself as 'Nemo' to my first etchings before adopting 'Phiz' as my soubriquet to harmonize. I suppose, better with Dickens' 'Boz.'" [David C. Thomson, *Life and Labours of Hablot Knight Browne "Phiz,"* Chapman & Hall, 1884.[1]]

1837-1839. Traveling companion of Charles Dickens.

1838. Began thirty year association as illustrator for the novelist, Charles Lever.

1840. Married Miss Reynolds and moved to rural Surrey due to wife's ill-health.

1840's. Illustrated for Dickens, Charles Lever and other novelists, creating illustration not merely as an adjunct but as an extension of the written text.

1844. Resident artist on *Ainsworth's Magazine*.

April, 1856. Seventh child born. "Doesn't the Pope say something to the effect that 'Man never is—but always to be blessed!' . . . I am inclined to think he is nearer the mark than the man . . . who sings about the blessed state of the man with a perambulator—quiverfull, I mean."[1]

1857. Rift with Dickens developed after publication of *Little Dorritt*. "Dickens probably thinks a new hand would give his old puppets a fresh look, or perhaps he does not like my illustrating Trollope neck-and-neck with him—though, by Jingo, he need fear no rivalry *there!* Confound all authors and publishers, say I. There is no pleasing one or t'other. I wish I had never had anything to do with the lot." [John Buchanan-Brown, *Phiz! Illustrator of Dickens World,* Scribner, 1978.[2]]

1859. Work, income, abilities declined. Dropped by Dickens', his illustrations became less relevant to novels of the time. "Some years ago, when I was about to remove from Croydon, I had a bonfire to lessen the lumber, and burnt a stock of papers containing all Lever's, Dickens', Ainsworth's, and other authors' notes."[1]

Returned to London.

1860. Engaged in assignments which he considered hackwork. "I am (at present) on a Sporting paper—supported by some high and mighty Turf Nobs, but, I fear, like everything I have to do with, now-a-days, it will collapse—for—some

The No-Popery Dance. ■ (From *Barnaby Rudge: A Tale of the Riots of Eighty* by Charles Dickens. Illustrated by Phiz.)

(From *A Tale of Two Cities* by Charles Dickens. Illustrated by Phiz.)

of the Proprietors of the Paper are also Shareholders, . . . in the Graphotype Co. so they want to work the two together.—I hate the process—it takes quite four times as long as wood—and I cannot draw and express myself with a nasty finking brush, and the result when printed seems to alternate between something all as black as my hat—or as hazy and faint as a worn-out plate. . . . O! I'm a weary, I'm a weary! of this illustration business." [Fred G. Kitton, *"Phiz" Hablot Knight Browne: A Memoir*, W. Satchell & Co., 1882.[3]]

1867. Contracted polio leaving his right side paralyzed—lost use of his right thumb and blinded his right eye. The illness aged him prematurely and drastically impaired his ability to draw.

1868. In his courageous return to illustration, Phiz insisted on being propped up at his table to draw with pencil between his fingers.

June, 1878. Unsuccessfully petitioned for a pension. "I am sixty-three years old, and have been before the public forty-five years as an artist, constantly illustrating from month to month all sorts of books and authors—Bulwer, Dickens, Lever, Ainsworth, and many others; magazines, papers, periodicals of all sorts, comic and serious. It is just possible I have helped to amuse a few in my time, and in the earliest days I was a bit of a favourite, I think, but the present generation 'knoweth not Joseph.' I have had a large family, nine still living—four girls and one boy still dependent on me. I have had one paralytic attack, and I have been blinded of one eye for five months by acute rheumatism, but I am all right now."[1]

March, 1879. Found himself lost in total despair. "I don't know where to turn or what to do. I have at last come to a full stop and don't see my way just yet to get on again. My occupation seems gone, extinct; I suppose I am thought to be used up, and I have been long enough before the public. I have not had a single thing to do this year, nor for some months previous in the past year."[1]

July 8, 1882. Died in West Brighton where he had lived on a small annuity granted by the Royal Academy.

FOR MORE INFORMATION SEE: Frederic G. Kitton, *Phiz: A Memoir*, G. Redway, 1882, reprinted, Haskell House, 1974; David C. Thomson, *Life and Labours of Hablot K. Browne, "Phiz"*, Chapman & Hall, 1884; Edgar A. Browne, *Phiz and Dickens as They Appeared to Edgar Browne* (with original illustrations by H. K. Browne), J. Nisbet, 1913, reprinted, Haskell House, 1972; Albert Johannsen, *Phiz Illustrations from the Novels of Charles Dickens*, University of Chicago Press, 1956; *The Comic World of Dickens*, selected by Bernard N. Schilling, J. Murray, 1959; Michael Steig, *Dickens and Phiz*, Indiana University Press, 1978; John Buchanan-Brown, *Phiz! Illustrator of Dickens' World*, Scribner, 1978.

There was an Old Man with a beard,
Who said, 'It is just as I feared!—
    Two Owls and a Hen,
    Four Larks and a Wren,
Have all built their nests in my beard!'

—Edward Lear

BRYCHTA, Alex 1956-

PERSONAL: Surname pronounced Bricktah; born January 13, 1956, in Prague, Czechoslovakia; son of Jan (a graphic designer) and Lida (a graphic designer; maiden name Ambroz) Brychta. *Education:* London College of Printing, B.A., 1977; attended National Film School, Buckinghamshire, England, 1977-80. *Politics:* Conservative. *Home:* 9 Links View, Dollis Rd., London N-3, England.

CAREER: Illustrator; artist. *Exhibitions:* (With his parents) Gallery Mensch, Hamburg, Germany, 1967, 1970; London and Preston, early 1970's. *Member:* British Film Institute.

WRITINGS—Self-illustrated: Numbers 1 to 10 and Back Again, Frank Book Corp., 1977.

Illustrator: Perrott Philips, *When in Spain,* Dent, 1974; Helen Hoke, compiler, *Ghostly, Grim and Gruesome,* Dent, 1976; Helen Hoke, compiler, *Eerie, Weird and Wicked,* Dent, 1977; Helen Hoke, *The Little Riddle Book,* R. Enslow, 1977; David English, *Bee Gees Legend,* Entertainers Merchandise Management Corp., (EMMC), 1979.

SIDELIGHTS: "I don't consider my experience as an illustrator wide enough to be able to comment on motivation or my modus operandi, except that up till now, my motivation has always been that of financial reward. The media I favor are virtually all, except oil. I prefer to draw in India ink and color the drawings with watercolors, inks, crayons or markers. Paul Peter Piech, Alen Hurlburt, Tom Eckersley were among my most favourite tutors.

ALEX BRYCHTA

"It may be of some interest to readers that I was born in Czechoslovakia where I lived until the age of twelve and where my enthusiasm for art was constantly supressed by the educational authorities. I attended two schools in Prague and was almost daily punished in one form or another for attempting to draw in exercise books, on blotters or just scraps of paper under the desk.

"Ironically, my personal 'liberation' came with the Soviet occupation of Czechoslovakia in the fall of 1968. My parents decided to leave the country and we settled down in London.

"Here things began to look up. The teachers at William Ellis School in Highgate soon realized that art was my strong subject, and I was gradually allowed to drop most of the subject in which I had no interest (math, chemistry, etc.) and substitute them with extra hours of drawing and painting.

"Due to my childhood in Czechoslovakia, I speak Czech without an accent. I had also studied Russian for several years, but without the opportunity to use the language I fear I have forgotten most of it.

"Apart from illustration, I'm very interested in film and film animation (cartoon and puppet) and have in the past worked on cartoons for children's television programs. I also produce a fair amount of poster design, magazine illustration, book jackets and commercial art (stationery, logo design, etc.)"

HOBBIES AND OTHER INTERESTS: "My avocational interests are numerous. I like photography, automobile body design, reading, music, sailing, swimming, squash, and badminton among others. I also love to travel, especially to the United States."

"At the next stop Mr. Wonderful, carrying his potted plant, got off." ■ (From *Numbers 1 to 10 and Back Again* by Alex Brychta. Illustrated by the author.)

CAPLIN, Alfred Gerald 1909-1979
(Al Capp)

OBITUARY NOTICE: Born September 28, 1909, in New Haven, Conn.; died November 5, 1979, in Cambridge, Mass. Columnist, television commentator, lecturer, and cartoonist best known for his comic strip "Li'l Abner," which featured a naive, nineteen-year-old Southerner living in the fictitious town of Dogpatch, Lower Slobbovia. The comic strip enjoyed a great deal of success from its beginning in the mid-1930's until the 1960's, when Capp's own political views, made obvious within the strip, changed from liberal to conservative. Because of the nature of "Li'l Abner," Capp is often compared to Mark Twain. Capp's strips have also been published in separate volumes, including *The Life and Times of the Shmoo, Fearless Fosdick,* and *The World of Li'l Abner. For More Information See: Current Biography,* Wilson, 1947; *Celebrity Register,* 3rd edition, Simon & Schuster, 1973; *Who's Who in American Art,* Bowker, 1973; *Contemporary Authors,* Volume 57-60, Gale, 1976; *Time,* October 17, 1977; *Newsweek,* October 17, 1977; *Who's Who in America,* 40th edition, Marquis, 1978. *Obituaries: New York Times,* November 6, 1979; *Time,* November 19, 1979; *Contemporary Authors,* Volume 89-92, Gale, 1980.

CHRISTY, Howard Chandler 1873-1952

PERSONAL: Born January 10, 1873, in Morgan County, Ohio; died March 4, 1952; son of F. M. Christy; married Nancy May Palmer, August 14, 1919; children: Natalie. *Home:* New York City.

CAREER: Illustrator for several leading periodicals, including *Scribner's* and the *Hearst's* magazines, New York City, beginning 1893; accompanied the 2nd United States Regulars and "Rough Riders" to Cuba, and witnessed the fighting

The boy was not more than twelve years old. He was seated on the river bank under a clump of sycamores....
■ (From "Ez," in *James Whitcomb Riley's Complete Works.* Illustrated by Howard Chandler Christy.)

before Santiago; resumed portrait painting, 1920, and painted the portraits of numerous well-known people, including Will Rogers, Amelia Earhart, and Presidents Warren G. Harding and Calvin Coolidge. *Awards, honors:* Awarded medals at the Paris Exposition, Chicago Exposition, and the National Academy of Design; received a special medal from the Society for Sanity in Art, 1941.

ILLUSTRATOR: Men of the Army and Navy, Scribner, 1899; *Pastel Portraits from the Romantic Drama,* Scribner, 1899; *Types of the American Girl,* Scribner, 1900; Thomas Page, *Old Gentleman of the Black Stock,* Scribner, 1900; Winston Churchill, *Crisis,* Macmillan, 1901; Anthony Hope Hawkins, *Dolly Dialogues,* Holt, 1902; James Whitcomb Riley, *Old Sweetheart of Mine,* Bowen-Merrill, 1902; John P. Sousa, *The Fifth String,* Bobbs-Merrill, 1902; Henry Wadsworth Longfellow, *Courtship of Miles Standish,* Bobbs-Merrill, 1903; J. W. Riley, *Out to Old Aunt Mary's,* Bobbs-Merrill, 1904; *Drawings by Howard Chandler Christy,* Moffat, Yard, 1905; H. W. Longfellow, *Evangeline,* Bobbs-Merrill, 1905; Meredith Nicholson, *The House of a Thousand Candles,* Bobbs-Merrill, 1905; *The American Girl as Seen and Por-*

HOWARD CHANDLER CHRISTY

**But home, with Aunty in nearer call,
That was the best place, after all!--**
■ (From *Out to Old Aunt Mary's* by James Whitcomb
Riley. Illustrated by Howard Chandler Christy.)

trayed by Howard Chandler Christy, Moffat, Yard, 1906; *The
Christy Girl,* Bobbs-Merrill, 1906; *The Christy Book of Draw-
ings,* Moffat, Yard, 1908; Hudson Douglas (pseudonym of
Robert Aitken), *The Lantern of Luck,* Watt, 1909; George
Eliot (pseudonym of Mary Ann Evans), *Two Lovers,* Moffat,
Yard, 1909; J. W. Riley, *Songs of Sentiment,* Moffat, Yard,
1910; Walter Scott, *Lady of the Lake,* Bobbs-Merrill, 1910;
Alfred Lloyd Tennyson, *The Princess,* Bobbs-Merrill, 1911;
Liberty Belles, Bobbs-Merrill, 1912; J. W. Riley, *Good-Bye
Jim,* Bobbs-Merrill, 1913.

SIDELIGHTS: **January 10, 1873.** Born in Morgan County,
Ohio. "I was four years old when Dad took me to Zanesville
to see Charley Craig, a fine painter in his day. He went up
a flight of stairs and there was Mr. Craig—a red-haired, bald-
headed man—busily engaged in the painting of a river scene.
The sight of that artist thrilled me like nothing I had ever
before encountered in my brief life. I demanded that Dad
buy me a set of paints. Mr. Craig advised him to let me learn
to draw with a pencil first, but just the same I insisted on a
set of watercolors. Dad broke down and bought them for me!

"The river boats were my first fascination. I made friends
with many of the captains and they would throw out a plank
and ferry me free from the farm to Duncan Falls, a couple
of miles away, where there was a grade school. The bliss of
those romantic early morning rides contrasted sadly with the
trudges home through the mud. Sometimes when the river
was high, we kids (there were five children in my family)
would be forced to walk the rail fences in many spots to
avoid the mud.

"I always liked to do stuff from life. My first model was a
cow. Old Bossy would hold her pose stolidly except when
the flies bothered her. So I used to give my sister a penny
to stand by and keep the flies away." [Susan E. Meyer,
America's Great Illustrators, Harry N. Abrams, Inc., 1978.[1]]

1883. Received his first commission—a picture for the sign
of a butcher shop. He was paid ten dollars for a black and
white bull silhouetted against a bright blue sky. "Some people
objected on the grounds that a bull was not the best kind of
meat, others declared that the position of the legs was wrong.
As to that, I said, 'get down on all fours and walk.' That
convinced them I was right.

"I always seemed to get in trouble at school. For one thing,
I was left-handed, and the teacher always tried to break me
of the practice."[1] Terminated his formal education at the age
of twelve in favor of helping his father with farming and
drawing during his leisure time.

(From "Life at the Lake," in *James Whitcomb Riley's
Complete Works.* Illustrated by Howard Chandler
Christy.)

"Yonder there, on the hill by the sea, lies buried Rose Standish." ■ (From *The Courtship of Miles Standish* by Henry Wadsworth Longfellow. Illustrated by Howard Chandler Christy.)

The *Toledo Blade* newspaper accepted a sketch of Christy's and in payment thereof, offered him a job. Because he was only thirteen at the time, it was felt that the offer was premature.

Christy's dream was to study art in New York. The first attempt failed after a few months for financial reasons. At age nineteen he returned to the Art Student's League and the National Academy where he became the private student of William Merritt Chase—a considerable honor.

1895. Sold a black and white sketch to *Life* magazine for six dollars. "It was a question of food and shelter. I couldn't call for further sacrifice from my family, so had to give up all art or adopt a form that would provide a living."[1] Enraged, his teacher refused to speak with him for having abandoned the pursuit of "fine art." For the next two years he sold sketches to the magazines for very meagre returns.

1898. Covered the Spanish-American War as commissioned by *Harper's, Scribner's* and *Leslie's Weekly.* Christy traveled with Teddy Roosevelt's Rough Riders and drew sketches of Roosevelt and his aides. These were included in his portfolio called *Men of the Army and Navy* which were published as a book the following year. His dramatic combat sketches were widely published enabling him to return to the United States as a well-known illustrator.

As a correspondent he wrote accounts of the events to be printed with his drawings. *Leslie's Weekly* reviewed: "Among the others who have written about their experiences in the tropics, the most interesting is Howard Chandler Christy, the young artist who went to Cuba to make pictures for *Leslie's Weekly.* Mr. Christy had approved himself an artist of genius before the war, but probably no one, not even himself, suspected that he could write. But he can write; he

can write in the best possible way, for he is entirely unaffected, and has told in words what he saw with the same fidelity he has employed with lines and shadows in his drawings. . . . It may be that in Christy we have another Remington."[1]

He was labled a military artist. " 'Surely by now I have served my apprenticeship and have earned an opportunity of just one girl—any girl,' I told the art editors, but they could not see it my way and handed me, this time, from *Scribner's* a story by Richard Harding Davis—a yarn as you can imagine, about more soldiers. But traditionally warriors must have loves and those loves must be left behind and worn on ragged sleeves whenever guns stop popping. So I portrayed this battle-scarred hero returning home, now that peace was in sight, to a girl whose features were radiantly discernible through the cloud of smoke from his pipe. She was everything my poor talent was able to make her—young, glowing, tender and infinitely sweet. Thus, out of my own dreams was fashioned the first 'Christy Girl,' whose reception turned me, almost overnight, into a painter of some of the world's most beautiful models."

"[The 'Christy Girl'] started out as an idea, turned into a dream, and eventually, because in those days I couldn't afford an exclusive model, became a composite of the girls who were posing for Gibson, Wenzell and Church. As one of them said facetiously at the time, 'She should have been good; she combined the best features of all of them.' "[1]

Married Maybelle Thompson, one of his "exclusive" models. According to newspaper accounts this was considered an extremely tumultuous relationship. It did not endure. The union bore one daughter, Natalie.

Returned to Ohio with his daughter to re-establish his roots and sort out his mental and emotional problems. He stayed for seven years during which time he had a house built— "The Barracks." Some of the best illustrations of his career were painted during this period when he worked daily in his studio from 9:00 to 4:00. "In one month I had four serials, either ending or beginning, and I had to paint twenty-seven pictures in twenty-eight days. And I got 'em all in on time."[1]

August 14, 1919. Married Nancy May Palmer, his model, making her face a popular commodity between 1916-1921. The most familiar example was Christy's famous poster of World War I, *Gee I Wish I Were a Man,* an overwhelming success for the Navy.

A fervent patriot, Christy devoted his talent to many causes— Red Cross, Police Athletic League, Salvation Army, and the Children's Humane Army.

1921. Invited to judge the first Miss America Beauty Contest in Atlantic City. Norman Rockwell, one of the other judges, reported on Christy at this event: "At the right moment, when the photographers were clustering around trying to get a good picture and shouting at us to smile, move in, move out, stand up, sit down, Christy would appear in a white suit and broad-brimmed Stetson with a beautiful contestant on each arm, and the photographers would leave us milling about and run to take his picture. . . .

"We couldn't dislike Christy for it. He had such a warm, jovial personality: flamboyantly good-natured, boomingly cheerful. And if he liked publicity so much and was so good at getting it, well, I couldn't hate him for it. It seemed to go with his character. It fed him and he fed it. Publicity and he were right for each other. Like pearls and duchesses or cole slaw and church suppers."[1]

Christy's own view and evaluation of American beauty remained consistent during his life as a painter and illustrator. "The ideal American woman adheres to certain standards. . . . One of the standards of beauty is health. We love pink cheeks, clear eyes, white teeth, firm slenderness, glossy hair, animation—all meaning health or imitating it. Health and pep are American ideals. An American who doesn't have them is out of balance, and therefore not up to American beauty standards . . . as an artist I personally admire grace and proportion above all, plus animation.

"Take it from me, women have not changed much. It is only superficialities that have altered. The girl who went down to the railroad station to wave good-by to the boy on his way to Cuba, to avenge the sinking of the Maine, did not have rouge on her face and her nails were the color God made them. If she was daring, perhaps a tiny speck of black court plaster on her cheek made her look paler. She wore long skirts and the curves of her figure were accentuated in a big way. But at heart she was the same as the slim girls, whose carmine-tipped fingers twisted radio dials, trying to find out about the 'boy friend' who was fighting for his country in Europe or the Pacific. Oh, yes, the young people nowadays think that they are much more sophisticated than their grandmothers whom I drew. Take it from one who knows, they are not. Sure, they know all about inhibitions, neuroses, and stuff like that. They are more outspoken, too, and delight in calling spades shovels. In some ways they are more honest. But believe me, grandma's charm or allure was not any different from granddaughter's 'it' or 'oomph.' Necking was an unknown work in the old days, but sparking wasn't and a crushed leg-of-mutton sleeve was as much of a give-away then as lipstick on the party of the second part is now. Summer breezes blew as soft, moonlight was just as romantic and human hearts responded with the same kind of throbs."[1]

1921. Announced his retirement from magazine illustration to devote himself entirely to the painting of portraits. He completed thirty canvases his first year. The list of luminaries was endless—Will Rogers, Fritz Kreisler, Mrs. William Randolph Hearst, the Prince of Wales, Benito Mussolini, Amelia Earhart, etc., etc., making him the most fashionable portrait painter of his day. The social life of this profession suited him very well.

His daily schedule deviated little over these work years. Up at 8 a.m. for a stroll in Central Park "to get the feeling of the people," then to his studio for six full hours of painting. Asked one time by Normal Vincent Peale if he ever *worried,* Christy replied: "No, not on your life. I don't believe in it. . . . I tried it once. I noticed that everybody else seemed to worry and I figured I must be missing something, so one day I made up my mind to try it. I set aside a day and said, 'That is to be my worry day.' I decided I would investigate this worry business and do some worrying just to see what it was like.

"The night before the day came I went to bed early to get a good night's sleep to be rested up to do a good job of worrying the next day. In the morning I got up, ate a good breakfast—for you can't worry successfully on an empty stomach—and then decided to get to my worrying. Well, I just couldn't make heads nor tails of it. It didn't make sense

She quickly rose in answer to my invitation and offered me her hand. ■ (From *Dorothy Vernon of Haddon Hall* by Charles Major. Illustrated by Howard Chandler Christy.)

to me, so I just gave it up." [Norman Vincent Peale, *The Power of Positive Thinking,* Fawcett Books, 1956.[2]]

In the late thirties Christy was commissioned to paint the Signing of the Constitution for the Capitol. He devoted more than two years to research, scouring libraries and picture collections for likenesses and descriptions of the Constitution's thirty-nine signers. The canvas was huge—twenty feet by thirty feet. He worked every day for eight months until it was complete. Twenty men carried it to its final location above the east Grand Stairway in the Capitol where it hangs today. Christy's career remained active until his eightieth year.

March 4, 1952. Died in his New York apartment at the Hotel des Artistes, an unfinished painting at his easel.

FOR MORE INFORMATION SEE: Bertha E. Mahony, editor, *Illustrators of Children's Books: 1744-1945,* Horn Book, 1947; Loring Holmes Dodd, *Generation of Illustrators and Etchers,* Chapman & Grimes, 1960; (for children) James A. Rhodes, *Teenage Hall of Fame,* Bobbs-Merrill, 1960. Obituaries—*New York Times,* March 4, 1952; *Newsweek,* March 10, 1952; *Time,* March 10, 1952; *Art Digest,* March 15, 1952; *Wilson Library Bulletin,* May, 1952.

COSGRAVE, John O'Hara II   1908-1968

OBITUARY NOTICE: Born October 10, 1908, in San Francisco, Calif.; died in May, 1968, in Pocasset, Mass. Freelance commercial artist and book illustrator. After leaving the University of California, where he majored in art, Cosgrave went to Paris in 1930 to study painting with André Lhote. Cosgrave returned to the United States in 1932 to begin his career as a commercial artist. He did magazine advertisements and book jackets as well as illustrations for many books, including Jean Lee Latham's *Carry On, Mr. Bowditch,* Robert Frost's *Road Not Taken,* and Stephen Meader's *Guns for the Saratoga.* Cosgrave also wrote two books, *America Sails the Seas* and *Clipper Ships. For More Information See: Contemporary Authors,* Volume 1-4, first revision, Gale, 1967; *Illustrators of Books for Young People,* 2nd edition, Scarecrow, 1975. *Obituaries: New York Times,* May 11, 1968.

CRUMP, J(ames) Irving   1887-1979

OBITUARY NOTICE: Born December 7, 1887, in Saugerties, N.Y.; died July 3, 1979, in Hackensack, N.J. Editor and author. For nearly twenty-five years Crump was editor of *Boy's Life,* the official magazine of the Boy Scouts of America. He was also the author of more than forty books for young people, including *The Pilot of the Cloud Patrol, Og: Son of Og, Our G-Men, Our Oil Hunters,* and *Our United States Coast Guard Academy. For More Information See: Junior Book of Authors,* 2nd edition, Wilson, 1951; *Authors of Books for Young People,* 2nd edition, Scarecrow, 1971; *Contemporary Authors,* Volume 73-76, Gale, 1978. *Obituaries: New York Times,* July 4, 1979; *AB Bookman's Weekly,* July 30, 1979; *Contemporary Authors,* Volume 89-92, Gale, 1980.

DALGLIESH, Alice   1893-1979

OBITUARY NOTICE: Born October 7, 1893, in Trinidad, British West Indies; died June 11, 1979, in Woodbury, Conn. Educator, editor, book reviewer, and author. Dalgliesh was an elementary school teacher for nearly seventeen years, and later taught a course in children's literature at Columbia University. From 1934 to 1960 she served as children's book editor for Charles Scribner's Sons. In addition to her book reviews for such magazines as *Saturday Review of Literature* and *Parents' Magazine,* Dalgliesh wrote more than forty books for children, including Newbery Honor Books *The Silver Pencil, The Courage of Sarah Noble,* and *The Bears on Hemlock Mountain.* She also served as the first president of the Children's Book Council. *For More Information See: Junior Book of Authors,* 2nd edition, Wilson, 1951; *Authors of Books for Young People,* 2nd edition, Scarecrow, 1971; *Contemporary Authors,* Volume 73-76, Gale, 1978. *Obituaries: New York Times,* June 13, 1979; *Publishers Weekly,* July 2, 1979; *AB Bookman's Weekly,* August 13, 1979; *Horn Book,* August, 1979; *School Library Journal,* September, 1979; *Contemporary Authors,* Volume 89-92, Gale, 1980.

Childhood shows the man as morning does the day.
—John Milton

VINE DELORIA, JR.

DELORIA, Vine (Victor), Jr.   1933-

PERSONAL: Born March 26, 1933, in Martin, S.D.; son of Vine (a clergyman) and Barbara (Eastburn) Deloria; married Barbara Jeanne Nystrom, June, 1958; children: Philip, Daniel, Jeanne. *Education:* Iowa State University, B.S., 1958; Lutheran School of Theology, Rock Island, Ill., M.Th., 1963; University of Colorado, J.D., 1970. *Politics:* Democrat. *Religion:* "Seven Day Absentist." *Office:* Department of Political Science, University of Arizona, Tucson, Arizona 85721.

CAREER: United Scholarship Service, Denver, Colo., staff associate, 1963-64; National Congress of American Indians, Washington, D.C., executive director, 1964-67. Lecturer, Western Washington State College, 1970-72, and University of California, Los Angeles, 1972-74. Chairman, Institute for the Development of Indian Law, 1970-78, University of Arizona, Tucson, Arizona, professor of political science, 1978—; chairman of American Indian Studies, 1979—. *Military service:* U.S. Marine Corps Reserve, 1954-56. *Member:* American Bar Association, American Judicature Society, Authors Guild, Amnesty International, Colorado Authors League. *Awards, honors:* Anisfield-Wolf Award, 1970, for *Custer Died for Your Sins;* D.H.Litt., Augustana College, 1971; Indian Achievement Award from Indian Council Lire, 1972; D.Hum., Scholastica College, 1976; Distinguished Alumni Award, Iowa State University, 1976; L.H.D., Hamline University, 1979.

WRITINGS: Custer Died for Your Sins: An Indian Manifesto, Macmillan, 1969; *We Talk, You Listen: New Tribes, New Turf,* Macmillan, 1970; (editor and author of introduction) Jennings Cooper Wise, *The Red Man in the New World Drama,* Macmillan, 1971; (compiler) *Of Utmost Good Faith,*

Straight Arrow Books, 1971; *God Is Red,* Grosset, 1973; *Behind the Trail of Broken Treaties,* Delacorte, 1974; *The Indian Affair,* Friendship, 1974; *Indians of the Pacific Northwest,* Doubleday, 1977; *The Metaphysics of Modern Existence,* Harper, 1979.

SIDELIGHTS: "A great deal of my time is now spent in trying to educate a new generation of Indian scholars who can take traditional customs and beliefs and apply them to the solution of contemporary problems. I am now a professor of political science at the University of Arizona where I am developing a complete graduate program for American Indian students. We are attracting good students from a variety of tribes and will shortly be producing people with advanced degrees who are well-trained in the political history of different tribes.

"My Irish setter became unruly and fought with my other dogs and so I had to give him away. Looking around to see who would accept the dog, I ran into an anthropologist who, being not as smart as the dog, was available to be trained by the dog; they make a very compatible pair as long as the anthro behaves himself. My other dogs love Arizona and spend their time chasing rabbits and ground squirrels but are not smart enough to catch them.

"I remain a loyal fan of the Denver Broncos although it does take the patience of Job to watch them Sunday after Sunday without seeing much in the way of visible results. But sports are relaxing and present sufficient challenge in a tactical sense to prove interesting over the long haul. Although Arizona is an outside state, I am content to sit on the patio and watch the clouds roll by.

"I still try and read Raymond Chandler, Jack Kerouac, and Ross MacDonald at least once a year because I like their writing styles and re-reading their books gives me a good perspective on writing and human personality and a bit of the emotion of history past. One consuming topic of reading interest is the large number of books that have been written dealing with ancient cosmic catastrophes and the possibility of reviving the historical basis of oral traditions of our ancestors. Immaneul Velikovsky, particularly his later books on the revision of ancient Near Eastern history, seems to me to have initiated a whole new look at the history of our species which will be critically important in helping us get a more mature perspective on things."

FOR MORE INFORMATION SEE: Publishers Weekly, February 28, 1977.

DODGE, Mary (Elizabeth) Mapes 1831-1905

PERSONAL: Born January 26, 1831 (or 1838, according to some sources), in New York City; died August 21, 1905, at Onteora Park, New York; daughter of James Jay (a scientist) and Sophia (Furman) Mapes; married William Dodge (an attorney), 1851 (died, 1858); children: Jamie, Harry. *Education:* Educated at home by her father and private tutors. *Home:* New York City and Onteora Park in the Catskill Mountains of New York State.

CAREER: Author of books for children; associate editor of *Hearth and Home Magazine,* 1870-73; first editor of *St.*

MARY MAPES DODGE

Nicholas Magazine, 1873-1905. *Awards, honors:* Montyon Prize of the French Academy, 1869, for *Hans Brinker.*

WRITINGS—All for children: *Irvington Stories* (illustrated by F.O.C. Darley), James O'Kane, 1864, revised and enlarged edition, W. L. Allison, 1898; *Hans Brinker; or, The Silver Skates: A Story of Life in Holland* (illustrated by F.O.C. Darley and Thomas Nast), James O'Kane, 1865 [numerous later editions include those illustrated by Allen B. Doggett, Scribner, 1896; Rudolph Mencl, Graham & Matlack, 1913; George Wharton Edwards, Scribner, 1915, reprinted, 1974; Milo Winter, Rand McNally, 1916; Sears Gallagher (edited by Orton Lowe), Ginn, 1917; Alice Carsey, Whitman, 1917; Maginel Wright Enright, McKay, 1918; Louis Rhead, Harper, 1924; Clara M. Burd (edited by Ruth Ewing Hilpert), Winston, 1925; Eva Noé, Sears, 1926; Violet Moore Higgins, Whitman, 1929; N. C. Wyeth and Peter Hurd, Garden City Publishing, 1932; George Lawson, Saalfield Publishing, 1933; B. F. McNaughton (retold), Whitman, 1934; Helen Sewell and Mildred Boyle (edited by Edward L. Thorndike), Appleton-Century, 1936; Sari (edited by Gladys Malvern), McLaughlin Brothers, 1940; Helen Osborne, Saalfield Publishing, 1943; Cyrus Leroy Baldridge, Grosset, 1945; Hilda Van Stockum, World Publishing, 1946; Norma Guthrie Rudolph (retold), Winston, 1953; Paul Galdone, Junior Deluxe Editions, 1954; Hans Baumhauer, Dutton, 1955; Pelagie Doane, Lippincott, 1957; Peter Spier, Scribner, 1958; Fritz Kredel, Grosset, 1963; Dennis A. Dierks, Childrens Press, 1969].

(From *The Irvington Stories* by Mary Mapes Dodge. Illustrated by F. O. C. Darley.)

A Few Friends; or, How They Amused Themselves: A Tale, Lippincott, 1868; *Rhymes and Jingles,* Scribner, circa 1874, new edition illustrated by Sarah S. Stilwell, 1904; *Theophilus and Others,* Scribner,1876; *Along the Way,* Scribner, 1879, revised edition published as *Poems and Verses,* Century, 1904; *Donald and Dorothy,* Roberts Brothers, 1883; (with Palmer Cox and others) *Childhood's Happy Day A.B.C. Book,* Star Publishing, 1893; *The Land of Pluck: Stories and Sketches for Young Folk,* Century,1894; *When Life Is Young: A Collection of Verse for Boys and Girls,* Century, 1894; *The Golden Gate* (originally published in *Irvington Stories*), M. A. Donohue, 1903; *Po-no-kah: An Indian Tale of Long Ago* (originally published in *Irvington Stories*), M. A. Donohue, 1903.

Editor: *Baby World: Stories, Rhymes, and Pictures for Little Folks; from "St. Nicholas,"* Century, 1884; *New Baby World: Stories, Rhymes, and Pictures for Little Folk,* Century, 1897; *The Children's Book of Recitations,* De Witt, 1898.

Contributor of several adult stories to *Atlantic Monthly, Harper's Magazine,* and *Century Magazine,* among others.

ADAPTATIONS—Movies and filmstrips: "Hans Brinker; or, The Silver Skates" (filmstrip), Eye Gate House, 1958; motion picture of the same title (originally telecast on Walt Disney's "Wonderful World of Color" series), Walt Disney Productions, 1961; "Hans Brinker, Boy of Holland" (filmstrip), Encyclopaedia Britannica Films, 1964; "Hans Brinker's Great Decision" (filmstrip), Encyclopaedia Britannica Films,

1964; "Hans Brinker" (filmstrip), Filmfax Productions, 1971; "Hans Brinker by the Zuider Zee" (filmstrip in both sound and captioned versions), Walt Disney Educational Materials Co., 1971.

Recordings: "Favorite Classical Stories" (includes "Hans Brinker or the Silver Skates"; eight cassettes), Miller-Brody Productions; "Hans Brinker or the Silver Skates" (parts 1 & 2, individual cassettes; audio disc), Spoken Arts.

SIDELIGHTS: **January 26, 1831.** Born into a wealthy New York family, the daughter of a scholarly-scientist who tutored his children at home. Dodge was an avid reader and eager listener of her father's stories.

1841. Celebrated family anniversaries with "poetic effusions." "Someday perhaps I shall write a book. There will be no murderers in it and no hangings. And the father in my book will be a nice father like ours. . . ." [Miriam E. Mason, *Mary Mapes Dodge, Jolly Girl,* Bobbs-Merrill, 1962.[1]]

1847. Contributed leading articles for *The Working Farmer,* her father's magazine. "Just imagine how upset the subscribers of Father's paper would be if they knew a girl of sixteen had written some of the articles they read so seriously." [Alice B. Howard, *Mary Mapes Dodge of "St. Nicholas,"* Julian Messner, 1943.[2]]

1851. Married William Dodge, an attorney.

1858. Widowed, Dodge went to live with her father in New Jersey where she turned to writing as a means of support for

(From the television special "Hans Brinker," starring Dick Button, Peggy King and Tab Hunter. Presented on NBC television, 1958.)

her two young sons. "This last winter without William has been harder than any time I have ever known. The boys helped to forget, a little."[2]

1864. Published *Irvington Stories,* her first book. "When I saw the boys enjoyed [the story], I wrote it down one night after they'd gone to bed. The actual work kept my mind away from things I didn't want to think about. Well, then, one evening, Mr. [Horace] Greeley came in to call. . . . To pass the time, I pulled out the story and read it aloud."[2]

1865. After extensive research on Holland and Dutch life, *Hans Brinker* was published. "This little work aims to combine the instructive features of a book of travels with the interest of a domestic tale. Throughout its pages, the descriptions of Dutch localities, customs, and general characteristics, have been given with scrupulous care. Many of its incidents are drawn from life; and the story of Raff Brinker is founded strictly upon fact.

"While acknowledging my obligations to many well-known writers on Dutch history, literature, and art, I turn with especial gratitude of those kind Holland friends, who, with generous zeal, have taken many a backward glance at their country for my sake, seeing it as it looked twenty years ago, when the Brinker home stood unnoticed in sunlight and shadow.

"Should this simple narrative serve to give my young readers a just idea of Holland and its resources, or present true pictures of its inhabitants and their every-day life, or free them from certain current prejudices concerning that noble and enterprising people, the leading desire in writing it will have been satisfied.

"Should it cause even one heart to feel a deeper trust in God's goodness and love, or aid any in weaving a life,

The Investigating Committee. ▪ (From *Hans Brinker* by Mary Mapes Dodge. Illustrated by Thomas Nast.)

wherein, through knots and entanglements, the golden thread shall never be tarnished or broken, the prayer with which it was begun and ended will have been answered." [Mary Mapes Dodge, *Hans Brinker,* Doubleday, 1954.[3]]

January, 1866. Grieved by her father's death, Dodge immersed herself in the work of producing stories and verses. "I will maintain our support by writing—stories, articles, poems, anything which anyone will buy. I like the task of writing. . . . I not only think in written words but the actual task of putting words on paper is fun, not work."[2]

1870. Associate editor of *Hearth and Home,* a weekly family paper edited by Harriet Beecher Stowe.

November, 1873. Became editor of *St. Nicholas,* a new juvenile magazine. "The child's magazine must not be a milk-and-water variety of the periodical for adults. In fact, it needs to be stronger, truer, bolder, more uncompromising than the other; its cheer must be the cheer of the bird-song; it must mean freshness and heartiness, life and joy. Therefore look to it that it be strong, warm, beautiful, and true. Most children of the present attend school. Their heads are strained and taxed with the days lessons. They do not want to be bothered nor amused nor taught nor petted. They just want to have their own way over their own magazine. They want to enter the one place where they may come and go as they please, where they are not obliged to mind, or say 'yes, ma'am' and 'yes sir,'—where, in short, they can live a brand-new, free life of their own for a little while, accepting acquaintances as they choose and turning their backs without ceremony upon what does not concern them. Of course they expect to

(From *Hans Brinker* by Mary Mapes Dodge. Illustrated by Jessie Willcox Smith.)

The old man eyed his visitor shrewdly. Having been for some time a dealer in rare bric-à-brac, he prided himself on being up to the tricks of persons who had second-handed treasures to sell.
■(From *Donald and Dorothy* by Mary Mapes Dodge.)

pick up old bits and treasures, and now and then to 'drop in' familiarly at an air-castle, or step over to fairyland. A child's magazine is its playground." ["In Memory of Mary Mapes Dodge," *St. Nicholas* Magazine, October, 1905.[4]]

"Beauty, there must be that. Beauty in the poems and stories and pictures but never a bit of moralizing and—most especially beauty in the make-up of the magazine."[2]

1874-1880. Delighted and almost surprised by the immediate success of *St. Nicholas.* "They like it. The children like it! That's most important, but the nice thing about it is the mothers and fathers like it too.

"You know almost everyone likes to write letters. And especially children. I remember when Jamie first learned to make scratches on paper he called them 'ledders.' . . . Later when he had conquered his alphabet he was continually writing notes and mailing them in the old elm tree by the side of the play-room window."[2]

1881. Following sudden death of her beloved son, Harry, Dodge gradually withdrew from active control of *St. Nicholas.* "I had to give up one of my boys, but I don't think God feels about death as we do."[4]

1888. Purchased "Yarrow," a cottage in the Catskills, which became a mecca for literary notables of the day.

1890's. Worked at attracting noted authors to contribute work to *St. Nicholas.* "Mr. Kipling, will you try an animal story— or one about India? With all you know about that country such tales would be strange and fascinating.

"The critics still say it's good? Well, let them. That doesn't matter for one single minute. Most important is that the children still read it and love it!"[2]

August 21, 1905. Died after a long illness; honored by a funeral procession of children. "I am going in to rest, now. Don't come—any of you. I'm all right."[2]

FOR MORE INFORMATION SEE: William Fayal Clarke, "In Memory of Mary Mapes Dodge," *St. Nicholas,* volume 32, 1905; Alice B. Howard, *Mary Mapes Dodge of "St. Nicholas,"* Messner, 1943; Elizabeth R. Montgomery, *Story behind Great Books,* McBride, 1946; Miriam E. Mason, *Mary Mapes Dodge, Jolly Girl,* Bobbs-Merrill, 1949, reprinted, 1962; William Oliver Stevens, *Famous Women of America,* Dodd, 1950; F. M. Sturges, "St. Nicholas Bequest," *Horn Book,* October, 1960; Edna Yost, *Famous American Pioneering Women,* Dodd, 1961; Eleanor Farjeon, "Comedy in Wax, or, Lucy and Their Majesties: With Correspondence between Mary Mapes Dodge and B. L. Farjeon," *Horn Book,* August, 1965; Laura Benet, *Famous Storytellers for Young People,* Dodd, 1968; Brian Doyle, editor, *The Who's Who of Children's Literature,* Shocken Books, 1968; Obituary— *New York Times,* August 22, 1905.

DOYLE, RICHARD 1824-1883

PERSONAL: Born in September, 1824, in London, England; died December 11, 1883, in London; son of John (an Irish artist, caricaturist, and author) and Marianna (Conan) Doyle. *Education:* Studied art and caricature under the direction of his father and his uncle, Michael Conan. *Religion:* Roman Catholic. *Home:* London, England.

CAREER: Artist and caricaturist. Published his first book of sketches, 1840; joined the staff of *Punch,* 1843; contributed decorations, illustrations, and satirical sketches to that publication until November, 1850, when he resigned in protest of the anti-Catholic statements that appeared in the magazine; after severing his relations with *Punch,* Doyle concentrated his attention on book illustration and water color painting, 1850-1883; exhibited paintings in the Grosvenor Galleries and the Royal Academy, 1871-1883.

WRITINGS: The Eglinton Tournament, J. Dickinson, 1840; *Rejected Cartoons,* T. M'Lean & F. Syrett, 1848; *Manners and Customs of Ye Englyshe Drawn from Ye Quick,* Bradbury & Evans, 1849, a new edition published as *God's Englishmen,* Avalon, 1948; *An Overland Journey to the Great Exhibition, Showing a Few Extra Articles and Visitors,* [London], 1851; *The Foreign Tour of Messrs. Brown, Jones and Robinson:*

Richard Doyle, a self-portrait.

Being the History of What They Saw and Did in Belgium, Germany, Switzerland, and Italy, Bradbury & Evans, 1854, D. Appleton, 1860, reprinted, Bradbury & Evans, 1973, Arno, 1976; *Birds-eye Views of Modern Society,* Smith, Elder, 1864; *Comic Histories, with Tommy and the Lion,* Pall Mall Gazette, 1885; *Dick Doyle's Journal: A Journal Kept by Richard Doyle in the Year 1840,* Smith, Elder, 1885; *Homer for the Holidays,* Pall Mall Gazette, 1887; *Jack the Giant Killer,* Eyre & Spottiswoode, 1888.

Illustrations: Jacob Ludwig Carl and Wilhelm Carl Grimm, *The Fairy Ring: A New Collection of Popular Tales* (translated by J. E. Taylor), J. Murray, 1846; Leigh Hunt, *A Jar of Honey from Mount Hybla,* Smith, Elder, 1847; Mark Lemon, *The Enchanted Doll,* Bradbury & Evans, 1849; Anthony R. Montalba, *Fairy Tales from All Nations,* Chapman & Hall, 1849; William M. Thackeray, *Rebecca and Rowena: A Romance upon Romance,* Bradbury & Evans, 1850; John Ruskin, *The King of the Golden River,* 2nd edition, Smith, Elder, 1851, reprinted, Dover, 1974; *The Story of Jack and the Giants,* Cundall & Addey, 1851; W. M. Thackeray, *The Newcomes: Memoirs of a Most Respectable Family,* Bradbury & Evans, 1853-1855, Harper & Brothers, 1855; Eleanora Louisa Montagu, *Juvenile Calendar and Zodiac of Flowers,* Low, 1855; T. Hughes, *The Scouring of the White Horse; or, The Long Vacation Ramble of a London Clerk,* Macmillan, 1859.

Gluck went to the window, opened it, and put his head out to see who it was. It was the most extraordinary looking little gentleman he had ever seen in his life.
■ (From *The King of the Golden River* by John Ruskin. Illustrated by Richard Doyle.)

Moxon's Miniature Poets: A Selection from the Works of Frederick Locher, E. Moxon, 1865; James Robinson Planche, *An Old Fairy Tale Told Anew in Pictures and Verse*, Routledge, 1865; *The Visiting Justices and the Troublesome Priest; or, Irish Biddy in the English Gaol*, R. Bentley, 1868; M. Lemon, *Fairy Tales*, Bradbury & Evans, 1868; William Allingham, *Fairy Land: Pictures from the Old World*, D. Appleton, 1869 (published in England as *In Fairy Land: A Series of Pictures from the Elf-World*, Longmans, 1870, reissued, Viking, 1979); Laurence Oliphant, *Piccadilly*, Blackwoods, 1870; *The Enchanted Crow, and Other Famous Fairy Tales*, Dean & Son, 1871; *Feast of the Dwarfs, and Other Famous Fairy Tales*, Dean & Son, 1871; *Fortune's Favourite, and Other Famous Fairy Tales*, Dean & Son, 1871; *Snow-White and Rosy-Red, with Other Famous Fairy Tales*, Dean & Son, 1871; Madeline P.C.B. Wyndham, *The Sad Story of a Pig and a Little Girl*, [Cumberland], 1876; Andrew Lang, *The Princess Nobody: A Tale of Fairy Land*, Longmans, 1884; James E. Doyle, *Scenes from English History*, Pall Mall Gazette, 1886; *Beauty and the Beast: A Manuscript*, Pierpont Morgan Library, 1973.

Works including illustrations by Doyle: *The Fortunes of Hector O. Halloran*, Routledge, 1842; Charles Dickens, *The Chimes*, Chapman & Hall, 1845; C. Dickens, *The Battle of Life*, Bradbury & Evans, 1846; C. Dickens, *The Cricket on the Hearth*, Bradbury & Evans, 1846; John Milton, *L'Allegro and Il Penseroso*, Art-Union of London, 1848; John Forster, *Life of Oliver Goldsmith*, Bradbury & Evans, 1848; Bon Gaultier, *The Book of Ballads*, W. S. Orr, 1849; *Merry Pictures by the Comic Hands of H. K. Browne, Crowquill, Doyle, Leech, Meadows, Hine, and Others*, W. Kent, 1857; Harry Cholmondely Pennell, *Puck on Pegasus*, [London], 1861; C. Dickens, *Christmas Books*, Chapman & Hall, 1869; *Benjamin Disraeli, Earl of Beaconsfield (in Upwards of 100 Cartoons)*, Punch Office, 1878; Charles Plumptre Johnson, *The Early Writings of William Makepeace Thackeray*, E. Stock, 1888; M. P. Toby, *The Queen and Mr. Punch*, Bradbury, Agnew, 1897; Douglas William Jerrold, *Mrs. Caudle's Curtain Lectures* (originally published in *Punch*), R. B. Johnson, 1902.

SIDELIGHTS: **September, 1824.** Born in Hyde Park, England, the son of an Irish artist and cartoonist, John Doyle, or ''H. B.'' as he was known.

1840. *The Eglinton Tournament*, burlesque of early days of chivalry, appeared. ''Oh my goodness me fifty hot pressed copies of *The Tournament*. I can't believe it.... As soon as I got up this morning I ran to have a look at the fifty copies to see how they looked on the second day of arrival. Of course they looked beautiful. I began the illustrations to the *History of Belgium* today but some how or other I could not work. I suppose that the publication has acted so powerfully on my system, that I am not able to do anything.

Butterfly chariot. ■ (From *In Fairy Land* by William Allingham. Illustrated by Richard Doyle.)

She threw her arms around the stony figure, which at that moment received life and movement. ■ (From *The Feast of the Dwarfs, and Other Famous Fairy Tales.* Illustrated by Richard Doyle.)

"If I were not going to be an artist, I would like best to be an officer in the lifeguards. There is scarcely anything so delicious to me as a review." [Richard Doyle, *A Journal Kept by Richard Doyle in the Year 1840*, Scribner & Welford, 1886.[1]]

December, 1840. Displayed a particular gift for painting parades, processions, and historical pageantry. "I really feel afraid I will never be able to put down a quarter of the ideas for my procession that crowd into my head every time I think of it. Sometimes after I am in bed at night some idea to my mind more remarkable in point of brilliancy, than any preceeding it, strikes me. . . . First jumping out of bed, I seize upon a chair by brute force and plant it in the middle of the floor, becoming possessed of a coat I then place it upon the back of the chair, a pair of trousers in a reclining posture adds to the picturesque effect already produced and I become enraptured at the sight, fetch four boots and place a leg in each . . . I seized a hat and placing it on one side of the gentleman's head, gave at once to the whole, a light, cheerful, and even playful appearance. By this time feeling myself rather cold than otherwise. I sprang into bed. Upon awakening in the morning I was immediately struck by the singular appearance in the middle of the room and from thence reminded of the reason that gave rise to it."[1]

1843. Regular contributor to *Punch,* a humor magazine, between 1843 and 1851, illustrating the cover for the periodical in 1849 which later became famous.

1849. Began *Manners & Customs* series, which were to earn him his greatest popularity. Doyle spoofed English society, while bemoaning his own perennial bachelordom. "Blanche, how unfortunately Lady Airlie, was invited but could not come. . . . I thought I should have bust. I, however, controlled my feelings and by countenance by a powerful effort and succeeded in looking as if nothing was the matter. But little did that imperious woman . . . know the workings of my innermost soul." [Daria Hambourg, *Richard Doyle: His Life and Work*, Pellegrini & Cudahy, 1948.[2]]

1850. Left *Punch* because of its anti-Catholic bias to become perhaps the most gifted and original of the younger illustrators of his era.

1870's. Leading illustrator of "fairyland" figures. Nixies and pixies, giants and dwarfs, trolls and kobolds, wood-sprites, birds and butterflies typically populated his supernatural world.

December 11, 1883. Seized with a fatal apoplectic fit.

FOR MORE INFORMATION SEE: Daria Hambourg, *Richard Doyle: His Life and Work*, Pellegrini & Cudahy, 1948; *Nymphets and Fairies: Three Victorian Children's Illustrators*, St. Martin's, 1976; D. B. Lambourne, "Two Books Full of Nonsense and Other Works by Richard Doyle," *Burlington Magazine*, May, 1978.

EDGEWORTH, Maria   1767-1849

PERSONAL: Born January 1, 1767, in Black Bourton, Oxfordshire, England; died May 22, 1849, in Edgeworthstown, County Longford, Ireland; daughter (and the second of the 21 children) of Richard Lovell Edgeworth (an Irish educator); aunt of Thomas Lovell Beddoes, the poet and dramatist.

CAREER: Novelist and author of moral tales for children.

WRITINGS—Fiction: Castle Rackrent: An Hiberian Tale, J. Johnson, 1800, reprinted, Norton, 1965; *Belinda*, J. Johnson, 1801 [another edition illustrated by Chris Hammond, Macmillan, 1896]; *The Modern Griselda: A Tale*, J. Johnson, 1805; *Adelaide; or, The Chateau de St. Pierre*, J. F. Hughes, 1806; *Leonora*, [London], 1806; *Tales of Fashionable Life*, Town & Milligan, 1809; *Idleness and Industry Exemplified in the History of James Preston and Lazy Lawrence*, Johnson & Warner, 1811; *The Absentee: A Tale*, W. Cooper, 1812; *Vivian*, [London], 1812; *Patronage*, J. Johnson, 1814; *Harrington*, [London], 1817; *Ormond*, [London], 1817, reprinted, Irish University Press, 1972 [another edition illustrated by Carl Scholoesser, Macmillan, 1895]; *Helen: A Tale*, R. Bentley, 1834 [another edition illustrated by C. Hammond, Macmillan, 1896]; *The Most Unfortunate Day in My Life* (illustrated by Norah McGuinness), Cobden-Sanderson, 1931.

For children: *The Parents Assistant; or, Stories for Children*, 6 volumes, J. Johnson, 1796-1800, reprinted, Garland, 1977 [other editions illustrated by L. Speed, Bell, 1890; C. Hammond, Macmillan, 1897]; *Moral Tales for Young People*, J. Johnson, 1801, reprinted, Garland, 1974 [another edition illustrated by F.O.C. Darley, Appleton, 1856]; *Early Lessons*, [London], 1801; *Popular Tales*, J. Johnson, 1804 [another edition illustrated by William H. Croome, Appleton, 1853]; *Harry and Lucy*, Babcock, 1821; *Rosamond: A Sequel to Early Lessons*, J. Maxwell, 1821; *Frank*, [London], 1822.

Other: *Letters for Literary Ladies*, J. Johnson, 1795, reprinted, University Microfilms, 1974; (with father, Richard Lovell Edgeworth) *Practical Education*, [London], 1798, reprinted, Garland, 1974; *An Essay on the Noble Science of Self-Justification*, J. Milligan, 1810; *Comic Dramas, in Three Acts*, [London], 1817; (editor) *Memoirs of Richard Lovell Edgeworth*, [London], 1820, reprinted, Irish University Press, 1969.

Collections and selections: *Tales and Novels*, 20 volumes, Harper, 1835-36, reprinted, AMS Press, 1967; *The Novels of Maria Edgeworth*, 12 volumes, Dodd, 1893; *The Life and Letters of Maria Edgeworth*, edited by Augustus J. C. Hare, Houghton, 1895, reprinted, Books for Libraries, 1971; *Maria Edgeworth: Selections from Her Works*, F. A. Stokes, 1920; *Maria Edgeworth: Chosen Letters*, Houghton, 1931, reprinted, AMS Press, 1976.

ADAPTATIONS—Plays: Marianne Moore, *The Absentee* (three-act), House of Books, 1962.

SIDELIGHTS: **January 1, 1767.** Born in Black Bourton, Oxfordshire, England into a family of predominately Irish extraction.

1773. Mother died. Father remarried.

1780. Stepmother, Honora, died. Father married Honora's sister, Elizabeth.

1782. Family established residence at Edgeworthstown, Ireland. "Some men live with their families without letting them know their affairs, and, however great may be their affection and esteem for their wives and children, think that they have nothing to do with business. This was not my father's way of thinking. On the contrary, not only his wife, but his children, knew all his affairs. Whatever business he had to do was done in the midst of his family, usually in the common sitting-room; so that we were intimately acquainted, not only with his general principles of conduct, but with the minute details of their every-day application. I further enjoyed some peculiar advantages: he kindly wished to give me habits of business, and for this purpose allowed me, during many years, to assist him in copying his letters of business, and in receiving his rents." [Augustus Hare, editor, *The Life and Letters of Maria Edgeworth*, Volume I, Houghton, 1895.[1]]

1791-1792. Series of family illness precipitated return visit to England. "We live just the same kind of life that we used to do at Edgeworthstown, and though we move amongst numbers, are not moved by them, but feel independent of them for our daily amusement. All the *phantasmas* I had conjured up to frighten myself vanished after I had been here a week, for I found that they were but phantoms of my imagination, . . . We live very near the Downs, where we have almost every day charming walks, and all the children go bounding about over hill and dale along with us.

"Since I have been away from home I have missed the society and fondness of my father, mother and sisters, more than I can express, and more than beforehand I could have thought possible; I long to see them all again. Even when I am most amused I feel a void, and now I understand what an aching void is perfectly well." [Helen Zimmern, *Maria Edgeworth*, Roberts Brothers, 1883.[2]]

1793. In the wake of Irish political unrest, family returned to Edgeworthstown. "All that I crave for my own part is that if I am to have my throat cut, it may not be by a man with his face blackened with charcoal. I shall look at every person that comes here very closely, to see if there be any marks of charcoal upon their visages. Old wrinkled offenders, I should suppose, would never be able to wash out their stains, but in others a *very* clean face will, in my mind, be a strong symptom of guilt—clean hands proof positive, and clean nails ought to hang a man."[2]

1795. Embarked on a literary career with *Letters to Literary Ladies*. ". . . I am sorry to say they [*Literary Ladies*] are not as well as can be expected, nor are they likely to mend at present; when they are fit to be seen—if that happy time ever arrives—their first visit shall be to Black Castle. They are now disfigured by all manner of crooked marks of papa's critical indignation, besides various abusive marginal notes. . . .

"Whenever I thought of writing anything I always told my father my first rough plans; and always, with the instinct of a good critic, he used to fix immediately upon that which would best answer the purpose. 'Sketch that, and show it to me.' The words, from the experience of his sagacity, never failed to inspire me with hope of success. It was then sketched. Sometimes, when I was fond of a particular part, I used to dilate on it in the sketch; but to this he always objected. 'I don't want any of your painting—none of your drapery! I can imagine all that. Let me see the bare skeleton.'

"It seemed to me sometimes impossible that he could understand the very slight sketches I made; when, before I was conscious that I had expressed this doubt in my countenance, he always saw it.

"'Now, my dear little daughter, I know, does not believe that I understand her.' Then he would, in his own words, fill up my sketch, paint the description, or represent the character intended, with such life, that I was quite convinced he not only seized the ideas, but that he saw with the prophetic eye of taste the utmost that could be made of them. After a sketch had his approbation, he would not see the filling up till it had been worked upon for a week or fortnight, or till the first thirty or forty pages were written; then they were read to him, and if he thought them going on tolerably well, the pleasure in his eyes, the approving sound of his voice, even without the praise he so warmly bestowed, were sufficient and delightful incitements to 'go on and finish.' When he thought that there was spirit in what was written, but that it required, as it often did, great correction, he would say: 'Leave that to me; it is my business to cut and correct, yours to write on.' His skill in cutting, his decision in criticism, was peculiarly useful to me. His ready invention and infinite resource, when I had run myself into difficulties, never failed to extricate me at my utmost need. It was the happy experience of this, and my consequent reliance on his ability, decision and perfect honesty, that relieved me from the vacillation and anxiety to which I was so much subject, that I am sure I should not have written or finished anything without his support. He inspired in my mind a degree of hope and confidence, essential in the first instance to the full exertion of the mental powers, and necessary to insure perseverance in any occupation. Such, happily for me, was his power over my mind, that no one thing I ever began to write was ever left unfinished."[2]

1797. Stepmother, Elizabeth, died.

1798. Collaborated with her father on *Practical Education.* Father married for fourth time. "We are indeed happy. The more I see of my friend and mother, the more I love and esteem her. . . . So little change has been made in the way of living, that you would feel as if you were going on with your usual occupations and conversation amongst us. We laugh and talk and enjoy the good of every day, which is more than sufficient. How long this may last we cannot tell. I am going on in the old way, writing stories. I cannot be a captain of dragoons, and sitting with my hands before me would not make any of us one degree safer. I have finished a volume of wee-wee stories about the size of the *Purple Jar,* all about Rosamond. . . ."[2]

1801. Wrote *Belinda,* also *Moral Tales* in five volumes, designed as a modern equivalent of parables. "Belinda is but an interesting personage after all. . . . I was not sufficiently aware that the *goodness* of a heroine interests only in proportion to the perils and trails to which it is exposed.

"I really was so provoked with the cold tameness of that stick or stone, Belinda, that I could have torn the pages to pieces; really I have not the heart or the patience to *correct* her. As the hackney coachman said, 'Mend *you!* Better make a new one.'"[2]

1802-1803. Fell in love with a Swedish chevalier in Paris during her European tour. ". . . I was interrupted in a manner that . . . surprised me, by the coming in of Monsieur Edelcrantz, a Swedish gentleman, . . . of superior understanding and mild manners: he came to offer me his hand and heart!!

". . . I persist in refusing to leave my country and friends to live at the court of Stockholm. And he tells me (of course) that there is nothing he would not sacrifice for me except his duty; he has been all his life in the service of the King of Sweden, has places under him, and is actually employed in collecting information for a large political establishment. He thinks himself bound in honor to finish what he has begun. He says he should not fear the ridicule or blame that would be thrown upon him by his countrymen for quitting his country at his age, but that he would despise himself if he abandoned his duty for any passion. This is all very reasonable, but reasonable for him only, not for me, and I have never felt anything for him but esteem and gratitude."[2]

1809-1812. Wrote *Tales of Fashionable Life* in two sets, six volumes. Combined prolificity and humility in attitude towards her work. "In novel-writing I certainly have from principle avoided all exaggerated sentiment; but I am well aware that many other writers possess in a much higher degree than I do the power of pathos and the art of touching the passions. As to how I should use these powers if I had them, perhaps I cannot fairly judge, but all I am at present sure of is that I will not depreciate that which I do not possess.

"If everybody were to wait till they could write a book in which there should not be a single fault or error, the press might stand still for ages yet unborn. Mankind must have arrived at the summit of knowledge before language could be as perfect as you expect yours to be. Till ideas are exact, just and sufficient, how can words which represent them be accurate? The advantage of the art of printing is that the mistakes of individuals in reasoning and writing will be corrected in time by the public—so that the cause of truth cannot suffer, and I presume you are too much of a philosopher to mind the trifling mortification to your vanity which the de-

MARIA EDGEWORTH

tection of a mistake might occasion. You know that some sensible person has observed, only in other words, that we are wiser to-day than we were yesterday. . . . I think that only little or weak minds are so dreadfully afraid of being ever in the wrong. Those who feel that they have resources, that they have means of compensating for errors, have never this horror of being found in a mistake."[2]

March, 1813. First introduction to London high society. "The brilliant panorama of London is over, and I have enjoyed more pleasure and have had more amusement, infinitely more than I expected, and received more attention, more kindness, than I could have thought it possible would be shown to me; I have enjoyed the delight of seeing my father esteemed and honored by the best judges in England; I have felt the pleasure of seeing my true friend and mother—for she has been a mother to me—appreciated in the best society; and now, with the fullness of content, I return home, loving my own friends and my own mode of life preferably to all others, after comparison with all that is fine and gay, and rich and rare.

"I feel that I return with fresh pleasure to literary work from having been so long idle, and I have a famishing appetite for reading. All that we saw in London I am sure I enjoyed, while it was passing, as much as possible; but I should be sorry to live in that whirling vortex, and I find my taste and conviction confirmed on my return to my natural friends and my dear home."[2]

"Ay," said Holloway, "learn to stand your ground and fight before you meddle with me, I advise you."
■ (From *Moral Tales* by Maria Edgeworth. Illustrated by F. O. C. Darley.)

1814. Father ill. "The spring of his mind has not recovered. He says that nothing excites him, that he feels no motive. This is so unlike him. And it is so very uncommon to see him sad and silent, and utterly passive that it is impossible to resist the contagion." [James Newcomer, *Maria Edgeworth*, Bucknell University Press, 1973.[3]]

June 13, 1817. Father died. "The tears, felt like the cutting of a knife."[3]

"I was always fond of being loved, but of late I am become more sensible of the soothing power of affectionate expressions. Indeed, I have reason, although much has been taken from me, to be heartily grateful for all I have left of excellent friends, and for much, much unexpected kindness which has been shown to me and mine, not only by persons unconnected by any natural ties with me or them, but from mere acquaintance become friends."[2]

1819. Returned to work to complete her father's memoirs. "We are looking to the bright side of every object that remains to us, and many blessings we have still. I am now correcting what I had written of my father's life, and shall be for some months. . . .

"Till now I have never on any occasion addressed myself to the public alone, and speaking in the first person. This egotism is not only repugnant to my habits, but most painful and melancholy. Formerly I had always a friend and father who spoke and wrote for me; one who exerted for me all the powers of his strong mind, even to the very last. Far more than his protecting kindness I regret, at this moment, the want of his guiding judgment now, when it is most important to me—where *his* fame is at stake.

"You would scarcely believe, my dear friends, the calm of mind and the sort of satisfied resignation I feel as to my father's life. I suppose the two years of doubt and extreme anxiety that I felt exhausted all my power of doubting. I know that I have done my very best, I know that I have done my duty, and I firmly believe that if my dear father could see the whole, he would be satisfied with what I have done."[2]

1826. Took over management of Edgeworthstown from brother, Lovell. "I really think that if my thoughts and feelings were shut up completely within me, I should burst in a week, like a steam engine without a snifting-clack, now called by the grander name of a safety-valve. 'You want to know what I am doing and thinking of: of ditches, drains and sewers, of dragging quicks from one hedge and sticking them down into another, at the imminent peril of their green lives; of two houses to let, one tenant promised from the Isle of Man, another from the Irish Survey; of two bullfinches, each in his cage on the table—one who would sing if he could, and the other who could sing, I am told, if he would. . . .' "[2]

1830-1831. Another visit to England. "It is always gratifying to find old friends the same after long absence, but it has been particularly so to me now, when not only the leaves of the pleasures of life fall naturally in its winter, but when the great branches on whom happiness depended are gone.

"Old as I am, and imaginative as I am thought to be, I have really always found that the pleasures I have expected would be great, have actually been greater in the enjoyment than in the anticipation. This is written in my sixty-fourth year. . . . The pleasures here altogether, including the kindness of old friends and the civilities of acquaintances, are still more enhanced than I had calculated upon by the home and the quiet library and easy-chair morning retreat I enjoy.

"My last visit to universal London confirms to my own feelings your eulogium. I never was so happy there in my life, because I had, besides all the external pleasures, the solid satisfaction of a home there, and domestic pleasures, without which I should soon grow aweary of the world, and wish the business of the town were done. It is most gratifying to me, at such a distance, to hear and to believe that such kind and cultivated friends as you miss my company and wish for my future return. I should be very sorry if I were told this minute that I was never to see London again, and yet I am wondrous contented and happy at home."[2]

1833. Tour of Connemara. ". . . I confess it was imprudent and very unlike my usual dislike to leave home without any of my own people with me. But upon this occasion I fancied I should see all I wanted to see of the wonderful ways of going on and manners of the natives better for not being with any of my own family, and especially for its not being suspected that I was an authoress and might put them in a book. In short, I thought it was the best opportunity I could ever have of seeing a part of Ireland which, from time immemorial, I had been curious to see. My curiosity had been raised even when I first came to Ireland fifty years ago, by hearing my father talk of the King of Connemara, and his immense territory, and his ways of ruling over his people with almost absolute power, with laws of his own, and setting all other laws at defiance. Smugglers, and caves, and murders, and mermaids, and duels, and banshees, and fairies, were all mingled in my early associations with Connemara and Dick Martin,—'Hair-trigger Dick,' who cared so little for his own life or the life of man, and so much for the life of animals, who fought more duels than any man of even his 'Blue-blaze-devil' day, and who brought the bill into Parliament for preventing cruelty to animals; thenceforward changing his cognomen from 'Hair-trigger Dick' to 'Humanity Martin.' He was my father's contemporary, and he knew a number of anecdotes of him. *Too besides,* I once saw him, and remember that my blood crept slow and my breath was held when he first came into the room, a pale, little, insignificant-looking mortal he was, but he still kept hold of my imagination, and his land of Connemara was always a land I longed to visit. . . .'' [Augustus Hare, editor, *The Life and Letters of Maria Edgeworth,* Volume II, Houghton, 1895.[4]]

1834. Wrote *Helen,* her last novel of love and manners. ''. . . In my whole life, since I began to write, which is now, I am concerned to state, upwards of forty years, I have had only about half a dozen little note-books, strangely and irregularly kept, sometimes with only words of reference to some book, or fact I could not bring accurately to mind. At first I was much urged by my father to note down remarkable traits of character or incidents, which he thought might be introduced in stories; and he often blamed that idleness or laziness, as he thought it in me, which resisted his urgency. But I was averse to noting down, because I was conscious that it did better for me to keep the things in my head, if they suited my purpose; and if they did not, they would only encumber me. I knew that, when I wrote down, I put the thing out of my care, out of my head; and that, though it might be put by very safe, I should not know where to look for it; that the labor of looking over a note-book would never do when I was in the warmth and pleasure of inventing; that I should never recollect the facts or ideas at the right time, if I did not put them up in my own way in my own head. . . .''

''I never could use notes in writing dialogues; it would have been as impossible to me to get in the prepared good things at the right moment in the warmth of writing conversation, as it would be to lug them in in real conversation, perhaps more so—for I could not write dialogues at all without being at the time fully impressed with the characters, imagining myself each speaker, and that too fully engrosses the imagination to leave time for consulting note-books; the whole fairy vision would melt away, and the warmth and the pleasure of invention be gone. I might often, while writing, recollect from books or life what would suit, and often from note-book; but then I could not stop to look, and often quoted therefore inaccurately. . . .''[4]

1843. Seriously ill with bilious fever, Edgeworth's interests remained lively. ''. . . I am six years beyond the allotted age and have had so many attacks of illness within the last two years . . . like one of those pith puppets that you knock down in vain; they always start up the same as ever. . . . I am obliged to repeat myself, 'advanced age,' because really and truly neither my spirits nor my powers of locomotion and facility of running up and down stairs would put me in mind of it. I do not find either my love for my friends or my love of literature in the least failing. . . .

''I am surprised to find how much more history interests me now than when I was young, and how much more I am now interested in the same events recorded, and their causes and consequences shown, in this history of the French Revolution, and in all the history of Europe during the last quarter of a century, than I was when the news came fresh and fresh in the newspapers. I do not think I had sense enough to take

The boy pulled off the cover, and saw a white pigeon painted upon the sign.... ■ (From *The Parent's Assistant or Stories for Children* by Maria Edgeworth. Illustrated by Chris Hammond.)

in the relations and proportions of the events. It was like moving a magnifying glass over the parts of a beetle, and not taking in the whole.''[2]

1847. Helped the poor during potato famine. Children of Boston contributed flour and rice inscribed ''To Miss Edgeworth for her poor.''

May 22, 1849. Died in Edgeworthstown in the arms of her devoted stepmother. ''There is something mournful, yet pleasingly painful, in the sense of the ideal presence of the long-loved dead. Those images people and fill the mind with unselfish thoughts, and with the salutary feeling of responsibility and constant desire to be and to act in this world as the superior friend would have wished and approved.''[2]

FOR MORE INFORMATION SEE: Grace Oliver, *A Study of Maria Edgeworth,* A. Williams, 1882, reprinted, R. West, 1973; Helen Zimmern, *Maria Edgeworth,* Roberts Brothers, 1883, reprinted, R. West, 1973; Augustus J. C. Hare, editor, *The Life and Letters of Maria Edgeworth,* Houghton, 1895, reprinted, Books for Libraries, 1971; Emily Lawless, *Maria Edgeworth,* Macmillan, 1904, reprinted, R. West, 1973; Theodore Goodman, *Maria Edgeworth, Novelist of Reason,* New York University Press, 1936; (for children) Elizabeth Rider Montgomery, *Story behind Great Stories,* McBride,

1947; W. F. Gray, "Maria Edgeworth and a Gentleman-Philosopher," *Fortnightly*, May, 1949; Percy Howard Newby, *Maria Edgeworth*, Swallow Press, 1950, reprinted, R. West, 1973; Isabel C. Clarke, *Maria Edgeworth, Her Family and Friends*, Hutchinson, 1950, reprinted, Folcroft, 1972; Elisabeth Inglis-Jones, *Great Maria: A Portrait of Maria Edgeworth*, Faber, 1959; Thomas J. B. Flanagan, *Irish Novelists, 1800-1850*, Columbia University Press, 1959.

Frank Swinnerton, *Galaxy of Fathers*, Doubleday, 1966; Mark D. Hawthorne, *Doubt and Dogma in Maria Edgeworth*, University Presses of Florida, 1967; James Newcomer, *Maria Edgeworth the Novelist, 1767-1849*, Texas Christian University Press, 1967; Brian Doyle, editor, *Who's Who of Children's Literature*, Schocken Books, 1968; Michael Hurst, *Maria Edgeworth and the Public Scene: Intellect, Fine Feeling, and Landlordism in the Age of Reform*, Macmillan, 1969; O. Elizabeth Harden, *Maria Edgeworth's Art of Fiction*, Humanities, 1971; Patrick Murray, *Maria Edgeworth: A Study of the Novelist*, Mercier Press, 1971; Marilyn Butler, *Maria Edgeworth: A Literary Biography*, Oxford University Press, 1972; J. Newcomer, *Maria Edgeworth*, Bucknell University Press, 1973.

ELISOFON, Eliot   1911-1973

OBITUARY NOTICE: Born April 17, 1911, in New York, N.Y.; died April 7, 1973, in New York, N.Y. Photo-journalist, documentary film-maker, painter, art collector, and author. From an early age, Elisofon was a professional photographer, an occupation which led him to varied assignments in many parts of the world. He began his career doing freelance commercial photography, and went on to become a staff photographer for the Museum of Modern Art in 1939, and for *Life* from 1942 until the mid-'60s. He was a research fellow in primitive art with Harvard's Peabody Museum and a curatorial associate at the Museum of African Art in Washington, D.C. Elisofon often focused on the art and architecture of ancient cultures, and did photographic studies of locales ranging from South America to India to Cambodia to Africa. He was particularly enthralled with the latter, which became the subject of "Africa," a comprehensive documentary for ABC television, for which he was director of creative production. Elisofon also did film work, most notably as color consultant for "Moulin Rouge," "Bell, Book, and Candle," and "The War Lord," and as a still photographer for other movies, including "Dr. Dolittle." His photographs have appeared in some dozen books, and they are in the permanent collections of such museums as the Chicago Art Institute and the Museum of Modern Art. For children, Elisofon produced several photo-documentary books on life in other countries, including *Zaire: A Week in Joseph's World*, a Notable Children's Trade Book in the field of social studies. *For More Information See: Current Biography*, Wilson, 1972; *Who's Who in American Art*, Bowker, 1973. *Obituaries: Current Biography*, Wilson, 1973; *New York Times*, April 8, 1973; *Washington Post*, April 9, 1973; *Time*, April 16, 1973; *Contemporary Authors*, Volume 41-44, Gale, 1974.

There is no frigate like a book to take us lands away,
Nor any coursers like a page of prancing poetry.
—Emily Dickinson

MILDRED ADAMS FENTON

FENTON, Mildred Adams   1899-

PERSONAL: Born in 1899, near West Branch, Iowa; married Carroll Lane Fenton (an author), 1921 (died November 16, 1969). *Education:* Attended the University of Iowa and the University of Chicago. *Residence:* New Brunswick, N.J.

CAREER: University of Cincinnati, Cincinnati, Ohio, acting curator, 1926-29; Rutgers University, New Brunswick, N.J., curator of Geological Museum, 1944-46; author.

WRITINGS—For adults; all with husband, Carroll Lane Fenton: *Records of Evolution*, Haldeman-Julius, 1924; *The Rock Book*, Doubleday, 1940; *The Story of the Great Geologists*, Doubleday, Doran, 1945, reprinted, Books for Libraries, 1969, revised and enlarged edition published as *Giants of Geology*, Doubleday, 1952; *Rocks and Their Stories*, Doubleday, 1951; *The Fossil Book: A Record of Prehistoric Life*, Doubleday, 1958.

For young people; all with C. L. Fenton: *Mountains* (illustrated by the authors), Doubleday, Doran, 1942, reprinted, Books for Libraries, 1969; *The Land We Live On*, Doubleday, Doran, 1944, reissued, Doubleday, 1966; *Worlds in the Sky* (illustrated by the authors), J. Day, 1950, revised edition, 1963; *Riches from the Earth* (illustrated by the authors), J. Day, 1953, reprinted, 1970; *Our Changing Weather*, Doubleday, 1954; *Prehistoric Zoo* (illustrated by C. L. Fenton), Doubleday, 1959; *In Prehistoric Seas* (illustrated by C. L. Fenton), Doubleday, 1963.

SIDELIGHTS: Fenton credits two college professors with developing her interest in geology and fossils. Upon her marriage to Carroll Lane Fenton, she began to co-author books in this field. An early effort, *Mountains*, was reviewed by a *Horn Book* critic, who wrote, "... In a clear, non-technical style, ... [the Fentons] tell of batholiths and blister mountains, of the origin of volcanoes and glaciers. Not only does this excellent guide book introduce the beginner to mountain structure, but it also throws a clear light on the formation and composition of many minerals. Graphic and beautiful illustrations give their vigorous aid to the young student." *Commonweal* added, "The text misses the happy medium between the use of technical terms and the supposed necessity of writing 'down' for the interested amateur. Nevertheless it is informative and unusually well illustrated. ..."

Kirkus called the Fentons' *Story of the Great Geologists* "a worthwhile compilation of unhackneyed material, which evades the dangers of too glossy popularization in keeping to a conservative interpretation of biographical and scientific importance of the subjects." Of *Our Changing Weather*, the *New York Herald Tribune Book Review* commented, "A handsomely made book, its generous pages give good space for the many dramatic photographs, very well printed, and the well drawn diagrams. The text is purely factual, its lure being entirely in the fascinating subjects well chosen and titles in the contents. ..." Added the *Springfield Republican*: "Although designed primarily for junior readers, this well-written book contains so much valuable information that it should be interesting also to many adults."

Diplodocus, a plant-eating dinosaur 87 feet long, had a slender neck and tail. This restoration of the reptile as it looked during life is based on skeletons found in northeastern Utah. ■ (From *The Fossil Book* by Carroll Lane Fenton and Mildred Adams Fenton. Illustrated by the authors.)

In a review of *The Fossil Book: A Record of Prehistoric Life*, the *Chicago Sunday Tribune* observed: "The fossil collectors now have for the first time a readable, handsomely illustrated and remarkably comprehensive survey of the realm of prehistoric life." Noted the *San Francisco Chronicle*: "The *Fossil Book* ... makes paleontology as interesting and dramatic to the layman as archaeology has become in recent years. ... This is a colorful, kaleidoscopic record of prehistoric life. It is generously illustrated with scores of photographs, drawings, and color plates."

One of the Fentons' most recent books, *Prehistoric Zoo*, was thus described by *Kirkus*: "A study in evolution and zoology, this text, generously illustrated in black and white, presents its subject in a vital manner, free from arid academies. ... An unusually original, informative and lively text."

FOR MORE INFORMATION SEE: Horn Book, September, 1942; *Commonweal*, December 4, 1942; *Kirkus*, April 1, 1945; *New York Herald Tribune Book Review*, May 16, 1954; *Springfield Republican*, June 13, 1954; *Chicago Sunday Tribune*, February 8, 1959; *San Francisco Chronicle*, August 23, 1959; Muriel Fuller, editor, *More Junior Authors*, H. W. Wilson, 1963.

FERRIS, Helen Josephine   1890-1969

PERSONAL: Born November 19, 1890, in Hastings, Neb.; died September 28, 1969; daughter of Elmer E. (a minister) and Minnie (Lum) Ferris; married Albert B. Tibbets, February 12, 1924. *Education:* Vassar College, B.A., 1912.

CAREER: Correspondent for a Poughkeepsie, N.Y., and a New Jersey newspaper during college, 1909-12; John Wanamaker stores, worker in educational department, 1912-18; editor, the *Guardian*, 1921-23, *American Girl*, 1923-28; *Youth's Companion*, associate editor, 1928-29; Junior Literary Guild, editor-in-chief, 1929-59; author. *Wartime service:* Served on the Commission on Training Camp Activities of the War Work Council, 1918-19. *Member:* Phi Beta Kappa. *Awards, honors:* Child Study Association Children's Book Committee award, 1950, for *Partners: The United Nations and Youth.*

WRITINGS: Girls's Clubs, Their Organization and Management: A Manual for Workers, Dutton, 1918, new edition, 1926; *Producing Amateur Entertainments: Varied Stunts and Other Numbers with Program Plans and Directions*, Dutton, 1921; (with Virginia Moore) *Girls Who Did: Stories of Real Girls and Their Careers* (illustrated by Harriet Moncure), Dutton, 1927; *This Happened to Me: Stories of Real Girls as Told to Helen Ferris*, Dutton, 1929; *Dody and Cap-tin Jinks* (illustrated by Grace Paull), Doubleday, Doran, 1939; *Tommy and His Dog, Hurry* (illustrated by Ruth Wood), Doubleday, 1944; *Watch Me, Said the Jeep* (illustrated by Tibor Gergely), Garden City Publishing, 1944; (with Eleanor Roosevelt) *Partners: The United Nations and Youth*, Doubleday, 1950; (with E. Roosevelt) *Your Teens and Mine*, Doubleday, 1961.

Editor: (With Alice M. Kimball) *Girl Scout Short Stories*, Doubleday, Page, 1925; *Adventure Waits: A Book of Adventure Stories for Girls* (illustrated by Beth K. Morris), Harcourt, 1928; *Loves Comes Riding: Stories of Romance and Adventure for Girls* (illustrated by B. K. Morris), Harcourt, 1929; *When I Was a Girl: Stories of Five Famous Women*

HELEN FERRIS

as Told by Themselves (illustrated by Curtiss Sprague), Macmillan, 1930; (with Anne H. Choate) *Juliette Low and the Girl Scouts*, Girl Scouts, 1931; *Five Girls Who Dared: The Girlhood Stories of Five Courageous Girls as Told by Themselves* (illustrated by Allan McNab), Macmillan, 1931, reprinted, Books for Libraries, 1971; *P. T. Barnum, Here Comes Barnum* (illustrated by Frank Dobias), Harcourt, 1932; (with Grace T. Huffard and L. M. Carlisle) *My Poetry Book*, Winston, 1934; *Challenge: Stories of Courage and Love for Girls* (illustrated by Marguerite de Angeli), Doubleday, Doran, 1936; *Love's Enchantment: Story Poems and Ballads* (illustrated by Vera Bock), Doubleday, 1944, reprinted, Books for Libraries, 1969; *Writing Books for Boys and Girls: A Young Wings Anthology of Essays*, Junior Literary Guild, 1952; *Favorite Poems, Old and New* (illustrated by Kay L. Smith and Leonard Weisgard), Doubleday, 1957; *Girls, Girls, Girls: Stories of Love, Courage, and the Quest for Happiness*, Watts, 1957; *Brave and the Fair: Stories of Courage and Romance*, Winston, 1960; *Time of Discovering: Stories of Girls Who Found Clues to Careers*, Watts, 1961; *Time of Starting Out: Stories of Girls on Their First Jobs*, Watts, 1962; *Time of Understanding: Stories of Girls Learning to Get Along with Their Parents*, Watts, 1963.

SIDELIGHTS: **November 19, 1890.** Born in Hastings, Nebraska; daughter of minister, Elmer Ferris. ". . . [My] two parents, loving poetry, made it as much a part of their children's every day as getting up in the morning, eating breakfast, going to school, playing outdoors until suppertime.

"It is evening. My brother Fred and I are in bed, propped up against the pillows. Mama is sitting by the table, with the

lamp's red shade throwing a rosy glow over her face and the book from which she is reading.

> *'Little Jack Horner*
> *Sat in a corner . . .'*

"Fred and I know it by heart, just as we know by heart all the others in the Mother Goose Book. But to have Mama read them aloud gives us a warm feeling of the day ending as it should end. And to our profound satisfaction in hearing the familiar words over and over again is added our pleasure in the cadence of her voice.

"When Papa can be with us, it is an event, all too seldom realized. For Papa is a minister with many evening meetings in the small Nebraska town where we live.

"Not even Mama can make the shivers run down our backbones as he does with:

> *''Twas a misty, moisty morning,*
> *And cloudy was the weather.'*

"There is ominous portent in his deep tones. Fred and I push closer together.

> *'I chanced to meet an old man,*
> *Clad all in leather.*
> *Clad all in leather*
> *With a STRAP beneath his chin.'*

"A strap—goodness! But the mood quickly brightens, for now Fred and I have our turn. . . .

"One night Papa came in to hear Mama read:

> *'Tom, Tom, the piper's son,*
> *Stole a pig and away he ran.'*

"'My dear Min,' he protested. Mama's name was Minnie. 'What are you doing? The word is "run."'"

"Mama's hazel eyes flashed, 'Elmer Ferris,' she told him firmly, 'if you think I am going to expose our children to bad grammar in this house, you are mistaken.'

"'Better that than expose them to bad rhyme,' declared Papa no less firmly.

"It was a difference of opinion that was never resolved. But, as with many such at our house, it became a source of merriment. Every now and then when supper was ready Mama would beckon to Fred and me, and the three of us would tiptoe to Papa's study, where he sat reading the paper. Soundlessly Mama's lips would form the words, 'Tom, Tom.'

"Then she would declaim: 'Tom, Tom, the piper's son, stole a pig and away he—'

"'Ran, ran, ran, ran,' Fred and I would shout, swarming over Papa to the definite detriment of the newspaper. Papa would throw back his head and laugh and laugh. And Fred and I were never to forget the importance either of good grammar or good rhyme.

"Memory of the poems that accompanied and followed Mother Goose in our bedtime hours is a tapestry, lovely but with no set design. Later I was to learn that Mama had an articulate theory about reading poetry aloud to children, a theory not surprising for she was a pianist. It did not matter, she was convinced, if we could not understand all the words. We could enjoy the beautiful sound of them. So it was that for Fred and me Mother Goose flowed easefully into Alfred Tennyson, Henry Wadsworth Longfellow into Shakespeare.

"Shakespeare was especially Papa's. . . . During many a family celebration Papa would take down the Shakespeare book, unerringly turn the pages to a certain passage, and new meaning was added to the occasion.

"Like the sunshine and the softness of twilight, like the wind and the rain and the snow, the poetry of the Bible belongs to the warp and woof of Fred's and my growing up. Mama, reading, 'I will lift up mine eyes unto the hills. . . .' She loved the Wisconsin hills of her girlhood and Fred and I were sure the Psalmist meant Wisconsin. Papa, slim and serious in the pulpit of the little prairie church: 'The Heavens declare the glory of God. . . .'

"I often wonder how Mama and Papa knew which of the new books to buy for us. There was no library in that small Nebraska town, no librarian to consult, no bookstore. Nor did the periodicals of those days carry many reviews of children's books. Yet new books regularly appeared for us, often those of poetry, which only rarely failed to enchant us. Perhaps Papa asked questions on his trips.

"From one of those trips Papa came home with exciting news. We were going to move to Wisconsin to live. 'In the city of La Crosse, which is on the mighty Mississippi River,' he told us. From then on it was one word to me, 'Mightymississippi.'

"Having the Mightymississippi so close was as exciting as Papa had predicted. 'Papa,' I asked him one morning at breakfast, 'does the Mightymississippi come from haunts of coot and hern?'

"'Certainly,' he replied, 'and it bickers down a valley, too—up North.'

"After that, whenever I went alone to the island out in the river, which was the city's Pettibone Park—as I was by then old enough to do—my routine was always the same. Hopping off my bike in the middle of the long bridge, leaning out over the railing, facing north, I told the Mightymississippi, so wide and ceaselessly flowing far below: 'You come from haunts of coot and hern. You bicker down a valley.'

"Friday afternoon at school was recitation time. Nor was there ever a lapse in any program when measles, mumps, or whooping cough laid low the scheduled performer. There was at hand an ever-eager, ever-ready volunteer named Helen to fill the gap. I loved reciting the dramatic poems—'One if by land, two if by sea'; "'But spare your country's flag,'' she said.' The sad ones—'The little toy dog is covered with dust.' Those with enviable elocutionary opportunity, 'Have you ever heard the wind go ''Yoooooooo?''' And the nonsense, ''Twas brillig, and the slithy toves.'

"To achieve effective rendition, rehearsing was called for. This took place in my room on the second floor of the parsonage. Standing by my bed, I faced the door, opened into the hall. But it was not the hall that was outside. It was a vast auditorium, crowded with an enrapt throng. And it was my pleasure—nay, my duty—to make certain that those in the most remote corners could hear me with ease.

(From "The Blind Beggar's Daughter of Bednall-Green," in *Love's Enchantment,* collected by Helen Ferris. Illustrated by Vera Bock.)

"Then one afternoon: 'Daughter!' It was Papa at the foot of the stairs. 'If you must bellow, kindly close the door. You are driving every idea out of my head.'

"Bellow! That was crushing. But without protest I closed the door. All the family knew the importance of ideas to Papa's sermons." [Introduction to *Favorite Poems, Old and New,* edited by Helen Ferris, Doubleday, 1957.[1]]

1912. Received her B.A. degree from Vassar College. "The years passed. Somewhere along the way 'Mama' became 'Mother' to Fred and me; 'Papa,' 'Dad.' But there was no change in our delight in bringing home new poetry that we had discovered. I from Vassar, with all the books by Sara Teasdale that I could squeeze out of my allowance. Fred from Brown, with William Henry Drummond and his *Wreck of the 'Julie Plante.'*

(From *Favorite Poems Old and New,* selected by Helen Ferris. Illustrated by Leonard Weisgard.)

Myself and I

"We moved to New York, on Morningside Drive, with the sweep of the great city beneath our windows and the sunrise on the distant horizon. One afternoon I opened the door of the apartment to see Dad pacing the floor, an open book in his hand. 'When I lived in Chicago,' he was telling Mother, 'the air was electric. I and my friends were young and going places. Chicago was young and going places. And this man Sandburg has caught it. What a poet! Listen to this. . . .'

"Mother liked Sandburg, too, but she preferred what she called his quiet poems. '"The fog comes in on little cat feet"—isn't that exactly the way it does down there in the street?'

"In time Fred's children stood beside her at the window. 'Look Helen. Look, Frederick. The stars! "Shall we ride to the blue star or the white star?"' And then to her and Dad's great-grandchildren at the same window: 'Look, Ricky. Look, Kimmy. The stars! "Shall we ride to the blue star or the white star?"'"[1]

1921-1923. Editor of the *Guardian.*

1923-1928. Editor of *American Girl* magazine. "There is always special excitement when an editor becomes editor of something new. It was this excitement that I felt when I entered upon my work of editing *The American Girl,* the magazine for all girls published by the Girl Scouts. And since,

further, an editor always has a special weakness for putting into any magazine that she edits those things that she herself especially loves, I quite naturally planned a poetry page for each issue of *The American Girl.*

"Right then I faced a question: Just what kinds of poems do girls in their early teens like best? My own love of poetry came, curiously, after I emerged from the teens—I think because in school I was always made to scan poetry, a process that eliminated the music and lyric joy for me.

"The answer to my question clearly lay with the girls themselves. Happily, very early in my *American Girl* editorship, Jane Deeter Rippin, the executive of the Girl Scouts, suggested that I visit a number of their summer camps. Into my suitcase I tucked my cherished volumes of poetry. And at each campfire out under the stars I told the girls that they were going to help me choose a poem for *The American Girl* poetry page. Then I read aloud many kinds of poems, glancing up to watch their faces.

"As is the way with many kinds of girls, they like many kinds of poems. But one kind never failed to arouse their unanimous enthusiasm—the poem that told a story. And of all the story poems I read, those that were their immediate delight were romantic poems. The princess in the beleaguered tower—that was it!"

1924. Married Albert B. Tibbets.

1928-1929. Became editor-in-chief of Junior Literary Guild. ''When, in time, I became editor of the Junior Literary Guild, there was for me but one way in which to start each issue of *Young Wings,* our Junior Guild magazine. Many a letter from our young members enthusiastically mentioned this poem and that, which had appeared on the inside front cover. 'Please have more like the one last month.' When we sent books of poetry to them, as Junior Literary Guild selections, their warm response was immediate. Of Ruth Barnes's collection of traditional poems from our country, *I Hear America Singing,* one boy wrote, 'These poems are swell.' Of Carl Sandburg's *Early Moon,* a girl said, 'I didn't know poetry could be like this. I have read *Early Moon* six times and am going to read it lots more.' The old and the new.''

1959-1969. Continued to write books for children and teenagers upon retirement from her career as an editor.

September 28, 1969. Died two months before her seventy-ninth birthday. Ferris' book, *Favorite Poems, Old and New,* a collection of her favorite poems and a living proof of her life-long enthusiasm for poetry, remains in print today.

Ferris' long and diverse career included both writing and editing. One of her earlier writing efforts was *Dody and Captin Jinks,* of which a *New York Times* critic commented, ''Dody, the publishers say, is the author's own mother, which may account for the perfect understanding of a little girl's desires and the intimate tone of family fun which runs through the story, but the skill with which it is told is the author's own. Grace Paull's illustrations, pleasantly reminiscent of the early nineteen hundreds, are as droll and sprightly as ever, although the ubiquitous smiles on all the faces are a trifle wearisome.'' Later, she collaborated with Eleanor Roosevelt to write *Your Teens and Mine.* A *Horn Book* reviewer noted, ''Out of her magnificent life, Mrs. Roosevelt offers, without preaching, some wisdom. . . . The compassion, warmth, humanity, and humor found here make the usual teen-age guides to life, popularity, and charm seem pallid indeed. . . . Girls fortunate enough to read this book will feel that they have talked directly with a real, living woman who cares about them, who in other times and circumstances faced problems and experiences basically the same as theirs.''

FOR MORE INFORMATION SEE: New York Times, January 7, 1940; Stanley J. Kunitz and Howard Haycraft, editors, *Junior Book of Authors,* second edition revised, H. W. Wilson, 1951; *Saturday Review,* November 16, 1957; *Library Journal,* December 15, 1957; *Horn Book,* December, 1957, December, 1961; Obituaries—*New York Times,* September 29, 1969; *Publishers Weekly,* October 13, 1969.

FOSTER, Margaret Lesser   1899(?)-1979

OBITUARY NOTICE: Born about 1899 in Montana; died November 21, 1979, in New York, N.Y. Foster was one of the pioneer editors of books for children in the United States. Trained as a journalist, she worked for the *Seattle Post-Intelligencer* and the *Seattle Times* early in her career. In the late 1920's she joined Doubleday and served as editor of its children's books department from 1934 to 1964. She was president of the Children's Book Council for two terms and served as editorial consultant to the Junior Literary Guild following her retirement from Doubleday. *Obituaries: New York Times,* November 23, 1979; *Publishers Weekly,* December 24, 1979; *School Library Journal,* January, 1980; *Contemporary Authors,* Volume 89-92, Gale, 1980.

IRA M. FREEMAN

FREEMAN, Ira M(aximilian)   1905-

PERSONAL: Born August 15, 1905, in Chicago, Illinois; married Mae Blacker, 1935; children: one son, one daughter. *Education:* University of Chicago, B.S., 1925, M.S., 1926, Ph.D. (physics), 1928.

CAREER: Author of books about science. Princeton University, Princeton, New Jersey, resident associate professor, 1943-45; Swarthmore College, Swarthmore, Pennsylvania, associate professor, 1945-47; Rutgers University, New Brunswick, New Jersey, associate professor, 1947-59, professor, 1959—. Fellow, Institute of International Education, Frankfort, Germany, 1928-29; fellow, von Humboldt Foundation, 1929-30; associate physicist, National Advisory Committee for Aeronautics, Langley Field, Virginia, 1930-31; visiting professor, Purdue University, 1942-43; National Defense Research Committee, 1944; science consultant, UNESCO, Paris, 1950-51; consultant on physics films to Coronet Instructional Films. *Member:* American Association for the Advancement of Science (fellow), American Association of Physics Teachers.

WRITINGS: Invitation to Experiment (photographs and drawings by the author and wife, Mae Freeman), Dutton, 1940; *Modern Introductory Physics,* McGraw-Hill, 1949; *Physics Made Simple,* Cadillac Publishing, 1954, revised edition, Doubleday, 1965; *All about the Wonders of Chemistry* (illustrated by George Wilde), Random House, 1954; *All about the Atom* (illustrated by G. Wilde), Random House, 1955; *All about Electricity* (illustrated by Evelyn Urbanowich), Random House, 1957; *All about Sound and Ultrasonics* (illustrated by Irving Geis), Random House, 1961, reissued as *Sound and Ultrasonics* (illustrated by George T. Resch), 1968; (with Arthur March) *The New World of Physics,* Random House, 1962; *All about Light and Radiation,* Random House, 1965, reissued as *Light and Radiation* (illustrated by G. T. Resch), 1968; (with Alva Rae Patton) *The Science of Chemistry* (illustrated by Zenowij Onyshkewych), Random House, 1968; *Physics: Principles and Insights,* McGraw-Hill, 1968; *The Look-It-Up Book of Space* (illustrated by John Polgreen), Random House, 1969; (with Sean Morrison) *Your Body: Bones and Muscles,* Random House, 1970.

With wife, Mae (Blacker) Freeman: *Fun with Science,* Random House, 1943, revised edition, 1956; *Fun with Chemistry,* Random House, 1944, reissued, 1967; *Fun with Figures,* Random House, 1946, reissued, 1963; *Fun with Geometry,* Random House, 1946, reissued, Kaye & Ward, 1969; *Fun with Astronomy,* Random House, 1953; *Fun with Your Cam-* *era,* Random House, 1955; *Your Wonderful World of Science* (illustrated by Rene Martin), Random House, 1957; *You Will Go to the Moon* (illustrated by Robert Patterson), Random House, 1959, revised edition, 1971; *The Sun, the Moon, and the Stars* (illustrated by R. Martin), Random House, 1959; *Fun with Scientific Experiments,* Random House, 1960; *The Story of the Atom* (illustrated by R. Martin), Random House, 1960; *The Story of Electricity* (illustrated by R. Martin), Random House, 1961; *The Story of Chemistry* (illustrated by Charles Goslin), Random House, 1962; *Fun with Photography* (edited by Gordon Catling), E. Ward, 1962; *Fun and Experiments with Light,* Random House, 1963, reissued as *Fun with Light,* Kaye & Ward, 1968.

SIDELIGHTS: Ira M. Freeman's *The Look-It-Up Book of Space* was described by *Library Journal* as a "well-illustrated, informative junior reference book. . . . Both theoret-

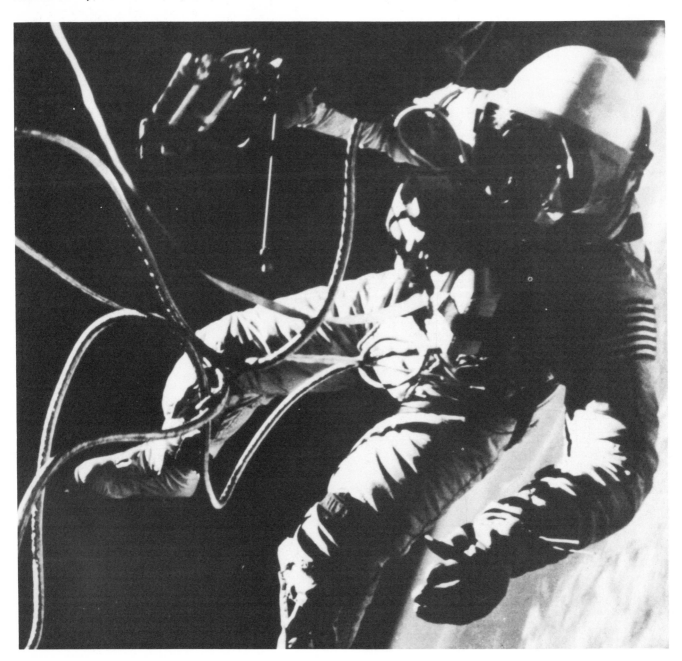

(From *The Look It Up Book of Space* by Ira M. Freeman. Illustrated by John Polgreen.)

ical and applied space science terms are included and are arranged in an encyclopedic format which frequently makes use of cross references. The discussions are detailed without being complex . . . [and there are many] color photographs and clear diagrams. . . ." Of *All about the Atom,* the *New York Times* said, "His explanations are, on the whole, lucid, easy to understand and his approach should help make young people feel at home in this strange new world. . . ."

A *Christian Science Monitor* reviewer said of *All about Sound and Ultrasonics,* "With the help of striking illustrations, this absorbing discussion of acoustics carries the 10-14 [year-olds] through all aspects of its subject. Here is an author who is not afraid to talk to his readers as intelligent young people. He has explained his subject simply and interestingly. . . ." Isaac Asimov, writing in *Horn Book,* reviewed *All about Light and Radiation* and called Freeman, "one of the most skillful of current science writers. His books have never failed to be both authoritative and well presented. And this book is no exception."

FOR MORE INFORMATION SEE: Muriel Fuller, editor, *More Junior Authors,* H. W. Wilson, 1963.

FULLER, Edmund (Maybank)   1914-
(Amicus Curiae)

PERSONAL; Born March 3, 1914, in Wilmington, Del.; married Ann Graham, 1936; children: four. *Residence:* Kent, Conn.

CAREER: Teacher, New Theatre School, New School for Social Research, 1940-43, South Kent School, Kent, Conn., 1952-63, Columbia University, New York, N.Y., 1952-54, St. Stephens School, Rome, Italy, 1965-66; author, editor,

(From *Poems of Henry Wadsworth Longfellow,* selected by Edmund Fuller. Etchings by John Ross and Clare Romano Ross.)

and literary critic. Trustee and chairman of the academic committee of Wykeham Rise School, Washington, Conn.; contributor of reviews to the *Wall Street Journal.*

WRITINGS—Fiction: *A Star Pointed North,* Harper, 1946, reissued, 1965; *Brothers Divided,* Bobbs-Merrill, 1951; *The Corridor,* Random House, 1963; *Flight,* Random House, 1970.

Nonfiction: *A Pageant of the Theatre,* Crowell, 1941, new revised edition, 1965; *John Milton* (juvenile; illustrated by Robert Ball), Harper, 1944, reissued, Seabury Press, 1967; *George Bernard Shaw: Critic of Western Morale,* Scribner, 1950; *Vermont: A History of the Green Mountain State,* State Board of Education, 1952; *Tinkers and Genius,* Hastings House, 1955; *Man in Modern Fiction: Some Minority Opinions on Contemporary American Writing,* Random House, 1958; *Peter the Apostle* (juvenile), Doubleday, 1961; *Books with Men behind Them,* Random House, 1962; *Successful Calamity: A Writer's Follies on a Vermont Farm,* Random House, 1966; *Charles Williams' All Hallows' Eve,* Seabury Press, 1967; (with David E. Green) *God in the White House: The Faiths of American Presidents,* Crown, 1968; *Prudence Crandall: An Incident of Racism in Nineteenth-Century Connecticut,* Wesleyan University Press, 1971; (with others) *Myth, Allegory, and Gospel: An Interpretation of J.R.R.*

EDMUND FULLER

Tolkien, C. S. Lewis, G. K. Chesterton, and Charles Williams, Bethany Fellowship, 1974.

Editor: *Thesaurus of Quotations*, Crown, 1941; *Thesaurus of Anecdotes*, Crown, 1942, reissued as *2500 Anecdotes for All Occasions*, Doubleday, 1961; *Thesaurus of Epigrams*, Crown, 1943; (under pseudonym Amicus Curiae) *Law in Action: An Anthology of the Law in Literature*, Crown, 1947; (with Hiram C. Haydn) *Thesaurus of Book Digests*, Crown, 1949, reissued, Bonanza Books, 1963; Leo Stein, *Journey into the Self: Being the Letters, Papers, and Journals of Leo Stein*, Crown, 1950; *Mutiny!*, Crown, 1953; Fedor Dostoyevsky, *The Brothers Karamazov*, Dell, 1956; *The Christian Idea of Education*, Yale University Press, 1957-62; Samuel Langhorne Clemens, *Mark Twain*, Dell, 1958; (with Olga Achtenhagen) *Four American Novels*, Harcourt, 1959; Plutarch, *Lives of the Noble Romans*, Dell, 1959; Plutarch, *Lives of the Noble Greeks*, Dell, 1959; Francois Voltaire, *Voltaire*, Dell, 1959; Thomas Bullfinch, *Mythology: A Modern Abridgement*, Dell, 1959.

(With Blanche J. Thompson) *Four Novels for Appreciation*, Harcourt, 1960; Honore de Balzac, *Balzac: Five Stories*, Dell, 1960; (with O. Achtenhagen) *Four Novels for Adventure*, Harcourt, 1960; (with O. B. Davis) *Four American Biographies*, Harcourt, 1961; *Schools and Scholarship: The Christian Idea of Education*, Yale University Press, 1962; (with B. J. Kinnick) *Adventures in American Literature*, Harcourt, 1963; (with O. B. Davis) *Three World Classics*, Harcourt, 1963; John Donne, *The Showing Forth of Christ: Sermons*, Harper, 1964; *The Great English and American Essays*, Avon Books, 1964; Samuel Johnson, *Selections from The Lives of the English Poets* [and] *Preface to Shakespeare*, Avon Books, 1965; William Shakespeare, *Hamlet*, Dell, 1966; Shakespeare, *Julius Caesar*, Dell, 1966; Shakespeare, *Macbeth*, Dell, 1966; Shakespeare, *The Merchant of Venice*, Dell, 1966; Henry W. Longfellow, *Poems* (illustrated by John Ross and Clare Romano Ross), Crowell, 1967; *Affirmations of God and Man: Writings for Modern Dialogue*, Association Press, 1967; (with O. B. Davis) *The Idea of Man: An Anthology of Literature*, Harcourt, 1967; Shakespeare, *Henry IV, Part One*, Dell, 1968; Shakespeare, *As You Like It*, Dell, 1968; Shakespeare, *Romeo and Juliet*, Dell, 1968; Shakespeare, *A Midsummer Night's Dream*, Dell, 1968; James Boswell, *The Life of Samuel Johnson, LL.D.*, Heron Books, 1969; (with O. B. Davis) *Introduction to the Essay*, Hayden Book Co., 1971; *Time of Turbulence: Research Cases of Freshman English*, Crowell, 1972.

SIDELIGHTS: Fuller's first novel, *Star Pointed North*, was reviewed by a *New York Times* critic who wrote, "With his fast-moving, well-written, at times beautiful historical novel based on the life of Frederick Douglass, Edmund Fuller has performed a double service. He has bridged an aching gap in American history; and he has done this in a thoroughly enjoyable book in which a great man is handled with dignity and warmth, in which a Negro hero is treated as the American hero that he was." *Kirkus* noted: "A biographical novel about the famous Negro abolitionist, Frederick Douglass, which reads more like history than fiction, but a pretty thrilling piece of history at that. The most vivid and engrossing part of the book deals with Douglass' life as a slave."

FOR MORE INFORMATION SEE: Kirkus, September 1, 1946, March 1, 1958; *New York Times*, November 3, 1946, June 1, 1958; *Saturday Review*, May 17, 1958; *Chicago Sunday Tribune*, May 18, 1958; *New Yorker*, May 25, 1963; *New York Times Book Review*, May 26, 1963; John Wakeman, editor, *World Authors, 1950-1970*, H. W. Wilson, 1975.

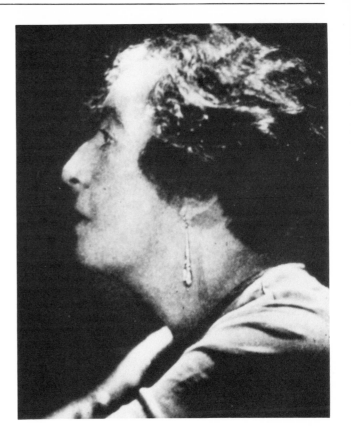

ROSE FYLEMAN

FYLEMAN, Rose   1877-1957

PERSONAL: Born in 1877, in Nottingham, England; died August 1, 1957. *Education:* Attended University College, Nottingham; Royal College of Music, A.R.C.M.; private study of voice in London, Paris, and Berlin. *Religion:* Jewish. *Home:* London, England.

CAREER: Began her career as a schoolteacher; later became a professional singer, making her first public appearance at Queen's Hall, London, 1903; voice teacher and lecturer; began her writing career about 1917; founded and edited the children's magazine, *Merry-Go-Round*, 1923; travelled through Europe and North America, including a lecture tour of the United States, 1929-30 and 1931-32.

WRITINGS: Fairies and Chimneys (poems), Methuen, 1918, G. H. Doran, 1920, reprinted, Core Coll. Books, 1976; *The Sunny Book* (illustrated by Millicent Sowerby), Humphrey Milford, 1918; *The Fairy Green* (poems), Methuen, 1919, G. H. Doran, 1923; *The Fairy Flute* (poems), Methuen, 1921, G. H. Doran, 1923; *The Rainbow Cat* (illustrated by Thelma Cudlipp Grosvenor), Methuen, 1922, G. H. Doran, 1923; *Forty Good-Night Tales* (illustrated by T. C. Grosvenor), Methuen, 1923, G. H. Doran, 1924; *The Rose Fyleman Fairy Book*, George H. Doran, 1923; *A Small Cruse* (poems), Methuen, 1923; *The Adventure Club* (illustrated by A. H. Watson), Methuen, 1925, G. H. Doran, 1926; *Fairies and Friends* (poems), Methuen, 1925, G. H. Doran, 1926; *Forty Good-Morning Tales* (illustrated by Erick Berry), Methuen, 1926, Doubleday, Doran, 1929; *Letty: A Study of a Child* (illustrated by Lisl Hummel), Methuen, 1926, G. H. Doran, 1927; *A Little*

Christmas Book (illustrated by L. Hummel), Methuen, 1926, G. H. Doran, 1927; *The Katy Kruse Dolly Book,* G. H. Doran, 1927; *A Princess Comes to Our Town* (illustrated by Gertrude Lindsay), Methuen, 1927, American edition illustrated by E. Berry, Doubleday, Doran, 1928; *A Garland of Rose's* (poems), Methuen, 1928; *Old-Fashioned Girls, and Other Poems* (illustrated by Ethel Everett), Methuen, 1928; *Gay Go Up* (illustrated by Decie Merwin), Methuen, 1929, Doubleday, Doran, 1930; *Twenty Tea-Time Tales,* Methuen, 1929.

The Doll's House (illustrated by E. Berry), Methuen, 1930, Doubleday, Doran, 1931; *The Katy Kruse Play Book* (illustrated by Katy Kruse), McKay, 1930; *Tea Time Tales* (illustrated by E. Berry), Doubleday, Doran, 1930; *Fifty-One New Nursery Rhymes* (illustrated by Dorothy Burroughes), Methuen, 1931, Doubleday, Doran, 1932; *Hey! Ding-a-Ding,* University of London Press, 1931; *The Strange Adventures of Captain Marwhopple,* Methuen, 1931, Doubleday, Doran, 1932; *The Easter Hare,* Methuen, 1932; *The Rose Fyleman Birthday Book,* Medici Society, 1932; *Jeremy Quince, Lord Mayor of London* (illustrated by Cecil Leslie), J. Cape, 1933; *The Princess Dances* (illustrated by C. Leslie), Dent, 1933; *Bears* (illustrated by Stuart Tresilian), Thomas Nelson, 1935; *Monkeys,* Thomas Nelson, 1936; (with E.M.D. Wilson) *Billy Monkey: A True Tale of a Capuchin* (illustrated by C. Leslie), Thomas Nelson, 1936; *A Book of Saints,* Methuen, 1939; *Folk-Tales from Many Lands,* Methuen, 1939.

Runabout Rhymes (illustrated by Margaret Tempest), Methuen, 1941; *Timothy's Conjuror,* Methuen, 1942; *Hob and Bob: A Tale of Two Goblins* (illustrated by Charles Stewart), Hollis & Carter, 1944; *The Timothy Toy Trust* (illustrated by Marjorie Wratten), Methuen, 1944; *Adventures with Benghazi* (illustrated by Peggy Fortnum), Eyre & Spottiswoode, 1946; *Number Rhymes,* E. J. Arnold, 1946; *The Smith Family* (Books 4-6; Books 1-3 by Enid Blyton), E. J. Arnold, 1947;

**Dance, dance, are we not fine
Laura, Sara and Nicholine?**
■ (From *Nursery Rhymes from Many Lands,* translated by Rose Fyleman. Pictures by Valery Carrick.)

Rose Fyleman's Nursery Stories, Evans Brothers, 1949; *Rhyme Book for Adam,* Methuen, 1949; *Lucy the Lamb,* Eyre & Spottiswoode, 1951; *The Sparrow and the Goat,* Eyre & Spottiswoode, 1951; *The Starling and the Fox,* Eyre & Spottiswoode, 1951; *Daphne and Dick,* Macdonald & Co., 1952; *White Flower* (illustrated by M. E. Stewart), E. J. Arnold, 1953.

Plays and operas: *Eight Little Plays for Children,* Methuen, 1924, George H. Doran, 1925; *Seven Little Plays for Children,* Methuen, 1928; *Happy Families* (three-act comic opera; music by Thomas F. Dunhill; first performed in Guildford, England, November, 1933), Methuen, 1933; *Nine New Plays for Children* (illustrated by Eleanor L. Halsey), Thomas Nelson, 1934; *Six Longer Plays for Children* (illustrated by E. L. Halsey), Thomas Nelson, 1936; *The Magic Pencil, and Other Plays from My Tales,* Methuen, 1938; *After All* (one-act play), Methuen, 1939; *The Spanish Cloak* (one-act play), Methuen, 1939; (librettist) *Red-Riding-Hood* (operetta; music by Will Grant, pseudonym of Wilhelm Grosz), Oxford University Press, 1949. Also author of the Christmas Play for the Old Vic Theatre, London, 1926.

Contributor to various London newspapers and periodicals, including *Punch* and *Joy Street Poems,* 1927.

Editor: *Round the Mulberry Bush,* Dodd, 1928; *Sugar and Spice* (illustrated by Janet Laura Scott), Whitman Publishing, 1935; *Here We Come a'Piping,* Basil Blackwell, 1936, Frederick A. Stokes, 1937, reprinted, Granger Books, 1978; *A'Piping Again,* Frederick A. Stokes, 1938; *Bells Ringing,* Basil Blackwell, 1938, Frederick A. Stokes, 1939; *Pipe and Drum,* Basil Blackwell, 1939, reprinted, Books for Libraries, 1972; *Punch and Judy* (photographs by Paul Henning), Methuen, 1944; *Over the Tree-Tops: Nursery Rhymes from Many Lands,* Basil Blackwell, 1949, reissued as *Nursery Rhymes from Many Lands,* Dover, 1971.

Translator: *Songs Translated,* J. Curwen, 1927; *Widdy-Widdy-Wurkey: Nursery Rhymes from Many Lands* (illustrated by Valery Carrick), Basil Blackwell, 1934, published in America as *Picture Rhymes from Foreign Lands,* Frederick A. Stokes, 1935, reprinted as *Nursery Rhymes from Many Lands,* Dover, 1971; Katharina Marie Bech Michaelis, *Bibi* (illustrated by Hedvig Collin), Allen & Unwin, 1933; K.M.B. Michaelis, *Bibi Goes Travelling* (translation of *Bibis Grosse Reise;* illustrated by H. Collin), Allen & Unwin, 1934; K.M.B. Michaelis, *The Green Island* (translation of *Die Gruene Insel;* illustrated by H. Collin), Allen & Unwin, 1935; Lida, *Pere Castor's Wild Animal Books,* Allen & Unwin, 1938; Jan Karafiat, *Fireflies* (translation of *Broucci;* illustrated by Emil Weiss), Allen & Unwin, 1942; Alfred Flueckiger, *Tuck: The Story of a Snow-Hare* (translation of *Mueck: Lebenstage eines Alpenhasen;* illustrated by Grace Huxtable), Bodley Head, 1949, Coward, circa 1953; Marie-Louise Ventteclaye, *Simone and the Lilywhites* (translation of *Simone et les Blanc-Blanc*), Museum Press, 1949; Lillian Miozzi, *The Adventures of Tommy: The Cat Who Went to Sea* (translation of *Le Avventure di Tommy;* illustrated by Charlotte Hough), Bodley Head, 1950; Lili Martini, *Peter and His Friend Toby* (translation of *Peter und Sein Freund Bulli;* illustrated by Wolfgang Felten), Bodley Head, 1955.

FOR MORE INFORMATION SEE: Stanley J. Kunitz, editor, *Twentieth Century Authors,* H. W. Wilson, 1942, reissued, 1973; Stanley J. Kunitz, editor, *Junior Book of Authors,* revised edition, H. W. Wilson, 1951; Brian Doyle, editor, *Who's Who of Children's Literature,* Schocken, 1968. Obituary: *New York Times,* August 4, 1957.

HELEN GARRETT

GARRETT, Helen 1895-

PERSONAL: Born in 1895.

CAREER: Author, educator. Taught in New York before becoming State Education supervisor, elementary division, State Education Department in Albany, New York. Has written eight books for children over a span of twenty-four years, and has also written several books in the field of education.

WRITINGS—For children: *Jobie* (illustrated by Connie Moran), Messner, 1942; *Angelo, the Naughty One* (illustrated by Leo Politi), Viking, 1944, reissued, 1966; *Rufous Redtail* (illustrated by Francis Jaques), Viking, 1947; *Mr. Flip Flop* (illustrated by Garry MacKenzie), Viking, 1948; *Tophill Road* (illustrated by Corydon Bell), Viking, 1950; *Polly Roughhouse* (illustrated by Myron S. Hall), Viking, 1951; *The Brothers from North Bay* (illustrated by Victor Mays), Westminster Press, 1966.

Other: *Play Is Learning Too*, University of the State of New York, 1948; *When Shall We Begin to Teach Reading?*, University of the State of New York, 1949; (with Gloria Gavan) *Not a Leg to Stand On*, Hale, 1967.

SIDELIGHTS: "My storytelling started years ago at bedtime. For quite awhile, one of my oldest sisters used to tell us stories about fairies and elves, pearls and diamonds and riches of all kinds. When she was twelve or thirteen, she felt herself too old for storytelling, and then I took up the task.

"I don't remember these first stories of mine in detail, but I do recall one night when my mother heard my seven-year-old voice going on and on, long after I should have been asleep. She came up to quiet me and found my five-year-old brother hugging his knees, spellbound. His eyes were as big as saucers, and tears rolled down his cheeks.

"'Helen,' my mother exclaimed, 'you mustn't tell such stories to your little brother.'

"'Oh, yes,' Oliver cried. 'They're horrible, but I like them. Oh, I do.'

"In the days since, I have gone to college and have been a teacher. I loved both, but especially teaching because I came to know so many wonderful boys and girls. Now I am busy writing, and I love it. It is fun and hard work combined, but then, many other things are like that. I especially enjoy writing stories because the characters I create remain my real friends long after the stories themselves are finished."

Garrett strives to create clear-cut characters in her books that come to have lives of their own. This sense of strong characterization extends even to the animals she creates, as in the case of the hawk in *Rufous Redtail*. Said the *Saturday Review of Literature*, "He is a lively, independent creature and the record of his adventures has humor and vitality." And to the *New York Times*, "The engaging personality of Rufous stays with one long after the book is closed."

So too do her children come alive. The *New York Herald Tribune* had this critique of *Jobie*, "Reduced to bare facts, nothing much happens, but none of these facts are bare; they are clothed in the emotions country children feel—and so

On the steep side of a tall mountain in Mexico there was once a lovely little city. ■ (From *Angelo the Naughty One* by Helen Garrett. Illustrated by Leo Politi.)

seldom have the power or even the desire to express—about the life that is their world. . . . ''

FOR MORE INFORMATION SEE: Books—New York Herald Tribune, November 8, 1942; *Saturday Review of Literature,* November 15, 1947; *New York Times,* November 16, 1947; *Horn Book,* January—December, 1948. Helen Garrett, ''Writing's Hard, but Fun,'' *Young Wings,* May, 1950.

GARRIGUE, Sheila 1931-

PERSONAL: Surname rhymes with ''intrigue''; born December 30, 1931, in England; came to the United States in 1956; daughter of Edward Donaldson (a salesman) and Kathleen Norah (Hayes) Hogg; married Paul Garrigue (an insurance broker), March 14, 1959; children: Matthew, Andrew, Elizabeth. *Education:* Educated in Canada and England. *Politics:* ''Citizen of the United Kingdom (with Democratic leanings).'' *Religion:* Presbyterian. *Home:* 17 Ludlow Dr., Chappaqua, N.Y. 10514.

CAREER: Lange Maxwell & Springer Ltd. (publishers of foreign scientific books), London, England, secretary, 1949-53; S. H. Benson Ltd. (advertising agency), London, England, secretary, 1953-56; KCBS-Radio, San Francisco, Calif., secretary to program director, 1957-58; Columbia Broadcasting System, New York, N.Y., administrative assistant to Edward R. Murrow, 1958-60; writer, 1973—. Vice-president of executive board of Chappaqua Drama Group, 1977. *Member:* Authors Guild of Authors League of America.

WRITINGS: All the Children Were Sent Away (children's novel), Bradbury, 1976; *Between Friends,* Bradbury, 1978.

WORK IN PROGRESS: A children's novel tentatively titled *The Peace Tree,* dealing with a child's adjustment to war, death, first love.

SIDELIGHTS: ''I grew up an only child in Beckenham, Kent, a suburb of London. When very young I had rickets and spent some years with my legs in splints. To amuse me during this inactive time, my parents did a lot of reading and storytelling. As soon as I could read myself, I became a bookworm.

''In 1940, I was evacuated to Vancouver, Canada, to escape the German bombing of London, and lived with my mother's older brother. This time in my life formed the basis for *All the Children Were Sent Away.* I was put in a boarding school in Vancouver and then, following Pearl Harbor, was evacuated again from Vancouver to Montreal, remaining there for two years. As a result, from the age of nine, I did a lot of letterwriting and I continue to do so to this day, since again I live far from my childhood home and friends.

''I returned to England in 1945, attended the local girls' grammar school, finished by specializing in French, German, Latin and English. My lowest marks were in English. We were unable to afford college, so my family sent me to a secretarial school. After working in London for several years, I came to the U.S.A. in 1956 as a first step, as I thought, to working my way around the world. Instead, I met Paul Garrigue and we were married in 1959. I left my job with Ed Murrow, CBS News, in 1960, when he joined the Kennedy administration in Washington and I was expecting our first son, Matthew.

SHEILA GARRIGUE

We lived in Brooklyn Heights at first and moved to Chappaqua, N.Y., about forty miles north of Manhattan, after Andrew was born.

''I began writing when my youngest child, my daughter Elizabeth, entered first grade. All my writing up to then had been letterwriting, personal or business, but that had been received well, and I thought I'd try writing for children since I was constantly among them and felt I was on their wavelength.

''However, I intend my books for children and adults, and try to make the stories funny and dramatic and sad in turn, to hold the interest of any reader. It is my belief that, in order to really touch the reader, the writer must believe and feel strongly about the point he is trying to make. His feelings will form the invisible bridge for his words to march across, straight into the hearts of his readers.

''I have come to another activity late in the game—acting. I joined the Chappaqua Drama Group to work backstage and have gradually become brave enough to venture onstage. I love it and I feel the two disciplines of acting and writing are similar, each requiring you to get under the skin of your character.''

Garrigue details the basis for her second book: *''Between Friends* has been a long time in the making. From the early

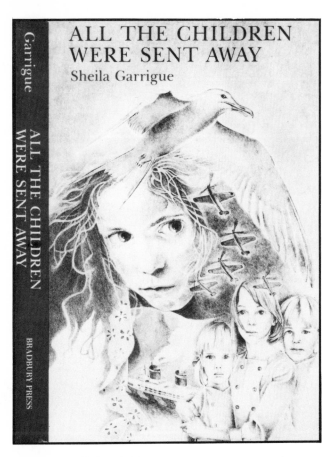

ALL THE CHILDREN WERE SENT AWAY
Sheila Garrigue

BRADBURY PRESS

(From *All the Children Were Sent Away* by Sheila Garrigue. Jacket illustration by Bernard Colonna.)

years of looking away, to the middle years of looking on, I finally arrived at the point of looking in.

"I've made progress since the day in my childhood when my mother and I passed a man twisted in his wheelchair, his hands flying about, his head rolling, and I said staring, 'What's the matter with him?' My mother replied in a whisper, 'He's an idiot, poor fellow. Look away, it's kinder.' I did as I was told and looked away not realizing until years later that cerebral palsy is not a form of idiocy.

"I don't remember seeing many handicapped people as I grew up. Perhaps I had perfected looking away to a fine art. Perhaps they were hidden in institutions or stayed home a lot. I didn't even notice that I wasn't seeing them. I had my own problems. I was Roman Catholic in an Anglican world. I wore steel-rimmed spectacles. My name was Sheila Hogg, and I ran home from school trying to escape the epithets—piggy, four-eyes, cat-licker. . . . I was the handicapped one, different in a world where everyone else was the same, or so it seemed. I survived of course and life was filled with school and travel and growing up. It was not until many years later when I was married and had children of my own, that I met Mimi Daly, who lived across the street from us in Chappaqua and who had Down's Syndrome.

"None of our family had known anyone with Down's Syndrome before, and, although Mimi was only about five years old at the time, it seems incredible to say it now—but the first time we met her, we were a little afraid of her. Adults and children alike, we felt the way one of the children in

Between Friends expresses it: 'Maybe it's because I don't know what she's going to do. . . . I mean, it's not like with a normal kid who acts the same way you do. Then, you can kind of look ahead and . . . be ready. Like, supposing I say to you "Are you going to watch the soccer game after school?" I know you're either going to say "Yes, I want to," or "No, I have too much homework," or anyway something that makes sense to me. But if I ask Dede that, she'll say "Yeh" and all the time not even know what soccer is. How can you talk to a person like that? I don't have any idea what she knows, and what she's thinking, or if she's thinking anything.'

"Well, we Garrigues were apprehensive in the same way that first time, but as we began to see more of the Dalys, we learned to relax and enjoy being with Mimi, just as she enjoyed being with us. Our fear vanished as soon as we knew her better.

"As our Elizabeth grew out of babyhood, she and Mimi became friends, spending a good deal of time together, sharing the pleasures of blocks, and puzzles and crayons. Elizabeth's other friends reacted to Mimi in a variety of ways. Some mimicked her behind her back. Some teased her to her face. Almost all of them were baffled as to why Elizabeth was a friend of Mimi's. I don't know whether Elizabeth ever explained her reasons to her friends, but I'd like to think she might have said, as Jill does about Dede in *Between Friends*:

"'Well, now I'm used to the way she is, she's sort of . . . comfortable to be with. She's quiet. She never wants anything. And she's never mean. I never heard her say one mean thing about anybody. And . . . well, I know it sounds funny . . . but she listens when I talk. But supposing I don't want to talk—say, just walk along—that's okay with her, too.'

"From time to time in those years, as I listened to the children talking about Mimi (and often what they said was mean and ignorant and made me angry), I'd speak to them sharply. They'd look at me without any real feeling for what they were doing to her or, just as importantly, to themselves. And I'd think, if only they could see themselves!. If they could only hear what they sound like!' So gradually the idea of putting it in a book began to seem the way to make the children see themselves. I hope that *Between Friends* has accomplished this purpose."

HOBBIES AND OTHER INTERESTS: Travel, embroidery, reading, acting, speaking in schools.

GOLD, Phyllis 1941-

PERSONAL: Name legally changed to Gold. Born in Long Island, N.Y.; daughter of James J. (a lawyer) and Blanche (Levenbron) Weissman; married Paul Goldberg (a mortgage banker); children: Mitchell, Lizbeth. *Education:* Attended Syracuse University; Hofstra University, B.A. *Office:* 17 Graystone Dr., East Northport, Long Island, N.Y. 11731.

CAREER: Has held positions as Family Court probation officer, casework therapist, photographer's fashion model in New York, N.Y., and agent for advertising photographers in New York; Photography Unlimited, New York, N.Y., owner of agency representing professional photographers, 1975—; private practice, Long Island, N.Y., certified hypnotist and psychotherapist, 1976—; Pickwick Inn, Plainview,

Long Island, director of "mindworks" self-actualization seminars. Is also on faculty of Hofstra University and New York Institute of Technology as a lecturer, teacher, and writer on the subjects of "Human Potential" and "Stress Control." *Member:* National Society for Autistic Children (founding president of New York chapter; past national vice-president).

WRITINGS: Please Don't Say Hello (on infantile autism; for children; with photographs), Human Sciences Press, 1975.

"Please Don't Say Hello," based on Gold's book was adapted into a television script. Author and photographer for filmstrips "Shoplifter" and "Deserted," both for Activity Records.

WORK IN PROGRESS: Somewhere a Place Far From Home; Long Distance (tentative title), a novel; audio-visual material aimed at teaching high school students about establishing ego strength and achieving genuine intimacy through real communication minus traditional courtship role-playing; adapting "Please Don't Say Hello" into a filmstrip.

SIDELIGHTS: "Being the mother of an autistic boy, *Please Don't Say Hello* was a labor of love. . . . I believe when one lives through difficult experiences which may be outside the rounds of the average person, one also gains in perspective and understanding. I think I should attempt to transmit some of the things I feel fortunate enough to have learned through my personal experiences and observations. I hope my new book, a novel, *Somewhere a Place Far From Home* will bring something substantial, also, to readers."

HOBBIES AND OTHER INTERESTS: Music, writing poetry, tennis, anything related to the ocean, gourmet cooking, photography, transcendental meditation.

GRANT, Myrna (Lois)   1934-

PERSONAL: Born March 9, 1934, in Hamilton, Ontario, Canada; daughter of Harold and Florence Reid; children: Christopher, Susan, Andrew, Jennifer. *Education:* Attended McMaster University, 1957; Moody Bible Institute, B.Sc., 1969; Wheaton College, Wheaton, Ill., M.A., 1971. *Religion:* Conservative Protestant. *Home:* 1218 Greenwood, Wheaton, Ill. 60187.

CAREER: Author of books, articles, and television, radio and film scripts. Actress on radio programs, narrator of sound recordings. Wheaton College Graduate School of communication, Wheaton, Ill., broadcast coordinator, 1974—. *Member:* Society of Children's Book Writers, Arts Centre Group (London, England), Fellowship of Christians in Arts, Media and Entertainment, Christian Communicators Fellowship, Christian Women in Media, Society for the Study of Religion under Communism (board of directors), Scholastic Honor Society (Wheaton College), 1978.

WRITINGS: Vanya (biography), Creation House, 1974; *Let's Put on a Play,* Moody, 1974; *Ivan and the Informer* (juvenile fiction), Moody, 1974; *Ivan and the Hidden Bible,* Tyndale, 1975; *Ivan and the Secret in the Suitcase,* Tyndale, 1976; *Ivan and the Daring Escape,* Tyndale, 1976; *Ivan and the Star of David,* Tyndale, 1977; *The Journey* (biography), Tyndale, 1978; *Ivan and the Moscow Circus,* Tyndale, 1980.

Ivan was so frightened he didn't know where to look to avoid the eyes of the officer. He gazed at the floor. He looked out of the window. He clenched his hands and stared at them. ■ (From *Ivan and the Secret in the Suitcase* by Myrna Grant. Illustrated by Joseph E. DeVelasco.)

Films: "Bright Gem of Hope," Evangelical Alliance Mission, 1971; "Love and the Little Ones," Compassion Child Care Agency, 1972.

Television scripts: "Treehouse Club" series, 1974.

Sound Recordings: "Happytime Stories for Children" and "More Happytime Stories for Children," Zondervan, 1970.

Radio script series: "The Monk of Wittenburg" (Martin Luther), 1960; "Beautiful Upon the Mountains" (Madam Guyon), 1961; "Thunder on the Heather" (John Knox), 1962; "Pilgrim's Progress" (adaptation), 1962; "Ranger Bill," 1963-66; "Sailor Sam," 1965-67; "This Is My Song" (Fanny Crosby), 1965; "Ninepence in Her Pocket" (Gladys Aylward), 1966; "Hudson and Maria" (Hudson Taylor), 1969; "Anthology," 1969-70; "Harriet" (Harriet Beecher Stowe),

MYRNA GRANT

1970, "Code Name Sebastian" (adaptation), 1975; "The Journey," 1980.

Author of a monthly column, "Since You Asked," for *Christian Life*, 1967-68. Contributor to *Eternity, Moody Monthly, Alpha* [Holland] *Christian Reader, Christian Life,* and *Spectrum.*

WORK IN PROGRESS: A history-fiction novel about a Russian pastor's single day, set in Leningrad.

SIDELIGHTS: "When I was a very young child in Canada, my mother became ill and my brother, five years my senior, and I were raised by a busy grocer and his wife who had no children of their own.

"I was left to myself a great deal and as soon as I learned to read the worlds and people I discovered in books became my worlds, my adventures, my family. I was enchanted forever by fairy tales and biographies and exotic places that seemed planets away from our grocery store and the neighborhood ladies who came to shop and gossip about their friends and families and to talk about their husbands' work in the steel factories of our city.

"Many of those women were immigrants who spoke Canadian English with mysterious accents and who talked about their joys and sorrows in 'the old country' which was often England or Eastern Europe.

"As a child I wrote stories and poems. I thought everyone did. It seemed a part of childhood, like 'hide and seek' or playing dolls with your best friend. As I grew older, teachers began to praise my school compositions. They were often, it seems to me, about handsome men falling in love with

orphan girls or the glories of nature, or people being rescued from terrible dangers.

"One of my chores as a child was to houseclean and to make it fun I always pretended I was a slave or a prisoner of war, or a peasant working for a grand European household. As I worked I pleaded with my oppressor, or plotted revenge with fellow sufferers, acting out all the parts as I polished and dusted the little rooms behind the grocery.

"In high school, acting was easy for me. I had been performing every Saturday for years and from school plays I went on to do drama for radio, professionally. Acting made writing dialogue easy and I began to write scripts.

"I came into the world of actors, writers, theatre, media almost unintentionally. Editors began asking me to write magazine articles and later, books.

"In the course of my writing, I've travelled to Japan, Brazil, Russia, Africa and many other countries.

"Writing has been the hardest work and the most fun of anything I've done in my life. It's taken me to Shinto shrines in Tokyo, the Golan Heights in Israel and tea in Buckingham Palace!"

Grant spends her summers in Europe, writing, teaching and "seeing."

FOR MORE INFORMATION SEE: Christian Bookseller, May, 1974; *Moody Monthly,* January, 1978; (Wheaton College) *Record,* January, 1980.

JOHN GROTH

"I am the Ghost of Christmas Present," said the Spirit. "Look upon me!" ■ (From *A Christmas Carol* by Charles Dickens. Illustrated by John Groth.)

GROTH, John 1908-

PERSONAL: Born February 26, 1908, in Chicago, Ill.; son of John and Ethel (Bragg) Groth; children: Tamara Collins. *Education:* Attended Chicago Art Institute, 1926-27; Art Students League, New York, N.Y., 1937-38. *Politics:* Democratic. *Religion:* Presbyterian. *Home and office:* 61 East 57th St., New York, N.Y. 10022.

CAREER: Esquire Magazine, art director, 1933-1937; Broun's Nutmeg, art director, 1939; *Parade* Magazine, art director, 1941-45; *Chicago Sun* syndicate, European war correspondent, 1944-45; Art Student's League, New York, N.Y., instructor, 1946-79; Metropolitan Group Syndicate, Korea, French-Indo China, artist, war correspondent, 1951; Pratt Institute, Brooklyn, N.Y., instructor, 1952-55; Parsons School of Design, New York, N.Y., instructor, 1954-55; *Sports Illustrated,* Asia, correspondent, 1954; U.S. Air Force correspondent, Congo-Central Africa, 1960; artist, war correspondent, Dominican Republic, 1965, Vietnam, 1967; University of Texas, artist-in-residence, 1970.

EXHIBITIONS: Rhoda Sande Gallery, New York, N.Y., 1978. Works are represented in Smithsonian Institution, Museum of Modern Art, Library of Congress, Metropolitan Museum of Art, Chicago Art Institute, Museum of Western

Art (Moscow), University of Texas collection and University of Georgia collection. *Member:* Oversees Press Club of America, Society of Illustrators, American Watercolor Society, Lotos Club, National Academy of Design. *Awards, honors:* Allied Artist award, 1961; honorary B.A. degree, Eastern Michigan University, Ypsilanti, Michigan, 1976.

WRITINGS—All self-illustrated: *Studio: Europe,* Vanguard, 1945; *Studio: Asia,* World, 1952; (with Pat Smith) *John Groth's World of Sports,* Winchester, 1970.

Illustrator: (Introduction) Ernest Hemingway, *Men Without Women,* World, 1946; John Steinbeck, *Grapes of Wrath,* World, 1947; Leo Tolstoy, *War and Peace,* Heinemann, 1961; Leon Uris, *Exodus,* Doubleday, 1962; Anna Sewell, *Black Beauty,* Macmillan, 1962; Charles Dickens, *A Christmas Carol,* Macmillan, 1963; Arnold Gingrich, *The Well-Tempered Angler,* Knopf, 1965; O. Henry, *The Stories of O. Henry,* Limited Edition Club, 1965; Martha Mitchell, *Gone with the Wind,* Limited Edition Club, 1967; Mark Twain, *The War Prayer,* Harper, 1968; Erich Maria Remarque, *All Quiet on the Western Front,* Limited Edition Club, 1969; Maia Wojciechowska, *Life and Death of a Brave Bull,* Harcourt, 1972; Giles Tippette, *The Brave Men,* Macmillan, 1972; Mark Twain, *Pudd'nhead Wilson,* Limited Edition Club, 1974; John Graves, *The Last Running,* Encino Press, 1974; Arnold

(From the short story, "The Last Leaf," in *The Stories of O. Henry*. Illustrated by John Groth.)

Gingrich, *The Fishing in Print*, Winchester, 1974; Kurth Sprague, *The Promise Kept*, Encino Press, 1975; Alice Hopf, *Biography of an American Reindeer*, Putnam, 1976. Currently doing all illustrations and cover for *Short Story International* magazine.

SIDELIGHTS: ''I work mainly in watercolor and pen and ink, occasionally in oil. The bulk of my work has been done based on sketches made in the field in the many assignments abroad for magazines and corporations, and during the six wars I have covered. The books I've illustrated have been done in pen and ink, also in wash, black and white, and in watercolor based on a pen and ink background. Working as I do in pen and ink, there is no erasing. When I strike a 'snag,' I begin the entire picture again, using the 'ruined' pictures as rehearsals for the final completed picture. I believe that this method gives my pictures the fresh and sketch-like quality I am striving to retain.''

Child! do not throw this book about;
Refrain from the unholy pleasure
Of cutting all the pictures out!
Preserve it as your chiefest treasure.

—Hilaire Belloc

HALL, James Norman   1887-1951
(Fern Gravel)

PERSONAL: Born April 22, 1887, in Colfax, Iowa; died July 6, 1951 (some sources cite July 5), in Papeete, Tahiti; buried in Arue, Tahiti; son of Arthur Wright and Ella Annette (Young) Hall; married Sarah Winchester in 1925; children: Conrad L. and Nancy E. Hall Rutgers. *Education:* Grinnell College, Ph.B., 1910. *Home:* Papeete, Tahiti.

CAREER: Novelist, short story writer, memoirist. Social worker, Society for the Prevention of Cruelty to Children, Boston, Mass., 1910-14; after serving in World War I, moved to Tahiti, 1920, and there entered into a long-standing and fruitful collaboration with Charles Nordhoff with the writing of *The Lafayette Flying Corps*. *Military service:* British Army, Lord Kitchener's Volunteers, 1914-16; machine gunner in France, 1915-16; enlisted, French Foreign Legion, Lafayette Flying Corps, 1916, which was later incorporated into the American Air Service; prisoner-of-war, Germany, 1918; became captain.

WRITINGS: Kitchener's Mob, Houghton, 1916; *High Adventure*, Houghton, 1918; *On the Stream of Travel*, Houghton, 1926; *Mid-Pacific*, Houghton, 1928; *Under the South* (includes chapters from *Faery Lands of the South Seas, Mid-Pacific*, and *On the Stream of Travel*), Chapman & Hall, 1928; *Flying with Chaucer*, Houghton, 1930; *Mother Goose Land* (for children; illustrated by Herman I. Bacharach), Houghton, 1930; *The Tale of a Shipwreck* (illustrated by W. Alister Macdonald), Houghton, 1934; *The Friends* (poem), Prairie Press, 1939; *Doctor Dogbody's Leg* (illustrated by Warren Chappell), Little, Brown, 1940; (under pseudonym Fern Gravel) *Oh Millersville!* (poem), Prairie Press, 1940; *Under a Thatched Roof*, Houghton, 1942, reprinted, Books for Libraries, 1970; *Lost Island* (novel), Little, Brown, 1944; *A Word for His Sponsor* (poem), Little, Brown, 1949; *The Far Lands* (novel; Literary Guild selection), Little, Brown, 1950; *The Forgotten One, and Other True Tales of the South Seas*, Little, Brown, 1952; *My Island Home* (autobiography), Little, Brown, 1952, reprinted, Greenwood Press, 1970.

With Charles Nordhoff: (Editors) *The Lafayette Flying Corps* (history), Houghton, 1920, reissued, Kennikat, 1964; *Faery Lands of the South Seas* (illustrated by George A. Picken), Harper & Brothers, 1921; *Falcons of France: A Tale of Youth and the Air* (illustrated by A. Vimnera), Little, Brown, 1929; *Mutiny on the Bounty* (novel), Little, Brown, 1932 [other editions include those illustrated by Fletcher Martin, Heritage Press, 1947; N. C. Wyeth, Franklin Library, 1978; school editions for children include those published by Globe Book, 1952, and Houghton, 1962], also published in England as *Mutiny!*, Chapman & Hall, 1933; *Pitcairn's Island* (novel), Little, Brown, 1934, reprinted, 1962; *The Bounty Trilogy* (includes *Mutiny on the Bounty, Men Against the Sea,* and *Pitcairn's Island*; illustrated by Henry C. Pitz), Little, Brown, 1936 [another edition illustrated by N. C. Wyeth, Little, Brown, 1940; a school edition for children published by Globe Book, 1953]; *The Hurricane* (novel), Little, Brown, 1936 [another edition with illustrations from the Samuel Goldwyn film production, Chapman & Hall, 1938]; *The Dark River* (novel), Little, Brown, 1938; *No More Gas* (novel), Little, Brown, 1940; *Botany Bay* (novel), Little, Brown, 1941, reissued, C. Chivers, 1973; *Men Without Country* (novel), Little, Brown, 1942; *The High Barbaree* (novel), Little, Brown, 1945.

Contributor of poems, short stories, and essays to numerous periodicals, including *Atlantic Monthly, Harper's Magazine,* and *Saturday Evening Post.*

ADAPTATIONS—Movies and filmstrips: "Mutiny on the Bounty" (motion pictures), Metro-Goldwyn-Mayer, starring Charles Laughton and Clark Gable, 1935, excerpts for school use, Teaching Film Custodians, 1944, Metro-Goldwyn-Mayer, starring Marlon Brando, Trevor Howard, and Richard Harris, 1962; "Mutiny on the Bounty" (filmstrip; excerpts from the 1962 motion picture), Films Inc., 1975; "The Hurricane" (motion pictures), United Artists, starring Dorothy Lamour and Mary Astor, 1938, Paramount Pictures Corp., starring Jason Robards, Mia Farrow, Max Von Sydow, Trevor Howard, and Timothy Bottoms, 1979; "The Tuttles of Tahiti" (motion picture), adaptation of *No More Gas,* starring Charles Laughton, RKO Radio Pictures, 1942; "Passage to Marseille" (motion picture), adaptation of *Men Without Country,* starring Humphrey Bogart, Sydney Greenstreet, Claude Rains, and Peter Lorre, Warner Brother Pictures, 1944; "High Barbaree" (motion picture) starring Van Johnson and June Allyson, Loew's Inc., 1947; "Botany Bay" (motion picture), starring Alan Ladd and James Mason, Paramount Pictures Corp., 1953.

SIDELIGHTS: **April 22, 1887.** Born in Colfax, Iowa.

1897. Yearned for both adventure and an expression for his love of the outdoor life. "Around my tenth year when I began my literary career, my model was James Whitcomb Riley,

JAMES NORMAN HALL

the Hoosier Poet, and my secret ambition was to be called, some day, the Hawkeye Poet. Despite my admiration for James Whitcomb Riley, I had no desire to follow him in writing dialect poems. I wished to write of real people and real events. . . .

"A great part of our enjoyment came from being so close to the bosom of Mother Earth, which gave us the keen sense of traveling at enormous speed and with effortless power. All the odors of the summer night were ours: the cool dank fragrance of bottom lands along the river, mingled with that of skunk, one of the healthiest of all smells; the perfume of drying clover hay; the pungent odors of weeds and field flowers lying in swathes along the right-of-way as the scythes of the section hands had left them; the mingled odors of manure, horse sweat and harness coming from barns. And, best of all, the deep-toned whistle of Number Six, and we traveling with it! It was splendid compensation for the many times when we heard train whistles from afar, the sound growing fainter and fainter until heard no more.

"Saturday night was bath night in the Hall family. We bathed in turn by the kitchen stove, the bathtub being an enameled dishpan; then, in clean nightgowns, the boys of the family— the girls were still too young—would gather in the sitting room around the hard-coal burner while Mother read to us from Dickens and Cooper, and the serial stories of *The Youth's Companion, The Old Curiosity Shop, Nicholas Nickleby, Oliver Twist* and *David Copperfield* were my Dickens favorites, and *The Last of the Mohicans, The Deerslayer* and *The Pathfinder,* of Cooper's works. Recently, glancing through *The Old Curiosity Shop* once more, I wondered

(From *The Tale of a Shipwreck* by James Norman Hall. Illustrated by Alister Macdonald.)

(From *Doctor Dogbody's Leg* by James Norman Hall. Illustrated by Warren Chappell.)

whether Mother had not done some judicious skipping in reading Dickens to us in the old days." [James Hall, *My Island Home*, Little, Brown, 1952.[1]]

1904. Graduated from Colfax, Iowa high school; worked in clothing store before making difficult decision to attend college. "One morning I 'rode the blind' of the local westbound passenger train (just to keep my hand in) to Des Moines, and spent a full day in the public library reading the poetry in the magazines received there. I returned home with the addresses of the *Atlantic Monthly*, *Harper's Magazine*, and half a dozen more.

"From that time on I lived a double life. By day I was a clothing salesman; by night a would-be poetry salesman. In the latter occupation I received such courteous rebuffs that I was encouraged rather than disheartened. . . .

"But what greater thrill, save an acceptance of a manuscript, could a woodshed poet have than that which comes with the taking-out, handling and reading of these printed cards that actually came from an editor's office and which may have been slipped into the envelopes by his very hands? The returned manuscript gains both dignity and merit because it has been read, he hopes, by the editor himself.

"Although the unbiased editorial opinions were all of a kind, I was not discouraged. With the coming of spring I went as usual to my Hill. The hepaticas were in glorious abundance. Their perfume alone convinced me that life was too precious to be spent in a clothing store, and that a young man who made the mistake of underestimating its value would have only himself to blame for the disillusionment of later years. I considered more and more seriously the prospect of going to college, and that meant Grinnell and no other place."[1]

1910. Graduated from Grinnell College. Hall set out for Boston to work for the Massachusetts Society for Prevention of Cruelty to Children. "For it was to be a high destiny—so with the assurance of youth I decided—none other than this: to wander over the earth as long as life should last. I would put aside all other desirable ends that might interfere; count other ambitions as nothing; be content to reap no rewards but one which seemed best of all: a growing delight in the new and strange; an appreciation, ripening as the years passed, of all the glories of earth seen at first hand. I would rest here and there for some brief time, then move on to vague and remote destinations. And, after long periods of wandering, returning to old haunts I would look upon them, too, with unaccustomed eyes, and be there, as elsewhere, a stranger and a guest.

"On the evening of the day before I set out for Boston we were all gathered in the sitting room around Mother's piano which her father, our Grandfather Young, had given her when she herself was a student at the Washington Academy, in Washington, Iowa. She played the songs we all loved, and later, when we went out to the front porch, she sang 'Last Night the Nightingale Woke Me,' which evoked for us so many happy memories of the summer nights of childhood. The illusion that time had rolled back was made all but perfect for me when the headlight of Number Six appeared over the horizon to the west, at the top of the Mitchellville grade, and I heard—

"' . . . the whistle far away Sounding through the air so still.'

"Later that night I walked east out the railway track to say good-by to my Hill. It looked more beautiful, if that is possible, than ever it had. The fireflies were everywhere, and I heard the stilly music of the frogs along the bottom lands and of the whippoorwills on the hill itself. I might have been the woodshed poet of the summer of 1904.

Of a sudden a great gun broke the silence with a reverberating roar. Against my will I turned my head. A cloud of smoke half hid the vessel, but as it billowed out and drifted slowly away I saw three small black figures suspended in mid-air, twitching as they swayed slowly from side to side. ■ (From *The Bounty Trilogy* by Charles Nordhoff and James Norman Hall. Illustrated by N. C. Wyeth.)

(From the movie "Botany Bay," starring Alan Ladd. Copyright 1953 by Paramount Pictures Corp.)

"The piercing squeak of the old hall door sounded mournful indeed upon this occasion as I went upstairs to bed, well after midnight. 'Here he is, Mother Hall,' it seemed to say; 'stealing up for the last time. I'm warning you.' Mother heard it as she had so often before, in earlier years, when I hoped that she wouldn't hear. We talked until nearly daylight, and a few hours later I set out for Boston, in quest of the Bird in the Bush."[1]

1910-1914. Strived to achieve literary recognition while earning his living as a social worker. " . . . I continued my double life throughout my four years in Boston: the hope of becoming a writer was the one I held in my heart of hearts. Knowing well by this time my limitations as a poet I did not aspire beyond them. I had what I thought was a splendid idea. I would be a newspaper poet, and so I consulted my friend, Laurence Winship, about the possibility of getting employment in this capacity on the Boston *Globe*. Winship was then only a cub reporter without much influence in the upper hierarchy of editors on the *Globe*. Nevertheless, he made inquiries in my behalf, but was obliged to tell me that the *Globe* did not require a poet. Had the decision been favorable I might have been a precursor of Eddie Guest, but I am sure that I could never have approached his versatility in writing newspaper verse—a poem a day, year in and year out.

"I had little encouragement from magazine editors. My collection of printed rejection slips would have covered one wall of my bedroom."[1]

May, 1914. Inspired by his favorite book *Lord Jim*, Hall sailed to England and joined the Royal Fusiliers. "I was not compelled to earn my living during the three months in England, but I still wanted to prove to myself that it could be done. Romanticists rarely profit by experience and I had been able to persuade myself that my luck would be better in England. It was a happy, hopeful woodshed poet who, early in June, arrived in London, a suitcase in one hand and a portable typewriter in the other.''[1]

1917. Became brevet pilot in Escadrille Lafayette, an adventure which included a near-fatal crash landing. '' . . . It was getting dusk and as I approached I lost sight of the plane lowest down; he was approaching at exactly my altitude and it is difficult to see a plane in that position, particularly in fading light. Suddenly he loomed up directly in front of me, and he was firing as he came. His tracer bullets were going by on the left side but he corrected his aim and my motor seemed to be eating them up. As I banked to the right I felt a smashing blow in my left shoulder accompanied by a peculiar sensation as though it had been thrust through by a white-hot iron. My left arm seemed to be off, but it was still there although there was no more feeling in it. Blood was trickling into my eyes so that I could scarcely see and my flying-goggles were hanging down over my ears in two parts; they had been cut through at the nosepiece. I have never been certain of this, but I don't believe I fired a single shot;

after the bullet that creased my forehead I couldn't see anything to shoot at. There followed a vacant period that I can't fill in, but when it passed I realized that I was falling in a kind of half-*vrille*—spinning nose dive—with my motor going full speed. The Boches were following me closely, judging by the sound of their machine guns. I fully expected to feel another bullet boring its way into me, and one did graze a very important part of my anatomy but I didn't know of this until later. Perhaps it was as well that I did fall out of control for a considerable distance, for the firing soon stopped; evidently the Germans thought, with good reason, that they had bagged me.

''I pulled out of the spin, got my stick between my knees, reached over with my right hand and throttled down the engine. The propeller stopped dead, and when that happened in the air with a Spad, there was no way of getting it turning again. I didn't much care at the moment, except for wondering in a kind of drowsy way whether I were on the French or the German side of the lines. I came out in *ligne de vol* at about a hundred and fifty meters from the ground. It was a wicked-looking place for landing: trenches and shell holes everywhere, dimly seen in the gathering dusk. I was still wondering in a vague way whether they were French or German when I fell into a most restful sleep.

(From the movie "The Hurricane," starring Raymond Massey, Dorothy Lamour and Mary Astor. Copyright 1938 by Samuel Goldwyn Inc.)

Nordhoff and Hall at work.

"I have no slightest recollection of the crash; I might have fallen as gentle as an autumn leaf. When I came to, it was at once, completely. . . . "[1]

1918. Commissioned as captain in U.S. Air Service. Hall was later shot down and taken prisoner of war. Wrote *High Adventure,* describing sensations of being an aviator. "At the front I found poetry a greater resource than ever. Sometimes at night as I lay hidden with my comrades in the tall grass and weeds of no man's land waiting for targets, I would sort over passages that I particularly loved.

"There were times when I would close my eyes and imagine that I was on my Hill at home, listening to the whippoorwills, or I would walk the G-Note Road toward Morning Sun Pond, trying to recapture, in the imagination, the feeling of 'sacredness' I had felt when viewing it as a child. I remember 'stilly' nights when the line was really quiet; when the stillness was accentuated by the occasional vicious, mournful whine of ricochets dying away in the distance. Nothing more weird and ghostly could be imagined than the light of trench rockets revealing briefly the desolate landscape with its tortured trees and ruined farm buildings, and, as the light faded, the shadows rushing back like the very wind of darkness.

"War has one compensation—a great one—which peace cannot provide to anything like the same extent; namely, the strength of the friendships formed among men sharing equally the misery, boredom, horror and danger of active service. . . . "[1]

1919. Ordered home to collaborate with Californian Charles Nordhoff on the history of Lafayette Flying Corps. "It's the fault of you so-called 'native sons.' Your Chambers of Commerce spend all of their time trying to persuade Middle Westerners to settle in California. You send out special trains filled with exhibits of your products: oranges, lemons, figs, English walnuts, and the like. You boast about your perfect climate; you beg, wheedle and cajole our people to move to California, and when they do you resent their coming. If you don't want them, why don't you stop advertising your wonderful Golden State?"[1]

January, 1920. Hall and Nordhoff set out for Tahiti. "Ever since boyhood the mere name, 'island,' has had a peculiar fascination for me. An inland birth was, doubtless, partly responsible for that; islands were far to seek on the prairies of Iowa, and yet they could be found, of a sort. A mudbank in the sluggish midstream of a prairie slough was enough; and if at the season of the spring rains I found one larger, with a tree or two, the roots undermined by the current, leaning across it, I asked nothing better than to halt there and moor my flat-bottomed skiff to the roots of one of the trees. Try as I would, though, I could not imagine the sea—any sea. . . .

"Who does not remember some day in boyhood, such as this one of mine, preserved, fragrant and memorable, between the covers of a book? *Typee* has my day safely hidden among its pages. There was a quality approaching the ideal in my experience; indeed, I cannot imagine anything lacking that

(From the movie "Mutiny on the Bounty," starring Marlon Brando and Trevor Howard. Released by Metro-Goldwyn-Mayer Corp., 1962.)

(From the movie "Passage to Marseille," adapted from the novel *Men Without Country*, starring Humphrey Bogart and Claude Rains. Copyright 1944 by Warner Brothers Pictures, Inc.)

(From the movie "Mutiny on the Bounty," starring Clark Gable and Charles Laughton. Copyright 1935 by Metro-Goldwyn-Mayer Corp.)

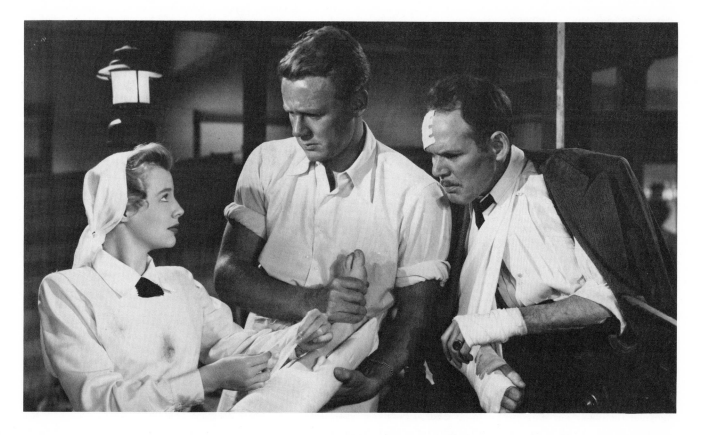

(From the movie "High Barbaree," starring June Allyson, Van Johnson and Henry Hull. Released by Metro-Goldwyn-Mayer Pictures, 1947.)

might have made it more so. It was my first authentic entrance, in literature, to the world of islands; and what more fitting vantage-point or vantage-time could I have had for the experience than the back room of Mrs. Sigafoos' shop, in a little farming town on the prairies on the afternoon of a snowy winter day? For the first time I believed in the sea—emotionally, I mean. That opening paragraph spread it out before me as something not to be questioned, like the sea of land rolling away to the horizons that bounded my home town. But, as I followed Melville across it, in the imagination, to Nuku Hiva in the Marquesas Islands, I little realized that the first gossamerlike thread of Chance was being spun which was to take me to the South Pacific, with my friend, Nordhoff, so many years later.

"Tahiti thirty years ago—to say nothing of other remote islands, both east and west in the Pacific—was a far different place from what it is today. Only the tips of the octopuslike tentacles of Western civilization, as we know it now, had reached this far into the Pacific, and the effect of them was scarcely felt. The character of the life was very much what it had been in the seventies and the eighties of the last century. There were, to be sure, a few motorcars, but not so many but what I could pretend not to see them."[1]

"I was to delve deeply, for the first time, into my own resources against loneliness. I had known the solitude of cities, but there one has the comfortable sense of nearness to others; the refuge of books, pictures, and music—all the distractions which prevent any very searching examination of one's capacity for a life of retirement. At Soul-Eaters' Island I would have no books, no pictures, excepting a colored postcard of the Woolworth Building which had won me this opportunity; and for music I was limited to what I could make for myself with my ocarina, my sweet-potato whistle which had a range of one octave. Thus scantily provided with diversions, I was to learn how far my own thoughts would serve to make a solitary life not only endurable, but pleasant." [Paul Briand, Jr., _In Search of Paradise_, Duell, Sloan and Pearce, 1966.[2]]

"I made excursions into the valleys and up the mountains, where no one lives, and at times prowled the streets of Papeete by day and by night. Having been inland born, with dreams of islands running through my head since boyhood days, I found that Tahiti surpassed my most hopeful expectations. Even with my feet on solid earth I could scarcely believe in the reality of the place. I liked being abroad at the time of the midday siesta when I had the streets almost to myself, and my first writing was a sketch in which I tried to put into words my feeling about that particular time of day.

"I love the hour between twelve and one when this island world falls under the enchantment of silence and sleep; but having been born in the higher latitudes, I can't accustom myself to the siesta. Sleep fails to come, and so, often, I set out for a stroll through the deserted streets.

"But my own wakefulness is only seeming. I too am under the midday enchantment which plays curious pranks with the senses, giving each of them the qualities of the others; and when a mynah bird, hidden in the deep shade of a mango tree, drops a single drowsy chirp into the pool of silence beneath and around him, I see, with my ears, so to speak, the silver splash it makes and the circles moving smoothly out over the placid surface. And, with my eyes, I hear the unfamiliar music of color that comes from gardens on either hand: the chiming of innumerable hibiscus bells; the clamorous trumpet-tones of the Bougainvillea; flamboyant trees

yearning like saxophones; and modest blossoms, deeply embowered in greenish gloom, giving forth arpeggios of cool notes like the tinkling of mandolins or the plucked strings of violins."[1]

1922. Left South Seas to write a travel book on Iceland, an assignment which he found particularly frustrating. In a letter to Nordhoff, Hall confessed: "I hope to get a good deal of work done this winter, despite the curse under which I seemed doomed to labor: the too-keen awareness of my feeble talents. Oh! that I had a great gift, or not the faintest glimmer of one! But how foolish and weak it is to complain! I must try and be content and make the most of one-tenth of a talent.

"What a pity it is that I must earn a living by writing! I do get so eternally sick of having to be eternally garrulous. My heaven is one where I may travel forever without ever being under the necessity of writing of my experiences.

" . . . How bitterly I regret my own folly now that it is too late! There is nothing for it now but to see the thing through, but to be deprived of Tahiti and your [Nordhoff] companionship—forgive me for speaking thus frankly—is almost too great a price to pay for even the most asinine folly. . . . When I have finished my work here, I shall return at once to Tahiti, never, I hope and believe, to leave the islands again."[2]

December, 1923. In deep despair over his lack of success, he returned to Tahiti. " . . . I have been going through a 'hellish crisis' and the end is not quite in sight. However, I think I shall win through eventually and gain the peace of mind which is necessary if one is to work to any purpose. As you know it has been almost impossible for me to write this long while. This has been horrible. To sit at one's desk day after day without being able to set down one decent paragraph—Lord! I hope that I shall never have to go through such a period again. It has been precisely as though a man, who had lost both of his legs, were under the absolute necessity of reaching a certain destination at a given time. . . . "[2]

1925. Married sixteen-year-old Sarah Winchester. "Well, well, here I am a married man of three months standing, and I haven't yet gotten over the shock. I keep on wondering in a sort of dazed way how the thing happened. . . . Sometimes, along about midday I hop on my bike and go into town for lunch, and usually, when I'm about halfway through the meal I remember that I have a wife, so I hop on my bike again and hurry home to another lunch which I attack with simulated enthusiasm. That's bad for the digestion."[2]

1926. Writing output improved with the birth of his son, Conrad, named for the author of _Lord Jim_.

1928-1934. Nordhoff and Hall teamed again to write the _Bounty_ trilogy. Hall concentrated on contributing descriptive passages. "It's three stories. First, the tale of the mutiny; then Bligh's open-boat voyage, and the third, the adventures of Fletcher Christian and the mutineers who went with him to Pitcairn Island, together with the Tahitian men and women who accompanied them. It's a natural for historical fiction. Who could, possibly, invent a better story? And it has the merit of being true.

"Although we saw, from the beginning, what a superb trilogy the _Bounty_ story would make, we could not assume that the general public would take the interest in it that we did; so our plan was, first, to write a tale concerned with Bligh's voyage to Tahiti, the collection there of the breadfruit trees, and the mutiny that followed on the homeward voyage, with just enough about Bligh's open-boat voyage and the later experiences of Christian and his men on Pitcairn to make an intelligible story of the whole *Bounty* affair, in case only one book was called for. But we hoped, of course, that there would be enough public interest in the story to warrant our going on with the two additional books we had planned: *Men Against the Sea* and *Pitcairn's Island.*"[1]

April, 1936. Returned with son to United States to seek medical treatment.

Late 1940's. From Tahiti Hall blasted Nordhoff in California for not returning to Tahiti to look after financial and family affairs. "You can understand the situation I have been placed in, having to take on the management of your affairs when you yourself should be here to do this. I can't understand why you don't come down, for a month or two at least, to set your Tahiti affairs in order. And, much more important than the land matters, what about the children? When I see two fine boys, Charley and Jimmie, simply vegetating here when they have reached an age when they should be receiving good schooling, I wonder that you can be so indifferent to their future. . . . Take them to the U.S.A. and give them an education that will fit them for life up there. I can see their future if they have to grow to manhood here with such little education as Tahiti schools can offer. I don't see how you can avoid longer the responsibility you have toward them. . . .

"You may say that all this is none of my business. But neither is it my business to have to take over the management of your land affairs which sorely need your own personal attention. . . . "[2]

1947. Nordhoff died in California. "Now that Nordy is dead, I write in a vacuum, so to speak. There is, actually, no one here to whom I can appeal for criticism and advice, and as I read over my stuff I often get discouraged and disheartened."[2]

June, 1950. Awarded honorary degree at his fortieth Grinnell College reunion. "My ideal, my companion I used to read poetry with in the library stockroom is here beside me; it's him, not me, the woodshed poet, who's receiving this honorary degree; and that's Old Man Diffidence on my back who was trying to hold off that cape, whispering in my ear: 'It's a certain thing, Norman Hall, no one knows better than yourself how little you deserve this.'"[2]

" . . . I contended that the places to avoid were those where one had been unhappy, and that happy memories could never be destroyed by a return to the old haunts concerned with them. But now, as I looked at the ruin of my Hill, I realized that I had returned once too often. Nevertheless, I still have it, in memory, just as it was in boyhood and youth. The stench of burned Diesel oil from all the Rock Island trains that pass and are yet to pass through it can never destroy, for me, the fragrance of the hepaticas that once grew on its slopes."[1]

1951. Reputation as a solo author was established with *The Far Lands.* Hall knew he was dying with an illness afflicting his legs. "My life is not so far different than what I had planned. Looking back over the years of my life I see how little I have changed. Wordsworth never wrote more truly than when he said the boy is father to the man. [I am] still

an idealist and a romanticist—and what misery these qualities have caused me!

"Men like myself who have no skill in practical matters are often seized by an almost unbearable sense of anguish thinking how useless their lives have been in comparison to men who build roads, bridges, lay water mains, etc., doing the practical work that has to be done in their time for the benefit of mankind."[2]

July 6, 1951. Died in Papeete, Tahiti. Buried on hill overlooking the bay where Bligh anchored *The Bounty.* "To most men, I believe, with the best of life before them, there is something terrible, infamous, in the thought of unrelieved blackness of an endless, dreamless sleep."[2]

FOR MORE INFORMATION SEE: James McConnaughey, "By Nordhoff and Hall," *Saturday Evening Post,* April 23, 1938; Robert Van Gelder, *Writers and Writing,* Scribner, 1946; Harvey Breit, "Talk with Mr. Hall," *New York Times Book Review,* January 14, 1951; E. Sedgwick, "James Norman Hall, 1887-1951," *Atlantic Monthly,* September, 1951, published in *Atlantic Monthly Jubilee,* Little, Brown, 1957; James Norman Hall, *My Island Home,* Little, Brown, 1952, reprinted, Greenwood Press, 1970; "Hall's Homes," *Newsweek,* November 13, 1952; Alice I. Hazeltine, *We Grew Up in America,* Abingdon, 1954; Paul L. Briand, *In Search of Paradise: The Nordhoff-Hall Story,* Duell, 1966; Robert L. Johnson, *American Heritage of James Norman Hall,* Dorrance, 1969; Robert Roulston, *James Norman Hall,* Twayne, 1978.

Obituaries: *New York Times,* July 7, 1951; *Newsweek,* July 16, 1951; *Time,* July 16, 1951; *Publishers Weekly,* July 28, 1951; *Wilson Library Bulletin,* September, 1951; *Americana Annual, 1952.*

HAWKINSON, Lucy (Ozone) 1924-1971

PERSONAL: Born in 1924, in California; died December 6, 1971; married John Samuel Hawkinson (an author and illustrator), September 20, 1954; children: Anne Miyo, Julia Eiko. *Education:* Studied at the Chicago Academy of Art. *Home:* Chicago.

CAREER: Author and illustrator of books for children. She was once employed by a publishing firm; she has illustrated the works of several well-known children's authors as well as those she has written herself and in collaboration with her husband.

WRITINGS—All self-illustrated except as indicated: *All in One Day,* A. Whitman, 1955; *Pockets,* A. Whitman, 1955; *Surprise!,* Rand McNally, 1956; *Dance, Dance, Amy-Chan!,* A. Whitman, 1964; *Days I Like,* A. Whitman, 1965; *That New River Train,* A. Whitman, 1970; *Picture Book Farm* (illustrated by Robert Pippenger), Childrens Press, 1971.

All illustrated and co-authored with John Hawkinson: *Winter Tree Birds,* A. Whitman, 1956; *City Birds,* A. Whitman, 1957; *Robins and Rabbits,* A. Whitman, 1960; *Birds in the Sky,* Childrens Press, 1965; *Little Boy Who Lives up High,* A. Whitman, 1967.

Illustrator: Jene Barr, *Good Morning, Teacher,* A. Whitman, 1957, 1966; Carla Greene, *I Want to Be a Fisherman,* Childrens Press, 1957; Jene Barr, *Miss Terry at the Library,* A. Whitman, 1962, 1967; (with John Hawkinson) Mabel Gee and Mary Bongiorno, *How Can I Find Out,* Childrens Press, 1963; Margaret Friskey, *Mystery of the Farmer's Three Fives,* Childrens Press, 1963; Jane Hefflefinger and Elaine Hoffman, *At the Pet Hospital,* Melmont, 1964; Dorothy Koch, *Up the Big Mountain,* Holiday House, 1964; Florence Schultz, *I Am Andrew,* CLC Press, 1965; Natalie Miller, *Story of the Statue of Liberty,* Childrens Press, 1965; Miriam Schlein, *Billy the Littlest One,* A. Whitman, 1966; M. Friskey, *Indian Two Feet and His Eagle Feather,* Childrens Press, 1967; Patricia Miles Martin, *One Special Dog,* Rand McNally, 1968; Muriel Novella Stanek, *Left, Right, Left, Right!,* A. Whitman, 1969; Fran Harvey, *Why Does It Rain?,* Harvey House, 1969; Patrick Mayers, *Just One More Block,* A. Whitman, 1970; M. N. Stanek, *Tall Tina,* A. Whitman, 1970; Helen Ross Russell, *The True Book of Buds: Surprise Packages,* Childrens Press, 1970.

ADAPTATIONS: "Birds in The Sky" (filmstrip), Westport Communications Group, 1969.

SIDELIGHTS: Hawkinson wrote and illustrated several books for children since the 1950's. Although she was quite active, critical reaction to her work has been scant and only mildly favorable. The *Chicago Sunday Tribune* has described *Winter Tree Birds,* written in collaboration with John Hawkinson, with conditional approval. "The text's flirting with being verse deserves little approval from the most uncritical of young readers, but it is accurate, set in large type, and accompanied by admirable pictures in a somewhat oriental style, and in color." *Birds in the Sky,* another husband-wife effort, has been praised a little more heartily by *Library Journal.* "Descriptive text is in close harmony with the illustrations. Fine for independent reading because it doesn't limit the child to a controlled vocabulary. In spite of the bird chart, this is not primarily for identification but for appreciation."

FOR MORE INFORMATION SEE: Chicago Sunday Tribune, November 11, 1956; *Library Journal,* December 15, 1965.

LUCY HAWKINSON

Some days the sky is gray, and I can watch the raindrops fall all the way down.

(From *Little Boy Who Lives Up High* by John and Lucy Hawkinson. Illustrated by the authors.)

HEUMAN, William 1912-1971 (George Kramer)

PERSONAL: Born February 11, 1912, in Brooklyn, N.Y.; died, August 21, 1971 in Huntington, N.Y.; son of John and Christine (Krauss) Heuman; married Esther Read, October 18, 1942; children: Robert, Janet. *Education:* Graduated from high school. *Religion:* Church of Christ. *Home:* Wyona Ct., Huntington, N.Y. *Agent:* Littauer & Wilkinson, 500 Fifth Ave., New York, N.Y. 10036.

CAREER: National Supply Corp., New York, N.Y., clerk for twelve years; free-lance writer, 1950—. Has taught private classes in writing.

WRITINGS: Fighting Five, Morrow, 1950; *Guns at Broken Bow,* Gold Medal Books, 1950; *Hunt the Man Down,* Gold Medal Books, 1951; *Roll the Wagons,* Gold Medal Books, 1951; *Red Runs the River,* Gold Medal Books, 1951; *Maverick with a Star,* Ace Books, 1952; *Secret of Death Valley,* Gold Medal Books, 1952; *South to Santa Fe,* Ace Books, 1952; *Keelboats North,* Gold Medal Books, 1953; *Junior Quarterback,* Morrow, 1953; *On to Santa Fe,* Gold Medal Books, 1953; *Captain McRae,* Morrow, 1954; *Range Buster,* Gold Medal Books, 1954; *Ride for Texas,* Gold Medal Books, 1954; *Gunhand from Texas,* Avon, 1954; *Bonanza on the Big Muddy,* Arcadia, 1955; *Girl from Frisco,* Morrow, 1955; *Nightstage,* Arcadia, 1955; *Wonder Boy,* Morrow, 1955; *Wagon Train West,* Gold Medal Books, 1955; *Man in Blue,* Ace Books, 1956; *Strictly from Brooklyn,* Morrow, 1956; *Little League Champs,* Lippincott, 1956; *Rocky Malone,* Steck, 1957; *Stagecoach West,* Gold Medal Books, 1957; *Violence Valley,* Gold Medal Books, 1957; *Guns of Hell Valley,* Arcadia, 1958; *Rustler's Range,* Arcadia, 1958; *Sabers in the Sun,* Arcadia, 1958; *Left End Luisetti,* Steck, 1958; *Wagon Wheel Drifter,* Arcadia, 1958; *Heller from Texas,* Gold Medal Books, 1958; *Then Came Mulvane,* Avon, 1959; *Rimrock City,* Arcadia, 1959; *Second String Hero,* Steck, 1959.

River Boy, Dodd, 1960; *Bullets for Mulvane,* Avon, 1960; *Mulane's War,* Avon, 1960; *Back Court Man,* Dodd, 1961; *King of the West Side,* Eerdmans, 1961; *Last Chance Valley,*

Arcadia, 1961; *Mulvane on the Prod,* Avon, 1961; *Guns Along the Big Muddy,* Arcadia, 1962; *Wonder Five,* Dodd, 1962; *Rookie Backstop,* Dodd, 1962; *Tall in the Saddle,* Jenkins, 1963; *Famous American Athletes,* Dodd, 1963; *Powerhouse Five,* Dodd, 1963; *City High Five,* Dodd, 1964; *Thorpe Halloran,* Ace Books, 1964; *The Horse That Played the Outfield,* Dodd, 1964; *Crossfire Creek,* Arcadia, 1964; *The Indians of Carlisle,* Putnam, 1965; *Horace Higby and the Field Goal Formula,* Dodd, 1965; *Hillbilly Hurler,* Dodd, 1966; *Tall Team,* Dodd 1966; *Famous Pro Football Stars,* Dodd, 1967; *Scrambling Quarterback,* Dodd, 1967; *Horace Higby and the Scientific Pitch,* Dodd, 1968; *Famous Coaches,* Dodd, 1968; *Backup Quarterback,* Steck, 1968; *Custer: Man and Legend,* Dodd, 1968; *Goofer Pitch,* Dodd, 1969; *Buffalo Soldier,* Dodd, 1969; *City High Champions,* Dodd, 1969.

Famous Pro Basketball Stars, Dodd, 1970; *Gridiron Stranger,* Lippincott, 1970; *Home Run Henri,* Dodd, 1970; *Horace Higby and the Gentle Fullback,* Dodd, 1970; *Fastbreak Rebel,* Dodd, 1971; *Horace Higby, Coxswain of the Crew,* Dodd, 1971; *Famous American Indians,* Dodd, 1972; *Little League Hotshots,* Dodd, 1972.

Under pseudonym George Kramer: *The Left Hander,* Putnam, 1964; *Kid Battery,* Putnam, 1968. Contributor of about 600 short stories and novelettes to *Saturday Evening Post, Collier's, Redbook, Sports Illustrated, Argosy, Bluebook, Boys' Life,* and other magazines, and several hundred juvenile short stories to religious publications.

SIDELIGHTS: Heuman was born and raised in Brooklyn and many of his short stories were set in this New York borough. He was also known for his popular sports novels for young people and for his books on the American West in which he was particularly interested.

He looked at Horace from the end of his chain. ■ (From *Horace Higby and the Scientific Pitch* by William Heuman. Illustrated by William Moyers.)

"... Some twenty years ago I wrote stories with many different backgrounds—Western, Northwestern, and even juvenile European stories—because I was convinced that my own background was completely dull, and in it could be found none of the elements of fiction.

"I lived for thirty years of my life in Brookyn, which most people view as a rather bizarre place. We who lived there did not share this view. The area of Brooklyn in which I lived was peculiarly quiet. There were no killings, robberies, or even juvenile delinquency, as I remember it. It was a work-aday life, with one day very much like the other, and you would hardly say that here could be found the germs of stories which would eventually appear in *The Saturday Evening Post....*

"It took me twenty years of writing western stories and novels, and other types of fiction, before I returned to my home locality and discovered the gold mine in the commonplace....

"I do not have to think when I write the speech of my characters from Brooklyn, because they speak most naturally. How valuable, then, is the admonition that we write about what we know best! For twenty years I had heard this, but didn't believe it....

WILLIAM HEUMAN

"We who seek to entertain through fiction must present persons who are different one from another. We can do this through a description of them, through mannerisms, but never so well as by their speech and by their actions, and speech can never be disassociated from action, as the one necessarily accompanies the other.

"Writing is hard work. Write about what you know, and the people you know, and you will give an air of authenticity to your writing. If you must go far afield, know your background, know it completely through the reading of hundreds of books, and if possible, by living there and becoming part of it for a time. Dialect in both cases will take care of itself." [William Heuman, "Dialect Does It," *The Writer,* June, 1956.[1]]

HOBBIES AND OTHER INTERESTS: Collecting guns and antique weapons; sports, especially baseball.

FOR MORE INFORMATION SEE: Saturday Evening Post, April 23, 1955; *The Writer,* June, 1956.

HEYWARD, Du Bose   1885-1940

PERSONAL: Born August 31, 1885, in Charleston, South Carolina; died June 16, 1940, in Tryon, North Carolina; son of Edwin W. and Jane (Du Bose) Heyward; descendent of Thomas Heyward, Jr. (a signer of the Declaration of Independence); married Dorothy Hartzell Kuhns (a playwright), September 22, 1923; children: Jenifer. *Education:* Attended public schools until age fourteen. *Politics:* Democrat. *Religion:* Episcopalian. *Home:* Charleston, South Carolina and Hendersonville, North Carolina.

CAREER: Novelist, poet, and playwright. Sold newspapers at age nine; other early jobs included hardware store clerk, warehouse clerk, cotton checker on the waterfront, and insurance salesman at age 21. With John Bennett and Hervey Allen, established the Poetry Society of South Carolina, 1920, becoming editor of its *Year Book,* 1921-24, and president, 1924. *Member:* National Institute of Arts and Letters, Poetry Society of America, MacDowell Colony, honorary Phi Beta Kappa. *Awards, honors:* Pulitzer Prize, 1927, for the dramatic version of *Porgy;* Litt.D. from University of North Carolina, 1928, College of Charleston, 1929, and University of South Carolina.

WRITINGS—Novels: *Porgy* (illustrated by Theodore Nadejen), G. H. Doran, 1925, reprinted, N. S. Berg, 1967 [another edition illustrated by Elizabeth O'Neill Verner, Doubleday, Doran, 1928]; *Angel,* G. H. Doran, 1926; *Mamba's Daughters,* Doubleday, Doran, 1929, reprinted, N. S. Berg, 1974; *The Half Pint Flask* (short story), Farrar & Rinehart, 1929; *Peter Ashley,* Farrar & Rinehart, 1932; *Lost Morning,* Farrar & Rinehart, 1936; *Star Spangled Virgin* (illustrated by T. Nadejen), Farrar & Rinehart, 1939.

Poems: (With Hervey Allen) *Carolina Chansons: Legends of the Low Country,* Macmillan, 1922, reprinted, Kraus Reprint, 1971; *Skylines and Horizons,* Macmillan, 1924; *Jasbo Brown and Selected Poems,* Farrar & Rinehart, 1931.

Plays: (With wife, Dorothy Heyward) *Porgy* (four-act; based on the author's novel; first produced in New York City at the Guild Theatre, October 10, 1927), Doubleday, Page, 1927; *Brass Ankle* (three-act), Farrar & Rinehart, 1931; (with D.

DU BOSE HEYWARD

Heyward) *Mamba's Daughters* (based on the author's novel), Farrar & Rinehart, 1939.

Other: (with Herbert Ravenel Sass) *Fort Sumter,* Farrar & Rinehart, 1938; *The Country Bunny and the Little Gold Shoes, as Told to Jenifer* (for children), Houghton, 1939, reprinted, 1974.

ADAPTATIONS—Movies: "Porgy and Bess" (musical; music by George Gershwin; words by Du Bose Heyward and Ira Gershwin), starring Sidney Poitier, Sammy Davis, Jr., and Dorothy Dandridge, Columbia Pictures, 1959.

Other: George Gershwin, *Porgy and Bess* (three-act opera; based on the play; music by G. Gershwin; libretto by Du Bose Heyward; lyrics by Heyward and Ira Gershwin; first performed in New York City at the Alvin Theatre, October 10, 1935), Random House, 1935.

SIDELIGHTS: **August 31, 1885.** Born into a leading family of Charleston, S.C., which experienced shocking economic setbacks when Heyward's father was suddenly killed in an accident.

Plagued with childhood illness and academic indifference, Heyward discontinued his formal education at the age of fourteen. During his eighteenth year he contracted polio which left him immobilized with temporary paralysis of his arms. Thereafter, he maintained several jobs as a cotton checker for a steamship line on the Charleston waterfront and as an insurance salesman. Again he was stricken with ill heath in the form of pleuresy.

Illness prevented his active participation in World War I. "[I'm] a poor bird who couldn't get by the physical and stayed home making speeches instead of getting first-hand experience in the trenches." [Frank Durham, *Du Bose Heyward, The Man Who Wrote Porgy,* University of South Carolina Press, 1854.[1]]

1917-1920. Concentrated on writing short stories. "*The Brute*" was the first of his stories to be published in 1918.

1918. Acquired a patron, John Bennett, who encouraged Heyward in his literary ambition. "The time was when I rather withered under [criticism]. Now I welcome it, and know that I must either admit its rightness, or offer good and sufficient reason for adhering to my own opinion.

"This summer especially I am trying out very different types of work. I want to find my vein, if possible. At present I have no idea what it is. . . ."[1]

1920. Turned exclusively to poetry writing. Helped organize the Poetry Society of South Carolina, an idea which blossomed into the genesis of a literary movement. "The Poetry Society of South Carolina is actively engaged in fostering literary activity throughout the South. This is not being done from a provincial or sectional spirit, but because . . . no one can deny that the world's most precious masterpieces . . . sprang out of local loyalties, and attained to universality because the locale, grandly handled, becomes as wide as the earth." [*Virginia Quarterly Review,* October, 1930.[2]]

August, 1921. Paid first of many visits to MacDowell Writers' Colony in New Hampshire.

September 22, 1923. Married Dorothy Kuhns, an aspiring playwright whom he met at the MacDowell Colony. ". . . Dorothy Kuhns and I decided that it was really no use trying to live apart any longer. We have tried it, and it does not work. And so, on the afternoon of the 22nd, I will march myself to 'The Little Church Around the Corner,' and into matrimony. . . ."[1]

1924. Abandoned the insurance business to devote full time to writing and the lecture circuit. ". . . I have fixed my plans to quit insurance and take the plunge. Very exciting, but a long story. . . .

"[I had set myself] the task of earning in eight months sufficient to support life for twelve [so that I might] write for four months. . . ."[1]

July, 1924. Interest sparked in the writing of novels, a new departure for him. "Dorothy and I are both off; she on a new play, and your humble (very much so in this case) servant hell bent on the negro novel. It is still so experimental. I am just feeling it out, and it may not come through to my satisfaction, in which case I will destroy, and await a return of the spirit with sufficient power. We all hate inquiries about brain children that came to still-birth. So let's wait and see whether it will breathe."[1]

October 20, 1924. Assumed Presidency of South Carolina Poetry Society.

May, 1925. Resigned from Society to pursue his own career interests as a potential novelist. "I have something of a plot in hand, and I will try to treat it simply, honestly, and directly, using some of the characters who have lived in my poems."[1]

...And the Jack Rabbits with long legs, who can run so fast, laughed at the little Cottontail and told her to go back to the country and eat a carrot. ■ (From *The Country Bunny and the Little Gold Shoes* by Du Bose Heyward. Pictures by Marjorie Flack.)

1925. Concluded *Porgy,* a novel which was to bring him acclaim. ". . . I am almost sure that I have closed my hands about something alive in my 'PORGO.' The Spirit of God has been perched upon the studio gable for a month, and where the stuff came from else, I can't imagine. It was not in me, I am sure. Terribly keen to get it under your knife, and listen to your comments. I might be all wrong. I am pretty drunk over it now. But anyway it is nearly done, right up to the last final copying, and I'll not do more to it now. I know that it needs a glance from the man who is 'Hell on commas.' But I think the stuff's there."[1]

October, 1926. Completed *Angel,* a novel compiled from short stories with mountain setting. ". . . I was scared blue of the reception it would receive, and I have been amazed at its press. Thank God, enough undiscerning, but recognized critics think it better than *Porgy,* and say so in print to give it a big publicity shove. . . . I did put my guts into it. It was a harder job technically than *Porgy,* and I think it helped to teach enough of the craft to prepare me for a real book."[1]

October 10, 1927. *Porgy,* adapted as a play, written in collaboration with his wife, opened to great success on Broadway.

1929. Wrote *Mamba's Daughter,* a Literary Guild selection. "Everything goes well here. We are both busy, and Dorothy is keeping in fine trim. I find, however, my old friend, that I am beginning to understand your own words of longing for the full power of the earlier years. Somehow I haven't the head of steam that once upon a time used to fairly blow the boiler head out. I am starting into some fairly intense stuff now. I start off sizzling in the morning, but it does not carry as it used to. Oh well, we have not said our say yet—neither of us.

". . . I have high hopes for this try. My canvas is broad, the dark shade predominates, but the white is coming up higher than in _Porgy_. I am almost afraid to whisper about it. It is still in such a touch and go state. But I have something big here if I can keep my hands on it."[1]

1932. Began formulating the idea of turning _Porgy_ into an opera with music by George Gershwin. "Statistics record the fact that there are 25,000,000 radios in America. Their contribution to the opera was indirect but important. Out of them for half an hour each week poured the glad tidings that Feenament could be wheedled away from virtually any drug clerk in America for one dime—the tenth part of a dollar. And with the authentic medicine-man flair, the manufacturer distributed his information in an irresistible wrapper of Gershwin hits, with the composer at the piano.

"There is, I imagine, a worse fate than that which derives from the use of a laxative gum. And, anyhow, we felt that the end justified the means, and that they also served who only sat and waited.

"I am offering a new idea for the opening of scene as you will see from the script. The play opened with a regular riot of noise and color. This makes an entirely different opening, which I think is important. What I have in mind is to let the scene, as I describe it, merge with the overture, almost in the sense of illustration, giving the added force of sight and sound. I think it would be very effective to have the lights go out during overture, so that the curtain rises in darkness, then the first scene will begin to come up as the music takes up the theme of jazz from the dance hall piano. The songs which I have written for this part will fall naturally into the action and mood of the separate flashes of negro life."[1]

October, 1932. _Peter Ashley,_ historical novel, published after a lengthy gestation period. "I want to tell you honestly, and really humbly, that I am not yet prepared to do the epic novel. I want to add that to do it is my greatest ambition. It is taking form slowly in my mind, and if I can afford to take the necessary time for research this winter, I will start to get my material. I am not sure that you will like what I will do. I do not even know myself what it will be like. But whatever it is it will be _myself,_ and not a meritritious (if that's the way you spell it) 'best seller.' I promise you that. I see the period just before, and during the war, and not the earliest time most clearly now. But I do not know how it will work out."[1]

(From the movie "Porgy and Bess," starring Sidney Poitier and Pearl Bailey. Released by Columbia Pictures Corp., 1959.)

Du Bose Heyward. Detail of a painting by George Gershwin.

1933. Wrote his first motion picture script for O'Neill's *Emperor Jones*. "Just what I will be doing next God knows. I am in the doldrums and feeling about for a current that will take me out and start me on my way. Nothing has come up from Hollywood that I would want to take, so I shall probably not be sitting on a California hillside with a screen beauty this summer while my wife and chieeld [*sic*] languish in the N.C. mountains."[1]

October 10, 1935. Opening of *Porgy and Bess*, the first American folk opera.

1939. Organized playwrights' group at Dock Street Theatre in Charleston.

April, 1939. Publication of his children's story, *The Country Bunny*.

June 16, 1940. Returned from visit to his beloved Carolina mountains. Suffered fatal heart attack in Tryon, North Carolina.

FOR MORE INFORMATION SEE: Hervey Allen, *Du Bose Heyward: A Critical and Biographical Sketch*, 1922, reprinted, Folcroft, 1973; Emily Clark, "Du Bose Heyward," in her *Innocence Abroad*, Knopf, 1931; Harlan H. Hatcher, "Exploiting the Negro," in his *Creating the Modern American Novel*, Farrar, Straus, 1935; Frank Durham, *Du Bose Heyward: The Man Who Wrote Porgy*, University of South Carolina Press, 1954.

HOFSINDE, Robert 1902-1973

PERSONAL: Born December 10, 1902, in Odense, Denmark; emigrated to the United States in 1922; married wife, Geraldine, 1937. *Education:* Attended Royal Art Academy, Copenhagen, Denmark, 1916-22, Minneapolis School of Art. *Residence:* Monroe, N.Y.

CAREER: Author and illustrator of books for children. With his wife, had daily radio program, "Gray-Wolf's Ti-pi" in Chicago, beginning 1937; through Junior Programs of New York, organized school assemblies on Indian lore throughout the country, beginning 1940. Has designed scenery for the Circus Saints and Sinners Club, illustrations for the New York Railroad Club, and numerous murals.

WRITINGS—All self-illustrated; all published by Morrow: *The Indian's Secret World*, 1955; *Indian Sign Language*, 1956; *Indian Games and Crafts*, 1957; *Indian Beadwork*, 1958; *Indian Picture Writing*, 1959; *The Indian and His Horse*, 1960; *The Indian and the Buffalo*, 1961; *Indian Hunting*, 1962; *Indian Fishing and Camping*, 1963; *Indians at Home*, 1964; *Indian Warriors and Their Weapons*, 1965; *The Indian Medicine Man*, 1966; *Indian Music Makers*, 1967; *Indian Costumes*, 1968; *Indians on the Move*, 1970; *Indian Arts*, 1971.

Illustrator: Allan A. Macfarlan, *Indian Adventure Trails*, Dodd, 1953.

Contributor of articles on Indian lore to *Popular Mechanics* and *Popular Science*.

ROBERT HOFSINDE

The headdress of the Chirichua was perhaps the most beautiful. It consisted of a buckskin skullcap ornamented with antelope fur, red cloth and beads. A pair of antelope pronged horns stood upright from its sides. ■ (From *Indian Costumes* by Robert Hofsinde. Illustrated by the author.)

SIDELIGHTS: Hofsinde was born next door to Hans Christian Andersen's house. His interest in the American Indian culture began with a painting trip to the north woods of Minnesota. One day, he came upon a young Indian boy who had fallen into a pit trap and suffered a compound fracture of the leg. Hofsinde rescued the boy, set the break, and carried him back to his village on a sled. In gratitude, Hofsinde was made a blood brother of the Ojibwa tribe and was given the name Gray-Wolf. He enjoyed sketching the Ojibwas and became so interested in their culture that he stayed with them for three years. He returned to Minneapolis, but still wanted to know more about the Indians. He set off on a research and sketching trip which lasted sixteen years. He visited the Ojibwa and Blackfeet tribes, traveling on horseback from Montana to Arizona. He was accepted among all the Indians as a friend, and allowed to participate in their ceremonies, sit in their councils, and smoke with the men. His wife often traveled with him, and the Indians gave her the name Morning Star.

FOR MORE INFORMATION SEE: Kirkus Reviews, July 1, 1955; *Chicago Tribune,* November 13, 1955; *Young Readers' Review,* May, 1967; *Christian Science Monitor,* June 22, 1967.

HOOD, Robert E. 1926-

PERSONAL: Born April 15, 1926, in Mildred, Pa., son of Charles E. (a coal miner) and Alice V. (Johnson) Hood; married Ann M. King, October 15, 1955; children: Carol Ann, Eric Charles. *Education:* Harpur College (now State University of New York at Binghamton), B.A., 1951; New York University, graduate study, 1951-53. *Politics:* Democrat. *Home:* 14304 Olympic Ct., Farmers Branch, Tex. 75234. *Agent:* Sterling Lord Agency, 660 Madison Ave., New York, N.Y. 10021. *Office: Boy's Life,* Boy Scouts of America, New Brunswick, N.J. 08903.

CAREER: Boy's Life, New Brunswick, N.J., editorial assistant, 1953-54, assistant editor, 1954-58, associate editor, 1958-62, executive editor, 1962-64, editor, 1964-70, editor-in-chief, 1970—. Special consultant for Community Relations Service, 1964. Volunteer speech and pamphlet writer for Senator John F. Kennedy, 1960; speech writer for Senator Harrison Williams, 1964, and Governor LeRoy Collins, 1964-66. *Military service:* U.S. Navy Reserve, 1944-46. *Member:* American Society of Magazine Editors.

WRITINGS—All published by Putnam except as indicated: *Find a Career in Photography,* 1959; *Twelve at War: Great Photographers under Fire,* 1967; *Let's Go to a Baseball Game,* 1973, 1976; *Let's Go to a Stock Car Race,* 1973; *Let's Go to a Football Game,* 1974; *Let's Go to a Basketball Game,* 1975; *The Gashouse Gang,* Morrow, 1976. Editor, Putnam's "Sport Series," 1958—, and Coward's "States of the Nation Series," 1964-66. Contributor of articles and reviews to *World Book Yearbook, New York Times, Popular Photography, American Swedish Monthly, Infinity, Famous Writers Magazine.*

ROBERT E. HOOD

In the air is the smell of racing, of new tires and burning rubber, of grease and oil and gasoline.
■ (From *Let's Go to a Stock Car Race* by Robert Hood. Illustrated by Paul Frame.)

WORK IN PROGRESS: The Withered Branch, a novel; *Beating the Bushes,* a baseball memoir.

SIDELIGHTS: "I am a lazy writer who'd rather play than work. When I wrote my juvenile books, my own children were at home, providing a background of noise and activity to offset the loneliness of composition. I like to hear people around me when writing, particularly young people having a good time. Silence makes me uneasy. Sounds odd, I know, because I do enjoy solitude, time for reading and thinking, but *not* when I write!

"Faced with a deadline, I'm able to write anywhere, on a bus or train, at a typewriter, or lying in bed scribbling on a yellow pad, which is how I wrote most of *The Gashouse Gang.*

"I've written for most ages—eight-ten year olds, eleven-fourteen year olds, young adults and adults. I don't vary my style and worry about the age of a reader. If one writes simply and doesn't patronize, both young and old will enjoy the work *if* it is interesting.

"As a youngster, my ambition was to play major league baseball. After failing at that, I sort of stumbled into writing via journalism courses and through working on a college newspaper. Several of my books were written for money (I didn't make it), and three of them from having something to say. They didn't make money either, but that doesn't trouble me. It's more important having published than having made money.

"*The Gashouse Gang* was fun to do because it included interviews with old players whom I admired. My best book is *Twelve at War,* also based on interviews with well-known people. I like people, so interviewing is fun for me."

HOBBIES AND OTHER INTERESTS: "Love to golf, fish, and watch baseball games."

HOOKER, Ruth 1920-

PERSONAL: Born April 30, 1920, in Rockville Center, N.Y.; daughter of John Wilhelm (an engineer) and Ruth (Garges) Hieronymus; married Harris Hooker (an electrical engineer), August 1, 1941; children: Charlotte (Mrs. Robert Kreamer), George, Jane (Mrs. Robert Hansen), Barbara (Mrs. William Shaw). *Education:* Attended Northern Illinois University, 1938-40; attended Moser Business College, 1940-41. *Home:* 1049 Sylvan Circle, Naperville, Ill. 60540.

CAREER: Children's librarian in Naperville, Ill., 1962-64; writer, 1964—. Trustee of Nichols Library (Naperville). *Member:* Society of Children's Book Writers, Children's Reading Round Table, Off-Campus Writers Workshop, Mystery Writers of America. *Awards, honors:* Award from Friends of American Writers, 1971, for *Gertrude Kloppenberg (Private).*

WRITINGS—All juveniles: *Gertrude Kloppenberg (Private)* (novel), Abingdon, 1970; *Gertrude Kloppenberg II* (novel), Abingdon, 1974; *Kennaquhair* (science fiction novel), Abingdon, 1976; (with Carole Smith) *Pelican Mystery,* A. Whitman, 1977; (with Carole Smith) *The Kidnapping of Anna,* A. Whitman, 1979. Contributor of stories to *Child Life, Boys and Girls, Red Cross Youth News, Trails, Twelve/Fifteen, Adventure,* and *Christian Science Monitor.*

WORK IN PROGRESS: Another mystery with Carole Smith; a story about a girl whose good deeds backfire; a nonfiction book about water towers.

SIDELIGHTS: "I did not start writing seriously until after my children were grown. Before that time, I wouldn't have believed anyone who might have predicted my becoming an author of children's books and stories. But looking back, I can see that my life had been pointing in that direction.

my life that has furnished ideas for background and characters.

"Until I was nine we lived in an apartment on the south side of Chicago. We visited museums, zoos, conservatories, rode on double-deck buses, and played in parks and on beaches, I thought it was an exciting and wonderful place to live.

"Summers were spent on Long Island in New York with grandparents. We lived in a house full of unmarried uncles and aunts and an airdale named Sandy and rode in a big touring car. The beaches had tall roaring waves that were salty and the carnivals had airplanes doing stunts not terribly high up in the air. I remember picking raspberries for breakfast and I remember the smell of the chicken coop where I was taken to gather eggs. But the chickens petrified me, just as they petrified Pummy in *Kennaquhair*.

"We moved to a suburb about the time the depression was beginning to be felt. My mother died and we were sad and lost, besides being very poor. I have written some stories based on those days when we had to learn to cook and clean and pinch pennies, and about the summer we spent with my aunt and three cowboy cousins in New Mexico.

"Not long after I was married we moved to Nevada and were fascinated with our new surroundings. We explored the desert, abandoned mines, and mountains. Many years later I wrote a science-fiction story about a bat cave and a dry lake, two boys and their amazing adventure there.

"During the war years we moved from coast to coast, following orders from the Navy. Afterwards we settled in the midwest where we have lived ever since. Camping throughout the United States and Canada, having an exchange stu-

They raced down the road until they reached the police car. ■ (From *The Pelican Mystery* by Ruth Hooker and Carole Smith. Illustrated by George Armstrong.)

"Books have always been a big part of my life. In my early years stories were read aloud, poems recited, and proverbs said. At around the age of nine I discovered the joy of reading. I read my older brother's books about Tarzan, trips to Mars, and other outlandish adventures. I exchanged books with friends, devoured library books by the dozen, and read the many magazines delivered to our house. I always read as much as I could, which was considered to be more than I should.

"I was a shy child, which gave me time to look and wonder and think; somewhat like *Gertrude Kloppenberg* who spent a whole recess being enchanted by single snowflakes. My shyness eventually left but there still remains the inclination for me to wonder and think, especially when I'm writing.

"These two things, love of books and introspection, gave me the temperament to be an author, but it was the variety of

RUTH HOOKER

dent from Sweden for a year, and renting boats to sail in the Caribbean and the Great Lakes added adventure to our lives and furnished me with many ideas for stories. The most essential ingredient, children themselves, has been plentiful throughout my life. Children to know, listen to, play with, care for, and love have always been near.

"But I believe being a children's librarian stirred me into action. I delighted in the children's reaction during story hour and the older children's reports about books they had read. I decided I wanted to make children laugh or sigh with contentment or wiggle with anticipation.

"I started writing picture books, which I mainly sold as short stories. I wrote stories for the middle grades and gradually worked into writing books for the same age.

"Usually I read reference books to double check myself as I write. I read about survival and handcrafts when I wrote *Kennaquhair,* and about Shakespeare's works and the Earl of Southampton when I wrote *Time Out of Joint.*

"Lately Carole Smith and I have been writing mysteries together. It works out very well because it's good to have two to keep track of the clues.

"When I am first planning a book my thoughts go so fast that I feel like a soaring bird, but when I write page after page, crossing out, rewriting, and correcting, I feel like a very slow turtle. In the end I am usually pleased and satisfied, but I do wish I could be a speedier turtle. There is so much I want to write."

HOBBIES AND OTHER INTERESTS: Sailing, reading, gardening.

FOR MORE INFORMATION SEE: Publishers Weekly, February 28, 1977.

"...Make this repulsive, stinking thing leave at once on his confounded magic horse." ■ (From *Ali Baba and the Forty Thieves and Nine Other Tales from the Arabian Nights,* retold by Ned Hoopes. Illustrated by Unada.)

NED E. HOOPES

HOOPES, Ned E(dward) 1932-

PERSONAL: Born May 22, 1932, in Safford, Ariz.; son of Cloyde M. and Pearl (Greenhalgh) Hoopes. *Education:* Brigham Young University, B.A., 1956, M.A., 1957; Northwestern University, M.A., 1958, Ph.D., 1967. *Home:* 205 Third Ave., Apt. #10U, New York, N.Y. 10003.

CAREER: Special lecturer, Evanston Township High School, Evanston, Illinois, 1959-62; Hofstra University, Hempstead, N.Y., instructor, 1962-63; Hunter College, New York, N.Y., lecturer in School of General Studies, and instructor, Hunter College High School, 1963-68; Pace University, New York, N.Y., professor of English, 1968—. Master teacher, Master of Arts Program, Harvard University, summer, 1962, Yale University, summer, 1963. Television host for "The Reading Room," Columbia Broadcasting System network show for children; narrator of poetry records for Macmillan, and children's stories records for Weston Studios. Former member of editorial board, Laurel Leaf and Mayflower libraries, Dell Publishing Co. *Member:* National Council of Teachers of English (formerly on the board of directors).

WRITINGS: (Editor with Diane W. Wilbur) *The Lighter Side,* Scholastic Book Services, 1964; (editor with Richard S. Beal) *Search for Perspective,* Holt, 1965; (editor) *Harte of the West: 17 Stories by Bret Harte,* Dell, 1966; (editor with Richard Corbin) *Incredible Tales by Saki,* Dell, 1966; (editor with R. Corbin) *Surprises: 20 Stories by O. Henry,* Dell, 1966; (editor) *The Wonderful World of Horses,* Dell, 1966; (editor with Richard Peck) *Edge of Awareness: 25 Contemporary Essays,* Laurel, 1966, Delacorte, 1970; (editor) *Famous Devil Stories,* Laurel, 1967; (retelling of *Arabian Nights*), *Ali Baba and the Thieves, and Other Stories,* Mayflower Book, 1967; (with Bernard Evslin) *Heroes and Monsters of Greek Myth,* Scholastic Book Services, 1967; (editor) *Stories to Enjoy,* Macmillan, 1967, new edition, 1974; (editor) *Ideas in Motion,* Holt, 1969; *Who Am I?,* Dell, 1969; (editor) *Great Television Plays,* Laurel, Volume I, 1969, Volume II (with Pat Gordon), 1975. Contributor to *Britannica Junior Encyclopaedia for Boys and Girls.* Former issue editor, *Scholastic Teacher.* Former television editor, *Media and Methods* (formerly *School Paperback Journal*). Former book editor, *Ingenue* Magazine.

WORK IN PROGRESS: A biography of Viola Bodenschatz, an American involved in the Nazi movement.

HULL, Eleanor (Means) 1913-

PERSONAL: Born August 19, 1913, in Denver, Colo.; daughter of Carleton Bell and Florence (an author; maiden name, Crannell) Means; married Angus Clifton Hull (a clergyman), January 9, 1938 (died January 15, 1974); children: Mary Margaret (Mrs. Joseph Philip Hammer), Angus Crannell, Stephen Carleton, Peter Henrich, Jeremy Robert. *Education:* Colorado Woman's College, A.A., 1930; University of Redlands, B.A., 1932; University of Denver, B.F.A., 1934. *Politics:* Democrat. *Religion:* Baptist. *Home:* Salino Star Rte., Gold Hill, Colorado 80302.

ELEANOR HULL

If he was ever going to leave, he'd have to do it before she came out and looked at him. ■(From *A Trainful of Strangers* by Eleanor Hull. Illustrated by Joan Sandin.)

CAREER: Department of Welfare, New York, N.Y., social caseworker, 1964-69. *Awards, honors:* Degree from Wilberforce College, Yellow Springs, Ohio.

WRITINGS: Tumbleweed Boy, Friendship, 1949; *The Third Wish,* Friendship, 1950; *Papi,* Friendship, 1953; *The Turquoise Horse,* Friendship, 1955; *Suddenly the Sun: A Biography of Shizuko Takahashi,* Friendship, 1957; *In the Time of the Condor,* Friendship, 1961; *Through the Secret Door,* Pilgrim Press, 1963; *The Sling and the Swallow,* United Church Press, 1963; *Moncho and the Dukes,* Friendship, 1964; *Everybody's Somebody,* Pilgrim Press, 1964; (with Elinor G. Galusha and Sarah D. Schear) *Let Us Worship God,* United Church Press, 1964; *The Church Not Made with Hands,* Judson, 1965; *A Trainful of Strangers,* Atheneum, 1968; *The Second Heart,* Atheneum, 1973; *Women Who Carried the Good News,* Judson, 1975.

WORK IN PROGRESS: A book on Mexico; a novel about a black welfare mother and her two sons called *The Birthright;* a novel entitled, *A Woman Alone.*

SIDELIGHTS: "When I was ten, I wrote a book that started, 'Diantha laid down her dustcloth in sheer amazement.'

"I didn't know what Diantha was amazed about, but I knew what a dustcloth was (it was my chore to ply one), and I hoped that the two were not totally incompatible.

"That book went to only four chapters; but the books my mother, Florence Crannell Means, wrote, which I read sheet by sheet as they came out of the typewriter, went to many chapters and many editions and finally totalled forty-one. *Candle in the Mist* was the first, and therefore, to me the most beloved.

"Later I had five children of my own who provided brisk competition to book-writing, but also a lot of ideas. I found time only for books that were commissioned and armed with deadlines, but enjoyed writing a number of them for junior age for Friendship Press and others about migrant children, Puerto Rican children in East Harlem, Navaho children, Indian children on the high plains of Ecuador, and others.

"My minister-husband gave me help and encouragement, and his life, first as a pastor and later as an executive secretary in Cleveland and New York City, brought us into contact with many different styles of life and people.

"My experiences in New York, which included social work among some very poor people, gave me material for a book about the different groups of children who live there: *A Trainful of Strangers,* published by Atheneum.

"My husband's Sabbatical provided us both with the opportunity for living for several months with a Mexican family in Cuernavaca, Mexico, and studying at CIDOC, the interesting learning center created by Ivan Illich. This resulted in a book for older young people, *The Second Heart,* also published by Atheneum; it was written in pursuit of an Indian maid in the household where we lived, whose mysterious background and puzzling personality stimulated me to study and observe the past and present of Mexican life until I could present a girl who might have felt and thought as that other girl felt and thought, hoping that I had gained understanding which would help other people to understand.

"Now, living by myself in the mountains near an old mining town, often visited by my six grandchildren, I am working on several novels and on a book about a boy and his grandmother.

"I no longer have to look hard to find things about which to be amazed!"

Books are keys to wisdom's treasure;
Books are gates to lands of pleasure;
Books are paths that upward lead;
Books are friends. Come let us read.
—Emilie Poulsson

The Love of Books, the Golden Key
That opens the Enchanted Door.
—Andrew Lang

JOANNE ISAAC

ISAAC, Joanne 1934-

PERSONAL: Born June 12, 1934, in New York, N.Y.; daughter of Morris and Maxine (Goodman) Goldman; married Charles D. Isaac (a lawyer); children: Jean, Rachel, Ruth, Paul. *Education:* Attended Parsons School of Design, New York, N.Y., 1953-54, and Yale University, 1955-57. *Home:* R.D. 4, Quakertown, Pa. 18951.

CAREER: Etcher, making own prints on a Charles Brand etching press. *Exhibitions*—One person shows: William Penn Memorial Museum, Harrisburg, Pa., 1975; Lock Ridge Furnace Museum, Alburtis, Pa., 1978. Group shows: Associated American Artists Collector's Show, New York, N.Y., 1978; Bologna Arte Fiera, Italy, 1978. Juried shows: American Institute of Graphic Arts, New York, N.Y., 1968; Society of Illustrators, New York, N.Y., 1969; Kemerer Museum, Bethlehem, Pa., 1973; Allentown Art Museum Shows, Allentown, Pa., 1973; Pennsylvania Printmakers, Lehigh University, Bethlehem, Pa., 1973; National Arts Club Graphics Show, New York, N.Y., 1974; Philadelphia Art Alliance Printmakers, Philadelphia, Pa., 1975; Contemporary Prints, Lehigh University, Bethlehem, Pa., 1975; Eleventh National Print Exhibition, Silvermine, Conn., 1976; International Print Bienalle, Cracow, Poland, 1978; Mid-Atlantic Drawing and Print Exhibition, Frostburg, Md., 1979; Saga National Print Collection, the Society of American Graphic Artists, New York, N.Y., 1979. Permanent collections: UNICEF—United Nations Children's Fund, New York, N.Y.; U.S. Department of State, Washington, D.C.; U.S. Embassy, Paris, France; New Ginkaku Yadoya, Kyoto, Japan; Free Library of Philadelphia, Illustrator's Collection; New York Public Library, Illustrator's Collection. *Awards, honors:* Awards from

(From *Amanda* by Joanne Isaac. Illustrated by the author.)

American Institute of Graphic Arts, Children's Book Show, and Society of Illustrators Show.

WRITINGS—Self-illustrated children's books: *Amanda*, Lerner, 1968; *Tom Thumb's Alphabet*, Putnam, 1970.

Illustrator: *Rhone, River of Contrasts*, Garrard, 1967; *Are You My Friend?*, Judson Press, 1968.

SIDELIGHTS: "As an artist—a professional printmaker—I work all the time. I just love what I do!"

ISHAM, Charlotte H(ickox) 1912-

PERSONAL: Surname is pronounced *Eye*-shum; born May 17, 1912, in Waterbury, Conn.; daughter of Austin (a farmer) and Sarah (Mattoon) Isham. *Education:* Danbury State Teachers College, B.E., 1940; Yale University, M.A., 1948; Harvard University, Ed.D., 1967. *Politics:* Republican. *Religion:* Congregationalist. *Home:* 153B Washington Rd., Woodbury, Conn. 06798 and 560 W. Graves Ave., Orange City, Fla. 32763 (winter). *Office:* Department of Education, Western Connecticut State College, 181 White St., Danbury, Conn. 06810.

CAREER: Elementary school teacher in Plymouth, Conn., 1935-36, Harwinton, Conn., 1936-39, and Litchfield, Conn., 1939-43; teacher and principal of elementary school in Newtown, Conn., 1943-47; elementary supervisor of region including Newtown, Southbury, Woodbury, and Bethlehem, Conn., 1947-50, region including Woodbury, Southbury, and Bethlehem, 1950-53, and region including Woodbury and Bethlehem, 1953-54; supervisor of instruction in Woodbury, Conn., 1954-64; Western Connecticut State College, Danbury, assistant professor, 1964-67, associate professor, 1967-71, professor of children's literature, 1971-76, professor emeritus, 1978—. Member of Waterbury Greater Chamber of Commerce Resource Center, 1972.

MEMBER: National Education Association (life member), Association for Supervision and Curriculum Development, American Association of University Women, New England Reading Association, New England Association for Supervision and Curriculum Development, Connecticut Teachers Association, Connecticut Department of Higher Education, Connecticut Association for Supervision and Curriculum Development, Old Woodbury Historical Society (librarian), Delta Kappa Gamma, Eastern Star (past matron), Orange City (Florida) Woman's Club, Orange City Library (board member), Orange City Shuffleboard Club. *Awards, honors:* Outstanding Educators Award, 1970, from Western Connecticut State College; Outstanding Educators of America Award, 1972.

CHARLOTTE H. ISHAM

Freddie was a little brown trout. ■ (From *Freddie* by Charlotte Isham. Illustrated by Carol A. Hoover.)

WRITINGS: The Face of Connecticut, Sugar Ball Press, 1952; *Now We Are Six*, privately printed, 1955; *The History of North Congregational Church*, privately printed, 1966; *Freddie* (juvenile), Franklin Publishing, 1972; *Freddie's Discoveries* (juvenile), Franklin Publishing, 1974; *Matilda Mae Manatee*, Volusia Graphics, 1978. Author of pamphlets for Old Woodbury Historical Society. Contributor to education journals.

WORK IN PROGRESS: Research on the anhinga (turkey bird).

SIDELIGHTS: "I retired from Western Connecticut State College in December, 1976. I had been professor the last few years and taught at the college twelve and one half years. In the spring of 1977 I was named professor emeritus.

"Last winter I discovered that there had been *no* story about the manatee. This fascinating mammal is on the endangered species list. The Blue Springs State Park is one of the few places where the manatee is protected. Well, I wrote *Matilda Mae Manatee*.

"Last winter I also wrote *A History of Western Connecticut State College*.

"Right now I am doing research on the anhinga—a most interesting bird. It has no oil in its wings so it can't stay in the water very long. When the anhinga climbs on a low bush to dry his wings he looks more like his other name—turkey bird. That just might be my next story!

"I am in Florida from early October until May. It's harder to write down here. It is so beautiful outdoors and I'm involved in so many activities.

"Late in April I go home to my farm in Woodbury. I have a big garden and much lawn. I enjoy taking care of the garden and the lawn. That keeps me outdoors and healthy."

Isham's children's books are set almost in her own back yard. She draws heavily on natural surroundings, especially the Weekeepeemee River near her home. Her books are intended to assist the beginning reader without boring him, and she insists that they be inexpensive and widely available to children.

FOR MORE INFORMATION SEE: News-Times, November, 1974; *Newton Bee,* June, 1975.

JACOB, Helen Pierce 1927-

PERSONAL: Born November 9, 1927, in Lakewood, Ohio; daughter of Clyde Cowan (a teacher) and Lena (a teacher; maiden name, Grafton) Pierce; married Louis Albert Jacob (a librarian), August 15, 1953. *Education:* Mount Union College, B.A., 1949; Case Western Reserve University, M.S.L.S., 1953. *Politics:* Liberal. *Religion:* Methodist. *Residence:* Kensington, Md.

CAREER: High school teacher and librarian in Hudson, Ohio, 1949-51; assistant librarian in junior high school in

HELEN PIERCE JACOB

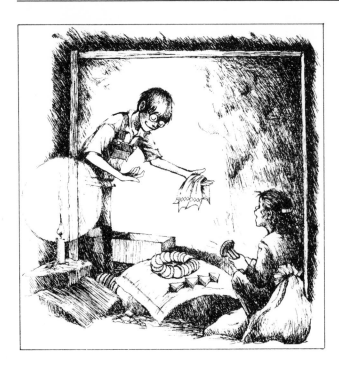

Finally with a bow, he handed an embroidered linen napkin to Kate and said, "Tea is served, M'Lady."
■(From *The Secret of the Strawbridge Place* by Helen Pierce Jacob. Illustrated by A. Delaney.)

Shaker Heights, Ohio, 1952-54; American University, Washington, D.C., associate librarian, 1954-55; University of California, Berkeley, reference and circulation librarian in education library, 1955-60; Parnassus Press, Berkeley, Calif., member of staff, 1960-61; junior high school librarian in Oakland, Calif., 1962-65, high school librarian, 1965-68; librarian in private school in Bryn Mawr, Pa., 1969-72; writer, 1972—. *Member:* Children's Book Guild (Washington, D.C.).

WRITINGS—For children: *A Garland for Gandhi* (picture book), Parnassus Press, 1968; *The Imperfect Princess,* Children's Book Trust (New Delhi, India), 1975; *The Secret of the Strawbridge Place,* Atheneum, 1976; *The Diary of the Strawbridge Place,* Atheneum, 1978. Contributor of articles, stories, and reviews to *Cricket, Harper's Weekly,* and *School Library Journal.*

WORK IN PROGRESS: Another Strawbridge book.

SIDELIGHTS: "I grew up in a century-old house in Ohio which was rumored to have been on the Underground Railroad, and my two elder brothers, my younger sister, and I spent years hunting for the secret hiding place. We never found it, but Kate, the heroine in my first *Strawbridge* book, does.

"My admiration for India, my husband's speciality, has produced two picture books and two stories.

"Working as a waitress, credit clerk, publisher's helper, teacher, and librarian, I *made* time to write. Every morning from 4:00 to 7:00 A.M. I wrote. I sent out manuscripts, all were rejected. It hurt, but failure became a goad to work harder. And to read harder too. I needed models: inspiration, excellent stylists, and wide reading helped—especially po-

etry. Style and imagination are so important, for there are no new ideas—just original variations of those universal themes of love (or the lack of it), death, friendship, mystery, etc.

"I write because I must. I keep a journal where I record many things, but, especially, where my writing ideas come from, how I develop them, and how the writing goes each day. Working out a plot begins in my head, but it is only when I pick up my pencil (longhand on the backs of junk mail) that the real organizing begins. I make false starts, have to write the first chapters two or three times before the story begins to take shape. Once started, the plotting gets easier for the characters become real. These pencil people plague me. I may be their creator, but they take over, and it is their growth, their ideas, their feelings which become the sinews of my stories.

"Books are important to me. I now write for young people because I hope that I can give pleasure to my readers as I derived pleasure from those authors I read in my young days. My heart is in both fields—writing and librarianship."

FOR MORE INFORMATION SEE: Sarah Lee Kennerly, "Mysteries too Good to Miss," *Cricket,* March, 1979.

JACOBS, Linda C.   1943-
(Tom Austin, Claire Blackburn)

PERSONAL: Born January 22, 1943, in Winston-Salem, N.C.; daughter of Lloyd Daniel and Elizabeth (Parker) Blackburn; married Thomas D. Austin (a psychiatric technician), September 25, 1961 (divorced, 1970); married Joseph D. Jacobs (a former social worker), October 9, 1972 (divorced); married Dr. Winthrop H. Ware (a psychiatrist); children: (first marriage) Brian Vincent. *Education:* Attended high school in San Bernardino, Calif. *Residence:* Ventura, Calif.

CAREER: Author. *Member:* Society of Children's Book Writers, Mythopoeic Society.

WRITINGS—Young adults; all published by EMC Corp., except as noted: "Women Who Win" series (biography): *Janet Lynn: Sunshine on Ice,* 1974; *Olga Korbut: Tears and Triumph,* 1974; *Shane Gould: Olympic Swimmer,* 1974; *Chris Evert: Tennis Pro,* 1974; *Laura Baugh: Golf's Golden Girl,* 1975; *Wilma Rudolph: Run for Glory,* 1975; *Evonne Goolagong: Smiles and Smashes,* 1975; *Cathy Rigby: On the Beam,* 1975; *Mary Decker: Speed Records and Spaghetti,* 1975; *Joan Moore Rice: The Olympic Dream,* 1975; *Annemarie Proell: Queen of the Mountain,* 1975; *Rosemary Casals: The Rebel Rosebud,* 1975; *Cindy Nelson: North Country Skier,* 1976; *Robyn Smith: In Silks,* 1976; *Martina Navratilova: Tennis Fury,* 1976; *Robin Campbell: Joy in the Morning,* 1976; *Barbara Jordan: Keeping Faith,* 1978; *Jane Pauley: A Heartland Style,* 1978.

"Winners All" series (fiction); all published by EMC Corp., 1974: *Ellen the Expert; In Tennis, Love Means Nothing; For One—Or For All, Go for Six.*

"Really Me" series (fiction); all published by EMC Corp., 1974, except as noted: *A Candle, a Feather, a Wooden Spoon; Will the Real Jeannie Murphy Please Stand Up?; Everyone's Watching Tammy; Checkmate, Julie; God, Why Is She The Way She Is?,* Concordia, 1979.

LINDA C. JACOBS

"Women behind the Bright Lights" series (biography); all published by EMC Corp., 1975, except as noted; *Olivia Newton-John: Sunshine Supergirl; Valerie Harper: The Unforgettable Snowflake; Roberta Flack: Sound of Velvet Melting; Cher: Simply Cher; Natalie Cole: Star Child,* 1977; *Lindsay Wagner: Her Own Way,* 1977.

"Men behind the Bright Lights" series (biography); all published by EMC Corp., 1975, except as noted: *Stevie Wonder: Sunshine in the Shadow; John Denver: A Natural High; Elton John: Reginald Dwight and Company; Jim Croce: The Feeling Lives On; Jimmy Walker: Funny Is Where It's At,* 1977; *John Travolta: Making an Impact,* 1977; *Henry Winkler: Born Actor,* 1978; *Gabe Kaplan: A Spirit of Laughter,* 1978.

"Black American Athletes" series (biography); all published by EMC Corp., 1976: *Madeline Manning Jackson: Running on Faith; Julius Erving: Dr. J. and Julius W.; Lee Elder: The Daring Dream; Arthur Ashe: Alone in the Crowd.*

Under pseudonym Claire Blackburn; all published by Bouregy: *Return Engagement,* 1970; *A Teacher for My Heart,* 1972; *Rainbow for Clari,* 1973; *Heart on Ice,* 1976. Contributor of articles to magazines under pseudonyms, Tom Austin and Claire Blackburn. Assistant editor for the fiction section of *Mythprint* and the Mythopoeic Society newsletter.

WORK IN PROGRESS: A youth novel researching fantasy and myth, for a series of fantasy books and a children's novel on child abuse.

SIDELIGHTS: "When I was four years old, I sat in my sandbox with new toys—the typical pail, shovel, sifter, kind of things—and I cried, because I wondered what would happen to them when I died. I thought that perhaps I could keep them from getting scratched and dented (they were metal in those days, not plastic). But even if I managed to keep them like new, there was still that problem—I would die and leave them.

"Since then, there has been a perfectionism in me, a searching for something that will last. It's not the easiest thing in the world to live with, and without my writing, would be downright impossible. I do not focus on my published works as something that will last and thereby make my tenure on this earth meaningful. I am well aware that—with the exception of a few classics—most books go 'the way of all flesh.' Rather, for me, writing itself is a means for searching, for trying to organize some meaning into a life view.

"This element is present even in my more frivolous works, for that, too, is part of life. I write primarily for children because I believe that this questioning, this 'why am I here, and what's it all about anyway' is most painful in childhood. Like my young readers, I have no answers—only questions.

"Lately, I have become interested in literary fantasy, for in the symbols of this genre I sense the potential for some deep exploration of the things that are truly important in human life. It has taken me a long time to come to this place, for I am only beginning to take myself seriously as a writer. Now I am coming to feel that perhaps this unrest I've known all my life can be put to good use. Perhaps, rather than mere therapy for me, my work can be a means of sharing the questions, sharing the thirst for meaningful answers.

"My interests outside my work are rather limited. I raised Lhasa Apso dogs and always seem to have a house full of animals, but I am not one for sports or extensive social activities. I have a few close friends with whom I would trust my very life, but not many casual associates. I do, however, take classes occasionally at the local college—mostly in philosophy and religious studies—and I find the conversations with fellow students very interesting."

JACOBSON, Morris K(arl) 1906-

PERSONAL: Born December 29, 1906, in Memel, Germany; son of George (a salesman) and Minna (Jakobsohn) Jacobson; married Lena Schechter, July 14, 1929; children: John Ernest. *Education:* New York University, B.S., 1928; Columbia University, A.M., 1930. *Politics:* Democrat. *Religion:* Jewish. *Home:* 865 Capon St., Palm Bay, Fla. 32905.

CAREER: John Adams High School, New York, N.Y., teacher of German, 1937-53; Andrew Jackson High School, New York, chairman of department of foreign languages, 1953-71. Associate in malacology, American Museum of Natural History. *Member:* American Malacological Union (president, 1955), Israel Malacological Society, Western Society of Malacologists, New York Shell Club (president, 1949-51). *Awards, honors:* National Science Foundation grant, 1966, to "write on land shells of Cuba"; National Science Teachers Association Children's Book Council certificates, 1977, for *Wonders of Sponges* and, 1978, for *Wonders of Jellyfish.*

WRITINGS: (With William K. Emerson) *Shells of the New York City Area,* Argonaut, 1961; *Shells from Cape Cod to Cape May,* Dover, 1971; *Wonders of the World of Shells,* Dodd, 1971; (with William K. Emerson) *American Museum of Natural History Guide to Shells,* Knopf, 1976; (with Rosemary K. Pang) *Wonders of Sponges,* Dodd, 1976; (with William K. Emerson) *Wonders of Starfish,* Dodd, 1977; (with David R. Franz) *Wonders of Jellyfish,* Dodd, 1978; (with David R. Franz) *Wonders of Corals and Coral Reefs,* Dodd, 1979; (with David R. Franz) *Wonders of Snails and Slugs,* Dodd, 1980.

SIDELIGHTS: "I write because I enjoy writing. My first published material consisted of specialized articles in the field of malacology. They appeared in *The Nautilus* (USA), *Archiv für Molluskenkunde* (Germany), *Revista de la Sociedad Malacológica* (Cuba), and elsewhere. Writing this sort of material proved to be excellent practice. I learned to write lean, clear, simple prose without recourse to unnecessary ponderous neologisms, so unfortunately common in much scientific writing.

"Since I retired from teaching (foreign languages), I have been writing books on natural history subjects for ten to fifteen year olds. Here, my experience working with children at school and my training in scientific writing have enabled me to develop a satisfactory style for this purpose. I love doing the research and then stating the facts in an interesting and attractive fashion to capture the attention of my readers. I am most contented when engaged in such a project. Any money that results from this is pure serendipity. I write as much or more for popular and professional seashell magazines without any pay—and have just as much fun. In children's books I make it a policy of collaborating with a professional in the field to make sure that no blatant misstatements slip by. When I am not writing for publication, I love to write long personal letters to friends and relatives. I am one of the persons whom Dr. Samuel Johnson stigmatized as fools for writing without the necessary hope of financial reward. But I love it—and hate typewriting.

"I am not aware of having any special writing habits. When I write for publication, I lay the first version aside for a week or so. Then I revise—often extensively.

"I have recently, as a hobby, learned to read—only read—Russian and have undertaken to translate Russian scientific articles into English for friends and/or scholars at the American Museum of Natural History and the Museum of Comparative Zoology in Harvard University. I enjoy the linguistic and scientific challenge. I also have the manuscript of a translation which I did of a highly successful Argentine novel by Jorge W. Abolos entitled *Shunko.* So far no luck in getting a publisher to accept it. But I keep trying."

Jacobson has travelled extensively in the Caribbean, Central America, and western Europe, collecting shells and studying languages.

FOR MORE INFORMATION SEE: Publishers Weekly, February 28, 1977; *Horn Book,* June, 1978.

Author Jacobson showing his grandchildren, Elana and Kenny, how to look for shells on the beach. ■ (From *Wonders of the World of Shells* by Morris K. Jacobson and William K. Emerson. Photograph courtesy of John E. Jacobson.)

MORRIS K. JACOBSON

JAQUES, Faith 1923-

PERSONAL: Born December 13, 1923, in Leicester, England; daughter of Maurice Thompson (a businessman) and Gladys Jaques. *Education:* Attended Leicester College of Art, England, 1940-41, and Central School of Art, London, England, 1946-48. *Home and office:* 16 Hillcrest, 51 Ladbroke Grove, London W11 3AX, England.

CAREER: Illustrator. Guildford School of Art, England, visiting lecturer, 1950-54; Hornsey College of Art, London, England, visiting lecturer, 1958-64. *Exhibitions:* The Workshop Gallery, London, 1972, 1976; Nicholas Hill Gallery, London, 1975; Chichester Gallery, Sussex, 1976; Piccadilly Gallery, London, 1977. *Military service:* Women's Royal Naval Service, petty officer, 1941-45. *Member:* Association of Illustrators, Society of Authors.

WRITINGS—Self-illustrated: Drawing in Pen & Ink, Studio Vista, 1964; *Tilly's House,* Atheneum, 1979.

Illustrator: Dorothy Wellesley, *Rhymes for Middle Years,* James Barrie, 1954; Jo Manton, *A Portrait of Bach,* Abelard, 1957; René Guillot, *The White Shadow,* Oxford University Press, 1959; Gaskell, *Lois the Witch,* Methuen, 1960; *The Hugh Evelyn History of Costume, 6th Century B.C.—1900 A.D.,* four volumes, Hugh Evelyn, 1960-1970; *A Peck of Pepper,* Chatto, 1961; Josephine Kamm, *Mrs. Pankhurst,*

Methuen, 1961; Eric Mathieson, *Jumbo the Elephant,* Hamish Hamilton, 1963, published in the U.S. as *The True Story of Jumbo the Elephant,* Coward, 1964; Henry Treece, *The Windswept City,* Meredith, 1967; Josephine Kamm, *Joseph Paxton,* Methuen, 1967; Roald Dahl, *Charlie and the Chocolate Factory,* Allen & Unwin, 1967; Ivan Turgenev, *The Torrents of Spring,* Folio Society, 1967; Samuel Butler, *The Way of All Flesh,* Heron Books, 1967; Henry James, *The Turn of the Screw,* (abridged version), Longman Books, 1967; R. D. Blackmore, *Lorna Doone,* Heron books, 1968; Robert Louis Stevenson, *Treasure Island,* Heron Books, 1968; Mary Treadgold, *The Humbugs,* Methuen, 1968; Charles Dickens, *The Magic Fish-bone* (picture book), Chatto, 1969, Harvey House, 1970.

Ursula Moray Williams, *Johnny Golightly and His Crocodile* (picture book), Chatto, 1970, Harvey House, 1971; Eric Houghton, *The Mouse and the Magician* (picture book), Lippincott, 1970; Monica Dickens, *The Great Fire,* Kaye & Ward, 1970; E. Nesbit, *The Island of the Nine Whirlpools,* Kaye & Ward, 1970; John Cunliffe, *The Giant Who Stole the World* (picture book), Deutsch, 1971; Arthur Ransome, *Old Peter's Russian Tales,* Nelson, 1971, new edition, 1976; Charles Dickens, *David Copperfield,* American Educational Publications, 1971; Gillian Avery, *A Likely Lad,* Collins, 1971; Philippa Pearce, *What the Neighbours Did and Other Stories,* Longman Young Books, 1972, Crowell, 1973; Jane Austen, *Persuasion* (abridged version), Longman Books, 1972; Margaret Crush, *A First Look at Costume,* Watts, 1972; Ursula Moray Williams, *A Picnic with the Aunts* (picture book), Chatto, 1972; John Cunliffe, *The Giant Who Swallowed the Wind* (picture book), Deutsch, 1972; Nina Bawden, *Carrie's War,* Lippincott, 1973; Margery Fisher, editor, *Journeys,* Brockhampton, 1973; Robert Newton Peck, *A Day No Pigs Would Die,* Knopf, 1973; John Cunliffe, *The King's Birthday Cake* (picture book), Deutsch, 1973; Kathleen Lines, editor, *The Faber Book of Greek Legends,* Faber & Faber, 1973; Roald Dahl, *Charlie and the Great Glass Elevator,* Allen & Unwin, 1973, Gallimard, 1978; Hilary Seton, *Beyond the Blue Hills,* Heinemann, 1973; Hilary Seton, *A Lion in the Garden,* Heinemann, 1974; Elizabeth Yandell, *Henry,* Bodley Head, 1974; Maurice Duggan, *Falter Tom and the Water Boy,* Kestrel, 1974; John Rae, *The Golden Crucifix,* Brockhampton, 1974; George Eliot, *The Mill on the Floss,* Collins, 1974; Margery Sharp, *The Magical Cockatoo,* Heinemann, 1974; Ursula Moray Williams, *Grandpapa's Folly and the Woodworm-Bookworm,* Chatto, 1974; Helen Cresswell, *Lizzie Dripping Again,* BBC Publications, 1974; John Rae, *The Treasure of Westminster Abbey,* Brockhampton, 1975; E. Nesbit, *The Old Nursery Stories,* Hodder and Stoughton, 1975; Barbara Willard, editor, *Field and Forest,* Kestrel, 1975; Eric Houghton, *A Giant Can Do Anything* (picture book), Deutsch, 1975; John Rae, *Christmas is Coming,* Brockhampton, 1976; Margery Sharp, *Bernard the Brave,* Heinemann, 1976; Andrew Lang, *The Red Fairy Book,* Viking, 1976; Alison Uttley, *A Traveller in Time,* Puffin, 1977; Gillian Avery, *Mouldy's Orphan,* Collins, 1978; Alison Uttley, *The Little Grey Rabbit Book,* Heinemann, 1980.

All by Leon Garfield, all published by Heinemann: *Moss & Blister,* 1976; *The Cloak,* 1976; *The Valentine,* 1977; *Labour in Vain,* 1977; *The Fool,* 1977; *Rosy Starling,* 1977; *The Dumb Cake,* 1977; *Tom Titmarsh's Devil,* 1977; *The Filthy Beast,* 1978; *The Enemy,* 1978. Regular contributor to *Cricket* Magazine since 1974.

WORK IN PROGRESS: A sequel to *Tilly's House.*

FAITH JAQUES

SIDELIGHTS: ''I care as much for the word as the picture, so far as possible I try to select the books I illustrate—the quality of the writing matters very much and I like to feel the book will stand the test of time. Fortunately the standard of writing in children's books is so high now that a degree of choice is possible. But I regret that the publishers are tending to neglect black and white illustration in favour of so many full-colour picture books. The latter are great fun to do, and a proportion of them are really worthwhile, but to me the problems are not so interesting as those of trying to complement a full-length text, strong in mood and characterization and with the author's particular 'flavour.' This requires *illustration* not *decoration,* which means abilities of draftsmanship and technique are necessary, as well as a wide background knowledge. I'm always thankful that I was trained at a time when life drawing was predominant, plus studies of architecture and perspective, and furniture and costume styles. I wouldn't consider myself as a 'documentary' illustrator, but I'm grateful for the work I had to put in years ago on these subjects and for the lifelong interest in social history that has resulted. I can't create in a void—I need practical knowledge as a jumping-off point for the imagination.

''My interests range far and wide—anything the eye can see or that can be read about. I like to walk a lot, both in the country and in towns—a slow ramble around a town with a long history is a great pleasure. Natural history and all animal life appeal to me; I could never live without a cat, and would dearly love a horse. All the arts give me pleasure, and crafts too. I like to know how things are made. Most of all, books

are my joy—I've read widely all my life and often think I was really educated by public libraries. I've many good friends who are very important to me, but at the same time I like to be alone a lot; I think artists and writers need plenty of solitude.

''The major influences on my work have stemmed from my childhood reading. I read Dickens, Thackeray, the Brontës and other Victorian writers when I was quite young and then became fond of the steel and wood-engraved pictures by Cruikshank, 'Phiz,' and so on, which accompanied the texts. I still love this sort of illustration because it accomplished so much in the way of mood and scene-setting, is capable of great subtlety, and never dominates the text.

''My favourite illustrator of all time is a Frenchman called Grandville; he is not as well-known in England as he ought to be, but in my view he was the precursor of the sort of illustration which in the late 19th century became known as 'typically English' (Tenniel's illustrations of 'Alice' are very influenced by him). Grandville was also a satirist, caricaturist and a true surrealist—highly original and given to marvellous flights of fancy. I never look at science fiction illustration, which is often so coarse and basically unimaginative, without reflecting how much better Grandville did it in the 1830's and 40's.

''I was born in Leicester, a rather dull town then, in the midlands. After the war came I left it as soon as I was old enough (seventeen) to join the WRNS (Women's Royal Naval Service), hoping I'd be posted to the coast, as I love the sea.

As it turned out I was sent to Oxford, very fortunately, as I was able to take part in university life to a certain extent. Most of all I was stunned by the beauty of the colleges and their gardens—coming from an industrial town it had never occurred to me that one could live in beautiful surroundings. So my adolescent years, though not without the usual problems, were spent in a very congenial place, with ready access to books, good conversation, theatre and music, museums and art classes. So Oxford had an important effect on me.

"I was demobbed in December, 1945 and started at the Central School of Art, London, in January, 1946, on a tiny ex-service grant of £3.15 shillings a week, lasting for four terms only. So my entire art school training was very short, but I made up for it by working about eighteen hours a day. I had to get any commissions I could while still a student, so I worked in every sort of illustration then and for the next fifteen years—newspapers, books, magazines, advertising, postage stamps, filmstrips, wallpapers, pottery, textiles, etc. Only in the last fifteen years have I been able to concentrate on book illustration, which is what I wanted to do ever since I was a child. I have also sold several illustrations to the British Museum, have work in various private collections, and did the four 1978 Christmas stamps on the theme of carol-singing (Great Britain issue)."

In an article, "Every Picture Tells a Story," the author wrote: "I think I'm rather an old-fashioned illustrator. I really like the picture in a book to have a degree of realism and I do try to create a 'you are there' feeling, to make the settings convincing and the characters as near as I can to the author's ideas. As a child I spent hours poring over the pictures in my books, stepping into them, placing myself within the scene and absorbing every detail. Whether children still do this I don't know—I suspect that, as with authors, we are really working out of our childhood memories and not at all for an anonymous group of people called 'children.'

"Naturally all illustrators will have different views on the subject, but my own feeling is that I'm there to interpret the author, to translate from the medium of words to the medium of pictures. To get on to the author's 'wavelength' is the first and essential thing to do; apart from anything else (I'm referring here to illustrated fiction, not picturebooks) I believe the words are most important. The plot, the invention, the mood, the ideas—all these things are created by the words: the pictures should complement, and with luck, enhance, everything the author is trying to say. A descriptive illustrator is always open to the charge that he or she is tediously putting into pictorial form what the author has already conveyed in words, but I believe the illustrator can be clear, accurate, faithful to the text, and still show a certain individual quality that *adds* to the author's intentions.

"Illustration is a minor art, and in many ways an art of compromise. I think it has an analogy with acting: in both cases one is there to interpret someone else's words, and the meanings behind the words—it's much more subtle than a literal translation. A play can appear to mean different things according to the way the actors play it—and several ways could be equally right. But with some methods you can feel an attempt to get at real truths, whereas with others you know that somewhere both production and acting are not true to the spirit of the play. Don't we all know actors who perhaps bring too much of themselves to a part, who are too mannered and quirky, who sometimes throw the whole play out of balance, even though their own performance, in itself, may be fascinating? This domination of the text can occur

So they all set off along the road to the candlemaker's house—the soldiers, their captain, and the sweep.... ■ (From *The King's Birthday Cake* by John Cunliffe. Illustrated by Faith Jaques.)

...The cockatoo was flying about with more than usual brio...as all the while it kept up a flow of anecdote about the French Revolution; never had there been such an accomplished bird! ■ (From *The Magical Cockatoo* by Margery Sharp. Illustrated by Faith Jaques.)

in illustration too, when the artist imposes his style and mannerisms too strongly on the book. It is not easy to find the balancing point between following the text too slavishly, and imposing oneself too aggressively. Sometimes, of course, the illustrator with an emphatic style is the right choice—the trick is to match the right book with the right artist. But when the text is gentle and quiet—implicit rather than explicit—I hate to see it knocked out of court by an over-theatrical performance from the artist.

"I feel quite strongly on the subject of accuracy; after all, if the author can bother to research his material, surely the illustrator must too? I don't see why factual accuracy should necessarily make one's work too literal—I know I need solid information to give my imagination something to build on and select from. (All knowledge is useful knowledge to the illustrator, and similarly a solid training in drawing will be always necessary; it's the vehicle by which we convey what we have to express.) The matter of references has to be taken seriously: apart from a houseful of books I also have about 10,000 pictures filed away under subject-headings. For a recent anthology requiring only twelve drawings, I needed pictures of an ox-cart, a Danish street, bicycles, a country bus, a market square, a barge, skating dress in 1895, a sledge,

elephants, a schooner, a canopied bed, a sixteenth-century London street, a pram, an Alken print called 'Full Cry,' a canal lock, a Midland village, and many other specific things, plus suitable trees and landscapes of various countries, street furniture, bridges, cars, domestic interiors, all the extras needed to make an illustration convincing. A quite straightforward book will often need at least 100 references, and there is not time to chase around museums and libraries. It is not a case of *copying* a reference. I simply need enough information to act as a base for my imagination. Even if I had a very stylised technique I would still have to know the structure of everything I draw—you can't simplify what you don't understand in the first place. Anyone who has read the notebooks and letters of eminent writers will know the immense amount of research and study that goes into the writing of a book; for writer or illustrator it doesn't stultify the imagination but creates the springboard from which ideas take flight.

"Illustrators are often asked what subjects they like best. In general it is the quality of the writing that makes the book good or bad, but like most illustrators I would always welcome a good collection of myths and legends, mainly because the images are usually so exciting and fantastic, so interesting in themselves that it hardly matters how one treats them. I think children automatically go to the subject portrayed, regardless of the manner in which it is handled, and this is right; *what* you do is often more important than *how* you do it. The really difficult books are the ones that are perfectly well written but lack interesting pictorial content. They are like modern structure—but not nearly so interesting as something more complicated, more earthy, more strange and individual. A really good book has a sort of personal conviction, and this is the most important requirement of all for an illustrator to do the job well." [Faith Jaques, "Every Picture Tells A Story," *Federation of Children's Book Groups Yearbook,* 1973-1974.]

FOR MORE INFORMATION SEE: Book Design and Production, Vol. 2, #3, 1959; *The Guardian,* February 10, 1975; *Mother* Magazine, September, 1975; Faith Jaques, "Every Picture Tells a Story," *Federation of Children's Book Groups Yearbook,* 1973-1974.

KATONA, Robert 1949-

PERSONAL: Accent is on second syllable; born March 16, 1949, in Athens, Ohio; son of Arthur (a professor) and Verna (a teacher; maiden name Wendelin) Katona. *Education:* Attended University of Colorado and Denver Community College. *Politics:* "Freedom for man in the space age." *Religion:* Humanist. *Home address:* 427 Plateau Pkwy., Golden, Colo. 80401.

CAREER: Artist; illustrator. *Exhibitions:* Denver Art Museum, Own Your Own, 1968, First Colorado Bicentennial, 1972; Gilpin County Arts Association, Central City, Colo., 1968-75; Gaslight Theater, Denver, Colo., 1970; Denver Metropolitan, 1972, 1974; Kennedy Galleries, New York, 1974; Carson Gallery, Denver, Colo., 1977-79; Union Art Gallery, San Francisco, Calif., 1978-79; Valhalla Gallery, Wichita, Kansas, 1980. Private collections: Royal Family of Saudi Arabia; H. E. Shaikh Hamed, Heir Apparent, Bahrain; Count Umberto Caproni, Milan, Italy; Lorant de Bastyai, London, England; James T. Ross, Zurich, Switzerland;

Lemon Saks, Denver, Colo.; Walt Poirer, Trinidad, Colo.; Shunichi Yamazaki, Osaka, Japan. *Awards, honors:* Jenkins Award, Gilpin County Arts Association, 1970, 1974; National Award, Society of Illustrators for *Golden Eagle Country,* 1976; represented in 19th Illustrators Annual; Outstanding Young Man of America, 1980.

ILLUSTRATOR: Richard Oldendorf, *Golden Eagle Country,* Knopf, 1975; Frances Hamerstrom, *Walk When the Moon is Full,* Crossing Press, 1975. Work has appeared in *Denver Post, Raptor Research Foundation Bulletin, North American Falconers Association Journal.*

SIDELIGHTS: Raised in Colorado, Katona is an artist-falconer working in oil, watercolor, pencil and etching. Essentially self-taught in both art and falconry, Katona has trained and flown many species of raptors including the endangered Peregrine Falcon.

A master of many styles including super-realism, drip-painting, and mono-print painting, his work has received critical acclaim from Angus Cameron of Alfred Knopf who described the drawings in *Golden Eagle Country* as "stunning, sensational and superlative," and Barbara Haddad of the *Denver Post* who spoke of his "remarkable drawing done with an incredibly sensitive hand."

Katona was influenced by Salvador Dali, Jimi Hendrix and Egon Schiele.

FOR MORE INFORMATION SEE: Southwest Art, July, 1978; *19th Illustrators Annual.*

(From *Walk When the Moon Is Full* by Frances Hamerstrom. Illustrated by Robert Katona.)

Robert Katona with trained falcon.

KERMAN, Gertrude Lerner   1909-

PERSONAL: Born August 29, 1909, in Quebec City, Quebec, Canada; daughter of Leon and Deborah (Ortenberg) Lerner; married Joseph Kerman, May 29, 1936 (died, 1964); married LeRoy S. Furman, November 28, 1969; children: Patricia Clare, Julie Beth. *Education:* McGill University, B.A. (summa cum laude), 1929; additional study at New School for Social Research, Columbia University, New York University and Lee Strasberg's Theatre Institute. *Home:* 21 Chapel Place, Great Neck, N.Y. 11021 and Kent Cliffs, N.Y.

CAREER: Former Broadway actress; associated with Producers Leland Hayward and Gilbert Miller; Adelphi University, Children's Center for Creative Arts, Garden City, N.Y., instructor-playwright; Off-Broadway Children's Theater, director. Adult Program of Great Neck (N.Y.) Schools, instructor in dramatic writing; Great Neck (N.Y.) School of Drama, director; Great Neck Community Theatre, executive producer, director. *Member:* Authors League of America, American Educational Theatre Association, Delta Phi Epsilon.

WRITINGS: Plays and Creative Ways with Children, Harvey, 1961; *Shakespeare for Young Players,* Harvey, 1964; *Cabeza de Vaca, Defender of the Indians,* Harvey, 1974. Author of radio plays, magazine articles on the theater.

WORK IN PROGRESS: An adult fiction book, currently untitled.

SIDELIGHTS: ''My love affair with theatre in all its forms began in my cradle. I can remember making up plays in which my fingers took on the roles of Daddy, Mommy, Sister, Brother, while my thumb invariably brought news of dire happenings offstage! The love affair continued throughout my developing years as the youngest in a household of five children. Here it often became a weapon in the hands of irate siblings. 'Oh you're just an actress!' they would fling whenever I was particularly exasperating, and reduce me to tears. Eventually, upon graduation from McGill University, it led me to New York and Broadway.

''My love affair with creative drama for young people specifically began when I left the professional theatre to raise a family. The need to express myself imaginatively led to a need to share my enthusiasm with my daughters, and later with boys and girls everywhere. Teaching, directing, lecturing, demonstrating creative techniques, and writing followed in due course; activities which engross me to this day.

'''You can see Mrs. Kerman loves children,' remarked a teacher at a recent demonstration.

'''You can see Mrs. Kerman loves *theatre*,' corrected a second.

'''No,' a third added wisely, 'you can see Mrs. Kerman loves *both children and theatre*.'

''What nicer recognition can one want for a love affair of a lifetime?''

FOR MORE INFORMATION SEE: Montreal Star, July 5, 1962; *Montreal Gazette,* July 5, 1962.

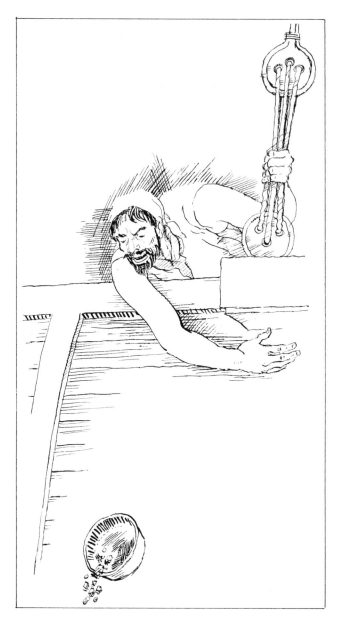

He hurled his meal into the sea. "Our horses eat better than this!" ■ (From *Cabeza de Vaca, Defender of the Indians* by Gertrude Kerman. Illustrated by Ray Abel.)

GERTRUDE LERNER KERMAN

Twinkle, twinkle, little bat!
How I wonder what you're at!
Up above the world you fly!
Like a teatray in the sky.

—Lewis Carroll
(pseudonym of Charles Lutwidge Dodgson)

IRENE KIEFER

KIEFER, Irene 1926-

PERSONAL: Born November 1, 1926, in Red Lodge, Mont.; daughter of John (a grocer) and Madalene (Giachino) Giovanini; married David Kiefer (a scientific journalist), April 9, 1955; children: Timothy, Katherine. *Education:* Montana State University, B.S. (honors), 1948. *Home:* 6917 Ayr Lane, Bethesda, Md. 20034.

CAREER: DuPont Co., chemist in Waynesboro, Va., 1948-50, and Wilmington, Del., 1950-51; *Chemical Engineering News*, Washington, D.C., assistant editor, 1952-57; free-lance writer, 1964—. Editorial consultant to U.S. Environmental Protection Agency and U.S. Department of Energy.

WRITINGS: Underground Furnaces: The Story of Geothermal Energy (juvenile), Morrow, 1976; *Global Jigsaw Puzzle: The Story of Continental Drift* (juvenile), Atheneum, 1978; *Energy for America* (juvenile), Atheneum, 1979. Author of public information booklets for several science-oriented federal agencies. Contributor to magazines, including *Smithsonian, Washingtonian, Maryland, Travel, Mosaic,* and to local newspapers.

WORK IN PROGRESS: Research on food problems and nuclear and chemical waste disposal.

SIDELIGHTS: "I grew up in Montana, but to find a job as a chemist I had to leave there following my graduation from Montana State University. My first job was in an industrial laboratory doing research on synthetic textile fibers. After three years, I realized that I didn't want to spend my life working in a laboratory—I found the 'view down the test tube too narrow.'

"I quit my job in the laboratory and traveled in Europe and the Near East for several months. I then spent a few more months with my family in Montana. During all this time, I was thinking about what I wanted to do. I decided I ought to try to use my education and experience in chemistry—this was, after all, the only skill I had that would be of any value to an employer. I had never thought particularly about writing as a career, althought I had always been an avid reader, even as a child. However, I jumped at the chance when I was offered a job on a magazine that published news about chemistry and the chemical industry. The policy of this magazine was to hire chemists and train them to be editors and writers. I finally had found a career—science writing.

"I met my husband on the magazine. His experience was similar to mine. He, too, was educated as a chemist but did not like working in a laboratory. Our experiences have led us to point out to our two children (and anyone else who will listen!) that combining two skills often opens doors to interesting careers.

"When our son was born, I resigned from the magazine and spent the next few years (until our daughter was four years old) at home. Visiting our local public library was a regular and important outing for our family. Being interested in science, mother and father always managed to include a children's science book or two in the armloads of books we carried away. From time to time, I was heard to say: 'I could write one of those!'

"I didn't try to 'write one of those' for several years, for I had started to free-lance as a science writer and editor. This enabled me to continue to be active in my field, but I could work largely at home at my own schedule. Over the years, my free-lancing has required me to explain to non-scientists various complex issues—energy and the environment, for example. These issues, of course, involve far more than sci-

(From *Underground Furnaces: The Story of Geothermal Energy* by Irene Kiefer. Illustrated by Terrence Fehr.)

ence and technology. They affect the very future of mankind, and it is vital in a democratic society that everyone—including our young people—understand them.

"So I finally tried my hand at writing children's science books. It was not easy, for the techniques and vocabulary were often quite different from those I had been using for years. Also, there are far more people who want to write books than there are publishers who want to publish them. I acquired a large collection of 'rejection' letters! But I was determined ('stubborn' is the word the family prefers!), and eventually I succeeded in getting my first 'acceptance' letter. I've had others since then, but I still agree with Snoopy in the 'Peanuts' comic strip: 'Good writing is hard work!' I'm fortunate in that my husband is also a science writer. He reads much of my work, and frequently is able to make suggestions that clarify and improve my writing."

HOBBIES AND OTHER INTERESTS: Traveling, attending concerts and plays, tennis, and birding.

FOR MORE INFORMATION SEE: Horn Book, April, 1977.

KOERNER, W(illiam) H(enry) D(avid) 1878-1938

PERSONAL: Born November 19, 1878, in Lunden, Schleswig-Holstein, Germany; emigrated to the United States in 1880; died August 11, 1938, in Interlaken, New Jersey; son of William Henry Dethlep and Margaret Anna (Williams) Koerner. *Education:* Attended the Francis Smith Art Academy; studied at the Art Students League in New York City, 1905-07; studied with Howard Pyle, 1907-11. *Home:* 209 Grassmere Ave., Interlaken, N.J.

CAREER: Artist and illustrator. Hired by the *Chicago Tribune* as staff artist, 1896; art editor of a literary magazine in Battle Creek, Michigan, 1904; worked as an illustrator in Wilmington, Delaware, 1907-11; after 1922, Koerner became well-known as an illustrator for *The Saturday Evening Post* and other prominent publications. *Exhibitions:* Montana Historical Society, 1971; Delaware Art Museum, Wilmington, 1977.

ILLUSTRATOR: Marie Manning, *Judith of the Plains,* Harper, 1903; Karl Edwin Harriman, *The Girl and the Deal,* W. Jacobs & Co., 1903; George Selwyn Kimball, *The Lackawannas at Moosehead,* Ball Publishing, 1908; Irving Bacheller, *Keeping Up with Lizzie,* Harper, 1911; Margaret Deland, *The Voice,* Harper, 1912; Grace S. Richmond, *Mrs. Red Pepper,* Doubleday, 1913; George Kibbe Turner, *The Last Christian,* Hearst's International Library Co., 1914; Margaret Deland, *Around Old Chester,* Harper, 1915; Stewart Edward White, *The Leopard Woman,* Doubleday, 1916; Anna Theresa Sadlier, *Gerald Delacey's Daughter,* Kennedy & Co., 1916; Burton E. Stevenson, *A King in Babylon,* Small, Maynard & Co., 1917; Harold MacGrath, *The Luck of the Irish,* Harper, 1917; George Van Schaick, *The Peace of Roaring River,* Small, Maynard & Co., 1918; William Patten, *Stories of Today,* P. F. Collier & Son, 1918; Jack Boyle, *Boston Blackie,* H. K. Fly Co., 1919; George Agnew Chamberlain, *White Man,* Bobbs-Merrill, 1919; Zane Grey, *The Desert of Wheat,* Harper, 1919.

Self-portrait of Koerner, age seventeen.

Earl Wayland Bowman, *The Ramblin' Kid,* Bobbs-Merrill, 1920; Elizabeth Dejeans, *The Moreton Mystery,* Bobbs-Merrill, 1920; Kennett Harris, *Meet Mr. Stegg,* Holt, 1920; Harold MacGrath, *The Pagan Madonna,* Doubleday, 1921; Eugene Manlove Rhodes, *Stepsons of Light,* Houghton, 1921; Rex Beach, *Flowing Gold,* Harper, 1922; Richard Matthews Hallett, *The Canyon of the Fools,* Harper, 1922; Emerson Hough, *The Covered Wagon,* D. Appleton & Co., 1922; Arthur Stringer, *The Prairie Child,* Bobbs-Merrill, 1922; Hal G. Evarts, *Tumbleweeds,* Little, Brown, 1923; Emerson Hough, *North of 36,* D. Appleton & Co., 1923; Emerson Hough, *The Ship of Souls,* D. Appleton & Co., 1925; Martha Ostenso, *Wild Geese,* Dodd, 1925; C. E. Scoggins, *The Proud Old Name,* Bobbs-Merrill, 1925.

Earl Derr Biggers, *The Chinese Parrot,* Bobbs-Merrill, 1926; Ben Ames Williams, *The Silver Forest,* Dutton, 1926; Hal G. Evarts, *The Painted Stallion,* Little, Brown, 1926; John Taintor Foote, *The Number One Boy,* D. Appleton & Co., 1926; Mary Roberts Rinehart, *Lost Ecstasy,* George H. Doran Co., 1927; D. Crockett, *The Life of Colonel David Crockett, An Autobiography,* A. L. Burt & Co., 1928; Hal G. Evarts, *Fur Brigade,* Little, Brown, 1928; Hal G. Evarts, *Tomahawk Rights,* Little, Brown, 1929; Arthur Stringer, *A Lady Quite*

Lost, Bobbs-Merrill, 1931; Zane Grey, *Sunset Pass,* Harper, 1931; Hal G. Evarts, *Shortgrass,* Little, Brown, 1932; Zane Grey, *The Drift Fence,* Harper, 1933; Eugene Manlove Rhodes, *The Trusty Knaves,* Houghton, 1933; Stewart Edward White, *Ranchero,* Doubleday, 1933; Eugene Manlove Rhodes, *Beyond the Desert,* Houghton, 1934; Eugene Manlove Rhodes, *The Proud Sheriff,* Houghton, 1935; C. E. Scoggins, *Pampa Joe,* Appleton-Century, 1936. Also created illustrations for *"Charge It"* by Irving Bacheller for Harper.

Work has appeared in *American* magazine, *Collier's Weekly, Cosmopolitan, Country Gentleman, Good Housekeeping, Harper's, Ladies' Home Journal, Metropolitan* magazine, *Pictorial Review, Redbook, Saturday Evening Post, Woman's Home Companion, The Pilgrim* and other magazines, as well as in various anthologies and compendiums. Created magazine covers and advertisements for Grape-Nuts, Postum, and Post Toasties.

SIDELIGHTS: **November 19, 1878:** Born in Lunden, Schleswig-Holstein, Germany.

1881. Emigrated to the United States with his parents and younger sister. Family settled in Clinton, Iowa.

1898. Enrolled in a local art school conducted by John M. Stich. "He taught me to *see* things, to remember what I saw, and to draw well, and to have a photographic mind.

"I drew everything I saw; used house paint, crayons, pencils; made my own canvas and sketched along the river. One canvas I began in Spring; next I painted it over in Summer with heavy green foliage; then came Autumn and I was still working on it, only now in vivid reds and yellows. It was to be my masterpiece but Mother used it to stop a leak in the roof of our hen house." [W. H. Hutchinson, *The World, the Work and the West of W.H.D. Koerner,* University of Oklahoma Press, 1978.[1]]

Autumn, 1898. Moved to Chicago where he secured a job on the Chicago *Tribune* as a staff artist. In that capacity Koerner accompanied reporters to do what today's news photographers do—record the visual impact of the story. "Once I got the cops to lock me in the cell with a particularly brutal murderer, for that was the only way I could get to see him. I didn't dare sketch him there or he would have had two murders to answer for instead of one. But I memorized his features and when the cops let me out after about ten minutes, pretending to take me to the Judge, I hustled back to the office and put his face down while it was fresh in my mind.

"Once I was sent down to the morgue to get the likeness of a criminal who had been killed in a brawl. The boys at the morgue would not help me find the body, so I went down to the slabs to look for myself. I went from body to body, lifting each sheet just a little to see if it was my man, and just

"Three days later I drove to the villa with my matron and the babies." ■ (From *Keeping Up with Lizzie* by Irving Bacheller. Illustrated by W. H. D. Koerner.)

The Leopard Woman stood just within the circle of illumination. ■ (From *The Leopard Woman* by Stewart Edward White. Illustrated by W. H. D. Koerner.)

as I started to lift one more, it moved! and a man rose up saying, 'What the Hell you doing here?' It was the night watchman.

"The son of one of the prominent citizens was involved in a scrape and our reporters were given the bounce every time they went to his home. I learned that he had attended the University of Chicago and went there but could not find a picture of him. So I collected a group of his student friends and went through some old yearbooks, asking them to pick out characteristics in the pictures that resembled the man I was after. From these I did a composite that was good enough to impress Wells and Keely that it was the lad in question.

"When the [newspaper] boys set up a hectic chase for the picture of a University professor [Jacques Loeb] who had

made himself famous overnight by some discovery or other. He was as shy as an unbroken colt and didn't want his picture in the papers. He slammed his door in my face when I called on him but I got a glimpse and drew a portrait of him that was printed. He protested vigorously to Keely but the picture had run and that's what counted. Then *McClure's* Magazine wired me to send them the picture to be used with an article they were going to run on him. I didn't want to use the same old picture, so I went down to the University one morning and went in with the students as they entered his classroom. I sat in the very back row and was busy sketching when he called on me to recite. I excused myself by saying I was unprepared. 'See that you are better prepared tomorrow,' was his rejoinder, but there wasn't any tomorrow as far as I was concerned. I had gotten enough notes to do a fine portrait and *McClure's* paid me a small fortune for it.''[1]

1901. Attended the Chicago Art Institute.

1902. Assistant art editor of the *Tribune*.

June 24, 1903. Married an artist, Lillian Lusk. ''. . . Went to art school one morning to study art; saw a girl instead of the model, drew the girl, stopped studying art to study the girl, drew a proposal. She accepted and my 'model' sweetheart became my 'model' wife; and, like a wedding gift to us, I became art editor of a Middle Western magazine and worked with such men as Willis J. Abbot and Karl K. Harriman as editors.'' [''Who's Who—And Why,'' *Saturday Evening Post*, August 22, 1925.[2]]

1903. Art editor of *Pilgrim: A Magazine for the Home*.

December 18, 1904. Resigned from *Pilgrim*, although his work continued to appear in it for the next twelve months.

October, 1905. Enrolled at the Art Students League in New York. ''Then we came to New York! Also down, down, down in our estimations of our success as artists. My wife quit art; I went doggedly on, drew on my imagination of what I might be, aimed high, worked hard, starved—a little, learned a lot, went to art school and studied hard this time, took scholarships, hoped, feared; look over a bunch of my illustrations; you'll see it all in them, for I've drawn my history.''[2]

December, 1905. Advertising work for Grape-Nuts, Postum, and Post Toasties.

Summer, 1906. Illustrated the fall-winter catalog for the Kalamazoo Suit Company. ''It was an order for twenty or thirty drawings of suits, for which I was to receive something like four or five dollars for each drawing. I put infinite pains and care into the first drawing and was pleased with it. BUT— it took me three days to make it. I worked faster on the second but it took me two days. I sat down to think. At the rate I was going and considering the extreme transience of feminine styles, I figured that by the time I completed the set I would be too aged and infirm to draw, even it should be the fashion to wear clothing. So I thought out a plan. I made two fine drawings: one with the left hand raised in a graceful gesture; the other with the right hand raised in an equally graceful gesture. Then I made tracings from these and added the details. I knocked off about three or four a day. There was a certain lack of variety, but the fashion man was more concerned about buttons and braid than originality so they were highly satisfactory.''[1]

Autumn, 1907. Accepted at Howard Pyle's art school in Wilmington, Delaware. "Howard Pyle taught, fought, sang, laughed and sobbed through his work. His pictures, in point of composition were simplicity itself, and in their straightforward way of appeal, one felt the frank, open-hearted sincerity of their creator. In color, he caught the rare and subtle tints of nature; he understood her moods, her shades, her tones, her atmosphere as one with less trained senses and grosser soul could never know or feel; and, although his imagination seemed boundless, yet it was always held true and wholesome by his sense of justice to his fellowmen, his reverence for high morals and religion and his love for truth.

"Howard Pyle was not a narrow specialist, and although he became the authority in his favorite field, he seemed to know the essential points of a subject upon whatever line he touched, or was called upon to discuss with his students. He understood the heart of things and he learned this great throbbing pulse, through his own personal efforts in untiring study and observation."[1]

1908. Illustrated for *Redbook* magazine and continued his cereal and beverage advertising work.

Autumn, 1909. Joined an artist's colony with his wife near Claymont, Delaware called Naaman's-on-Delaware. "Four years is quite a long time for four fellows to bind themselves to keep a house because of the chance of change, marriage, or family affairs, and to us it seems rather a long period to bind ourselves for we do not know how things would work out if we should have a family or if either of our mothers should need our help and home. . . . So much depends on the manner and ability Mrs. Koerner has in running such a house. The aim of all is to have it a success—professionally and domestically—and if a success, then a continuance. . . ."[1]

1911. Left Naaman's and moved to Wilmington.

October 18, 1913. Daughter, Ruth Ann, born.

April 27, 1915. Son, W. H., Jr., born.

1919-1922. Illustrated western books and articles by Emerson Hough. Hough's reaction to one of Koerner's illustrations: "I don't know when an illustration has hit me in the face th[e] way that one has. Tell Koerner that this is the first time in my career that an artist has really pleased me with his work. Here we have imagination and fidelity both. . . ."[1]

May, 1924. With his family and close friends took a trip West. Koerner's wife recalled the manner in which they traveled: "On the running boards of our seven-passenger, open Buick, we carried a Brooks Umbrella Tent for four people; four 'blowbeds' [air mattresses] that were pumped up by a device attached to the engine which saved William from blowing his lungs out, and on the front bumper we carried a two-burner gasoline stove, that was filled each night from our gas tank to cook dinner and breakfast. Pots and pans and bedding were wrapped in tarpaulins on the running boards and back bumper. A set of three cans went on one running board: one gallon of oil, one of water, one of gasoline for emergency use. Gas stations were far apart. Inside the car, made out of khaki cloth and fastened to the back of the front seat, was a car-wide deep bag with separate places for clothing. The four side pockets on the doors and the dashboard were filled. We never hunted where to find what, for the children saw to it that everything was perfectly packed where it belonged. Canvas bags filled with water hung on the outside door han-

(From *The Covered Wagon* by Emerson Hough. Illustrated by W. H. D. Koerner.)

dles and we carried canteens inside the car for drinking water, which we had to use carefully, not wasting a drop. We had agreed before we left home that neither car would travel over thirty-five miles per hour; that we would never look at the other family when discipline was in progress, and that we would never interfere or argue with each other—almost!

"William was continually sketching and painting. His oils and paint box with a stretched canvas inside, his colored crayons and water colors, and his book in which he drew his compositions for his illustrations were always with him, ready for notes or scenes or people who wanted to pose. An old army scout who remembered Jim Bridger had his log cabin lined with William's illustrations, especially those from *The Covered Wagon*. He followed William wherever he went and swore his approval."[1]

1934. Suffered from arthritis. The manner in which Koerner bore this debilitating malady was best described in a letter from a friend: "I can't tell you Bill how glad I was to see you. I've been thinking of you so much this week and wish I lived a little closer so I could run in to talk over old times. You know I've been worrying a lot the past six years, and then after I saw the fine courage with which you face life, I felt so ashamed of my own petty troubles. . . . I have always admired your work so much, and now we have something even finer to admire. There is so much I would like to say but I don't know how to say it. I can only hope that because we are both a little older and understand things a little better, that words are not so necessary to express our feelings."[1]

W. H. D. Koerner in his Interlaken studio.

August 1, 1938. A series of minor strokes culminated in a massive and fatal cerebral hemorrhage at his home in Interlaken, New Jersey.

June 17, 1978. Koerner's re-constructed studio was dedicated as a permanent part of the Whitney Gallery of Western Art, Cody, Wyoming.

FOR MORE INFORMATION SEE: Saturday Evening Post, August 22, 1925; Bertha E. Mahony, and others, compilers, *Illustrators of Children's Books, 1744-1945,* Horn Book, 1947; "The Mythic West of W.H.D. Koerner," *The American West,* May, 1967; William Henry Hutchinson, *W.H.D. Koerner: Illustrating the Western Myth,* Amon Carter Museum of Western Art, 1969; *Western Horseman,* Volume 39, October, 1974; W. H. Hutchinson, *The World, the Work and the West of W.H.D. Koerner,* University of Oklahoma Press, 1978.

LAMB, Beatrice Pitney   1904-

PERSONAL: Born May 12, 1904; daughter of Mahlon (a justice of the U.S. Supreme Court) and Florence (Shelton) Pitney; married Horace R. Lamb (a lawyer), February 8, 1930; children: Barbara (Mrs. Tristam Johnson), Dorothy (Mrs. John C. Crawford). *Education:* Attended Westover School, Middlebury, Conn.; Bryn Mawr College, B.A., 1927; Geneva School of International Studies; Columbia University, M.A., 1956. *Home:* 672 Oenoke Ridge, New Canaan, Conn. 06840.

CAREER: League of Women Voters, Washington, D.C., secretary, national staff, 1928-33, writer of pamphlets, 1928-36; *United Nations News,* editor, 1945-49; New School for Social Research, New York, N.Y., lecturer, 1955-56; New York University, New York, N.Y., lecturer, 1959-65; author, professional lecturer and photographer. Has sold slides and pictures to *Time, American Oxford Encyclopedia,* and other publications. *Member:* American Association of Asian Studies, Asia Society (member of India Council), Society of Women Geographers.

WRITINGS: (With Allen W. Dulles) *The United Nations,* Foreign Policy Association, 1946; *Introduction to India,* American Association of University Women, 1960; *India—A World in Transition,* Praeger, 1963, 4th edition, revised, 1974; *India,* Macmillan, 1965; *The Nehrus of India: Three Generations of Leadership,* Macmillan, 1967. Twice revised the article on India for the *World Book Encyclopedia;* author of a public affairs pamphlet and of pamphlets on international relations and consumer problems for League of Women Voters.

SIDELIGHTS; "My desire to become a writer began, I believe, on the very first day that I discovered, when I was about four years old, that I myself could actually read a real story, not merely sentences like 'See Spot run.' What I was reading was a story about a child who somehow managed to float through the sky aboard a puffy white cloud and see many fascinating new sights passing by below him. It gave me a feeling of unlimited freedom and joy. From then on, when asked what I wanted for Christmas or as a birthday present, I always answered, 'just give me books.'

"Although I read and read, I was also a very active child. In school and college I was on every athletic team from field hockey to basketball to water polo to lacrosse and especially tennis, in which I won countless tournaments. I have inter-

(From *India: A World in Transition* by Beatrice P. Lamb.)

spersed my writing with many other interests, perhaps especially traveling, photography, lecturing and teaching. I have continued to be physically active and even now in my mid-seventies am a strong, enthusiastic swimmer and still play tennis.

"From 1930 until his death in 1977, I was married to a wonderful man, Horace R. Lamb, a lawyer of distinction whose biography has been included in the *National Cyclopedia of American Biography*. He shared my interest in traveling and in international affairs and loved to operate the projector when I showed my slides of India in illustrated lectures. Although I had had to fight hard in my youth for the right to a college education, I never had to fight him for the right to a career. He always aided and abetted it.

"My three most important books all deal, at different levels, with subject matter relating to India, a country which I visited seven times and studied intensively. One of them, *India—A World in Transition,* has been widely used as compulsory reading in college and high school classes. My other two books are for young people's enjoyment outside the classroom. My complete bibliography includes many pamphlets on international affairs, written for adult audiences.

"As most young people would probably agree, the most notable fact about me at this time perhaps is the fact that my oldest grandson is the famous Christopher Reeve, a committed actor since he was age thirteen, who rose to international stardom playing the title role in the 1979 movie, 'Superman.'"

BEATRICE PITNEY LAMB

KEO FELKER LAZARUS

LAZARUS, Keo Felker 1913-

PERSONAL: Born October 22, 1913, in Callaway, Neb.; daughter of John Edwin (a rancher and jeweler) and Nola (Smith) Felker; married Arnold Leslie Lazarus (a professor of English), July 24, 1938; children: Kearvelle (Mrs. John B. Friedman), Dianne (Mrs. James Runnels), J. David, Peter D. *Education:* University of California, Los Angeles, B.E., 1938; Purdue University, Indiana, graduate study. *Home:* 945 Ward Dr. #69, Santa Barbara, Calif. 93111.

CAREER: Physical education teacher in Los Angeles, Calif., 1939-41, 1955-59. *Member:* Chicago Children's Reading Round Table, Tippecanoe County Historical Association, Society of Children's Book Writers.

WRITINGS—Juvenile: *Rattlesnake Run*, Follett, 1968; *The Gismo*, Follett, 1970; *Tadpole Taylor*, Steck, 1970; *The Billy Goat in the Chili Patch*, Steck, 1972; *The Shark in the Window*, Morrow, 1972; *A Totem for Ti-Jacques*, Waveland Press, 1977; *The Gismonauts*, Follett, 1980; *A Message from Monaal*, Follett, 1980. Contributor to *Jack and Jill*, *Cricket*, and *Highlights for Children*.

WORK IN PROGRESS: *Dragon in the Eagle's Nest; Secret of the Lucky Blue;* and *You've Got a Pet What?.*

SIDELIGHTS: "I grew up on a lemon ranch in Santa Barbara, California. Books, books, and more books filled my life, as we carted home armloads of them from our local public library.

"My father was an inventive soul in whose vocabulary the word 'impossible' didn't exist. He involved my younger brother and me in building a clay tennis court by the blackberry bushes, modeling concrete into statues, and gazing at the stars through a homemade telescope constructed from a hand-ground concave mirror and an old hot water heater.

Mother filled us with the love of music and art. We were a happy family and did lots of things together.

"Because of my enjoyment of outdoor sports and dance I became a physical education teacher. Just out of college, I married and had two girls and two boys. We continued the weekly visits to the libraries, always reserving one book to be read aloud in the evenings. We resisted buying a TV. It was during these reading sessions that I became interested in writing for children.

"My attempts, however, were unappreciated by the editors, until I took a course in directed writing from Caroline Gordon, the novelist, who was writer-in-residence at Purdue University, Lafayette, Indiana. My husband was a professor there at the time. Miss Gordon tore my writing to shreds, then began building it up sentence by sentence, paragraph by paragraph. I learned many writing techniques which I found, as in any art, needed to be practiced to develop a professional responsibility to one's art.

"I often tell children in the schools that books are like airplanes—they take you places and show you things you could never learn any other way. Writing a book is like piloting a plane. Just as a pilot has to know those instruments on the instrument panel in front of him, so a writer needs to know ways of writing that will put the reader right into the story.

"Each letter I receive from a child who has enjoyed one of my books, spurs me on to write better and better stories. My readers send me with a bucket to that ocean of ideas awaiting anyone who dares to dip in."

HOBBIES AND OTHER INTERESTS: Archeology ("I work on summer digs whenever I can."), swimming, hiking, painting, and working in the garden.

FOR MORE INFORMATION SEE: Book World, May 5, 1968.

His captors hoisted him out of the pirogue and carried him to a small campsite cleared in the thicket. ■(From *A Totem for Ti-Jacques* by Keo Felker Lazarus. Illustrated by the author.)

LENARD, Alexander   1910-1972

OBITUARY NOTICE: Born March 9, 1910, in Budapest, Hungary; died April 14, 1972, in Brazil. Scholar, translator, and author. Lenard is best known for his Latin translation of A. A. Milne's *Winnie the Pooh,* entitled *Winni Ille Pu,* which he wrote to interest young people in the study of Latin. The book unexpectedly became an international best-seller. Lenard also translated Francoise Sagan's *Bonjour Tristesse* into Latin and wrote several volumes of poetry in both German and Italian. He contributed articles on medical subjects to numerous international publications. *For More Information See: Contemporary Authors,* Volume 5-8, revised, Gale, 1969. *Obituaries: New York Times,* May 3, 1972; *AB Bookman's Weekly,* May 15, 1972.

LeSHAN, Eda J(oan)   1922-

PERSONAL: Born June 6, 1922, in New York, N.Y.; daughter of Max (a lawyer) and Jean (Schick) Grossman; married Lawrence L. LeShan (a psychologist), August 19, 1944; children: Wendy Jean. *Education:* Columbia University, B.S., 1944; Clark University, M.A., 1947. *Home and office:* 263

EDA J. LeSHAN

Many of our feelings are wonderful and the best thing we can do is let them flow freely. ■(From *What Makes Me Feel This Way?* by Eda LeShan. Illustrated by Lisl Weil.)

West End Ave., New York, N.Y. 10023. *Agent:* Ann Elmo, 52 Vanderbilt Ave., New York, N.Y. 10017.

CAREER: Worcester Child Guidance Clinic, Worcester, Mass., diagnostician and play therapist, 1947-48; Association for Family Living, Chicago, Ill., parent education discussion leader, 1949-51; Guidance Center, New Rochelle, N.Y., director of education, 1955-60; Manhattan Society for Mental Health, New York, N.Y., educational director, 1960-62, consultant, 1962—; Pengilly Country Day School, New Rochelle, N.Y., consulting psychologist, 1962—. New York State Regent's Committee on Parent Education, member 1963-66; PBS, WNET-TV, moderator of "How Do Your Children Grow?," 1970-72; WCBS-TV, co-host of "In Tune," 1976. Currently contributing editor of *Woman's Day* magazine and consultant for ABC-TV children's program, "Alex and Annie." *Member:* American Psychological Association, Association for Humanistic Psychology, Authors League, New York Academy of Television Arts and Sciences (board of governors).

WRITINGS: How to Survive Parenthood, Random House, 1965; *The Conspiracy Against Childhood,* Atheneum, 1967; *Sex and Your Teen-ager: A Guide for Parents,* McKay, 1969; *Natural Parenthood: Raising Your Child Without a Script,* New American Library, 1970; *How do Your Children Grow?,* McKay, 1971; *On "How do Your Children Grow?": A Dialogue with Parents,* McKay, 1972; *What Makes Me Feel This*

Way?: Growing Up With Human Emotions (juvenile), Macmillan, 1972; *The Wonderful Crisis of Middle Age: Some Personal Reflections,* McKay, 1973; *You and Your Feelings* (juvenile), Macmillan, 1975; *In Search of Myself and Other Children,* Evans, 1976; *Learning to Say Good-bye: When a Parent Dies* (juvenile), Macmillan, 1976; (with Lee Polk) *The Incredible Television Machine* (juvenile), Macmillan, 1977; *What's Going to Happen to Me?: When Parents Separate and Divorce,* Four Winds, 1978. *Winning the Losing Battle,* Crowell, 1979.

Author of public affairs pamphlets. contributor to *Parents' Magazine, New York Times Magazine, Redbook, McCall's, Reader's Digest,* and many other publications.

WORK IN PROGRESS: The Roots of Crime for Four Winds and a book for teen-agers.

SIDELIGHTS: "I write books for children that I wished *I'd* had as a child. I've worked very hard at remembering the feelings of childhood, and all my children's books are about feelings."

HOBBIES AND OTHER INTERESTS: Theatre, travel, opera, reading. "I've become a bird watcher and feed ducks on a lake all summer."

FOR MORE INFORMATION SEE: "If There's a Death in the Family, Don't let Kids Bottle up Their Grief, Warns Eda LeShan," *People,* January 31, 1977; *Horn Book,* February, 1977.

MEYER LEVIN

LEVIN, Meyer   1905-

PERSONAL: Born October 8, 1905, in Chicago, Ill.; son of Joseph (a tailor) and Goldie (Basiste) Levin; married Mabel Schamp Foy, 1934 (divorced, 1944); married Tereska Szwarc (a French novelist, known under name Tereska Torres), March 25, 1948; children: (first marriage) Eli; (second marriage) Gabriel, Mikael; (stepchildren) Dominique. *Education:* University of Chicago, Ph.B., 1924; attended Academie Moderne art school, Paris, 1925. *Religion:* Reform Judaism. *Home:* Street of the Blue Waves, Herzlia-on-Sea, Israel and Apt. 13, 65 Blvd. Arago, Paris 13, France. *Agent:* Scott Meredith, 845 Third Ave., New York, N.Y. 10022.

CAREER: Chicago Daily News, Chicago, Ill., reporter, feature writer, and columnist, 1923-29; one-time member of collective farm community in Palestine (pre-Israel); producer of marionette plays at New School for Social Research, New York, N.Y.; *Esquire,* Chicago, Ill., associate editor, 1933-38, film critic, 1933-39; U.S. Office of War Information, film writer, producer, and director, 1942-43; later war correspondent for Overseas News Agency and Jewish Telegraphic Agency, with special assignment to discover and document the fate of European Jewry; film producer and writer. *Member:* American War Correspondents Association, Authors League, Dramatists Guild. *Awards, honors:* Harry and Ethel Daroff Fiction award, 1966, for *The Stronghold;* Isaac Siegel Memorial Juvenile award of Jewish Book Council of America, 1967, for *The Story of Israel;* special citation by World Federation of Bergen/Belsen Associations, 1969, for "excellence and distinction in literature of the Holocaust and Jewish destiny."

WRITINGS: Reporter (novel), John Day, 1929 (withdrawn shortly after publication); *Frankie and Johnnie: A Love Story,* John Day, 1930, revised edition published as *The Young Lovers,* New American Library, 1952; *Yehuda,* J. Cape & H. Smith, 1931; *The Golden Mountain* (folk tales retold from Hebrew, Yiddish, and German sources), Behrman, 1932, reissued as *Classic Hassidic Tales,* Citadel, 1966, Penguin, 1975; *The New Bridge* (novel), Covici, Friede, 1933; *The Old Bunch* (novel), Viking, 1937; *Citizens* (novel), Viking, 1940; *My Father's House* (novel), Viking, 1947; *If I Forget Thee: A Picture Story of Modern Palestine* (synopsis of the author's film, "My Father's House," with photographs), Viking, 1947; (translator) Sholem Asch, *Tales Of My People,* Putnam, 1948; *In Search* (autobiography), Horizon, 1950; *Compulsion* (novel), Simon & Schuster, 1956; *Eva* (novel); Simon & Schuster, 1959; *The Fanatic* (novel), Simon & Schuster, 1964; *The Stronghold* (novel), Simon & Schuster, 1965; *Gore and Igor: An Extravaganza* (novel), Simon & Schuster, 1968; *The Haggadah Retold* (original paperback), music by Harry Coopersmith, design and illustrations by Miriam Woods, Behrman, 1968, hardcover and paperback editions published as *An Israel Haggadah for Passover,* Abrams, 1970; *Beginnings in Jewish Philosophy,* Behrman, 1971; *The Settlers* (novel), Simon & Schuster, 1972; *A Spell of Time* (novella), Praeger, 1975; *The Obsession,* Simon & Schuster, 1976; *The Harvest* (novel, sequel to *The Settlers*), Simon & Schuster, 1978.

Juveniles: (With Toby K. Kurzband) *The Story of the Synagogue*, Behrman, 1957; (with Kurzband) *The Story of the Jewish Way of Life*, Behrman, 1959; (with Dorothy K. Kripke) *God and the Story of Judaism*, Behrman, 1962; *The Story of Israel*, includes photographs by Archie Lieberman, sketches by son, Eli Levin, Putnam, 1966.

Editor: (And translator) *Selections from the Kibbutz Buchenwald Diary*, Zionist Organization, 1946; (and author of introduction) David S. Kogan, *Diary*, Beechhurst Press, 1955; Arthur D. Goldhaft, *Golden Egg*, Horizon, 1957; (with Charles Angoff) *The Rise of American Jewish Literature* (anthology of selections from major novels), Simon & Schuster, 1970.

Translator from the French—all written by Levin's wife, under name Tereska Torres: *Not Yet*, Crown, 1957; *Dangerous Games*, Dial, 1957; *The Golden Cage*, Dial, 1959; *Women's Barracks*, Allen, 1960; *The Only Reason*, Allen, 1962.

Plays: "The Good Old Days," first produced in Paris, 1951; *Compulsion* (two-act; revised version first produced on Broadway at Ambassador Theatre, October 24, 1957), original typescript, M. McCall, 1958. Also author of dramatization of *The Diary of Anne Frank*, privately printed "for literary discussion," 1967, produced by The Israel Soldiers Theatre, 1966, and Brandeis University, 1972, although forbidden by the *Diary* owners.

Films: (Writer and co-producer, with Herbert Kline) "My Father's House," feature film produced in Palestine, 1947; "The Illegals," feature-length documentary filmed in Eastern Europe, 1948. Also author of documentary films, "The Falashas," "Bus to Sinai," "The Mountain of Moses," and "The Unafraid." Author of a report entitled "Another Kind

of Blacklist," *Congress Bi-Weekly*, 1961. Contributor of articles and short stories to *New Yorker, Reporter, New Republic, Nation, Travel, Saturday Evening Post, Menorah Journal, Commentary, Collier's*, and other periodicals.

SIDELIGHTS: "I grew up on Chicago's turbulent old west side in a neighborhood then turning from Jewish to Italian, it was to become the notorious Chicago gangland of the twenties. Though bookish, timid, and maybe even a bit cowardly, I have from then on found myself pictured as a scrappy, tough fellow—even in the literary world, where, as in my Chicago childhood, I've at times had to fight a gang-up. I always wanted to be a writer, and even in grammar school started publishing myself because I was a shark in the printshop and could run off my own poems. Many years later, after I had become a newspaper columnist, a novelist, and a war correspondent, I again found myself publishing my own work, because an autobiography I wrote in 1950 proved too outspoken, so I had it printed in Paris. This book, called *In Search*, was republished in America and is a kind of early example of the search-for-roots that is important today. In my childhood and youth, in the flood tide of immigration, the 'melting pot' idea was the dominating image of our American civilization, and it is only comparatively recently that we have, in reverse, become interested in ethnic themes.

"Yet, for me the ethnic background was central; one wrote about what one knew, and thus, I became dominantly a writer about American Jewish life, at least a generation before American Jewish writers became a dominant category. My biggest novel, *The Old Bunch*, published in the mid-Thirties, would, I suppose, today be regarded as a foundation book in ethnic literature. At the time I simply regarded it as an American novel, although, paradoxically, I now see myself as a Jewish novelist, even more than as an American or American, Jewish novelist. This is because, in my mature experience, the Jewish influence became dominant.

(From the movie "Compulsion," starring Bradford Dillman, Dean Stockwell and Orson Welles. Copyright © 1959 by Twentieth Century-Fox Corp.)

"Just out of college in 1924, I found myself, at the end of a wander-year abroad, visiting Palestine, where I became fascinated by pioneer life in the settlers' communes, the kibbutzim. A few years later I returned to Palestine to live in a kibbutz and write a novel about it, called *Yehuda*. Thus began my seesaw between America and Palestine-Israel. Even when I worked, during the depression, on a new American magazine called *Esquire,* so as to support myself while writing *The Old Bunch,* Jewish life was my theme. With the coming of World War II, I became haunted by the question of the fate of Europe's Jews, and eventually secured a post as war correspondent, with the special assignment of searching out that fate. Thus I became a 'specialist' in death camps. After the war, I followed the fates of the survivors, filming them as they were led across secret routes to board illegal ships on the way to Palestine. Later I conceived what I saw as my 'big work' around the experience of the Jews of our century; in Europe with the Holocaust, in America with the development of the American Jewish community, in Palestine with the birth of Israel. This resulted in the duonovel, *The Settlers* and *The Harvest.*

"As another result—again paradoxically—of this ethnic or particularist interest, I lead a rather cosmopolitan life, living part of each year in America, and part in Israel, with intervals in Paris. For as our family grew up, a daughter and son settled in Paris, where my wife—a French novelist—was born and raised. So, in between America and Israel, we spend time with them. My eldest son is an artist living in Santa Fe. He is the son of my first marriage; the daughter of my wife's first marriage is married to a Frenchman and is a television reporter in Paris. Our middle son is a poet and clinical psychologist in Jerusalem. Our youngest son is an art photographer based in Paris; his wife is an artist from Sweden. Thus, we are pretty well safe-guarded against ultra-nationalism and chauvinism.

"In my literary development I found myself drawn more and more to identification with Jewish culture, rather than the English culture in which I was schooled. The Bible became a source of literary structure to me, from the parable-tale to the prototype of the modern novel, the story of Joseph. In the early thirties, when Hassidic literature was unknown in America, in Europe I became interested in Yiddish folktales of the legendary Hassidic wonder-working rabbis, and this resulted in my translation and re-telling of the basic tales, at first called *The Golden Mountain* and today published by Penguin books as *Classic Hassidic Tales.* The influence on my own writing can be readily seen in a kind of science-fiction mystical, love story called *A Spell of Time,* set in Jerusalem.

"Because of my documentary film work during the war, writing with a camera, as I call it, has remained a side-occupation—more than a hobby—with me, and in this, too, I have followed my ethnic bent, for one of my most gratifying films is 'The Falashas,' the story of the oldest existing tribe of Jews, the black communities in Ethiopia. Another is 'The Mountain of Moses,' tracing the known and legendary sites of the Exodus, in the Sinai. Sometimes, indeed, I'm seen as an educator more than as a literary personage, for when an educational publisher asked me to work on a series called *The Jewish Heritage,* I felt it indeed appropriate for me to do so, and an entire generation in America has used these books, and grown up to read my novels. There is nothing more gratifying, for a writer, than to know that his work continues after many years to be read.''

TED LEWIN

LEWIN, Ted 1935-

PERSONAL: Born May 6, 1935, in Buffalo, N.Y.; son of Sidney (a retail jeweler) and Bernece (Klenn) Lewin; married Betsy Reilly (an artist). *Education:* Pratt Institute of Art, B.F.A., 1956. *Home and office:* 152 Willoughby Ave., Brooklyn, N.Y. 11205.

CAREER: Professional wrestler, 1952-65; artist and freelance illustrator, 1956—. *Exhibition:* One man show, Laboratory of Ornithology, Cornell University, 1978. *Military service:* U.S. Army, 1958.

WRITINGS—Self-illustrated: World Within a World: Everglades, Dodd, 1976; *World Within a World: Baja,* Dodd, 1978; *World Within a World: Pribilofs,* Dodd, 1980.

Illustrator: Wyatt Blassingame, *Look-It-Up Book of Presidents,* Random House, 1968; George S. Trow, *Meet Robert E. Lee,* Random House, 1969; Margaret T. Burroughs, *Jasper the Drummin' Boy,* Follett, 1970; Janet H. Ervin, *More Than Half Way There,* Follett, 1970; Donald Cox, *Pioneers of Ecology,* Hammond, 1971; Nellie Burchardt, *Surprise for Carlotta,* Watts, 1971; Gene Smith, *Visitor,* Cowles, 1971; Betty Horvath, *Not Enough Indians,* Watts, 1971; Maurine H. Gee, *Chicano, Amigo,* Morrow, 1972; Rose Blue, *Grandma Didn't Wave Back,* Watts, 1972; Michael Capizzi, *Getting It All Together,* Delacorte, 1972; Rose Blue, *A Month of Sundays,* Watts, 1972; Rita Micklish, *Sugar Bee,* Delacorte, 1972; Darrell A. Rolerson, *In Sheep's Clothing,* Dodd, 1972; Charlotte Gantz, *Boy with Three Names,* Houghton, 1973; William MacKellar, *The Ghost of Grannoch Moor,* Dodd, 1973; Marian Rumsey, *Lion on the Run,* Morrow, 1973, Grosset, 1974; Rose Blue, *Nikki 108,* Watts, 1973; Darrell A.

Rolerson, *A Boy Called Plum*, Dodd, 1974; Jean S. Doty, *Gabriel*, Macmillan, 1974; Gene Smith, *The Hayburners*, Delacorte, 1974; Matt Christopher, *Earthquake*, Little, Brown, 1975; Patricia Beatty, *Rufus, Red Rufus*, Morrow, 1975; Charles Ferry, *Up in Sister Bay*, Houghton, 1975; Jean S. Doty, *Winter Pony*, Macmillan, 1975; Scott O'Dell, *Zia*, Houghton, 1976; Lynne Martin, *Puffin, Bird of the Open Seas*, Morrow, 1976; Laurence Pringle, *Listen to the Crows*, Crowell, 1976; Patricia Clyne, *Ghostly Animals of America*, Dodd, 1977; Mildred Teal, *Bird of Passage*, Little, Brown, 1977; Marian Rumsey, *Carolina Hurricane*, Morrow, 1977; Nigel Gray, *The Deserter*, Harper, 1977; Robert N. Peck, *Patooie*, Knopf, 1977; Philippa Pearce, *The Shadow Cage and Other Tales of the Supernatural*, Crowell, 1977; Helen Hill, *Straight on Till Morning: Poems of the Imaginary World*, Crowell, 1977; Rose Blue, *The Thirteenth Year: A*

Bar Mitzvah Story, Watts, 1977; Leslie Norris, *Merlin and the Snake's Egg: Poems*, Viking, 1978; William MacKellar, *The Silent Bells*, Dodd, 1978; Robert N. Peck, *Soup for President*, Knopf, 1978; William MacKellar, *The Witch of Glen Gowrie*, Dodd, 1978; Anne E. Crompton, *A Womans Place*, Little, Brown, 1978; David Stemple, *High Ridge Gobble: A Story of the Eastern Wild Turkey*, Collins, 1980; Jean Doty, *Can I Get There by Candlelight*, Macmillan, 1980; Rose Blue, *My Mother the Witch*, McGraw, 1980.

WORK IN PROGRESS: Illustrating books.

SIDELIGHTS: "I am primarily an artist-illustrator, and my writing has grown out of an interest in the natural world which, until my first book, I confined to graphic form only. I am a deeply concerned environmentalist and conserva-

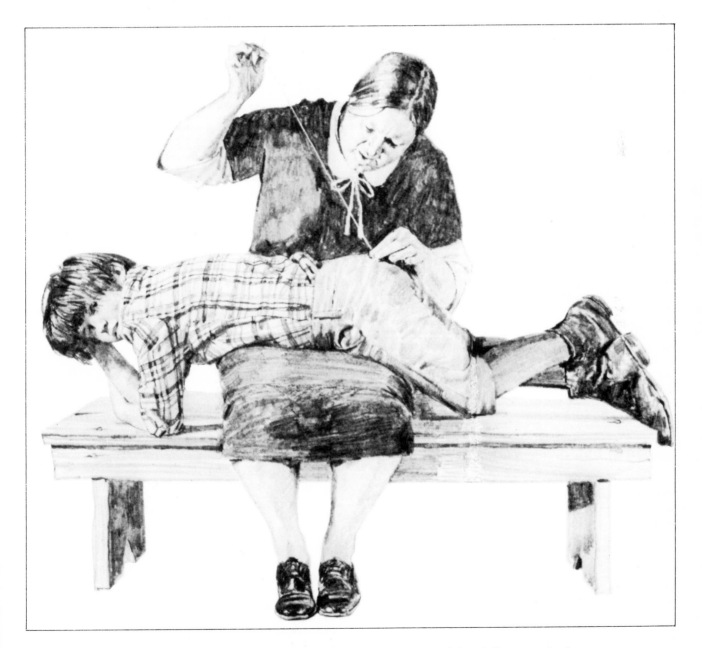

Her hand touched my face. Then she went inside to get a needle and thread. I lay across her lap while she sewed up a rip in the seat of my trousers. ■ (From *Hub* by Robert Newton Peck. Illustrated by Ted Lewin.)

(From *Soup for President* by Robert Newton Peck. Illustrated by Ted Lewin.)

tionist, and travel to wilderness areas around the world for both graphic and literary material.''

Lewin was born in Buffalo where he attended public schools and earned a B.F.A. from Pratt Institute in Brooklyn, receiving the Dean's Medal upon graduation in 1956. While he was in school he supported himself by wrestling professionally. A free-lance illustrator, his pictures have appeared in *Boy's Life* and other publications and in several books, among them the Junior Literary Guild selection, *Not Enough Indians* by Betty Horvath.

FOR MORE INFORMATION SEE: Horn Book, August, 1977.

LEYDON, Rita (Flodén)   1949-

PERSONAL: Born December 24, 1949, in Sweden; daughter of Björn F. (an engineer) and Gun-Britt (a draftsman; maiden name Ullberg) Flodén; married Christopher F. Leydon (a vintage auto restorer), August 25, 1973; children: Krispin Johan, Lars Kristofer. *Education:* Moore College of Art, 1968-69; Philadelphia College of Art, B.F.A., 1972. *Religion:* Bahá'í. *Home address:* Box 127, Lahaska, Pa. 18931.

CAREER: Child's Way magazine, Bahá'í Publishing Trust, Wilmette, Ill., art director, 1978—.

ILLUSTRATOR: Carol Barkin and Elizabeth James, *Slapdash Sewing,* Lothrop, 1975; C. Barkin and E. James, *Slapdash Cooking,* Lothrop, 1976; C. Barkin and E. James, *Slapdash Alterations: How to Recycle Your Wardrobe,* Lothrop, 1977; C. Barkin and E. James, *Slapdash Decorating,* Loth-

rop, 1977; Lillian Morrison, *Who Would Marry a Mineral? Riddles, Rones & Love Tunes,* Lothrop, 1978; (with Lou Jacobs, Jr.), Marilyn Gould, *Playground Sports, a Book of Ball Games,* Lothrop, 1978; Helen Roney Sattler, *Dollars from Dandelions: 101 Ways to Earn Money,* Lothrop, 1979; C. Barkin and E. James, *Babysitter's Handbook,* Simon & Schuster, 1980.

SIDELIGHTS: ''Being an illustrator/designer is only a small, although, very important corner of my present life. Being a mother of two very young children occupies a lot of time and energy with only nap-time and late evenings left over for mother's other interests and duties. Of necessity, my illustration ambitions are on the slow burner at this time—meaning that I do, perhaps, two books a year and put out a children's magazine six times a year. The magazine is called *Child's Way* and is published by the Bahá'í Publishing Trust. There is plenty of time later to become more aggressive and pound the pavement as I did after college.

''Home life is on a sixty-five acre farm in Bucks County, Pennsylvania. My husband works at home also—he owns and operates a vintage sport and race car restoration center of the highest caliber. My involvement in Leydon Restoration is as bookkeeper and upholsterer when need arises.

''My own creative juices flow exhuberantly at the loom. I have an antique loom of questionable make and am anticipating graduating soon to a modern Swedish countermarch loom that I have stashed away in our barn.

''Another interest that propelled me forward until time and finances didn't allow was soaring. (Both my parents are very accomplished soaring enthusiasts.) My husband shares my enthusiasm for flight, but his dream is old bi-planes (we own a 1929 Parks Speedster). I soloed on my eleventh flight but never did finish with a license.

RITA LEYDON

You and your best friend can have a great time making matching peasant dresses. ■ (From *Slapdash Sewing* by Carol Barkin and Elizabeth James. Illustrated by Rita Flodén Leydon.)

"I was born and lived my first ten years in Sweden. So my first language is Swedish and I am certain that most of my solutions to design and illustrative problems are filled through those early impressions.

"The most important and influential aspect of my whole life and being is my faith. I am a Bahá'í. It is an every-day-every-moment faith whose key word is UNITY. A famous quote from the prophet founder Bahá'u'lláh is 'The earth is but one country, and mankind it's citizens.' My outlook on everything, from world circumstances to the food I eat to how to raise my children to how I treat the delivery man, is colored by the Bahá'í teachings, not to mention my approach to my art. First I am a Bahá'í, then I am a wife/mother and last I am an illustrator/artist."

Fairy land,
Where all the children dine at five,
And all the playthings come alive.

—Robert Louis Stevenson

LIPMAN, David 1931-

PERSONAL: Born February 13, 1931, in Springfield, Mo.; son of Benjamin (a grocer) and Rose (Mack) Lipman; married Marilyn Lee Vittert, December 10, 1961; children: Gay Ilene, Benjamin Alan. *Education:* University of Missouri, B.J., 1953. *Religion:* Jewish. *Home:* 122 Plantation Dr., St. Louis, Mo. 63141. *Office: St. Louis Post-Dispatch,* 900 North Twelfth Blvd., St. Louis, Mo. 63101. *Agent:* McIntosh & Otis, Inc., 18 East 41st St., New York, N.Y. 10017.

CAREER: Springfield Newspapers, Inc., Springfield, Mo., reporter and sportswriter, 1953-54, 1956-57; *Kansas City Star,* Kansas City, Mo., reporter and then copy editor, 1957-60; *St. Louis Post-Dispatch,* St. Louis, Mo., assistant sports editor, 1960-68, news editor, 1968-71, assistant managing editor, 1971-79, managing editor, 1979—. *Military service:* U.S. Air Force, 1954-56; became first lieutenant. *Member:* Football Writers Association of America (member of board of directors), Society of Professional Journalists/Sigma Delta Chi (former president; St. Louis chapter), Mid-America Press Institute (board member and former chairman).

WRITINGS: Maybe I'll Pitch Forever: The Autobiography of LeRoy (Satchel) Paige as Told to David Lipman, Doubleday, 1962; *Mr. Baseball: The Story of Branch Rickey,* Putnam, 1966; *Ken Boyer,* Putnam, 1967; *Joe Namath: A Football Legend,* Putnam, 1968; (with Ed Wilks) *Speed Kings: The Story of Bob Hayes,* Putnam, 1971; (with Ed Wilks) *Bob Gibson: Pitching Ace,* Putnam, 1975; (with wife, Marilyn Lipman) *Jim Hart: Underrated Quarterback,* Putnam, 1977.

DAVID LIPMAN

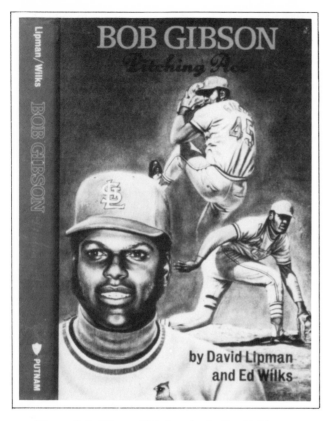

(From *Bob Gibson: Pithcing Ace* by David Lipman and Ed Wilkes. Jacket illustrated by Barbara Higgins Bond.)

WORK IN PROGRESS: A biography of Bob Hayes, for Putnam; a biography of Bob Gibson, for Putnam.

HOBBIES AND OTHER INTERESTS: Hunting.

LOEB, Robert H., Jr.   1917-

PERSONAL: Born November 1, 1917, in New York, N.Y.; son of Robert H. (a stockbroker) and Irma (Fried) Loeb; first marriage, 1937, ended in divorce; married Bette Harmon, September 6, 1943 (deceased); married Jeanne Starr (a dance teacher), July 2, 1964; children: (second marriage) Karen, Robert H. III. *Education:* Attended schools in Switzerland for four years as a boy; student at Brown University for three and one-half years (quit in senior year); later took courses at Columbia University. *Politics:* "Cultural Materialist." *Religion:* Episcopalian. *Home address:* R.R. 2, Box 88, Pomfret Center, Conn. 06259. *Agent:* Raines & Raines, 475 Fifth Ave., New, York, N.Y. 10017.

CAREER: Worked on Wall Street for several years; *Esquire,* Chicago, Ill., 1944-47, began as promotion man, became aviation, games, cook, and drink editor; Pegasus Books, Inc. (mail order publishing business), Chicago, president, 1947-50; Norman, Craig & Kummel Agency, New York City, copywriter, 1952-54; Ted Bates & Co., New York City, copywriter, 1954-66; full-time writer, 1966—. *Military service:* Royal Canadian Air Force and U.S. Army Air Forces during World War II (long since a pacifist). *Member:* Episcopal Peace fellowship.

WRITINGS: Wolf in Chef's Clothing: The Picture Cook and Drink Book for Men, Wilcox & Follett, 1950, published as *The New Wolf in Chef's Clothing,* Follett, 1958; *Date Bait: The Younger Set's Picture Cookbook,* Wilcox & Follett, 1952; *She Cooks to Conquer,* Funk, 1952; *He-Manners* (juvenile), Association Press, 1954, revised edition, 1970; *Nip Ahoy: The Picture Bar Guide,* Wilcox & Follett, 1954; *Mary Alden's Cook Book for Children,* Wonder Books, 1955; *She-Manners* (juvenile), Association Press, 1959, revised edition, 1970; *Manners for Minors,* Association Press, 1964; *How to Wine Friends and Affluent People,* Follett, 1965; *Manners at Work: How They Help You Toward Career Success,* Association Press, 1967; *The Sins of Bias* (juvenile), M. Evans, 1970; *His and Hers Dating Manners* (juvenile), Association Press, 1970; *Manners to Love by for Young Couples,* Association Press, 1971; *Your Legal Rights as a Minor,* F. Watts, 1974; *New England Village: Everyday Life in 1810,* Doubleday, 1977; *Your Guide to Voting,* F. Watts, 1977; *Breaking the Sex-Role Barrier,* F. Watts, 1977; *Crime and Capital Punishment,* F. Watts, 1978; *Meet the Real Pilgrim,* Doubleday, 1979; *Marriage: For Better or Worse,* F. Watts, 1980.

WORK IN PROGRESS: The Gynecological Hex—from Eve to Today, a study of the effects of macho medicine from prehistoric times to today and what women can do, an adult book; *Ms. or His: Your Right to Be You,* a book for young adults about the biological and social pressures which determine one's gender, for F. Watts; a satirical novel subsidized by a small grant from the Connecticut Commission on the Arts.

ROBERT H. LOEB, JR.

SIDELIGHTS: "All of my nonfiction books since 1971 (with the exception of the novel for which I received a grant from the Connecticut Commission on the Arts) have been for the young adult and juvenile audiences and have tried to instill these readers with an awareness of social trends and problems of the past and those of the present. I feel very strongly that the great majority of our schools do little, if anything, to make students aware of the realities which exist in today's world. Television and the mass media only add to the 'myth-conceptions.' All of the additional titles I have listed, are an attempt to pierce through this fog of misinformation. Unfortunately, because of my approach, none of these books enjoy great sales. And in the majority of instances, their distribution is limited to schools and libraries.

"Furthermore, the line of demarcation between young adult and adult reading material is tenuous. Consequently, I am now switching to doing adult books (with the same purpose) in the hope that they will be given greater distribution.

"I have been greatly influenced in my approach by the late Professor Ernest Becker and currently by Professor Marvin Harris. I consider my nonfiction writing as ninety percent research and scholarship and ten percent writing craftsmanship. My creative outlet is fiction writing, none of which has ever been published. Why? I look at the current, popular fiction list and shudder. And still hope to find a sensitive, literate editor who'll take a chance and possibly lose his job.

"In 1972 my wife and I fled from southern Connecticut to northeast Connecticut and a rural area. We try to heat our house as much as possible with a wood stove which entails 'harvesting' one's own wood—exercise. In addition, I work out at a gym three times a week, play tennis (singles, despite my venerable years). My reading is chiefly confined to sociological subjects. I have a son and daughter each of whom have two children. I am not an ideal grandfather as I'm too preoccupied with my writing and envisioning the end of the world. Situated less than forty miles from two nuclear power plants adds little optimism."

LORD, John Vernon   1939-

PERSONAL: Born April 9, 1939, in Glossop, England; son of Herbert Vernon (a baker) and Isobel Marjorie (a hairdresser; maiden name, Smith) Lord; married Lorna Deanna Trevelyan (a nurse and artist), August 20, 1961; children: Rachel Joanna, Katie Ruhamah, Corin Derry. *Education:* Salford Art School, D.A., 1960; attended Central School of Arts and Crafts, London, England, 1960-61. *Home and office:* Upwell, 4 Orchard Lane, Ditchling, Hassocks, Sussex BN6 8TH, England.

CAREER: Has worked as a chef, sandwich-board man, postman, factory worker; free-lance book illustrator, 1960—; Brighton Polytechnic, Faculty of Art & Design, Brighton, England, principal lecturer in drawing and illustration, 1961—. Member of graphic design panel of National Council for Diplomas in Art and Design. *Member:* Society of Illustrators.

WRITINGS—Self-illustrated children's books: (with Janet Burroway) *The Giant Jam Sandwich*, J. Cape, 1972, Hough-

ton, 1973; *The Run-away Rollerskate*, Houghton, 1974; *Mr. Mead and His Garden*, Houghton, 1974; (with Conrad Aiken) *Who's Zoo*, Atheneum, 1977; (with Fay Maschler) *Miserable Aunt Bertha*, J. Cape, 1980.

Illustrator: Lena F. Hurlong, *Adventures of Jaboti on the Amazon*, Abelard-Schuman, 1968; Joseph Jacobs, *Reynard the Fox*, as retold by Roy Brown, Abelard-Schuman, 1969; Janet Burroway, *The Truck on the Track*, J. Cape, 1970, Bobbs-Merrill, 1971; Ann Coates, *Dinosaurs Don't Die*, Longman Young, 1970; Joel Chandler Harris, *The Adventures of Brer Rabbit*, British Broadcasting Company, 1972; Rosemary Sutcliffe, *Sword at Sunset*, Heron Books, 1975.

WORK IN PROGRESS: Certain aspects of children's literature, a short lecture course; illustrating Edward Lear's verses.

SIDELIGHTS: "A good children's book should appeal to child, uncle, Mum, Dad, Grandma, teenager alike and should not be self-consciously written with just the child in mind." *The Giant Jam Sandwich* was dramatized on BBC-TV.

HOBBIES AND OTHER INTERESTS: Music (especially English Tudor composers, Monteverdi, Bach, Purcell), gardening, natural history (especially bird-watching), walking in the country, keeping geese and hens.

JOHN VERNON LORD

(From *The Giant Jam Sandwich,* story and pictures by John Vernon Lord. Verses by Janet Burroway.)

LUGARD, Flora Louisa Shaw   1852-1929
(Flora Louisa Shaw)

PERSONAL: Born in 1852, in Dublin, Ireland; died January 25, 1929, in Surrey, England; daughter of a British Army general; married Frederick Lugard (a colonial administrator), June, 1902. *Education:* Educated at private schools. *Home:* Little Parkhurst, Abinger Common, Surrey, England.

CAREER: Journalist, novelist, and author of books for children. Member of the staff of the *Pall Mall Gazette, Review of Reviews,* where she edited French periodicals, and the London *Times,* later becoming head of its colonial department. During World War I, she worked on behalf of Belgian refugees as co-founder of the War Refugees Commission and founder of the Lady Lugard Hospitality Commission. *Awards, honors:* Dame Commander of the Order of the British Empire, 1918.

WRITINGS—For children: *Castle Blair: A Story of Youthful Days,* [London], 1878, Roberts Brothers, 1881 [other editions illustrated by I. and H. Whitney, D. C. Heath, 1902; George Varian, Little, Brown, 1923; Carol Everest, Hart-Davis, 1966]; *Phyllis Browne,* [London], 1882, Roberts Brothers, 1886; *Hector: A Story for Young People* (illustrated by W. J. Hennessy), G. Bell, 1883, Roberts Brothers, 1887.

Other: *A Sea Change* (story), G. Munro, 1885; *Colonel Cheswick's Campaign* (novel), Longmans, 1886; *Letters from South Africa,* Macmillan, 1893; *Letters from Queensland,* Macmillan, 1893; *The Story of Australia,* H. Marshall, circa 1898; *A Tropical Dependency: An Outline of the Ancient History of the Western Soudan with an Account of the Modern Settlement of Northern Nigeria,* J. Nisbet, 1905, reissued, Barnes & Noble, 1965; *The Work of the War Refugees Committee* (address given to the Royal Society of Arts, March 24, 1915), G. Bell, 1915.

SIDELIGHTS: **1852.** Born in Dublin, Ireland, the third of fourteen children. Lugard was educated primarily by her mother (to read French), governess and older brother and sister. At the age of thirteen, she and sister, Mimi were responsible for the education of their younger siblings, for

housekeeping duties, and for the care of their ailing mother. These burdens led Lugard to an exhausted state of health that left her lungs in a seriously weakened condition. She was sent to her aunt in France to recuperate.

According to her biographer, literary associate, and friend, C. Moberly Bell: ''In 1869 Flora came out, and plunged into the gaieties of her first season. That these were extensive and delightful may well be believed. All the circumstances were favorable. At Woolwich she was the daughter of a distinguished senior officer, at Kimmage the grand-daughter of a much respected landowner. She shared the pleasures and excitements with Mimi, best of sisters and companions. She was a lovely girl, with her vivid colouring, her charming voice and manners and graceful figure. She was intelligent without a trace of the blue-stocking, and bore herself with a childish dignity entirely devoid of self-consciousness which was very captivating. It was no wonder that she was much in demand, that more than one young man wanted to marry her. Perhaps she was not heart whole, perhaps there was a certain fastidiousness in her taste which made it difficult to satisfy. Be that as it may, she would have none of them.'' [C. Moberly Bell, *Flora Shaw,* Constable and Co., Ltd., 1947.[1]]

1870. Sister Mimi, married and mother died.

Lugard worked in the East London slum section. ''It is not possible to look round in this part of London without a numbing sensation of despair. . . . The beauty of many of the children, the brightness of the young people, only seems in one mood to make it worse. Notwithstanding the natural human charm they are to be drawn into the whirlpool of sin, they are to become inhuman and degraded, and the laws which make this so are too strong for us. Private charity, while I admire it, seems to me utterly insufficient. It is like bailing out the sea with a tea-cup, or trying to sweep up the sands of the shore . . . the head tells me all the time that this kind of work is a satisfaction of the heart, but no real remedy.

''It is not the sacrifice of one life which will suffice, but the sacrifice, the aspirations, and the efforts of perhaps many, in many ages; yet the sacrifice of one has its place in the universal movement.''[1]

1886-1888. Traveled to Spain. "The effect of crossing the Straits appeared not unlike the effect of crossing the Flood." She felt herself to be "wandering through history so old that England became a modern intruder."[1]

Wrote travel articles for the *Pall Mall Gazette*.

1892. Traveled to Africa. ". . . Ordinary dirt is no name for the condition in which you descend from an African coach on a dusty day. Hair, eyes, teeth are full of gritty sand, and so far as your appearance goes, you might be carted away by mistake for a roadside sweeping.

"The streets [of Praetoria] are planted largely with weeping willows, and in the summer I am told that every garden hedge is a mass of roses. Children are coming out from school. There is a generally settled, quiet domestic aspect which contrasts strangely with Johannesburg. I observe that most of the advertisements are in English.

"I doubt whether in Johannesburg you would find a dozen men who, if they know, care for the difference between a violin and a vegetable.

"Johannesburg at present has no politics. It is much too busy with material problems. It is hideous and detestable, luxury without order, sensual enjoyment without art, riches without refinement, display without dignity. Everything, in fact, which is most foreign to the principles alike of morality and taste by which decent life has been guided in every stage of civilisation."[1]

Of a farm outside of Johannesburg, she wrote: "The fence is 24 miles round, so you can imagine the size. If I were to tell you all that grows within the fence and the rapidity with which it grows you would think I am romancing; acres of corn and wood and root crops, acres, too, of vines and monkey nuts besides acres of peach and apricot, apple, quince, orange and plum. There were fields of melon, which are used for feeding cattle, and hedges of fruit trees along the running streams. There were tea and sugar cane as well as turnips and mangold wurzel. There seemed to be no product of any climate from the Arctic to the Tropical which did not thrive. Nothing seemed to impress on me more vividly the rapidity with which the place had sprung into being than the simple fact that after hours of driving through vineyards, trees and cornfields we were met at the door of the house by a baby of 2½ who was older than everything we had seen. When she was born the spot on which it stands was nothing but bare veldt."[1]

1893. Traveled to Australia as a correspondent for *The Times*. ". . . A long wearisome journey, hour after hour through grass and gum trees with occasionally a station or a township with surrounding downs to break the solitude. The sum of isolation and monotony strangely depressing, almost—one could easily fancy—brutalising. The townships and stations the ugliest things in the way of human habitation that I have seen, for they haven't even the picturesque character of a Native African Settlement. . . .

"Hideously ugly, fairly clean, people most kindly. Building like a stable of corrugated iron, standing without garden yard or other approach upon ground which a shower of rain had turned into mud. Bedrooms like loose boxes with partitions that didn't go up to the roof and had the advantage of giving air combined with the publicity of hearing any sound in your neighbour's division. Food is everywhere plentiful and rough.

FLORA LOUISA SHAW LUGARD

"Every day we were up at sunrise and out as soon as the horses could be caught. There were days in which we did 70 miles driving all day till evening, and others on which we did only 30. The short days usually included sights to see in the shape of shearing sheds or a Bush township with perhaps an artesian bore—and generally much talk."[1]

Father died. "I am glad to be alone, to try to realise all by myself what has happened, and that another chapter of life is finished. One death brings all deaths so close."[1]

Sent to Canada for *The Times* with a stop over in San Francisco. "Women of apparently the upper classes outrageously dressed, covered with diamonds on all possible occasions, everybody flashed and glittered till you resented the fact that you were driven to dislike the sight of a stone which is in itself so beautiful. Of the men, I took my impression, I must admit, largely from the newspapers, edited presumably to suit their taste, and filled with pages and pages of police court, racing and mining records, but scarcely a paragraph of serious news or political information. Scarcely a sign of any interest whatsoever in the great world outside California; and as though the vulgarity of their own society were not quite enough, foreign telegrams, when they did appear, were usually headed 'Fiendish Crime,' 'Shocking Outrage!,' 'Social Scandal!' The multitude, as you meet it in the streets and trains and tramcars, with its women and children incessantly chewing gum, men spitting . . . does not tend to modify the disagreeable impression of having got hopelessly astray in one vast servants' hall from which there was no escape. However, of course, I am well aware that this is only a first and uncharitable impression which would wear off under the human influence of closer acquaintance. I fancy, also, that the special vulgarity is peculiar to San Francisco, a town which, with one of the loveliest situations in the world, with all its wealth, its palatial hotels, its gaudy dress—and I must admit its delicious food—has not a single public square or monument that reserves the name. Portland, only a quarter the size, was already different. There, to my relief, I saw women wearing shabby clothes, the broad streets were planted with trees, the finest buildings were neither hotels nor private houses and life seemed to get back to human dignity again."[1]

1893. The four Shaw sisters established themselves in an old-fashioned house in Cambridge Street, Warwick Square, London. Lugard was financially responsible for the venture. This household arrangement survived happily for eight years.

1896. Sister, Mimi, died. C. Moberly Bell related that: "For weeks Flora was entirely absorbed in her anxiety for her beloved sister, and when Mimi died Flora was for a moment stunned by the loss. Mimi had meant more to her than any member of the family; in the last few years, indeed, Lulu had been a closer companion and perhaps a more intimate friend, but Mimi was the sister of her youth; they had grown up together, they had been little girls together at Kimmage, and shared the joys of 'coming out' and the excitement of early love affairs; together they had nursed their ailing mother and looked after the younger sisters and brothers. There is a closeness in such a relationship that nothing can disturb; though Mimi's marriage and Flora's career had led them in widely different directions the bond had remained and its severance was a very real grief. In losing Mimi, Flora lost a part of herself, and it was the final closing of the door on her youth."[1]

1898. Sent by *The Times* to Canada to make a serious five month study of industry. All of this was prompted by the discovery of gold in the Klondike.

She wrote to her sister Lulu: "I want you fully to realise that I shall take every necessary precaution, and if you have any qualms reassure yourself by remembering that what *The Times* has sent me for is to send them good letters. If I were to allow myself to come to grief either through exposure or violence, they would get no letters, therefore my first plain duty is to take excellent care of myself. They have not gone to the expense of my journey for the purpose of leaving my bones in Canada."[1]

Her impressions of the semi-arctic landscape were "permanently grey and the whole scene in half-ghostly, dove-coloured tones, grey sea, grey sky, grey hills, dark at the base, which is generally crowded to the water edge and white on the snow-capped tops. To-day we have been passing glaciers by the dozen, and this evening a faint glimmer of the Aurora Borealis came to light the scene. . . . The land is bare of any habitation except a rare Indian settlement upon an island. We seem at times to have left the world behind us and to be steaming solitarily into the Northern sky. There is, however, plenty of animal life, whales spouting round the ship all day, wild duck, geese, puffins, and sea eagles."[1]

1900. Resigned from *The Times* staff. "The strain of the work if I do it seriously, has become too much for my strength, and unless I do it seriously I don't care for it. The doctors have been telling me for some time past that if I go on a breakdown can be only a question of time, it would be so inconvenient to my family if I did break down that it is not weakness but wisdom to withdraw in time."[1]

June, 1902. Married Sir Frederick Lugard, a colonial administrator stationed in Nigeria. Of their journey to West Africa, Lugard wrote: "For the first time in my life, I am in no particular hurry for the voyage to end. . . .

"Time passes on board our own boat rather like a dream. I get often an illusion that we are ourselves standing still and that the scenes on the bank are defiling before us, and it seems to me in my present passive mood to be somewhat typical of life. It's all very gentle and kind and restful and unreal. I have only the dreamish perception of what the next turn in the channel may bring. In the meantime there is much that is pleasant, and I have no wish for to-morrow.

"It is only here that I am able to see what Sir Frederick has really done, and I may confess to you that it satisfies my pride. He has nearly killed himself, and I think a fair proportion of his staff too, with overwork—yet they like it— after all, they are working for an idea—that is more than all men can say. It is a great idea, too, and fills one more and more as one thinks of it—this conception of an Empire which is to be the best place for the exercise of justice and liberty and individual effort which the world has ever seen."[1]

1907. Hilda, Mimi's daughter, to whom Lugard had been a surrogate mother died. According to C. Moberly Bell, "Flora was stunned by the blow. There had not then been two wars to school the older generations to endure the loss of those on whom their hopes for the future are centred, and Hilda's death, at the moment when she was standing on the threshold of a new life promising her so much, seemed almost intolerable. Flora had been present at Hilda's birth, with Mimi she had watched the child grow into girlhood; since Mimi's death she had taken the place of a mother to her. Hilda had learned much from her aunt, her interests and her tastes were greatly influenced by Flora, there had been a close intimacy between them not always realised by mothers and daughters. It is not surprising that in the first hours of her loss she said, 'I don't yet quite know how the future *can* go on without her.'"[1]

1919. Sir Frederick's governship of Nigeria came to an end, and they retired to little Parkhurst Abinger, where family and friends could gather. Easily accessible from London the house was rarely without guests, among them the Joseph Chamberlains, Winston Churchill and old friends from *The Times*.

1926-1927. Recurrence of illness and exhaustion. From this point on her health continued failing. "By the end of the day I am usually tired, and I don't feel like anything but an armchair and a book. In fact, for the body I think as one grows older there is only about half a day. The mind goes on for all the waking hours, but the body gives out.

"Our little home is ever more beautiful to my eyes; I have a penetrating sense of having come at last to the haven where I would be.

"I am so happy that nothing seems to matter. A peace which passeth understanding seems to have come to me. Of course

I don't mean to say that if an Angel came down and said 'Would you like to be strong again?' or 'Would you like to have your sight back?' that I should not be glad. But these things don't seem to matter. I am quite content."[1]

January 25, 1929. Died at Abinger Common, Surrey, England. Bell provided a final profile. "Flora was seventy-six when she died, and though she lived far into the reign of George V, she may fairly be reckoned as a Victorian, and not the least remarkable of the women of that great age. It was an age in which a woman was expected to comport herself with dignity, to make herself as little conspicuous as possible, to value family life above all else, to accept first and foremost the obligations of a wife, a mother, a daughter or a sister, and to regard any other duty as subordinate to these.

"The surprising thing about Flora was that she managed at the same time to fulfil these ideals and to do public work of great importance, gaining for herself an international reputation as a journalist and publicist. . . .

"She made journeys such as no other woman had then made, filled a position in journalism unique for a woman, wrote articles which had a real influence on the course of public affairs, worked early and late, driving with matchless courage a body ill-adapted for such labours in order to support more than one family, while she kept her private life out of the public eye. She enjoyed her work, and since it is not in human nature to be indifferent to success, she enjoyed also the knowledge that among all connected with public affairs her reputation stood high."[1]

FOR MORE INFORMATION: Stanley J. Kunitz and Howard Haycraft, editors, *Junior Book of Authors,* H. W. Wilson, 1934; S. J. Kunitz, editor, *British Authors of the Nineteenth Century,* H. W. Wilson, 1936; C. Moberly Bell, *Flora Shaw— Lady Lugard D.B.E.,* Constable, 1947.

MARSHALL, S(amuel) L(yman) A(twood) 1900-1977

PERSONAL: Born July 18, 1900, in Catskill, N.Y.; died December 17, 1977 in El Paso, Texas; son of Caleb Carey (a brickmaker) and Alice Medora (Beeman) Marshall; married Ruth Elstner (deceased); married Edith Ives Westervelt (died, 1952); married Catherine Finnerty, March 10, 1954; children: (first marriage) Samuel Lyman Atwood, Jr.; (third marriage) Sharon, Catherine, Bridget; (stepdaughter) Mrs. Pat Troiano. *Education:* Attended Texas College of Mines (now Texas Western University). *Religion:* Episcopalian. *Residence:* 2909 Stone Edge, El Paso, Tex. 79904.

CAREER: As a youth, Marshall acted for the Western Essanay Co., 1913-15; during most of his life, his careers in the military and writing have run parallel to each other; U.S. Army, enlisted, June 11, 1917, participating, during World War I, in campaigns in the Soissons, St. Mihiel, Meuse-Argonne, and Ypres-Lys, as well as instructor in grenades, gas warfare, bayonets, demolitions, and minor tactics; commissioned first lieutenant, 1921, resigning, November 11, 1922; served in the Texas National Guard, 1922-27; *El Paso Herald,* El Paso, Tex., sports editor, later city editor, 1923-27; North American Newspaper Alliance, foreign correspondent, 1927-35; *Detroit News,* Detroit, Mich., editorial writer, military

S. L. A. MARSHALL

critic, and foreign correspondent, 1927-62; war correspondent during the Spanish Civil War, 1936-37; consultant to the Secretary of War, 1942; reentered the Army during World War II as a major and was assigned Chief of Orientation; transferred to the Historical Division of the War Department; appointed Chief Combat Historian and served in the Central Pacific, 1943, participating in the invasions of the Gilbert and Marshall Islands; transferred to Europe, 1944, covering all airborne operations of the Normandy invasion; named Chief Historian of the European Theater of Operations, serving on the staff of the supreme commander, 1945-46; participant in the campaigns of Normandy and Brittany, the Siege of Brest, the Airborne Invasion of Holland, the Ruhr Encirclement, and battles in East Germany; returned to the U.S., 1946, and left the Army on May 8, 1946; recalled to active duty, May-July, 1946, to research the formation of the North Atlantic Alliance; served in Korea, 1950-51, as an infantry operations analyst with the Eighth Army, and with the Operations Research Office; commissioned as Brigadier General, August 1, 1951; retired, 1960; war correspondent, Korea, 1953, Sinai War, Israel-Egypt, 1956, Lebanon, 1958, South Vietnam; correspondent in the Middle East and Congo, 1961; with the U.S. Army in Vietnam, 1966-67, and consultant to the Pentagon during the war. Member of the U.S. Army Historical Advisory Commission, the Public Relations Commission, the Michigan Civil Defense Commission, the Chancellor's Council of the University of Texas, and a trustee of the Detroit chapter of the American Red Cross.

MEMBER: Sons of the American Revolution, Society of American Historians, Military Order of World Wars, Association of the U. S. Army, American Legion, Veterans of Foreign Wars, Coffee House Club (New York City), Detroit

Press Club, Bloomfield (Mich.) Hunt Club. *Awards, honors—* Military; U.S.: Distinguished Service Medal; Legion of Merit; Bronze Star medal with oak leaf cluster; Citation Medal with oak leaf clusters; Combat Infantry Badge; German Occupation World War I; German Occupation World War II; Pacific Theater; Vistory, Pacific, Africa-Middle East-European, Korean, and UN Korean medals; France: Legion of Honor; Croix de Guerre with Palm; Ordre d'Armee; Belgium: Order d'Leopold with Palm; Croix de Guerre with Palm; Ardennes medal; Italy: Croci di Guerra; Fatigue di Guerra; Ethiopia: Infantry Combat medal; Israel: Medallion of Valor. Civilian: Elected to the National Cowboy Hall of Fame, 1972; honorary fellow, Bar Ilan University; L.H.D., Wayne State University; LL.D., St. Bonaventure University.

WRITINGS: Blitzkrieg: Its History, Strategy, Economics, and the Challenge to America, W. Morrow, 1940; *Armies on Wheels,* W. Morrow, 1941; *Island Victory,* Penguin, 1944; *Bastogne: The Story of the First Eight Days in Which the 101st Airborne Division was Closed within the Ring of German Forces,* Infantry Journal Press, 1946; *Men Against Fire: The Problem of Battle Command in Future War,* Infantry Journal Press, 1947, reissued, W. Morrow, 1961; (contributor) Leonard Rapport, *Rendezvous with Destiny,* Infantry Journal Press, 1947; *The Price of Peace,* Washington and Jefferson College Press, 1948; *The Soldier's Load and the Mobility of a Nation,* Combat Forces Press, 1950; *The Armed Forces Officer,* Department of Defense, 1950, reissued as *The Officer as a Leader,* Stackpole Books, 1966; *The River and the Gauntlet: Defeat of the Eighth Army by the Chinese Communist Forces, November, 1950, in the Battle of the Chongchon River,* W. Morrow, 1953, reprinted, Greenwood Press, 1970; *Pork Chop Hill: The American Fighting Men in Action, Korea, Spring, 1953,* W. Morrow, 1956; *Sinai Victory: Command Decisions in History's Shortest War, Israel's Hundred-Hour Conquest of Egypt East of Suez, Autumn, 1956,* W. Morrow, 1958.

Night Drop: The American Airborne Invasion of Normandy (preface by Carl Sandburg; illustrated by H. Garver Miller), Little, Brown, 1962; (with Al Hine) *D-Day: The Invasion of Europe* (juvenile), Harper, 1962; *The Military History of the Korean War* (juvenile), F. Watts, 1963; *Battle at Best* (illustrated by H. G. Miller), W. Morrow, 1964; *The American Heritage History of World War I,* American Heritage Press, 1964, reissued as *World War I,* 1971 (an edition adapted by Robert Leckie for young children published as *The Story of World War I,* Random House, 1965); *The War to Free Cuba: The Military History of the Spanish-American War,* F. Watts, 1966; *Sinai Victory: Command Decisions in History's Shortest War,* W. Morrow, 1967; *A Special Study of South Africa: The Strategic View,* American-African Affairs Association, 1967; *Swift Sword: The Historical Record of Israel's Victory, June, 1967,* American Heritage Press, 1967; *Battles in the Monsoon: Campaigning in the Central Highlands, Vietnam, Summer, 1966,* W. Morrow, 1967; *West to Cambodia,* Cowles, 1968; *Bird: The Christmastide Battle,* Cowles, 1968; *Ambush: The Battle of Dau Tieng,* Cowles, 1969; (with Stephen Sears) *The Battle of the Bulge* (juvenile), American Heritage Press, 1969; *The Fields of Bamboo: Dong Tre, Trung Luong, and Hoa Hoi, Three Battles Just beyond the South China Sea,* Dial, 1971; *Crimsoned Prairie: The Wars between the United States and the Plains Indians during the Winning of the West,* Scribner, 1972.

Also author of *Makin,* 1947; *The Mobility of One Man,* 1949; *Critique of Weapons and Tactics in Korea,* 1952; *Hill 440,* 1952; *Tactics in Defense against Atomic Attack,* 1954; *First*

Book on Korea, 1964; *Vietnam Primer,* 1967; *History of World War II,* 1969; and *On Urban Warfare,* 1973; and numerous military texts and manuals.

Military contributor to *American College Dictionary, Crowell-Collier Encyclopaedia, Encyclopaedia Britannica,* and *U.S. Navy Annual Review;* contributor of articles on technical studies to *Combat Forces Journal, Marine Corps Gazette, Military Quarterly,* and other military periodicals; also contributor to *Reporter, New York Times Book Review, Collier's,* and *Harper's;* syndicated newspaper columnist, with articles appearing in the *Washington Post, Los Angeles Times,* and others; lecturer at the National War College, Air University, Armed Service Information School, the Infantry School, and the Armored School.

ADAPTATIONS—Movie: "Pork Chop Hill" (motion pictures), United Artists, starring Gregory Peck, 1959.

SIDELIGHTS: **July 18, 1900.** Born in Catskill, New York, Marshall was the son of a British born brickmaker. His mother was a member of an old American family that dated to the Revolutionary period. Marshall described his father as a man who could do all things well "but make money."

By the age of five Marshall had taught himself to read and write by copying tombstones in a local churchyard. By age seven he was reading Doyle, Dickens, Haggard, Hocking, Alger, and Henry.

June 11, 1917. Enlisted in the United States Army. During World War I Marshall gained distinction as the youngest second lieutenant in the Army. Five years later, in November, 1922, he resigned his commission and began his career as a reporter on the El Paso *Herald.* From 1923 to 1927 he worked on the *Herald* as a sports and city editor, and was also a member to the Texas National Guard.

1936-1937. Served as a war correspondent during the Spanish Civil War.

1942. Named chief of orientation for the Army. Marshall established the Army News Service and was credited with organizing the Army's wartime research methods in the development of tactical weapons.

April, 1945. Named Chief Historian, European Theater of Operations and served on the staff of the Supreme Commander.

1946. Left the army to write, but was recalled in 1948.

1951. Commissioned as Brigadier General. As a correspondent or active participant, Marshall claimed to have gone to twenty-one wars.

1960. Retired from active service, but continued as a consultant to the Pentagon in the Vietnam War. The author of nearly thirty books and hundreds of articles, Marshall wrote extensively on World War II, the Korean and Vietnam Wars, conflicts in the Middle East and other major battles. "I am described as a hawk by a lot of people, but I have not been a hawk. I can't think in those terms. I can only think in terms that are practical in the waging of warfare against an enemy of the United States. You don't play around with war." [Tom Ferrell, "If the Silent Majority Could Talk, What Would It Say?" *Esquire,* May, 1970.[1]]

1966-1967. Consultant to the Pentagon during the Vietnam War. Marshall stirred criticism by attacking the American press corps in Saigon in his book, *Battles in the Monsoon.* "I have noticed one thing in this war that I did not note in any other, and that is that when a paper takes an anti-war position, its correspondents get the idea and go down the line looking for stories that are going to color public opinion against the war. I've never seen this before."[1]

1974. Moved to El Paso, Texas. Marshall once remarked of his four children that they satisfied his only boyhood ambition—to have a family.

December 17, 1977. Died of heart failure at the William Beaumont Army Medical Center at Fort Bliss in El Paso, Texas, after a year of hospitalization. "I don't want to be misunderstood. I never qualify with 'maybes,' 'buts,' and 'on-the-other-hands.' I'd rather be proved wrong than vague." ["Who's Retiring?," *Newsweek*, August 15, 1960.[2]]

Marshall developed the technique of doing battlefield history by interviewing survivors about its operations soon after an encounter. "Marshall specialized in the small-unit type of action where he would talk to the people involved and elicit the details of what had happened," explained Brigadier General James L. Collins, Jr. to the *Washington Post.* "He was very good at putting it down in a vivid way, and made people read things that professional historians might make dry as dust." According to *Time,* "His writing was distinguished by narrative drive, a gritty attention to the details of combat, and a plain-spoken sympathy for the men who suffered on the front lines."

Pork Chop Hill, Marshall's account of the Korean War is probably his best known work. Called a "moving and stirring record," by *Kirkus,* the *New York Times* went on to describe it as "a distinguished contribution to the literature of war. It may be doubted whether Stephen Crane or Ambrose Bierce have ever written with such sustained realism about combat. . . ."

In critiquing *Battle at Best,* a *Reporter* critic made the following observations, which can also apply to Marshall's intentions in all of his books: "What S.L.A. Marshall writes about is rarely to be found in legend, traditional history, or fiction. His soldiers are not protagonists who inferentially represent all who fight in a war or battle. Marshall fills the gap between the impersonality of history and the overpersonality of fiction. He writes not of representative heroes but of all the soldiers in their own terms. He records deeds of heroism and acts of cowardice, and the far more common combat situation of inexplicable inactivity and misdirected overactivity. . . ."

HOBBIES AND OTHER INTERESTS: Polo, horse show judging, music, and collecting porcelains.

FOR MORE INFORMATION SEE: Current Biography, H. W. Wilson, 1953; "Grand Slam," *Newsweek,* June 13, 1955; *Kirkus,* October 1, 1956; *New York Times,* November 18, 1956; "Who's Retiring?" *Newsweek,* August 15, 1960; *Reporter,* May 7, 1964; T. Ferrell, "If the Silent Majority Could Talk, What Would It Say?" *Esquire,* May, 1970; John Wakeman, editor, *World Authors: 1950-1970,* Wilson, 1975.

Obituaries: *New York Times,* December 18, 1977; *Washington Post,* December 18, 1977; *Time,* December 26, 1977; *Newsweek,* January 2, 1978.

MARTIN, Lynne 1923-

PERSONAL: Born August 8, 1923, in Flushing, N.Y.; daughter of Charles J. (a carpenter) and Lee (Steurer) Svec; married Joseph B. Martin (an engineer), September 11, 1948; children: Peter, Priscilla, Laura, Joe, Jim, Ursula, Pamela. *Education:* Educated in public high school in Flushing, N.Y. *Residence:* Roslyn Heights, N.Y.

CAREER: Publicity writer for advertising agencies and public relations firms, 1942-50; free-lance writer, 1950—.

WRITINGS—Juvenile: *Amazing Animal Appetites,* Criterion, 1966; *Museum Menagerie,* Criterion, 1971; *The Giant Panda* (Junior Literary Guild selection), Addison-Wesley, 1972; *The Orchid Family,* Morrow, 1974; *Peacocks,* Morrow, 1975; *Bird of the Open Seas,* Morrow, 1976. Author of monthly column "Diary of a Mother," in *Modern Baby,* 1950-55. Contributor of articles to popular magazines and to *Science Digest* and *International Wildlife.*

SIDELIGHTS: Martin writes that she spends her time "introducing our children to the world."

The peacock is famous for his fancy feathers, proud bearing and stately strut. ■(From *Peacocks* by Lynne Martin. Illustrated by Lydia Rosier.)

McMURTREY, Martin A(loysius) 1921-

PERSONAL: Born April 16, 1921, in East St. Louis, Ill.; son of Martin William (a clerk) and Alice (Coever) McMurtrey. *Education:* University of Dayton, B.A., 1942; St. Louis University, M.Ed., 1949. *Religion:* Roman Catholic. *Home:* 808 Camden, San Antonio, Tex. 78215. *Office:* Central Catholic High School, 1403 North St. Marys, San Antonio, Tex. 78215.

CAREER: Entered Brothers of Mary, 1939; teacher in St. Louis, Chicago, and Belleville, Ill., 1939-50; Central Catholic High School, San Antonio, Tex., teacher of English, creative writing, and drafting, and football coach, 1945-54.

WRITINGS: Loose to the Wilds (novel for young people), Harper, 1976.

WORK IN PROGRESS: Us, a novel for young people and *Las Posadas* (title means "The Shelters"), a novel about a boy Mexican wetback trying to come in to the United States.

SIDELIGHTS: "I have been very fortunate in my relatives, particularly brothers and sisters, aunts, and grandparents. As far back as I can recall, I see myself trotting after my grandfather along the Mississippi River bluffs of Monroe County, Illinois. The world he introduced me to was a great green forest overlooking a wide brown river. He knew each wild bird and made me acquainted with it so that I might have another everlasting friend. Indian mounds, steamboats, river barges, bootlegger stills—for all of these my grandfather had a special story.

"Later his daughter, my aunt, continued my education in a very practical way: we went fishing, picked blackberries, and found mushrooms together. Her story I idealized and fictionalized in the juvenile novel, *Loose to the Wilds.* The character Aunt Jay in that book is not my real aunt, but she could have been; the boy she civilizes and educates in that story is not myself, but I wish he were. Still, there are some incidents, even some complete chapters in this book when my real aunt and I might have been photographed as we walked the Levee Road home from a day of fishing—and she caught more fish than I.

"I like to build characters by composites: they walk like this person, talk like that one; have this one's blue eyes, that one's half smile. Then, the soul I breathe into them is part of myself. Though I make long graphs of character traits that run throughout the planned book, still, I hope for my characters to come alive themselves and rebel or reject my contrivances. I plan their lives minutely, but they must fight free to independence. Until my characters reject my providence, they do not achieve their own personality.

"There is much ado these days about conservation and ecology. In my stories nature is a character itself. I don't intend any kind of pantheism. Still, because the stories take place in this time and that place, even the trees sometimes have names and effect actions in the story. A flower is important not only because it is part of a pretty setting but also because it helps form the personality of someone like my Aunt Jay. If my story sometimes dips into fantasy, I don't mind."

MONTANA, Bob 1920-1975

OBITUARY NOTICE: Born October 23, 1920, in Stockton, Calif.; died January 4, 1975 of an apparent heart attack while cross-country skiing, near Meredith, N.H. Cartoonist who created the syndicated comic strip "Archie," Montana led his teenage character Archie, along with rival girlfriends Veronica and Betty and friend Jughead, through thirty years of humorous high school shenanigans by pitting them against each other and such establishment foils as Miss Grundy and Principal Weatherbee. *For More Information See: Who's Who in America,* 38th edition, Marquis, 1974; *Who's Who in American Art,* Bowker, 1973. *Obituaries: New York Times,* June 6, 1975; *Newsweek,* January 20, 1975; *Time,* January 20, 1975; *Who Was Who in America,* 6th edition, Marquis, 1976.

MORRISON, Velma Ford 1909- (Hildegarde Ford)

PERSONAL: Born April 30, 1909, in Madrid, Iowa; daughter of William Bruce and Hildegarde Maria (Berg) Ford; married Hugh Pritchard Morrison (president of Pioneer Hi-Bred Corn Co. of Illinois), November 8, 1930; children: Hugh Pritchard, Jr., Mary (Mrs. James Anderson), Sarah (Mrs. Douglas Criner), John. *Education:* Graduated from Drake University, 1928. *Home and office:* Route 5, Princeton, Ill. 61356.

CAREER: Under the direction of Henry Wallace in Des Moines, Iowa, research in genetics, 1927-28, scientific breeding of corn and chicks, 1933-37; elementary teacher in Iowa schools, 1928-33, organizing "opportunity rooms" for teaching physically and mentally handicapped children, 1929-30; Morrison Book Co. (publishers specializing in children's books), Princeton, Ill., president and manager, 1953-70. American Cancer Society, Bureau County chairman, 1955-58, member of Illinois board of directors, 1959-63, district lay director, 1959—; member of county board of directors, Camp Fire Girls, 1950-60. *Member:* Woman's National Book Association, Phi Mu, Woman's Club (Princeton, Ill.; president, 1940-45).

WRITINGS: "My Book" series, five volumes, Morrison Book Co., 1953-54; *Bow Wow,* Morrison Book Co., 1955; *Meow, Meow,* Morrison Book Co., 1955; *My Go to Bed Book,* Morrison Book Co., 1955, revised edition, 1956; *Baby's Animal Book,* Morrison Book Co., 1957, Broadman Press, 1976; *Pat Little Puppy,* Morrison Book Co., 1958; *Herbie,* Morrison Book Co., 1961, revised edition, Harvey House, 1969; *Twinkle, Little Star,* Morrison Book Co., 1961; *Baby's Book,* Morrison Book Co., 1962; *Scrambola,* Harvey House, 1970; *There's Only One You,* Messner, 1978.

WORK IN PROGRESS: Biographical novel about a noted scientist.

SIDELIGHTS: "I have always been fascinated by the wonders of nature. As a young child I had my own experimental garden. I also raised rabbits, bees, and unusual breeds of poultry.

"My first introduction to the science of genetics and to the practical application of Mendel's Laws of Heredity occurred during my freshman year in college when a friend (who later became my husband) and I did some scientific cornbreeding work for the late Henry A. Wallace, one of the foremost

VELMA FORD MORRISON

plant breeders in the country at that time and who would one day become Secretary of Agriculture and Vice-President of the United States. Little did I realize then that my husband and I were beginning an exciting career involving the manipulation of genes.

"Soon thereafter, my husband and I formed a partnership with Henry A. Wallace and Raymond Baker, noted geneticist and head of research for Pioneer Hi-Bred International, to develop the *first true* hybrid chicks by scientific breeding. The chicks we developed are now known all over the world by the trade name, *Hy-Line Chicks*.

"Through this and other work involving the application of the Laws of Heredity, I have been in close touch with the science of genetics.

"My interest in genetics grew with the years. I read and studied everything I could find on the subject and related subjects including medicine, anthropology, archaeology, and agriculture. I studied the works of Darwin, Mendel, Huxley, Dunn, Dobzansky, Stebbins, Emerson, Montagu, and many others.

"My studies of human heredity, anthropology, archaeology, and plants include travels to Mexico, South and Central America, Africa (North, South and East including Egypt), Australia (including The Outback), New Zealand, New

Guinea, the South Pacific Islands, the U.S.S.R. from West Russia to Siberia, the Orient, Thailand, Nepal, India, Iran, Alaska and other places.

"There's a great deal of misunderstanding about human heredity and evolution. Why? First, it has been only in very recent years that the knowledge of heredity has come to us. Second, there are too few trained geneticists, and these few have concentrated on plants, crops and livestock rather than on human beings. Third, *all* levels of our educational system have failed to give adequate training in genetics and human heredity. Most text books are grossly outdated, and most teachers have little if any understanding of the subject. Fourth, most text books have been written in scientific language that only an advanced student of molecular biology can understand. And last, but not least, the mobilization of orthodox religion against the teaching of evolution and the biological sciences has succeeded in depriving much of the public of this knowledge.

"In my writings about heredity I try to separate myth from fact; and to explain in *simple language* what heredity is and how it works. Our young people need to understand how human life takes form and develops. Such understanding when properly used, can help control many of humanity's physical and mental disorders, and help make this world a better place in which to live."

O'CONNOR, Richard　1915-1975
(Frank Archer, John Burke, Patrick Wayland)

OBITUARY NOTICE: Born March 10, 1915, in La Porte, Ind.; died February 15, 1975, in Ellsworth, Me. Author of mysteries, histories, western sagas, and biographies, many of them under the pen names John Burke, Patrick Wayland, and Frank Archer. After a brief career as a Broadway actor, Richard O'Connor worked as a newspaperman in various cities throughout the United States. He published his first biography, *Thomas: Rock of Chickamunga,* in 1948. In the years that followed, O'Connor wrote about 50 books including biographies of such personalities as Patt Garrett, Jack London, Ambrose Bierce, and Alfred E. Smith. For children he also wrote biographies such as *Young Bat Masterson, Gentleman Johnny Burgoyne,* and *The Common Sense of Tom Paine.* The manuscripts of his works have been collected in the University of Maine Library. *For More Information See: Who's Who in the East,* 14th edition, Marquis, 1973; *Who's Who in America,* 38th edition, Marquis, 1974; *Contemporary Authors,* Volume 61-64, Gale, 1976. *Obituaries: Publishers Weekly,* March 3, 1975; *AB Bookman's Weekly,* March 17, 1975; *Contemporary Authors,* Volume 57-60, Gale, 1976.

Between the dark and the daylight,
　When the night is beginning to lower,
Comes a pause in the day's occupations,
　This is known as the Children's Hour.

—Henry Wadsworth Longfellow

JOHN EDWARD OLIVER

OLIVER, John Edward   1933-

PERSONAL: Born October 21, 1933, in Dover, Kent, England; son of Albert Edward and Florence (Allen) Oliver; married Sylvia Oberholzer, August 17, 1957; children: Frances Janine, Andrea Leigh. *Education:* University of London, B.Sc., 1956; University of Exeter, postgraduate certificate in education, 1957; Columbia University, M.A., 1966, Ph.D., 1969. *Religion:* Episcopalian. *Home:* 8282 S. 30 St., Terre Haute, Ind. 47809. *Office:* Department of Geography-Geology, Indiana State University, Terre Haute, Ind. 47809.

CAREER: Willesden Technical College, London, England, lecturer in geography and geology, 1957-58; Warwick Academy, Bermuda, senior master in geography and geology, 1958-65; Columbia University, New York, N.Y., lecturer, 1965-68, assistant professor of physical geography, 1968-72, associate professor, 1973; Indiana State University, Terre Haute, Ind., professor of physical geography, 1973—. *Member:* Royal Geographical Society, American Geographical Society, Association of American Geographers, Sigma Xi, Indiana Academy of Science, American Meteorological Society.

WRITINGS: (With Wreford Watson) *A Geography of Bermuda,* Collins, 1965; *What We Find When We Look at Maps* (juvenile), McGraw, 1970; *Climate and Man's Environment,* John Wiley, 1973; *Perspectives on Applied Physical Geography,* Duxbury, 1977; *Physical Geography: Principles and Applications,* Duxbury, 1979. Contributor to *Cowles Comprehensive Encyclopedia, Encyclopedia of Earth Sciences, Saturday Review, The Hoosier Science Teacher, Alumni*

Magazine, and geography journals. Editor, *Physical Geography,* a quarterly journal.

WORK IN PROGRESS: Climatology: Selected Applications for Winston-Halstead; *Modern Climatology,* for Duxbury.

ORBACH, Ruth Gary   1941-

PERSONAL: Born January 16, 1941, in New York, N.Y.; daughter of Joseph and Francis (Lahn) Gary; married Laurence Orbach (a historian); children: Shannah. *Education:* Attended Antioch College, 1959-61; Boston Museum School of Fine Art, 1961-62; New York University, 1964-69; City University of New York, B.A., 1972; Middlesex Polytechnic, art teacher's certificate, 1978. *Home:* 21 Hartham Rd., London N.7, England.

CAREER: Weaver and fabric designer in New York, N.Y., 1962-63; art teacher and painter in New York City, 1963-68; free-lance designer in New York City and London, England, 1963—; illustrator of children's books in London, England, 1970—; Incident School, New York, N.Y., art teacher,, 1971-72; Quarto Publishing Ltd., London, England, art editor, 1976—; currently teaching illustration at a local art college.

WRITINGS—All self-illustrated children's books: *One Eighth of a Muffin and That Was That,* J. Cape, 1974; *Acorns and Stew,* Collins, 1975, Collins World, 1976; *Apple Pigs,* Collins, 1976, Collins World, 1977; *Please Send a Panda,* Collins World, 1978.

(From *Please Send a Panda* by Ruth Orbach. Illustrated by the author.)

RUTH GARY ORBACH

Illustrator: Brothers Grimm, *Grimm's Fairy Tales,* Ward Lock, 1978.

WORK IN PROGRESS: Two new books for Collins.

SIDELIGHTS: "I write so that I can illustrate—this fact is often overlooked because reviewers tend to be literary people and look only at the words. For young children, however, pictures always come first."

PECK, Robert Newton, III   1928-

PERSONAL: Born February 17, 1928; son of F. Haven and Lucile Peck; married Dorothy Houston (a librarian and painter), 1958; children: Christopher Haven, Anne Houston. *Education:* Rollins College, A.B., 1953; Cornell University, law student. *Religion:* Protestant. *Home:* 500 Sweetwater Club Circle, Longwood, Fla. 32750.

CAREER: Author. *Military service:* U.S. Army, Infantry, 1945-47; served with 88th Division in Italy, Germany, and France.

WRITINGS: A Day No Pigs Would Die, Knopf, 1973; *Path of Hunters:Animal Struggle in a Meadow,* Knopf, 1973; *Millie's Boy,* Knopf, 1973; *Soup,* Knopf, 1974; *Fawn,* Little, Brown, 1975; *Wild Cat,* Holiday House, 1975; *Bee Tree and Other Stuff* (poems), Walker, 1975; *Soup and Me,* Knopf, 1975; *Hamilton,* Little, Brown, 1976; *Hang for Treason,* Doubleday, 1976; *Rabbits and Redcoats,* Walker, 1976; *King of Kazoo* (musical) Knopf, 1976; *Trig,* Little, Brown, 1977; *Last Sunday,* Doubleday, 1977; *The King's Iron,* Little,

Brown, 1977; *Patooie,* Knopf, 1977; *Soup for President,* Knopf, 1978; *Eagle Fur,* Knopf, 1978; *Trig Sees Red,* Little, Brown, 1978; *Basket Case,* Doubleday, 1979; *Hub,* Knopf, 1979; *Mr. Little,* Doubleday, 1979; *Clunie,* Knopf, 1979; *Soup's Drum,* Knopf, 1980.

ADAPTATIONS: Soup and Me was shown as an ABC-TV "After School Special."

SIDELIGHTS: "I am tall and angular, and don't always stand up to a full six-feet-four. I wear mule-ear boots, a ten-gallon hat, Western shirts and weigh not quite 200 pounds.

"Socially, I'm about as sophisticated as a turnip. I play rag-time piano (can't read a note), sing in a barbershop quartet, and have a speaking voice with a Vermont twang that is often akin to a Southern drawl. I'm an expert skier, a dismal dancer, and I love horses.

"I didn't start out to write for any particular age group. I only write about what I know, and if my books turn out to be right for teenagers and/or younger kids as well as for adults, it just happens that way.

"My first book, *A Day No Pigs Would Die,* was influenced by my relationship with my father, an illiterate farmer and

Critters

(From *Bee Tree and Other Stuff* by Robert Newton Peck. Illustrated by Laura Lydecker.)

ROBERT NEWTON PECK III

pig-slaughterer whose earthy wisdom continues to contribute to my understanding of the natural order and the old Shaker beliefs deeply rooted in the land and its harvest.

"Respect for living creatures led to *Path of Hunters,* which examines the poetic yet brutal life and death struggle for survival among small animals in a meadow.

"*Millie's Boy* is a novel that begins with a murder on a cold Vermont night in 1898. It's the story of a boy's search for his mother's killer and for his own identity.

"My *Soup* books reflect my boyhood on a Vermont Farm. I believe that educators are akin to farmers—both are custodians of the green and growing. My first schoolteacher, Miss Kelly, used to say that her garden came to her each morning. In the *Soup* books, Rob and Soup, though abrim with rascality, respect their beloved Miss Kelly, her Vermont virtue—and her ruler.

"Country humor helped produce *Patooie,* the story of a small-town crisis over a most unusual contest—spitting watermelon seeds. Country music and its foot-tapping lyrics helped to inspire *King of Kazoo*, my first musical, written to be produced on stage by children. It's a fantasy about a cantankerous old cowpuncher, a pretty plumber, and a handsome drummer.

"It's not easy writing four books a year, but it sure beats killing hogs."

Peck, his wife, who is a librarian and painter, and their two children, live in Longwood, Florida. He describes his daughter as an 'angelic ballerina'' and his son as a ''noise with dirt on it.'' Peck, who is an alumnus of Rollins College, is director of the Rollins College Writers Conference each February.

FOR MORE INFORMATION SEE: Horn Book, August and October, 1973, April and December, 1976.

PERKINS, Marlin   1905-

PERSONAL: Born March 28, 1905, in Carthage, Mo.; son of Joseph Dudley (a judge) and Mynta Mae (Miller) Perkins; married Elise More, September 12, 1933 (divorced October, 1953); married Carol M. Cotsworth, August 13, 1960; children: (first marriage) Suzanne. *Education:* University of Missouri, student, 1924-26. *Politics:* Republican. *Religion:* Episcopalian. *Address:* 520 N. Michigan Ave., Chicago, Ill. 60611.

CAREER: St. Louis Zoo, St. Louis, Mo., curator of reptiles, 1926-38, director, 1962-70, director emeritus, 1970—; Buffalo Zoo, Buffalo, N.Y., curator, 1938-44; Lincoln Park Zoo, Chicago, Ill., director, 1944-62. Originator of the television programs ''Zoo Parade,'' 1949-57, and (with Don Meier) ''Wild Kingdom,'' 1962—; member of Hillary's Expedition on Yeti Investigation, Himalayas, 1960. *Member:* International Union of Zoological Gardens Directors, World Wildlife Fund, East African Wildlife Society, American Society of

How wonderful it was to play, cool and secret, in a clean, new house. The pale yellow grass smelled of the sun and the wind; the red sand was soft and warm.
■(From *I Saw You from Afar* by Carol Morse Perkins and Marlin Perkins.)

MARLIN PERKINS

Ichthyologists and Herpetologists, American Association of Zoological Parks and Aquariums, Adventurers Club (Chicago), Explorers Club (New York City). *Awards, honors:* Perkins' television program "Zoo Parade" won numerous awards, including the Peabody award, 1950, Look Award, and Sylvania Award; his television series, "Wild Kingdom," was also the recipient of several awards, including four Emmy Awards; honorary doctorate, University of Missouri, 1971, Rockhurst College, Northland College.

WRITINGS: Animal Faces (photographs by the author), Foster & Stewart, 1944; (with Peggy Tibma) *One Magic Night: A Story from the Zoo* (illustrated by Katherine Evans), Regnery, 1952; *Zoo Parade* (illustrated by Paul Bransom and Seymour Fleishman), Rand McNally, 1954, (with his wife, Carol M. Perkins) *"I Saw You from Afar": A Visit to the Bushmen of the Kalahari Desert*, Atheneum, 1965; (author of introduction) Richard Cromer, *The Miracle of Flight* (illustrated by Joseph Cellini), Doubleday, 1968; (author of introduction) Allan W. Eckert, *Bayou Backwaters* (illustrated by J. Cellini), Doubleday, 1968; (author of introduction) A. W. Eckert, *In Search of a Whale* (illustrated by J. Cellini), Doubleday, 1970; (author of introduction) Robert Martin, *Yesterday's People* (illustrated by Richard Cuffari), Doubleday, 1970; (author of introduction) Lewis Wayne Walker, *Survival under the Sun* (illustrated by Jean Zallinger), Doubleday, 1971.

SIDELIGHTS: Perkins' interest in animals began when he was a young boy growing up in the Midwest. At the age of twenty-one, Perkins was hired as a workman at the St. Louis Zoo, and within two weeks was put in charge of the reptiles. During his stay as curator of the reptiles, the young zoologist expanded the snake collection by going on numerous hunting expeditions to Illinois and the Southern States. Perkins used

his unique flair for combining the entertainment and educational aspects of zoos at each of the wildlife parks where he was employed.

While working at the Buffalo Zoo, Perkins organized the material for his first book entitled *Animal Faces*. In this publication Perkins studied and compared various facial expressions of animals. A *New York Times* critic observed, "The photographs are beautifully done, and they go far toward proving the author's contention that the faces of animals are just as revealing as are those of human beings." In an article for *Weekly Book Review*, May Lamberton Becker commented, "I have seen many good books about wild animals, but none has interested me more than this. . . ."

Perkins later utilized the theatrics of animal behavior in putting together the television program "Zoo Parade." A zoologist always runs the risk of being injured while handling wild animals, and Perkins was no exception. It was during a rehearsal for the television show in April, 1951 that Perkins encountered one of several close calls with death after being bitten by a three-and-a-half foot rattlesnake.

In 1962 Perkins and producer, Don Meier, developed the television series "Wild Kingdom." Acclaimed for its emphasis on animal conservation, "Wild Kingdom" has been honored by almost every wildlife oganization in the United States. In an article for *Variety,* a critic noted, "Superb photography and editing and the actual physical participation of the narrators keep the show at high tempo."

The author-zoologist departed from the world of animals and wrote about a primitive African civilization in *"I Saw You from Afar": A Visit to the Bushmen of Kalahari Desert.* "A fine example of a book about another people which has beauty and authority as well as simplicity," commented a reviewer for *Horn Book.* A *New York Times* critic wrote, "This delightful little book, 50-odd pages of well-chosen words and photographs, opens a window on the world of the Bushmen. . . . The Perkinses admired these resourceful nomads, and their enthusiasm is contagious."

HOBBIES AND OTHER INTERESTS: Photography, archeology, scuba diving, and music.

FOR MORE INFORMATION SEE: Weekly Book Review, March 19, 1944; *New York Times,* April 16, 1944; *Current Biography Yearbook 1951;* Lynn and Gray Poole, *Scientists Who Work Outdoors,* Dodd, 1963; *Horn Book,* April, 1965; *New York Times Book Review,* May 9, 1965; *Variety,* January 15, 1969.

Come away, O human child!
To the waters and the wild
With a faery, hand in hand,
For the world's more full of weeping than you can
    understand.

—William Butler Yeats

VERNON PIZER

PIZER, Vernon   1918-

PERSONAL: Born February 20, 1918, in Boston, Mass.; son of Jack and Florence (Stearns) Pizer; married Marguerite Langdale, April 12, 1941. *Education:* George Washington University, student, 1939-42. *Home and office:* 2206 Newbern St., Valdosta, Ga. 31601.

CAREER: U.S. Army, 1941-63; attained rank of lieutenant colonel. Served as World War II infantry officer in North Africa and Europe, and subsequently in public affairs and information assignments including: chief of information, North Atlantic Treaty Forces in Turkey and Greece; executive officer, Public Information Division, Supreme Headquarters Allied Powers Europe, in Paris, France; and chief, Army Magazine and Book Branch, Pentagon, Washington, D.C. Simultaneously pursued part-time free-lance writing commencing in 1950. Full time writer, 1963—. *Member:* American Society of Journalists and Authors, Authors Guild National Press Club.

WRITINGS: (With Perry H. Davis III) *Your Assignment Overseas,* Norton, 1953; *Rockets, Missiles and Space,* Lippincott, 1962; (with William R. Anderson) *The Useful Atom,* World, 1966; *The United States Army,* Praeger, 1967; *The World Ocean,* World, 1967; *Glorious Triumphs* Dodd, 1968; *Ink, Ark., and All That* (Junior Literary Guild selection), Putnam, 1976; *You Don't Say,* Putnam, 1978; *Shortchanged By History,* Putnam, 1979. Author of more than three hundred articles for leading magazines in the U.S., Europe and the Far East, as well as author of numerous books and pamphlets for government agencies and non-profit institutions.

WORK IN PROGRESS: A revised, updated edition of *Glorious Triumphs,* for Dodd; an "off-beat, non-fiction" book, for Dodd.

SIDELIGHTS: "I can remember the day I decided to become a writer. I was all of eleven years old and the grade school I attended was holding an election for officers of the student government. Each nominee for office was allotted three minutes to address the student body in his quest for votes. One of the two candidates for president asked me to write his speech for him. I did, he won, and I was convinced it was the words I had written for him that did the trick. I can't recall at this late date whether or not he turned out to be a good class president but I do recall that I came away hooked on words and their ability to inform and influence when put together soundly. Now, countless thousands of words later, I am still hooked on words, still according them the full measure of respect and admiration they merit.

"As a young writer I was certain that the pen is mightier than the sword. Today, a considerably older writer, I retain that certainty. So it may seem odd that I pursued two careers simultaneously—one with the sword and the other with the pen. Actually, I found that the sword enabled me to grasp the pen more firmly, more surely. My military service in a number of European countries, in the Middle East, and in Africa—in peace and in war—exposed me to a variety of cultures, outlooks, and situations. This broad exposure gave me an informed awareness of the world around me—and of the attitudes, the hopes, and the needs of the peoples who inhabit it—and this made me a more sensitive, better balanced writer. It also created in me a great curiosity about the constantly developing human drama and a wish to understand it better. This, too, plays a major role in shaping a writing career.

"I try my level best to make my words perform a pleasing and useful service for my readers. I feel I owe that to them both. Between them—the words and those who read them—they have made it possible for me to put my typewriter to work enjoyably, satisfyingly, in some thirty different countries. Happily for me, there are still a lot of places and a lot of words to go.

A President Takes a Hand

(From *Ink, Ark., and All That* by Vernon Pizer. Illustrated by Tom Huffman.)

"Recently, while sorting through the effects of my late mother, I came across a folder containing a half-dozen sheets of composition paper covered by a schoolchild's scrawled writing. It was a hand that I recognized immediately because I have never out-grown that scrawl. And when I read the words I recognized them, too, across the chasm of the half-century-plus since I had penned them. It was an account of the life and times of my shoe cobbler grandfather. Re-reading it, I was struck by the fact that even as a child I must have realized the writer's obligation to commence with an idea worth recording and then to express it with honesty and clarity. Throughout my adult career as author and journalist in the United States and abroad I have always sought diligently for ideas worth recording. It has led me to plant explorers striving to save endangered species, to scientists striving to roll back the frontiers of knowledge, to humanitarians striving to blunt the barbs that lacerate the spirit of man. It has been an exciting quest, immensely satisfying when I have succeeded in communicating it to others in words that captured its essence faithfully, meaningfully, clearly.

"But if much of my writing has dealt with serious subjects I've always made an effort not to take myself too seriously, not to become a 'precious' writer who neglects his obligation to convey worthwhile information fully, comprehensibly and animatedly because he is too intent on dancing a linguistic minuet. I think my cobbler grandfather, who was impatient with pretension and peacockery, would have approved. Because he had a special fondness for the young, he would have been particularly pleased that several of my books have been intended for teenage audiences and that one of them, *Ink, Ark., and All That,* was a Junior Literary Guild selection."

FOR MORE INFORMATION SEE: Horn Book, February, 1977.

"Don't eat too much," said Jumbo. **"Or I won't be able to carry you back to Pooka Pooka."** ■ (From *Big Man* by Kin Platt. Pictures by Robert Lopshire.)

KIN PLATT

PLATT, Kin 1911-

PERSONAL: Born December 8, 1911, in New York, N.Y.; son of Daniel (a singer) and Etta (Hochberg) Platt; divorced; children: Christopher. *Agent:* Ruth Cantor, 120 West 42nd St., New York, N.Y. 10036.

CAREER: Cartoonist, painter and sculptor, and writer. New York Herald Tribune Syndicate, New York, N.Y., cartoonist (writer and illustrator) of comic strip. "Mr. and Mrs." 1947-63, and "The Duke and the Duchess," 1950-54. Sometime theatrical caricaturist for New York newspapers, including *Village Voice,* and for *Los Angeles Times. Military service:* U.S. Army Air Force, Air Transport Command, 1943-46; served in China-Burma-India theater; received Bronze Star. *Member:* Writers Guild of America, Mystery Writers of America, National Cartoonist Society. *Awards, honors:* Mystery Writers of America "Edgar" award for juvenile mystery, 1967.

WRITINGS: The Blue Man (juvenile), Harper, 1961; *Big Max* (juvenile), Harper, 1965; *Sinbad and Me* (juvenile), Chilton, 1966; *The Boy Who Could Make Himself Disappear,* Chilton, 1968; *Mystery of the Witch Who Wouldn't,* Chilton, 1969; *The Pushbutton Butterfly,* Random House, 1970; *The Kissing*

Gourami, Random House, 1970; *Hey, Dummy,* Chilton, 1971; *Dead As They Come,* Random House, 1972; *The Princess Stakes Murder,* Random House, 1973; *Chloris and the Creeps,* Chilton, 1973; *Headman,* Greenwillow, 1975; *Chloris and the Freaks,* Bradbury, 1975; *Run for Your Life,* Watts, 1977; *The Doomsday Gang,* Greenwillow, 1978.

SIDELIGHTS: "[I] would like to see less genteel supervised attitude toward books for children and more imaginative approaches welcomed. *Blue Man* was popular with children, not librarians, and lost the battle, for example." His novel, *The Boy Who Could Make Himself Disappear,* was adapted for a film entitled "Baxter," 1973.

POLHAMUS, Jean Burt   1928-

PERSONAL: Surname is pronounced Paul-haý-muss; born April 30, 1928; in Miss.; daughter of John Owen (a farmer) and Ellen (Sanders) Burt; married John Polhamus (an engineer), May 10, 1952; children: Jean Ellen, John Burt. *Education:* University of Arizona, B.S., 1950. *Home:* 4056 Honeycutt St., San Diego, Calif. 92109.

CAREER: U.S. Naval Station, San Diego, Calif., technical librarian, 1950-52; copywriter for an ad agency, Tucson, Ariz., 1952-53; U.S. Park Service, Dinosaur National Monument, Utah, fireguard, summer, 1953; Hughes Aircraft, Tucson, Ariz., technical librarian, 1953-55; homemaker/mother, 1956—. *Awards, honors:* Received honorary life

membership in the PTA for volunteer service in school library, 1974.

WRITINGS: Dinosaur Funny Bones, Prentice-Hall, 1974; *Dinosaur Dos and Don'ts,* Prentice-Hall, 1975. Author of an article in *Good Housekeeping,* June, 1973.

WORK IN PROGRESS: Several humorous dinosaur books, including *Beulah Brontosaurus,* a story-poem about a brontosaurus who yearns and tries to be skinny; *Dinosaur Holiday Book,* twelve poems just for fun (one for each month); *A Houseful of Dinosaurs and Pten Pteranodons; Dinosaur Safety Bones.*

SIDELIGHTS: "I write for fun, to inspire laughter, to nudge people's funny bones, including my own. I don't write exclusively in rhyme, but I lean toward it because I enjoy the meter and precision, as well as the challenge of creating a story or an idea with comparatively few words.

"The idea of treating lightly such awesome, exciting creatures as the formidably named dinosaurs occurred to me when I was a PTA volunteer librarian in my children's elementary school. I discovered that dinosaurs fascinated almost every child and that humor delighted even more. Therefore, why not funny dinosaurs? I began creating some, and found it so much fun, I'm still at it!

> "The dinosaurs were funny folks
> About whom we can make some jokes.
> (Especially since they're not around
> To pound us right into the ground!)"

When Allosaurus rode his bike,
Pedestrians stayed out of sight;
His ten-speed had just what it takes,
Except for one small thing—no brakes.

DO ride carefully and make sure your brakes are good. Pedestrians are an endangered species.

(From *Dinosaur Dos and Don'ts* by Jean Burt Polhamus. Illustrated by Steve O'Neill.)

JEAN BURT POLHAMUS

POTTER, Margaret (Newman) 1926-
(Anne Betteridge, Anne Melville)

PERSONAL: Born June 21, 1926, in London, England; daughter of Bernard and Marjory (Donald) Newman; married R. Jeremy Potter (a publisher), 1950; children: Jocelyn, Jonathan. *Education:* St. Hugh's College, Oxford, M.A. *Residence:* London, England.

CAREER: King's Messenger (children's magazine), England, editor, 1950-55; novelist. Citizens Advice Bureau, London, former staff member. *Awards, honors:* Romantic Novel Major Award, 1967, for *The Truth Game.*

WRITINGS—Novels; all under pseudonym Anne Betteridge; all published by Hurst & Blackett: *The Foreign Girl,* 1960; *The Young Widow,* 1961; *Spring in Morocco,* 1962; *The Long Dance of Love,* 1963; *The Younger Sister,* 1964; *Return to Delphi,* 1964; *Single to New York,* 1965; *The Chains of Love,* 1965; *The Truth Game,* 1966; *A Portuguese Affair,* 1966; *A Little Bit of Luck,* 1967; *Shooting Star,* 1968; *Love in a Rainy Country,* 1969; *Sirocco,* 1970; *The Girl Outside,* 1971; *Journey From a Foreign Land,* 1972; *The Sacrifice,* 1973; *A Time of Their Lives,* 1974; *The Stranger on the Beach,* 1974; *The Temp,* 1976; *A Place for Everyone,* 1977; *The Tiger and the Goat,* 1978.

Under pseudonym Anne Melville; all published by Doubleday: *The Lorimer Line,* 1977; *Alexa,* 1979.

Children's Books—all under name Margaret Potter: *The Touch-And-Go Year,* Dobson, 1968; *The Blow-And-Grow Year,* Dobson, 1970; *Sandy's Safari,* Dobson, 1971; *The Story of the Stolen Necklace,* Dobson, 1974; *Trouble on Sunday,* Methuen, 1974; *The Motorway Mob,* Methuen, 1976; *Tony's Special Place,* Bodley Head, 1977.

WORK IN PROGRESS: Lorimers at War, under pseudonym Anne Melville.

SIDELIGHTS: "I am a start-of-the-day writer, preferring to sit down at the typewriter as soon as the rest of the family has left the house. The housework has to wait until late afternoon. I find that if I undertake any other duty first thing in the day—even though there may still be four or five hours working time left when I am ready to begin writing—I find it extremely difficult to settle down to work.

"What I find most important in planning a book is to find exactly the right place in which to set it. A plot is something which always has to be invented; and I am one of those writers who likes to invent all her characters out of her head, rather than basing them on anybody known, because that act of creation is the main pleasure of writing. But places are different. Some areas—especially those which were inhabited many years ago but have been deserted for centuries—have such intense atmospheres that they impose themselves on a book, demanding to be included even if that was not in the original plan. But even where a more ordinary town or country area is concerned, I need to visit the place in which my characters are going to live before I can write about them successfully. I can often pick out one particular house as being exactly what I am looking for—and will do my best to get inside, if possible, to confirm the feeling."

HOBBIES AND OTHER INTERESTS: Tennis, gardening, travel abroad.

READ, Piers Paul 1941-

PERSONAL: Born March 7, 1941, in Beaconsfield, England; son of Herbert (a poet) and Margaret (Ludwig) Read; married Emily Boothby, July 28, 1967. *Education:* St. John's College, Cambridge, B.A., 1961, M.A., 1962. *Religion:* Roman Catholic. *Home:* Stonegrave, Yorkshire, England. *Agent:* Deborah Rogers Ltd., 5-11 Mortimer St., London W.1., England.

CAREER: Times Literary Supplement, London, England, sub-editor, 1964-65; novelist. *Awards, honors:* Ford Foundation fellow in Berlin, 1963-64; Harkness fellow in New York and Lexington, Mass., 1967-68; Somerset Maugham Award; Sir Geoffrey Faber Memorial Prize; Hawthornden Prize.

WRITINGS: Game in Heaven with Tussy Marx, Weidenfeld & Nicolson, 1966, McGraw, 1967; *The Junkers,* Secker & Warburg, 1968, Knopf, 1969; *Monk Dawson,* Lippincott, 1969; *The Professor's Daughter,* Lippincott, 1971; *The Upstart,* Lippincott, 1973; *Alive: The Story of the Andes Survivors,* Lippincott, 1974; *Polonaise,* Lippincott, 1976; *The Train Robbers,* Lippincott, 1978; *A Married Man,* Lippincott, 1980. Author of a television play, "Coincidence," produced by British Broadcasting Corp.

PIERS PAUL READ

SIDELIGHTS: Read's stay in Germany provided him with the background for *The Junkers*. David Williams says it is a novel of "very high quality indeed." He handles the material "with a sure and satisfying sense of form." Martin Seymour-Smith calls the book "cool and clever."

Read has traveled in the Far East, Indochina, Africa, and Europe; he lived in Munich and Berlin over a two-year period and now lives in North Yorkshire, England.

FOR MORE INFORMATION SEE: Spectator, June 21, 1968; *Punch,* July 17, 1968, January 1, 1969.

Dear little child, this little book
  Is less a primer than a key
To sunder gates where wonder waits
    Your "Open Sesame!"

                    —Rupert Hughes

The hills are dearest which our childish feet
Have climbed the earliest; and the streams most sweet
Are those at which our young lips drank.

              —John Greenleaf Whittier

REED, Gwendolyn E(lizabeth) 1932-

PERSONAL: Born June 27, 1932, in Louisville, Ky.; daughter of Henry Morrison (a businessman) and Cecelia (Zawatski) Reed. *Education:* Radcliffe College, B.A., 1954. *Home:* 2837 Riedling Dr., Louisville, Ky. 40206. *Agent:* Curtis Brown Ltd., 60 East 56th St., New York, N.Y. 10022.

CAREER: Worked for Institute of International Education, New York City, 1956-58, and Museum of Fine Arts, Boston, Mass., 1959-61; Grolier, Inc., New York City, associate editor of *Book of Knowledge,* 1962-64.

WRITINGS: (Editor with Sara Hannum) *Lean Out of the Window: An Anthology of Modern Poetry,* Atheneum, 1965; (compiler) *Out of the Ark: An Anthology of Animal Verse,* Atheneum, 1968; *The Sand Lady,* Lothrop, 1968; *Adam and Eve,* Lothrop, 1968; (compiler) *Bird Songs* (poems), Atheneum, 1969; *When the Assyrians Came Down from the Trees,* Lothrop, 1969; *The Talkative Beasts: Myths, Fables, and Poems of India,* Lothrop, 1969; (compiler) *Songs the Sandman Sings,* Atheneum, 1969; (compiler) *Beginnings,* Atheneum, 1971.

FOR MORE INFORMATION SEE: Young Readers' Review, June, 1968, November, 1968.

Wee, sleekit, cow'rin, tim'rous beastie,
O, what a panic's in thy breastie!
Thou need na start awa sae hasty,...

■ (From *Out of the Ark: An Anthology of Animal Verse,* compiled by Gwendolyn Reed. Drawings by Gabriele Margules.)

When she saw her nest, the queen ant came up and said: "Thank you, good man! If you ever need us, we will come to help you!" ■ (From *The Cobbler's Reward* by Barbara Reid and Ewa Reid. Illustrated by Charles Mikolaycak.)

REID, Barbara 1922-

PERSONAL: Born April 18, 1922, in New York, N.Y.; daughter of Louis Raymond (a newspaperman) and Helen (Dickey) Reid. *Education:* Wheaton College, Norton, Mass., B.A. (magna cum laude), 1942. *Politics:* Registered Democrat. *Religion:* Episcopalian. *Home:* 138 West 11th St., New York, N.Y. 10011. *Office:* Frederick R. Rinehart Co., 516 Fifth Ave., New York, N.Y. 10036.

CAREER: Secretary and editorial assistant, Frederick R. Rinehart Co., New York, N.Y. *Member:* Author's Guild of America, Poets and Writers, Phi Beta Kappa. *Awards, honors:* Grant from Mary Roberts Rinehart Foundation, 1967.

WRITINGS: (Ghost writer) *Horace Havemeyer, 1886-1956*, privately printed by Havemeyer family, 1957; *Carlo's Cricket* (juvenile), McGraw, 1967; *Miguel and His Racehorse* (juvenile), Morrow, 1974; (with Julia Markus) *Two Novellas*, Applewood, 1977; (with sister-in-law, Ewa Reid) *The Cobbler's Reward*, Macmillan, 1978. Contributor of articles and stories to *Harper's Bazaar*, *Ladies' Home Journal*, *Quixote*, *Descant*, *The Hudson Review*, *The Friend*, *Sewanee Review*, *Mississippi Review*, and *Quartet*.

WORK IN PROGRESS: A novel, *Moon in the Yellow River;* a juvenile book for Macmillan.

SIDELIGHTS: "In October, 1978, I was interviewed by Lester Strong for the 'Top of the Day' show on Station WBTV, Channel 3 in Charlotte, North Carolina. I was asked questions mostly about children's books and I said that 'it is a journey of awareness that children especially are traveling. They go on a quest . . . and they like to identify with the hero or heroine who must overcome difficulties.' Then I added: 'I think of writing as like making a bridge—we make a bridge between people, one of understanding, of filling the loneliness. It is communicating and the pleasure of reading is one with the pleasure of writing. I know when I am moved by something I am reading I think, yes, that is true, and it illuminates my vague feelings and helps me understand.' I recalled what Eudora Welty said on television, that 'writing is the response of love, we need to write with love, with internal vision. We need to see and radiate.' Quoting her on the program, I concluded, 'This is what I feel building the bridge between people is about—it is a bridge of love.'"

Reid has traveled and lived abroad a good deal, particularly in France, Italy, and England.

BARBARA REID

REID, John Calvin

PERSONAL: Born in Charlotte, N.C.; son of John Calvin and Ximena (Hunter) Reid; married Charlotte Boyce Orr, November 15, 1935. *Education:* Erskine College, B.A., 1922; Pittsburgh Theological Seminary, Th.M., 1926; New College Edinburgh and Oxford, post graduate studies, 1928; Southern Baptist Theological Seminary, Louisville, Ky., Ph.D., 1930. *Home:* 14 Spotted Sandpiper, Hilton Head Island, S.C. 29928.

CAREER: Presbyterian clergyman. Minister in Louisville, Ky., 1926-29, Butler, Pa., 1930-39, Columbus, Ga., 1940-45, and Pittsburgh, Pa., 1945-67; United Presbyterian Church, New York, N.Y., vice-moderator, 1958; Presbyterian Church, Hilton Head Island, S.C., minister, 1967-73. Interim supply minister: First Presbyterian Church, Alberquerque, N.M., 1967; Grosse Pointe Memorial United Presbyterian Church, Detroit, Mich., 1972; Menlo Park United Presbyterian Church, California, 1974; Memorial Drive Presbyterian Church, Houston, Tex., 1975; Walnut Creek United Presbyterian Church, California, 1976; Eastminster Presbyterian Church, Columbia, S.C., 1977; First Presbyterian Church, Aiken, S.C., 1978; Shandon Presbyterian Church, Columbia, S.C., 1979. Moderator of Pittsburgh Presbytery, 1966. Lecturer, under auspices of United Presbyterian Church in the U.S.A., Egypt, Spain, Iran and Lebanon, 1965. *Awards, honors:* D.D. from Muskinghum and Tarkio Colleges; Algernon Sydney Sullivan Award from Erskine College, 1979.

Mrs. Crow did not move over. ■ (From *Bird Life in Wington* by J. Calvin Reid. Illustrated by Reynold H. Weidenear.)

WRITINGS: Reserves of the Soul, John Knox Press, 1942; *Parables from Nature,* Eerdmans, 1945; *Birdlife in Wington,* Eerdmans, 1948; *On Toward the Goal,* John Knox Press, 1949; *We Knew Jesus,* Eerdmans, 1954; *Prayer Pilgrimage Through the Psalms,* Cokesbury, 1963; *War of the Birds* (juvenile), Eerdmans, 1963; *Surprise for Dr. Retriever* (juvenile), Eerdmans, 1963; *Frisky Finds a Treasure* (juvenile), Eerdmans, 1963; *We Spoke for God,* Eerdmans, 1967; *B.C.— A Digest of the Old Testament,* Regal, 1971; *His Story,* Word Books, 1971; *Come Be My Guest,* Regal, 1975; *Blessed Are Those Who Morn,* Regal, 1975; *Proverbs to Live By,* Regal, 1975; *Psalms to Live By,* Regal, 1975; *Green Fields of Promise,* Master's Press, 1978; *Secrets from Field and Forest,* Tyndale, 1979; *My Favorite Old Testament Stories,* Beka Books, 1980.

ADAPTATIONS—Cassettes: From *Birdlife in Wington,* produced by Word Books.

REIT, Seymour (Sy Reit)

CAREER: Surname sounds like "right." Author, animated cartoonist, editor. Has served on the faculty of Bank Street College of Education, as writer and editor, New York City; as an animated cartoonist, created the character "Casper the Friendly Ghost" for television. Has contributed to the Pre-School Library for Encyclopaedia Britannica, to the television show "Captain Kangaroo" and to magazines; has written scripts for movies and radio. He has also appeared on television for the New York Board of Education.

WRITINGS—For children: *The King Who Learned to Smile* (illustrated by Gordon Laite), Golden Press, 1960; (with Fred Dietrich) *Wheels, Sails, and Wings* (illustrated by Harald Bukor, Karl Peschke and Oswald Voh), Golden Press, 1961; *Where's Willie?* (illustrated by Erik Blegvad), Golden Press, 1961; (with Frances Giannoni) *The Golden Book of Gardening* (illustrated by William Sayles and Tom Tierney), Golden Press, 1962; *Look! Look! A Clown Book* (illustrated by Joanne Nigro), Golden Press, 1962; *Coins and Coin Collecting* (illustrated by W. T. Mars), Golden Press, 1965; (editor) *America Laughs: A Treasury of Great Humor* (illustrated by Huehnergarth), Crowell-Collier, 1966; *Count, Write and Read About What Goes Up and Down* (illustrated by Dorothy C. Fago), Golden Press, 1966; *Read and Write About What Is Big and Little* (illustrated by Julian Paul), Golden Press, 1966; (with Anne Bailey) *The West in the Middle Ages,* Golden Press, 1966; *Growing Up in the White House,* Crowell-Collier, 1968; *Dear Uncle Carlos* (illustrated by Sheldon Brody), McGraw, 1969; *Jamie Visits the Nurse* (illustrated by S. Brody), McGraw, 1969; *Round Things Everywhere* (illustrated by Carol Basen), McGraw, 1969; *A Week in Hagar's World: Israel* (illustrated by Louis Goldman), Crowell-Collier, 1969.

Animals Around My Block (illustrated by Alex V. Sobolewski), McGraw, 1970; *A Week in Bico's World: Brazil* (illustrated by Claudia Andujar), Crowell-Collier, 1970; *Child of the Navajos* (illustrated by Paul Conklin), Dodd, 1971; *The Easy How-To Book* (illustrated by William Dugan), Golden Press, 1973; *Rice Cakes and Paper Dragons* (illustrated by P. Conklin), Dodd, 1973; *Benvenuto* (illustrated by Will Winslow), Addison-Wesley, 1974; *Benvenuto and the Car-*

(From *Sails, Rails and Wings* by Seymour Reit. Illustrated by Roberto Innocenti.)

nival (illustrated by Marilyn Miller), Xerox Education Publications, 1976; *Race Against Death: A True Story of the Far North,* Dodd, 1976; *Bugs Bunny's Space Carrot* (illustrated by Ralph Heimdahl and William Lorencz), Golden Press, 1977; (under name Sy Reit) *The Ginghams,* Golden Press, 1977; *Ironclad!: A True Story of the Civil War,* Dodd, 1977; (under name Sy Reit) *Tiny and Tony* (illustrated by Jack Kent), Golden Press, 1977; *Tweety and Sylvester: Birds of a Feather* (illustrated by Lou Cunette), Golden Press, 1977; *All Kinds of Planes,* Golden Press, 1978; *All Kinds of Ships,* Golden Press, 1978; *All Kinds of Trains,* Golden Press, 1978; *Bugs Bunny Goes to the Dentist* (illustrated by L. Cunette), Golden Press, 1978.

Other: (Under name Sy Reit; with Frank Jacobs) *Canvas Confidential: A Backward Glance at the World of Art* (illustrated by Kelly Freas), Dial, 1963; *Masquerade: The Amazing Camouflage Deceptions of World War II,* Hawthorn, 1978.

SIDELIGHTS: Reit, who was born and raised in New York City, received his education at New York University. He began his writing career while an undergraduate, serving as editor and contributor to the monthly humor magazine *Varieties.*

Reit's interest in writing, coupled with artistic talent, led to a job with the Max Fleischer Studios, where he worked as writer and artist on a series of animated films.

SEYMOUR REIT

With the advent of World War II, Reit enlisted in the army, serving from 1942 to 1946 as a photo-intelligence officer in Europe and later on the personal staff of General Hoyt Vandenberg. He was awarded the Bronze Star Medal in 1945.

Following his discharge from the Army, Reit resumed his career as writer/artist on a free-lance basis, gradually devoting more and more of his time to writing. To date he has over thirty industrial films to his credit, numerous radio plays, magazine articles, a "Maggie" award winning educational comic book based on a trip to the United Nations, a humorous book for adults, as well as his many Golden Books. Among these are *The King Who Learned to Smile, Look! Look! A Clown Book, Where's Willie?, The Golden Book of Gardening* and *Wheels, Sails and Wings.*

As a free-lance author, Reit (whose middle name is Victory in honor of his birthdate—Armistice Day) does most of his work in the study of his Manhattan apartment. This, he feels, has both advantages, i.e. being able to wander through Central Park on a sunny afternoon and visit museums when *no one else is there,* and disadvantages, such as researching and writing late, late into the night to meet deadlines. The former far outweigh the latter, however, judging from his emphatic "No!" when asked if he would exchange his way of life for a more regimented one.

Seymour Reit's wide range of books have gathered mixed reviews from critics. The *Library Journal,* in writing about *A Week in Bico's World: Brazil,* a 1971 publication, said, "The easy text and appealing photos of [this book] will interest young readers and listeners as they follow Bico through his weekly routine. Some of the unique aspects of Brazilian life are shown, but this is more the story of a happy young boy growing up in a loving middle-class family in modern Sao Paulo."

Elaborating on this last point, the *Times Literary Supplement* said, "Bico's week in Brazil is . . . indistinguishable from any week in a North American city; as he lives in Sao Paulo in affluent circumstances, this is probably true, but it is not

And finally he even turned up his nose at Mrs. Bruno's ravioli. ■ (From *Benvenuto* by Seymour Reit. Illustrated by Will Winslow.)

very interesting. A book illustrating the similarities of life in all large cities would be valuable, but a book about life in another country in which anonymity predominates seems an uneconomic purchase."

A book in a completely different vein, *Coins and Coin Collecting* was received favorably by the *Library Journal.* "A comprehensive, up-to-date introduction to the subject, including a good history of coins, told interestingly and accurately. . . . Black-and-white photographs of coins are especially clear and there are colorful sketches showing pertinent historical settings. A sound guide for the beginner, and one seasoned collectors will want to see."

And a recent book, *Race Against Death,* was written about in *Booklist.* "This semi-fictionalized chronicle of the rigorous sled relay which delivered medicine in record time compels the reader in spite of Reit's superfluous dramatization and a secondary story thread that somewhat anthropomorphizes the dog's personality. The vivid descriptions of natural threats—wind, blizzards, cold, and dampness—generate enough real tension to counteract the book's flaws."

FOR MORE INFORMATION SEE: Library Journal, July, 1965; *Library Journal,* December 15, 1970; *Times Literary Supplement,* July 2, 1971; *Booklist,* February 15, 1976; *Authors of Books for Young People,* second edition, supplement, Scarecrow, 1979.

ROBERTS, Willo Davis   1928-

PERSONAL: Born May 29, 1928, in Grand Rapids, Mich.; daughter of Clayton R. and Lealah (Gleason) Davis; married David W. Roberts (a building supply salesman), May 20, 1949; children: Kathleen, David M., Larrilyn (Mrs. Eric Lindquist), Christopher. *Education:* Graduated from high school in Pontiac, Mich., 1946. *Religion:* Lutheran. *Residence:* Granite Falls, Wash. 98252. *Agent:* Curtis Brown Ltd., 575 Madison Ave., New York, N.Y. 10022.

CAREER: Writer of novels. Has worked in hospitals and doctors' offices in a paramedical capacity. Frequent lecturer and workshop leader at writers' conferences and schools. *Member:* Mystery Writers of America, Science Fiction Writers of America, Authors Guild of Authors League of America, Seattle Freelancers. Also member of the executive board of the Pacific Northwest Writers' Conference, held annually in the Puget Sound area.

WRITINGS: Murder at Grand Bay, Arcadia House, 1955; *The Girl Who Wasn't There,* Arcadia House, 1957; *Murder Is So Easy,* Vega Books, 1961; *The Suspected Four,* Vega Books, 1962; *Nurse Kay's Conquest,* Ace Books, 1966; *Once a Nurse,* Ace Books, 1966; *Nurse at Mystery Villa,* Ace Books, 1967; *Return to Darkness,* Lancer Books, 1969.

Shroud of Fog, Ace Books, 1970; *Devil Boy,* New American Library, 1970; *The Waiting Darkness,* Lancer Books, 1970; *Shadow of a Past Love,* Lancer Books, 1970; *The House at Fern Canyon,* Lancer Books, 1970; *The Tarot Spell,* Lancer Books, 1970; *Invitation to Evil,* Lancer Books, 1970; *The Terror Trap,* Lancer Books, 1971; *King's Pawn,* Lancer Books, 1971; *The Gates of Montrain,* Lancer Books, 1971; *The Watchers,* Lancer Books, 1971; *The Ghosts of Harrel,* Lancer Books, 1971; *Inherit the Darkness,* Lancer Books, 1972; *Nurse in Danger,* Ace Books, 1972; *Becca's Child,*

WILLO DAVIS ROBERTS

Lancer Books, 1972; *Sing a Dark Song,* Lancer Books, 1972; *The Nurses,* Ace Books, 1972; *The Face of Danger,* Lancer Books, 1972; *Dangerous Legacy,* Lancer Books, 1972; *Sinister Gardens,* Lancer Books, 1972; *The M.D.,* Lancer Books, 1972; *The Evil Children,* Lancer Books, 1973; *The Gods in Green,* Lancer Books, 1973; *Nurse Robin,* Lennox Hill, 1973; *Didn't Anybody Know My Wife?,* Putnam, 1974.

White Jade, Doubleday, 1975; *Key Witness,* Putnam, 1975; *The View from the Cherry Tree* (juvenile), Atheneum, 1975; *Expendable,* Doubleday, 1976; *The Jaubert Ring,* Doubleday, 1976; *Don't Hurt Laurie!* (juvenile), Atheneum, 1977; *Act of Fear,* Doubleday, 1977; *Cape of Black Sands,* Popular Library, 1977; *The House of Imposters,* Popular Library, 1977; *The Minden Curse* (juvenile), Atheneum, 1978.

Destiny's Women, Popular Library, 1980; *More Minden Curses* (juvenile), Atheneum, 1980; *The Search for Willie,* Popular Library, 1980; *The Girl With the Silver Eyes* (juvenile), Atheneum, 1980.

"Black Pearl" series; all published by Popular Library: *Dark Dowry,* 1978; *The Stuart Stain,* 1978; *The Cade Curse,* 1978; *The Devil's Double,* 1979; *The Radkin Revenge,* 1979; *The Hellfire Heritage,* 1979; *The Macomber Menace,* 1980.

SIDELIGHTS: "I don't think I ever wanted to be anything but a writer. My first imaginary creation was a companion, Bobby, who 'lived' with me from the time I was two until

Laurie stopped, for she recognized the murderous rage in Annabelle's face. She had seen it often enough.
■ (From *Don't Hurt Laurie* by Willo Davis Roberts. Illustrated by Ruth Sanderson.)

I was about three and one-half. My first story was written down when I was nine, and I've been writing ever since.

"Like many writers, I was pretty much of a loner as a child. Part of this was because I was shy, but probably most of it was because we moved so frequently that I seldom had a chance to get acquainted with other children—I was enrolled in six different schools during the fourth grade and never did learn the multiplication tables!

"I grew up loving the woods and the water in Northern Michigan, and even after I'd moved away from them always longed to be back. We have found the next best thing to returning to childhood (for my husband, too, grew up in the wild woods) was when we moved to Washington state in 1975. We now have a home overlooking the Stilliguamish River and Mt. Pilchuck, about fifty miles northeast of Seattle. My husband, David, has retired from the building supply business and is now a freelance writer and photographer. We have a fifth-wheel trailer with an office in it, and are making plans for extensive traveling from now on. We have been to Alaska and Georgia (to research books) and expect to see a good deal of the rest of the country.

"It was a great surprise to me when I became a writer for children. *The View from the Cherry Tree* was intended to be an adult suspense novel. My agent suggested trying it as a juvenile, for which I shall forever bless her. It has just gone into its fourth printing, and the many letters it has generated from kids have been pure delight. If it had not been for the success of *Cherry Tree*, I probably would never have undertaken anything more for kids, but now I'm firmly hooked. Kids write and tell you what they think about a book, and sometimes, so do their teachers and librarians.

"To now be able to devote full time to doing what I do best—writing—and what I've always wanted to do—traveling—promises to be a lot of fun."

FOR MORE INFORMATION SEE: The Calendar, September, 1975, February, 1976; *Publishers Weekly,* February 28, 1977; *New York Times Book Review,* April 17, 1977.

RODOWSKY, Colby 1932-

PERSONAL: Born February 26, 1932, in Baltimore, Md.; daughter of Frank M. Fossett and Mary C. Fitz-Townsend; married Lawrence Rodowsky (a lawyer), August 7, 1954; children: Laurie, Alice, Emily, Sarah, Gregory, Katherine. *Education:* College of Notre Dame of Maryland, B.A., 1953. *Religion:* Roman Catholic. *Home:* 4306 Norwood Rd., Baltimore, Md. 21218. *Agent:* Theron Raines, Raines & Raines, 475 Fifth Ave., New York, N.Y. 10017.

CAREER: Teacher in public schools in Baltimore, Md., 1953-55, and in a school for special education, 1955-56; Notre Dame Preparatory School, Baltimore, assistant librarian, 1974-79.

*WRITINGS—*For children: *What About Me?,* F. Watts, 1976; *P.S. Write Soon,* F. Watts, 1978; *Evy-Ivy-Over,* F. Watts, 1978; *A Summer's Worth of Shame,* F. Watts, 1980. Author of a regular column, "The Children's Place," for the Baltimore *Sun.* Also contributor of essays and short stories for the Baltimore *Sun, McCall's* and *Good Housekeeping.*

WORK IN PROGRESS: A novel for young people; short stories.

SIDELIGHTS: "I live in a very noisy house with my husband, five children (a sixth is married and lives close by) and two dogs and two cats. People often ask me if I write about my own children, but I find that my characters are more apt to come from the child that I was rather than from those I observe. I also find I know far more about my 'book children' than I do about my real life children—but even my book children have been known to surprise me at times.

"One thing that children often ask me is how much in a book is real and how much is made up. I enjoy 'dissecting' a book with them and showing how it is a combination of reality and imagination."

ROJANKOVSKY, Feodor (Stepanovich) 1891-1970 (Rojan)

PERSONAL: Surname is pronounced Roh-jan-*koff*-skee; born December 24, 1891, in Mitava, Russia; died, 1970; came to the United States in 1941; son of a school administrator; children: Tanya. *Education:* Moscow Fine Arts Academy, student, 1912-14. *Residence:* Bronxville, N.Y.

CAREER: Began illustrating children's books during the Russian Revolution; art director of both a fashion magazine and a book publishing company, also stage decorator in Poland, beginning 1920; worked for an advertising agency, motion pictures, and several publishing firms in Paris, 1927-41; associated with the Artists and Writers Guild, New York City, 1941-51. *Military service:* Russian Imperial Army, infantry reserve officer, 1914-17. *Awards, honors:* Limited Edition Club's Silver Medal of the Silver Jubilee, 1953; Caldecott medal, 1956, for *Frog Went A-Courtin'* edited by John Langstaff; Art Directors Club Gold Medal.

WRITINGS—All self-illustrated: *The Great Big Animal Book,* Simon & Schuster, 1950; *The Great Big Wild Animal Book,* Simon & Schuster, 1951; *Animals in the Zoo,* Knopf, 1962, reissued, Random House, 1973; *Animals on the Farm,* Knopf, 1967; *F. Rojankovsky's ABC: An Alphabet of Many Things,* Golden Press, 1970.

Illustrator: Esther Holden Averill and Lila Stanley, editors, *Daniel Boone: Historic Adventures of an American Hunter among the Indians,* Domino Press (Paris), 1931; E. H. Averill, *Powder: The Story of a Colt, a Duchess and the Circus,* H. Smith & R. Haas, 1933; Rose Celli, *Les Petits et les Grands,* Flammarion (Paris), 1933, translation published as *Wild Animals and Their Little Ones,* Artists & Writers Guild (Poughkeepsie, N.Y.), 1935; E. H. Averill, *Flash: The Story of a Horse, a Coach-Dog and the Gypsies,* Faber, 1934; E. H. Averill, *The Voyages of Jacques Cartier,* Domino Press, 1937, reissued as *Cartier Sails the St. Lawrence,* Harper, 1956; Jean Mariotti, *Tales of Poindi* (translated from the French by E. H. Averill), Domino Press, 1938.

Hans Christian Andersen, *Old Man Is Always Right,* Harper, 1940; Algernon Blackwood, *Adventures of Dudley and Gilderoy* (edited by Marion B. Cothren), Dutton, 1941; *The Tall Book of Mother Goose,* Harper, 1942; Rudyard Kipling, *How the Camel Got His Hump,* Garden City Publishing, 1942; R. Kipling, *How the Leopard Got His Spots,* Garden City Publishing, 1942; R. Kipling, *How the Rhinoceros Got His Skin,* Garden City Publishing, 1942; R. Kipling, *The Elephant's Child,* Garden City Publishing, 1942; Hazel Lockwood, *Golden Book of Birds,* Simon & Schuster, 1943; *Tall Book of Nursery Tales,* Harper, 1944; Georges Duplaix, *Animal Stories,* Simon & Schuster, 1944, reissued as *Animal Tales,* Golden Press, 1971; *Pictures from Mother Goose,* Simon & Schuster, 1945; H. C. Andersen, *Ugly Duckling,* Grosset, 1945.

Bible, *Golden Bible: From the King James Version of Old Testament* (edited by Jane Werner Watson), Simon & Schuster, 1946, reissued as *The Golden Bible: Stories from the Old Testament,* Golden Press, 1966; R. Kipling, *Butterfly That Stamped,* Garden City Publishing, 1947; R. Kipling, *The Cat That Walked by Himself,* Garden City Publishing, 1947; Covelle Newcomb, *Cortez: The Conqueror,* Random House, 1947; *The Three Bears,* Simon & Schuster, 1948 [another edition edited by Kathleen N. Daly, Golden Press, 1967]; G. Duplaix, *Gaston and Josephine,* Simon & Schuster, 1948;

FEODOR ROJANKOVSKY

(From *Cricket in a Thicket* by Aileen Fisher. Illustrated by Feodor Rojankovsky.)

Kathryn and Byron Jackson, *Big Farmer Big,* Simon & Schuster, 1948; Phyllis McGinley, *A Name for Kitty,* Simon & Schuster, 1948; Elsa Ruth Nast (pseudonym of Jane Werner Watson), *Our Puppy,* Simon & Schuster, 1948; *Favorite Fairy Tales,* Simon & Schuster, 1949; K. and B. Jackson, *The Big Elephant,* Simon & Schuster, 1949, reissued, Western Publishing, 1974.

Mikhail Mikhailovich Prishvin, *Treasure Trove of the Sun* (translated from the Russian by Tatiana Balkoff-Drowne), Viking, 1952; Claire Huchet Bishop, *All Alone,* Viking, 1953; Elizabeth Jane Coatsworth, *Giant Golden Book of Cat Stories,* Simon & Schuster, 1953; E. J. Coatsworth, *Giant Golden Book of Dog Stories,* Simon & Schuster, 1953; Nicholas Kalashnikoff, *My Friend Yakub,* Scribner, 1953; Florence Esther Tchaika, *Trouble at Beaver Dam,* Messner, 1953; E. J. Coatsworth and Kate Barnes, *Horse Stories,* Simon & Schuster, 1954; Dorothy Clarke Koch, *I Play at the Beach,* Holiday House, 1955; John Langstaff, editor, *Frog Went A-Courtin',* Harcourt, 1955, reissued, 1972.

Felix Riesenberg, *Balboa: Swordsman and Conquistador,* Random House, 1956; J. Langstaff, *Over in the Meadow,* Harcourt, 1957, reissued, 1972; Jane Thayer (pseudonym of Catherine Woolley), *The Outside Cat,* Morrow, 1957; *More Mother Goose Rhymes,* Simon & Schuster, 1958; Kathleen Daly, *Wild Animal Babies,* Western Publishing, 1958; Jean Fritz, *The Cabin Faced West,* Coward-McCann, 1958; Bible,

Catholic Child's Bible (edited by J. W. Watson and Charles Hartman), Simon & Schuster, 1958; Ann Rand, *Little River,* Harcourt, 1959.

Daniel Defoe, *Robinson Crusoe* (edited by Anne-Terry White), Golden Press, 1960; Bible, *Holy Bible* (edited by J. W. Watson and C. Hartman), Guild Press, 1960; Carl Memling, *Ten Little Animals,* Golden Press, 1961; Dimitry Varley, *The Whirly Bird,* Knopf, 1961; A. Rand, *So Small,* Harcourt, 1962; *The Dog and Cat Book,* Golden Pleasure, 1963; Aileen Lucia Fisher, *A Cricket in a Thicket,* Scribner, 1963; Jeanette Krinsley, *The Cow Went over the Mountain,* Western Publishing, 1963; C. Memling, *I Can Count,* Golden Press, 1963; (illustrator with others) *The Tall Book of Let's Pretend,* E. Ward, 1964.

Marie Colmont (pseudonym of Marie Collin Delavaud), *Christmas Bear* (translated by Constance Hirsch), Golden Press, 1966; John Graham, *A Crowd of Cows,* Harcourt, 1968; Guy Daniels, editor and translator, *The Falcon under the Hat: Russian Merry Tales and Fairy Tales,* Funk, 1969; Carol E. Lester, *To Make a Duck Happy,* Harper, 1969; Nina Rojankovsky, editor, *Rojankovsky's Wonderful Picture Book: An Anthology,* Golden Press, 1972; Bill Hall, *A Year in the Forest,* McGraw, 1975.

Under pseudonym Rojan: Lida, *Panache l'Ecureuil,* Flammarion (Paris), 1934, translation by G. Duplaix published as *Pompom, The Little Red Squirrel,* Harper, 1936; Lida, *Froux, Le Lievre,* Flammarion, 1935, translation by G. Duplaix published as *Fluff; The Little Wild Rabbit,* Harper, 1937; Lida, *Plouf, Canard Sauvage,* Flammarion, 1935, translation by G. Duplaix published as *Plouf, The Little Wild Duck,* Harper, 1936, reissued, Golden Press, 1966; Lida, *Bruin, The Brown Bear* (translated from the French by Lily Duplaix), Harper, 1937, reissued, Golden Press, 1966; Lida, *Scuff, The Seal* (translated from the French by J. Duplaix), Harper, 1937, reissued, Golden Press, 1966; Y. Lacote, *Children's Year* (adapted from the French by Margaret Wise Brown), Harper, 1937; Lida, *Spiky, The Hedgehog* (translated from the French by L. Duplaix), Harper, 1938, reissued, Golden Press, 1966; Lida, *The Kingfisher* (translated from the French by L. Duplaix), Harper, 1940; Lida, *Cuckoo* (translated from the French by L. Duplaix), Harper, 1942.

SIDELIGHTS: **December 24, 1891.** Born in Mitava, Russia. "... The roots of my vocation are to be traced back to my childhood and to my family. I must say that we were quite a family. When people ask me, 'Where are you from?' I answer, 'From Russia.' Then I feel that I owe them an explanation. My father was a teacher and administrator of high schools and his changing jobs took him across imperial Russia. My sister was born in Kishinev, which meant that she became Rumanian when the city was taken by the Rumanians. One of my brothers was born in Odessa and therefore became a Ukrainian or a 'Little Russian'; the other brother was born near Moscow and therefore he was a 'Great Russian.' My second sister was born in Estonia, and I in Mitava, Latvia. So we had five nationalities in one family. When I tried to explain that to an officer of the Immigration and Naturalization Service, he held his head with both hands and then grabbed an aspirin. I told him the story of a Jew who tried to explain that he was not a Pole. 'But weren't you born in Poland?' asked the officer. 'Listen,' answered the poor man, 'if a sparrow is born in a stable, that does not mean he is a horse.'

"Despite the fact that we were Rumanian, Ukrainian, Estonian and Latvian, we felt very much like Russians and there was a remarkable unity of atmosphere and spirit in our multi-national family. 'I do not want you to become rich,' my father used to say, 'but I want you to be well educated.' There was no danger of our becoming rich, with five children who were all to receive the best education on a teacher's salary which in those times was no higher than it is today. Yet we were all happy, and we were all extremely interested in the arts. Music, painting, literature were the family's daily and most beloved fare. My sister Alexandra went to St. Petersburg Conservatory. She had a lovely contralto voice. My brother Sergei studied law but he was a brilliant draughtsman and made excellent posters. The other brother, Pavel, an engineer, devoted his leisure to painting, and his water colors were so good that the Imperial Academy bought them. And my other sister Tatiana, who was a pupil in the aristocratic Catherine Institute for Noble Women, became a concert soloist and conducted church choirs.

"My father did not want his children to become professional artists because at that time Russian gentlemen looked down their noses at artists, but he could not help dabbling himself in painting and drawing. I remember that he accompanied his translations of Greek and Latin poets by naive and sometimes funny illustrations or made jocular portraits of his sons—in one of his drawings he represented me as gobbling buckwheat porridge.

"Two great events determined the course of my childhood. I was taken to the zoo and saw the most marvelous creatures on earth: bears, tigers, monkeys and reindeer, and, while my admiration was running high, I was given a set of color crayons. Naturally, I began immediately to depict the animals which captured my imagination. Also when my elder brothers, who were in schools in the capital, came home for vacation, I tried to copy their drawings and to imitate their paintings.

"There was another source for my artistic inspiration. After the death of my father . . . the family passed through hard times but we never parted from Father's valuable library. We kept it up and stuck to it in all our wanderings and misfortunes—and it took a revolution to destory it. There were big books in this library and I sat for hours admiring them. I remember so vividly Milton's *Paradise Lost* and *Don Quixote* with the magnificent illustrations by the great French artist Gustave Doré. And, of course, there was the Bible with the impressive drawings by the same Frenchman. One does not need to study Freudian psychology to understand the impact of these early experiences on the formation of artistic imagination and sensitivity. The whole environment in which I was brought up pushed me toward artistic expression." [Bertha Mahony Miller and Elinor Whitney Field, editors, *Caldecott Medal Books: 1938-1957,* Horn Book, 1957.[1]]

1900. "I was eight or nine when I started, together with my sister, to draw illustrations for Defoe's *Robinson Crusoe,* one of my favorite books. I am sorry to say that this first great work of mine was lost during the turbulent years of war and revolution.

"Later when I went to school in Reval Tallinn, an ancient town on the shores of the Baltic sea, my love for art was enhanced and strengthened by a passion for nature. Tallinn was surrounded by forest. The sea presented wonderful opportunities for excursions and study of sea life. But there were also steamers, sailboats, flags, and all the excitement

And then, when spring is not-quite warm
and days are not-quite mellow,
they poke up little goblets full
of yellow, yellow, yellow.
■ (From *Cricket in a Thicket* by Aileen Fisher. Illustrated by Feodor Rojankovsky.)

of a port. This was no less exciting than playing Red Indians or reading James Fenimore Cooper, the beloved author of all Russian children before, during, and after the Revolution."[1]

"My world was limited first to the apartment of the school's headmaster, and then to the yard surrounded by stunted trees and school buildings with their noisy and gay inhabitants. As soon as the bell rang at noon, I would reach up to the window, like Pavlov's dog, from where I could already hear the noise and hubbub of boys running through the yard at such speed that the eye could not follow them. They ran after each other, they ran in zig-zags, jumping, falling, leaping, and jumping again. My ears would ring from their shouts, but I could not move away from that window. When the bell rang again, this mass of boys, all dressed the same way in dark jackets with silver buttons, crowded near the main entrance and disappeared into the building." [Lee Bennett Hopkins, *Books Are by People,* Citation Press, 1969.[2]]

"What helped me enormously in my attachment to nature was an excellent teacher in high school who initiated his students into the secrets of woods and fields and lakes, and developed in us the power of observation. While I was rather poor in classes of design because I did not relish copying clay models of a pseudo-classical kind, I put all my ardor into compositions we had to write for the class in natural history, and I accompanied my enthusiastic descriptions of

(From *Frog Went A-Courtin'* by John Langstaff. Illustrated by Feodor Rojankovsky.)

plants and animals and insects with no less enthusiastic images of what I saw and loved. One such illustrated composition received the highest grade. This was my first award in art, and I was then thirteen. . . .

"I think that my training in observing nature—including such innocent things as collecting butterflies and minerals and plants and leaves, and fussing around with pet animals, and spending hours in observing wild life in forests or in Reval's 18th-century park—that all these early contacts with nature played a decisive role in my development as an artist. All my life I continued to be interested in those very things I became spellbound by as a child and as an adolescent. I believe that children who like my books feel instinctively that I see nature with the same wonder and thrill that they do.

"Later other factors were added to my first initiation into the mysteries of art and nature. I worked hard to acquire skills and techniques, and this work filled me with joy. I always loved my profession and my work. I found that creativity, particularly artistic creation, is a real blessing, and nothing else gave me such pleasure and satisfaction in life, even though I like all the good things on this earth.

"I was full of joy when . . . I was painting murals for a small theater in the Crimea, the Russian Florida, or doing some other half-professional jobs. By that time—on the eve of the First World War—everything became clear to me. I wanted to be a painter. An exhibition of paintings I saw in Moscow made me so happy and enthusiastic that I decided to present

myself in the examination contest for the Moscow Fine Arts Academy. . . ."[1]

1912. "I entered the Moscow Fine Arts Academy but two years later I was serving as an officer in the 1914-17 campaign. My regiment traveled through Poland, Prussia, Austria and Rumania. My war sketches were reproduced by art magazines. During the Revolution I started to make children's book illustrations for the young Ukrainian Republic. In 1919 I was mobilized by the 'Volunteer Army' (White Army), and soon my military career was finished behind barbed wire in Poland. Since then I have seen many countries and had many occupations." [Lee Kingman and others, compilers, *Illustrators of Children's Books: 1957-1966,* Horn Book, 1968.[3]]

1931. "In Paris, I met my first American publishers, Miss Esther Averill and Lila Stanley who were organizers of the Domino Press. I did *Daniel Boone* for them."[2]

1941. After the German occupation of Paris, Rojankovsky emigrated to the United States.

1956. Illustrations for editor John Langstaff's *Frog Went A-Courtin'* received the Caldecott Medal.

1970. Died.

Some of Rojankovsky's most noteworthy illustrations appeared in the *Tall Book of Mother Goose.* "A Mother Goose which fairly sparkles with life and color in the freshest of hues. . . . There are humor and a great zest as well as the fine artistry in these pictures," observed a critic for the *New*

York Times. A *Horn Book* reviewer commented, "Rojankovsky's pictures are on every page, gay, colorful, and above all sincere. The settings are drawn from the artist's childhood memories, the children are real and the animals are true to character."

Several of the author-illustrator's picture books were centered around the wildlife he had grown to respect as a child. A critic for the *San Francisco Chronicle* described Rojankovsky's *Animals in the Zoo* as being an alphabet book that is "simple [and] straightforward." Virginia Haviland further observed in *Horn Book:* "Mr. Rojankovsky is at his best drawing animals. The idea of an animal alphabet book has been overworked, but here he has produced something which a small child might well find memorable—lithographs in rich browns and blacks, notable for texture, expression, and liveliness."

F. Rojankovsky's ABC: An Alphabet of Many Things was the artist's last book for children. "Small children, just beginning to discover the fun of matching new words with the objects they identify, are sure to find delight in Mr. Rojankovsky's choices and his illustrations, from his spirited acrobats to his staring zebras," wrote a critic for *Publisher's Weekly.*

A reviewer for the *Bulletin of the Center for Children's Books* observed, "Although the variety and gaiety of the book are appealing, some of the pictures (and their labels) may be confusing, such as the use of 'uakari' for a monkey or 'Xantus murrelet' for a sea bird. . . ."

FOR MORE INFORMATION SEE: Bertha Mahony Miller and Elinor Whitney Field, editors, *Caldecott Medal Books: 1938-1957,* Horn Book, 1957; Lee Kingman and others, compilers, *Illustrations of Children's Books: 1957-1966,* Horn Book, 1968; Lee Bennett Hopkins, *Books Are by People,* Citation Press, 1969.

ROSENBLOOM, Joseph 1928-

PERSONAL: Born June 28, 1928, in New York, N.Y.; son of Jacob and Annie (Heck) Rosenbloom. *Education:* Attended New York University, 1946-48; University of Chicago, M.A., 1951; Rutgers University, M.S.L.S., 1965. *Religion:* Jewish. *Home:* 58 Middagh St., Brooklyn, N.Y. 11201.

CAREER: Einstein Free Public Library, Pompton Lakes, N.J., library director, 1965-67; Piscataway Township Libraries, Piscataway, N.J., library director, 1967-74; Macmillan Publishing Co., New York, N.Y., editorial researcher, 1974—. *Member:* Authors Guild.

*WRITINGS—*Adult non-fiction: *Consumer Complaint Guide,* Macmillan, 1972, 6th edition, 1979; *Kits and Plans,* Oliver Press, 1972; *Craft Supplies Supermarket,* Oliver Press, 1973; *Consumer Protection Guide,* Macmillan, 1977, 2nd edition, 1979.

For children: *Biggest Riddle Book in the World,* Sterling, 1976; *Dr. Knock-Knock's Official Knock Knock Dictionary,* Sterling, 1977; *Daffy Dictionary,* Sterling, 1978; *The Gigantic Joke Book,* Sterling, 1978; *Twist These on Your Tongue,* Thomas Nelson, 1978; *Bananas Don't Grow on Trees,* Sterling, 1979; *Silly Verse and Even Worse,* Sterling, 1979; *Maximillan You're the Greatest,* Grosset, 1979; *How Do You*

JOSEPH ROSENBLOOM

Make an Elephant Laugh?, Sterling, 1979; *Polar Bears Like it Hot,* Sterling, 1980; *Dictionary of Dinosaurs,* Messner, 1980.

SIDELIGHTS: "I have always been a closet creator. It has had a nasty way of popping up at the wrong moment, however. There I was in Piscataway, New Jersey, with a perfectly good job as director of the Piscataway Township Libraries, when it struck. I found myself mooning over being a writer rather than focusing my undivided attention on budgets, staff scheduling, monthly reports, annual reports, and the like. My job was beginning to suffer.

"Friends advised me to write part-time. Perhaps I would write myself out, or the desire would of itself go away, they suggested. I agreed not to do anything rash. I began to search for possible projects. After several abortive attempts, I hit on the idea of going to the reference desk and by listening to people I could find out what it was that they wanted to know about. If the information existed, all well and good; if the information did not exist, or did not exist in an accessible form, perhaps I could write it. This is how *Consumer Complaint Book Guide,* my first book, came about.

"I had also been drawn to the children's room. On those occasions when I needed relief from the arduous responsibilities of my position as library director, I found the children's room a relaxing place. It was there that I discovered that I had a real gift as a storyteller. I also began to look into the world of children's books of which I knew little. My visits

Why did the hippie like to stand in front of the electric fan?
It blew his mind.
■(From *Biggest Riddle Book in the World* by Joseph Rosenbloom. Illustrated by Joyce Behr.)

to the children's room grew more frequent. I realized that besides adult reference books, I was very much interested in writing for children.

"As I got deeper into the business of writing, I found a growing resentment building up inside of me against the time needed by my job. The urge to create books was driving me smack into a mid-life crisis. In order to write well, I felt it was best to devote full time to writing. If I did that, however, I would have to stop being a librarian. It was one or the other. The mid-life crisis was triggered by the realization that I did not have all the time in the world in which to make up my mind. If I waited too long, it might be too late. I became very much aware of the brevity of human life and the diminution of possibilities as time went on.

"I talked it over with friends. I consulted my bankbook and found it healthy. I also recognized that I had no responsibilities to anyone else. And so, after weighing all the pros and cons, I resigned from my position and struck out as a professional, full-time writer. That was five years ago. I must say that I have never been happier nor felt more fulfilled since. I would not necessarily recommend the same course to anyone else. I can only say that it has worked for me.

"With the exception of one title, all my books have been compilations of one kind or another. This reflects my years of experience as a professional librarian. I know where to look for things, and if I can't find them, I know who to ask. With the recent publication of *Maximilian You're the Greatest,* I've entered the world of fiction. The experience in writing this book was pure joy. I will be doing more fiction in the future, without doubt. As to the direction my fiction will take, I do not know at this moment. The lack of certitude about the future does not really bother me. I find it exciting not to know exactly where I am heading. It is all part of the discovery process, and I would not have it otherwise."

FOR MORE INFORMATION SEE: Horn Book, October, 1976.

'Tis the good reader that makes the book.
—Ralph Waldo Emerson

ROTH, Arnold 1929-

PERSONAL: Born February 25, 1929, in Philadelphia, Pa.; son of Louis (a salesman) and Rose (Paris) Roth; married Caroline Wingfield, October 26, 1952; children: Charles Perino, Adam Wingfield. *Education:* Philadelphia Museum College of Art, student, 1946-48. *Residence:* Princeton, N.J.

CAREER: Free-lance cartoonist and illustrator.

WRITINGS—Self-illustrated: *Pick a Peck of Puzzles,* Grosset, 1966; *Crazy Book of Science,* Grosset, 1971; *A Comick Book of Sports,* Scribner, 1974; *A Comick Book of Pets,* Scribner, 1976.

Illustrator: *Grimm's Fairy Tales,* Macmillan, 1963; Clifton Fadiman, *Wally the Word Worm,* Macmillan, 1963; Bennett Cerf, *Houseful of Laughter,* Random House, 1963; Jane Yolen, *The Witch Who Wasn't,* Macmillan, 1964; Richardson, Smith, and Weiss, *Six in a Mix,* Harper, 1965; Joseph Rosner, *The Hater's Handbook,* Delacorte, 1965; Holiday Magazine, *Choosing and Enjoying Wine,* Curtis, 1965; Julius Schwartz, *Go On Wheels,* McGraw, 1966; *Kids' Letters to the FBI,* Prentice-Hall, 1966; F. D. Roosevelt and others, *The President's Mystery Plot,* Prentice-Hall, 1967; Donald Pearce, *In the President's and My Opinion,* Prentice-Hall, 1967; Samuel Blum, *What Every Nice Boy Knew about Sex,* Geis, 1967; Jane Yolen, *Isabel's Noel,* Funk, 1967; Brock Brower, *The Inchworm War and the Butterfly Peace,* Doubleday, 1970; Ralph Schoenstein, *Little Spiro,* Morrow, 1971; Schoenstein, *I Hear America Mating,* St. Martin's, 1972. Contributor of illustrations to magazines, including *Punch, Holiday, Saturday Evening Post, Playboy, Look, Life, Sports Illustrated, Esquire, Show Business Illustrated.*

HOBBIES AND OTHER INTERESTS: Playing saxophone ("quite loudly").

FOR MORE INFORMATION SEE: Punch, August 31, 1966; *Horn Book,* December, 1974.

(From *A Comick Book of Sports* by Arnold Roth. Illustrated by the author.)

ROTH BY ROTH

RUDOLPH, Marguerita 1908-

PERSONAL: Born March 14, 1908, in Chernigov, Russia; married Joseph Rudolph, July, 1930; children: Alicia (Mrs. John Kaufmann). *Education:* University of Kansas, B.A., 1929; University of Minnesota, graduate study, one year; Bank Street College of Education, M.S., 1954. *Home address:* 192-20 B 64th Circle, Fresh Meadows, N.Y. 11365.

CAREER: Great Neck Community School, Great Neck, N.Y., director, 1957-70. Instructor in preschool education for summer sessions or extension courses at Adelphi University, Long Island University, and Hampton Institute. Consultant to Head Start Program, Nassau-Suffolk counties, N.Y., 1966-69; Instituto Allende, Mexico, juvenile literature workshop, teacher, 1973—. *Member:* National Association for the Education of Young Children, United Nations Association, Authors' Guild. *Awards, honors:* Citation from Writers' Union of U.S.S.R. for translation of Russian classical and contemporary children's fiction, 1979.

WRITINGS—Juvenile: *Masha, the Little Goose Girl,* Macmillan, 1939; *The Great Hope,* John Day, 1948; *You Can Learn Russian,* Little, Brown, 1964; *Look at Me,* McGraw, 1967; *The Magic Sack,* McGraw, 1967; *I Like a Whole One,* McGraw, 1968; *I Am Your Misfortune* (Latvian folktale retold), Seabury, 1968; *Brave Soldier and a Dozen Devils* (Latvian folktale retold), Seabury, 1970; *Sharp and Shiny,*

McGraw, 1971; *A Present for You*, McGraw, 1971; *The Magic Egg and Other Folk Tales of Rumania* (retold), Little, Brown, 1971; *Today Is Not My Birthday*, McGraw, 1973; *The Squeaky Machine*, McGraw, 1974.

Adult: *Living and Learning in Nursery School*, Harper, 1954; *From Hand to Head*, McGraw, 1973; (with Dorothy Cohen) *Kindergarten and Early Schooling*, revised edition, Prentice-Hall, 1977; *Should the Children Know?*, Schocken, 1978; *Include Me! Children of Special Need*, Schocken, 1981.

Translator from the Russian: Evgenli I. Charushin, *Baby Bears*, Macmillan, 1944; Charushin, *Little Grey Wolf*, Macmillan, 1963; Vsevolod Garshin, *The Traveling Frog*, McGraw, 1966; K. Ushinsky, *How a Shirt Grew in the Field*, McGraw, 1967; B. Zakhoder, *Star Bright*, Lothrop, 1969; Boris V. Zakhoder, *Rosachok*, Lothrop, 1970; Zakhoder, *How a Piglet Crashed the Christmas Party*, Lothrop, 1971; Konei Chukovsky, *Telephone*, Bobbs-Merrill, 1971; B. Zakhoder, *Crocodile's Toothbrush*, McGraw, 1973.

Stories included in a number of anthologies for children. Contributor of adult nonfiction to professional journals and popular magazines.

SIDELIGHTS: "Till the age of nine I lived in a primitive Ukrainian village among peasants, with *none* of modern technology or conveniences known to us. The native singing, local crafts and ethnic traditions left a profound impression on me and exerted a strong cultural influence. I lived through the exciting changes and turbulence of the Russian revolution, the tragedies of the civil war, and the breaking up of my family through violent death and dispersion. This is described in an autobiographical narrative, *The Great Hope*, to which Pearl Buck wrote a sympathetic introduction. Published in 1948, the book is no longer in print. My Russian education in the Soviet school in the city of Chernigov, my

"Maybe you can grind up some cracker crumbs," grandma said, and she attached a metal grinder to the kitchen table. ■ (From *The Sneaky Machine* by Marguerita Rudolph. Illustrated by Linda Strauss Edwards.)

exposure to literature, theatre and music—all contributed greatly to my development and taste.

"When I was young I do not think I showed any promise as a writer, although at age eleven I was so inspired by the Ukrainian poet Shevchenko that I wrote a biography of him, in imitative verse, and read it at a school assembly. As I was growing up—a rather shy, unassertive person—I never dreamed of becoming a writer, and most certainly not a writer in English! Yet. . . .

"When I finally emigrated to America, and started high school in Lawrence, Kansas at the age of sixteen, I naturally did not know a word of English. A little French, a bit of German, but no English—and everybody around me knew nothing else. I, therefore, found myself a deaf-mute, and a curiosity to all students, who tried to teach me. Thus, my profound ignorance of English, plus my urgent need of the language for all essentials of living gave me the incentive to learn English and the determination to master it. I also had the stamina and linguistic capacity of youth to persevere with so formidable a task. And it's interesting that my knowledge and use of Russian language makes me a more searching writer and enables me to derive greater pleasure from English.

"If I were asked what helped me most in the struggle to learn and to appreciate the English language I'd say it was first the patient, encouraging high school teachers in Kansas, and

MARGUERITA RUDOLPH

second, the study of Latin at the same time. . . . Being a writer is indeed a happy occupation as one grows older!

"*Should the Children Know?* is now published in five foreign countries—Germany, Sweden, Norway, Japan, and Australia."

Rudolph's works are included in the Kerlan Collection at the University of Minnesota and in the de Grummond Collection at the University of Mississippi.

FOR MORE INFORMATION SEE: Horn Book, April, 1968.

RYDBERG, Ernest E(mil)   1901-

PERSONAL: Born August 9, 1901, in Central City, Neb.; son of Frank Emil and Laura (Brouillette) Rydberg; married Louisa Hampton (an executive secretary and writer); children: Sonya (Mrs. Terry Cuclis). *Education:* University of Arizona, A.B., 1927. *Home:* 3742 Tennyson, San Diego, Calif. 92107.

CAREER: Along with free-lance writing, has worked in many fields—in sales, collections, banking, and in aircraft and ship-building plants; case reviewer, researcher, and writer for San Diego (Calif.) Department of Public Welfare, 1949-67. Full-time writer, 1967—. Began writing for magazines and now concentrates on juvenile books.

WRITINGS—Juvenile books: *Bright Summer,* Longmans, Green, 1953; *Sixteen Is Special,* Longmans, Green, 1954; *The Silver Fleet,* Longmans, Green, 1955; *The Golden Window,* Longmans, Green, 1956; *Conquer the Winds,* Longmans, Green, 1957; *The Mystery in the Jeep,* Longmans, Green, 1959; *The Day the Indians Came,* McKay, 1964; *The Dark of the Cave,* McKay, 1965; *The Yellow Line,* Meredith, 1969; *Footsy,* Bobbs-Merrill, 1973, large-type edition, G. K. Hall, 1973; (with wife, Louisa Hampton Rydberg) *The Shadow Army,* Thomas Nelson, 1976. Writer of about four hundred short stories for magazines and several radio scripts.

Co-author with Granville Baysee, "The Third Monkey" (three-act play), produced in 1944.

WORK IN PROGRESS: "Two books completed but not yet sold."

His arms and legs were long and thin. He was dressed in white leotards with a frilly little white skirt.
■(From *Footsy* by Ernie Rydberg. Illustrated by Charles Shaw.)

ERNEST E. RYDBERG

SIDELIGHTS: "I 'inherited' writing from relatives on my father's side of the family and also on my mother's side. I am sure this situation started me thinking of writing.

"Since I was married and had a family to support, I played it safe. I always worked at a job that would assure food and shelter. That isn't exactly true. Two or three times I broke away from this security and tried to make it on my own, but in a year or so I was back on a job.

"However, I always selected a job that would allow me to more or less forget it when I left the office, thus, allowing me to think of writing instead of unfinished business downtown. This did not lead to great advancement. In fact, I turned down many offers of advancement because I knew it would encroach on my writing time.

"I endeavored to take jobs that added to my knowledge and, if possible, to my imagination—ship building, purser on a very short run—San Diego across the Bay to Coronado. Actually, all I did was provide change for boat passengers to get through the turnstiles. You can imagine how busy I was when liberty broke for a few thousand sailors on weekends. I learned a bit here and there in banking and in building and loan associations, in furniture stores, in an aircraft factory and on and on and on. I am sure I used some of what I learned on each job in some book or another.

"I would look for story ideas much like one would pan for gold, always hoping that the next idea would be a real find. Although I started out doing adult stories, I soon found I had much more luck with juveniles, and I have done little else during the past twenty-five years."

Rydberg is a descendent on paternal side from Victor Rydberg, the Swedish writer, and on maternal side from John Watson (Ian Mclaren), a Scottish writer. Of his hopes to surpass his writing ancestors, Rydberg says: "So far it hasn't worked out quite that way."

SAUNDERS, Rubie (Agnes) 1929-

PERSONAL: Born January 31, 1929, in New York, N.Y.; daughter of Walter St. Clair and Rubie (Ford) Saunders. *Education:* Hunter College (now Hunter College of City University of New York), B.A., 1950. *Home:* 26 Glenwood Ave., New Rochelle, N.Y. 10801. *Office:* Parents' Magazine Enterprises, Inc., 52 Vanderbilt Ave., New York, N.Y. 10017.

CAREER: Parents' Magazine Enterprises, Inc., New York, N.Y., member of editorial staff, 1950-54, managing editor, 1955-60, editor of *Young Miss,* 1960-67, editorial director of *Humpty Dumpty* and *Children's Digest,* 1967—. *Awards, honors:* Outstanding Graduate award, Hunter College, 1960.

WRITINGS—For young people: *Calling All Girls Party Book,* Parents' Magazine Press, 1966; *Marilyn Morgan,*

You can't use rollers alone because they can't get into corners the way brushes can. ■ (From *Quick and Easy Housekeeping* by Rubie Saunders. Illustrated by Yvette Santiago Banik.)

R.N., New American Library, 1970; *Marilyn Morgan, Cruise Nurse,* New American Library, 1971; *Nurse Morgan Sees It Through,* New American Library, 1971; *The Franklin Watts Concise Guide to Baby Sitting,* F. Watts, 1972, published as *Baby Sitting: A Concise Guide,* Pocket Books, 1974; *The Franklin Watts Concise Guide to Good Grooming for Boys,* F. Watts, 1973; *The Franklin Watts Concise Guide to Smart Shopping And Consumerism,* F. Watts, 1973; *Quick and Easy Housekeeping,* F. Watts, 1977.

WORK IN PROGRESS: A novel, *City Summer,* and numerous articles.

SIDELIGHTS: "I write because I have something to say; I write for children and young adults because they are the most appreciative (and most critical) audience and also because I like them. Then, too, I have a strong feeling that working with youngsters, even indirectly, keeps one young in spirit."

SCHAEFFER, Mead   1898-

PERSONAL: Born July 15, 1898, in Freedom Plains, New York; son of Charles T. (a minister) and Minne (a painter; maiden name, Mead) Schaeffer; married Elizabeth Swyers (deceased); children: Lee (Mrs. Robert A. Goodfellow), Pa-

(From *Moby Dick; or, The White Whale* by Herman Melville. Illustrated by Mead Schaeffer.)

tricia (Mrs. Harry Robinson). *Education:* Attended Pratt Institute for two years; studied art under Dean Cornwell and Harvey Dunn. *Religion:* Methodist. *Home address:* 129-7th Ave., Sea Cliff, New York 11579.

CAREER: Illustrator and painter. War correspondent for the *Saturday Evening Post,* 1941-43. Illustrated books, 1921-53; painted, 1921-76. His paintings have appeared in numerous exhibitions. *Member:* Society of Illustrators, Salmagundi Club, Dutch Treat Club. *Awards, honors:* Gold Medal of the Academy of Philadelphia.

ILLUSTRATOR: Herman Melville, *Typee,* Dodd, 1922; Melville, *Moby Dick,* Dodd, 1922; Melville, *Omoo,* Dodd, 1923; Hector H. Malot, *Adventures of Remi,* Rand McNally, 1923; William C. Russell, *Wreck of the Grosvenor,* Dodd, 1923; Louis Tracy, *Wings of the Morning,* Clode, 1924; John Masefield, *Jim Davis,* F. A. Stokes, 1924; Victor Hugo, *Les Miserables,* Dodd, 1925; Frank T. Bullen, *Cruise of the Cachalot,* Dodd, 1926; Michael Scott, *Tom Cringle's Log,* Dodd, 1927; Alden A. Knipe and Emilie Knipe, *The Story of Old Ironsides: The Cradle of the United States Navy,* Dodd, 1928; Alexandre Dumas, *The Count of Monte Cristo,* Dodd, 1928; Stephen W. Meader, *Black Buccaneer,* Harcourt, 1929; A.

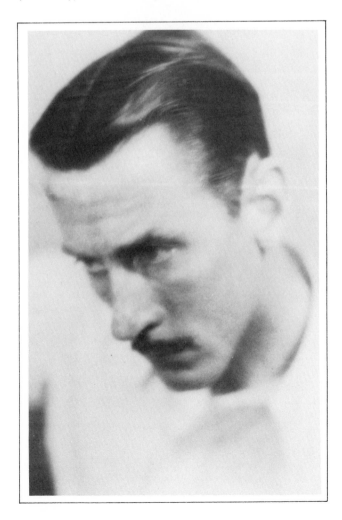

MEAD SCHAEFFER

Here the poor fellow choked, could not go on, but started up, swung the book into the sea, and vanished into his stateroom.

(From *The Man without a Country* by Edward Everett Hale. Illustrated by Mead Schaeffer.)

"If I find you here five minutes from now, you'll have to settle with me," said the innkeeper. ■ (From *The Adventures of Remi* translated by Philip Schuyler Allen. Illustrated by Mead Schaeffer.)

Dumas, *The Three Musketeers*, Dodd, 1929; Richard D. Blackmore, *Lorna Doone*, Dodd, 1930; A. A. Knipe, *Everybody's Washington*, Dodd, 1931.

Also contributor of illustrations to several magazines, including *American*, *Blue Book*, *Colliers*, *Cosmopolitan*, *Country Gentleman*, *Delineator*, *Designer*, *Everybody's*, *Farm & Fire Side*, *Harper's*, *Holiday*, *Ladies' Home Journal*, *McCall's*, *Red Book*, *St. Nicholas*, *Saturday Evening Post*, *Scribner's*, *True*, and *Woman's Home Companion*.

SIDELIGHTS: Schaeffer was born in Freedom Plains, New York. He studied at Pratt Institute and privately with Harvey Dunn and Dean Cornwell. His career in magazine illustration began at a young age and before long his works appeared in most major magazines. His World War II *Saturday Evening Post* covers of the branches of the service, as well as his other *Post* artwork, formed an exhibit which toured the United States and Canada. He lived for some time in Arlington, Vermont, a lifelong friend and neighbor of Norman Rockwell.

SCHEMM, Mildred Walker   1905-
(Mildred Walker)

PERSONAL: Born May 2, 1905, in Philadelphia, Pa.; daughter of Walter M. (a minister) and Harriet (Merrifield) Walker; married Ferdinand Ripley Schemm, 1927; children: Margaret Ripley Hugo, George W., Christopher M. *Education:* Wells College, B.A., 1926; University of Michigan, M.A., 1934. *Office:* Wells College, Aurora, N.Y. *Agent:* James Brown Associates, Inc. 25 W. 43rd St., New York, N.Y. 10036.

CAREER: John Wanamaker Co., Philadelphia, Pa., advertising copy writer, 1926-27; Wells College, Aurora, N.Y., professor of English literature, 1955-68. *Member:* American Association of University Professors.

WRITINGS:—All published by Harcourt, except as indicated: *Fireweed*, 1934, *Light from the Arcturus*, 1935, *Dr. Norton's Wife*, 1938, *The Brewers' Big Horses*, 1940, *Unless the Wind Turns*, 1941, *Winter Wheat*, 1944, *The Quarry*, 1947, *Medical Meeting*, 1949, *The Southwest Corner*, 1951, *The Curlew's Cry*, 1955, *The Body of a Young Man*, 1960, *If a Lion Could Talk*, 1970; *A Piece of the World*, Atheneum, 1972.

WORK IN PROGRESS: Novel about life and death and the importance of human relationships.

SCHILLER, Andrew   1919-

PERSONAL: Born February 1, 1919, in Hlomovec, Czechoslovakia; naturalized U.S. citizen; son of Kalman (an accountant) and Theresa (Prezlmayr) Schiller; married Evelyn Kovacs (an art instructor), February 24, 1944; children: Stephanie Maria, Geoffrey Coleman. *Education:* College of the City of New York (now City College of the City University of New York), B.S.S., 1942; University of Iowa, M.A., 1946, Ph.D., 1952. *Politics:* Liberal. *Religion:* Jewish. *Home:* 1030 North Kenilworth, Oak Park, Ill. 60302. *Office:* University of Illinois at Chicago Circle, Chicago, Ill. 60670.

CAREER: Has worked as free-lance writer and staff writer for various radio stations in New York, N.Y., University of Rochester, Rochester, N.Y., instructor in English, 1946-47; Ohio State University, Columbus, instructor in English, 1947-48; Wayne State University, Detroit, Mich., instructor in English and linguistics, 1952-55; University of Illinois at Chicago Circle, Chicago, assistant professor, 1955-61, associate professor, 1961-65, professor of English and linguistics, 1965-73, head of department of linguistics, 1973—. *Military service:* U.S. Army, Signal Corps and Military Intelligence, 1942-46.

Member: Linguistic Society of America, Modern Language Association of America, National TESOL, American Association for Applied Linguistics, U.S. Chess Federation, Chicago Linguistic Society. *Awards, honors:* Award from Standard Oil Corp. for contribution to teaching undergraduates, 1966.

WRITINGS: In Other Words, Scott, Foresman, Volume I: *A Beginning Thesaurus*, 1968, Volume II: *A Junior Thesaurus*, 1969; *Language and How to Use It*, Scott, Foresman, Books 1 and 2 (with Marion Monroe, Ralph Nichols, William Jenkins, and Charlotte Huck), 1970, Books 3, 4, 5 and 6 (with

save
preserve
conserve

hold

tend

protect
guard

Karen **keeps** goldfish.

(From *In Other Words: A Beginning Thesaurus* by Andrew Schiller and William A. Jenkins.)

Monroe, Nichols, Jenkins, and Huck), 1969, Books 7 and 8 (with Nichols, Jenkins, and Doris Welch), 1972; (with Monroe and W. C. Greet) *My Pictionary*, Scott, Foresman, 1970; (with Jenkins and Greet) *My First Picture Dictionary*, Scott, Foresman, 1970; (with Jenkins and Greet) *My Second Picture Dictionary*, Scott, Foresman, 1971. Co-author of Scott, Foresman series "Reading Systems," "Open Highways" and "Spelling Our Language." Contributor to anthologies; contributor to a variety of magazines, including *Harper's, Panorama, Kentucky Law Journal, Carleton Miscellany, Papers of the Michigan Academy of Science, Arts and Letters, Publication of the Modern Languages Association, Language and Style,* and English journals.

WORK IN PROGRESS: A book on relationships between structure of language and prose style; a book on relationships between linguistics and poetics.

SCHILLER, Barbara (Heyman) 1928-

PERSONAL: Born April 14, 1928, in Chicago, Ill.; daughter of Edward and Sarah May (Brisk) Heyman; married Hillel Schiller (an educational consultant) December 28, 1952; children: Thomas Samuel, Reuel Edward. *Education:* Syracuse University, B.A., 1948. *Politics:* Democrat. *Religion:* Jewish. *Residence:* Brooklyn, N.Y.

CAREER: Doubleday & Co., Inc., New York, N.Y., assistant editor, 1951-54; Pocket Books, Inc., New York, N.Y., associate editor, 1954-57; free-lance writer and editorial consultant, 1957—.

WRITINGS: The White Rat's Tale, Holt, 1967.

Author of folktale adaptations: Sir Thomas Malory, *The Kitchen Knight,* Holt, 1965; *The Vinlanders' Saga,* Holt, 1966; *Audun and His Bear,* Holt, 1968; *Erec and Enid,* Dutton, 1970; *The Wandering Knight,* Dutton, 1971; *Hrafkel's Saga: An Icelandic Story,* Seabury Press, 1972; *Eric the Red and Leif the Lucky, the Viking Adventure,* Troll, 1978.

SIDELIGHTS: "I wrote *The Kitchen Knight* because my five year old son was interested in knights and there was nothing for his age group. My other books grew out of an interest in medieval literature and history. I like old things and live in an old house in a well-preserved neighborhood of Victorian houses.

"I am currently at work on a book for adults interested in old houses. Possibly my interest in the old and well-established stems from a family that moved a great deal. I lived in six towns by the time I was six . . . and felt a definite lack of permanence."

FOR MORE INFORMATION SEE: Horn Book, December, 1970, February, 1973.

The crew looked in silence at the flat, wooded land before them. ■(From *The Vinlander's Saga* by Barbara Schiller. Illustrated by William Bock.)

SCHMIDT, James Norman 1912-
(James Norman)

PERSONAL: Born 1912, in Chicago, Ill.; son of Hugo and Laura (Blais) Schmidt; married Margaret Fox, 1961; children: Paul, Melissa Thompson (stepdaughter). *Education:* Loyola University, Chicago, Ill., B.A., 1932; Ecole des Beaux Arts (France), certificat, 1934; Centro Universitario Mexico, student, 1953-54. *Residence:* Athens, Ohio.

CAREER: Chicago Tribune and United Press, Paris, France, reporter, 1933-36; free-lance writer, 1936—. Lecturer on Mexican history and customs, Academia Hispano-Americana, Mexico; writer in residence, Hanover College, Hanover, Ind., spring, 1965; lecturer on English literature, Ohio University, Athens, 1965-66. *Military service:* U.S. Army, three years, attained rank of first lieutenant; awarded Bronze Star.

WRITINGS: Little Bosses, Ziff-Davis, 1934; *Murder Chop Chop,* Morrow, 1941, *An Inch of Time,* Morrow, 1942; *The Nightwalkers,* Ziff-Davis, 1946; *A Little North of Everywhere,* Pellegrini and Cudahy, 1950; *Father Juniper and the General,* Morrow, 1953; *In Mexico,* Morrow, 1956, revised edition, Doubleday, 1965; *The Fell of Dark,* Lippincott, 1960; *Terry's Guide to Mexico,* Doubleday, 1962; *The Valley of Lotus House,* P. Davies, 1962; *Navy That Crossed Mountains,* Putnam, 1964; *The Forgotten Empire,* Putnam, 1965; *The Strange World of Reptiles,* Putnam, 1966; *The Young Generals,* Putnam, 1968; *The Riddle of the Incas,* Hawthorn, 1968; *Great True Adventures,* Putnam, 1968; *Kearney Rode West,* Putnam, 1971; *Ancestral Voices,* Scholastic, 1975; *The Obsidian Mirror,* Carpenter Press, 1977. Television writer; contributor to *Saturday Evening Post, Cosmopolitan, Holiday, National Geographic,* and other journals.

WORK IN PROGRESS; Biography of Cassius Marcellus Clay.

SIDELIGHTS: "My father first stimulated my imagination and sense of wonder, setting the course that led me into professional writing. When I was a child he spent countless evenings telling me wonderful stories, mostly of adventure in far places—the Trojan War, the travels of Ulysses, the tales about Seigfried and about Sinbad. When I learned to read he gave me a beautifully-bound collection of books called *Journey Through Bookland.* It included many of the stories my father had told me, as well as simplified versions of the great epics and classic novels.

"Such reading bent me toward literature, arousing my interest in people living in distant lands. Later I was able to travel and enjoy the flavor of the places that had so intrigued me. Everywhere that I went—Europe, Norh Africa, Japan, China and Latin America—I collected information about the customs, the folk arts, the legends, and the history of people in these regions.

"All this, of course, filtered into my writing. As a result my novels and short-stories (adult fiction) were usually set in France, Spain, China or Latin America. My young adult books, all true stories about remarkable men and stirring happenings range widely—the conquest of Mexico and Peru, the adventures of our Civil War generals as young men in Mexico, the discovery of Machu Pichu, the story of the men who deciphered ancient 'lost' languages.

"Although I enjoy producing an adult novel, the task is a painful and lonely one. I'm locked up with my characters, sometimes for too long a period. I much prefer everything that is involved in doing a young adult book—the digging for information which becomes a fascinating quest, travel in the region where the story occurred, and the glimpses into the life of an interesting man or woman.

"Next best is an occasional assignment from the *National Geographic* Magazine which sends me backpacking into the sierras of Mexico to spend time with some remote Indian tribe."

FOR MORE INFORMATION SEE: Horn Book, February, 1976.

JAMES NORMAN SCHMIDT

GWEN SCHULTZ

SCHULTZ, Gwendolyn

PERSONAL: Born in Milwaukee, Wis.; daughter of Herbert (a judge) and Aurelia (an organist and teacher; maiden name, Nickel) Schultz. *Education:* University of Wisconsin, Madison, B.A. and M.A. *Religion:* Church member. *Home:* 111 West Wilson St., Madison, Wis. 53703. *Office:* University of Wisconsin, 1815 University Ave., Madison, Wis. 53706.

CAREER: University of Wisconsin, Madison, assistant professor, 1959-74, associate professor of geography, 1974—. *Member:* Authors Guild, National Writers Club, National League of American Pen Women, American Association of University Professors, Association of American Geographers, American Quaternary Association, Council of Wisconsin Writers (member of board of directors, 1976—), Wisconsin Academy of Sciences, Arts and Letters, Wisconsin Archaeological Society, Alaska Geographic Society. *Awards, honors:* Council for Wisconsin Writers best nonfiction book by Wisconsin writer, 1975, for *Ice Age Lost,* best juvenile book by Wisconsin writer, 1976, for *Icebergs and their Voyages;* Children's Reading Round Table Midwest Authors and Artists Tribute, 1979, for *The Blue Valentine;* National League of American Pen Women first-place award for best short story, 1979, for ''Return of the Wolves.''

WRITINGS: Glaciers and the Ice Age, Holt, 1963; *The Blue Valentine* (juvenile fiction), Morrow, 1965, reissued, 1979; *Colorprint World Atlas,* Fawcett, 1966; *Ice Age Lost* (nonfiction), Doubleday, 1974; (compiler) *Atlas of Wisconsin,*

University of Wisconsin Press, 1974; *Icebergs and Their Voyages* (juvenile), Morrow, 1975. Contributor of articles, reviews, and poems to periodicals, including articles for *Cricket* and *Highlights for Children.*

WORK IN PROGRESS; A book on the geology of Wisconsin tentatively titled *Wisconsin's Foundations* for the Wisconsin Geological and Natural History Survey.

SCHULTZ, Pearle Henriksen   1918-
(Marie Pershing)

PERSONAL: Born September 10, 1918, in Havre, Mont.; daughter of Louis G. (an architect) and Anne (Jacobson) Henriksen; married Harry Pershing Schultz (a professor of chemistry), September 25, 1943; children: Stephanie, Tor and Alison (twins). *Education:* University of Wisconsin, B.S., 1939; University of Miami, Coral Gables, Fla., M.Ed., 1951. *Politics:* Republican. *Religion:* Methodist. *Home:* 5835 Southwest 81st St., South Miami, Fla. 33143. *Agent:* McIntosh & Otis, Inc., 475 Fifth Ave., New York, N.Y. 10017.

CAREER: Teacher of English and history and guidance counselor in Racine, Wis., Middleton, Wis., Rahway, N.J., and Dade County, Fla., 1940-51; Cutler Cove Preparatory School, Miami, Fla., principal, 1956-63; Dade County Public Schools, Miami, Fla., supervisor of curriculum publications, 1963-72;

full-time writer in South Miami, Fla., 1972—. Florida Independent School Council, director, 1961-63.

WRITINGS: Sir Walter Scott: Wizard of the North, Vanguard, 1968; (with husband, Harry P. Schultz) *Isaac Newton: Scientific Genius,* Garrard, 1972; *Paul Laurence Dunbar,* Garrard, 1974; *The Generous Strangers: Six Heroes of the American Revolution,* Vanguard, 1976.

Under pseudonym Marie Pershing; all adult; published by Dell: *First a Dream,* 1979; *Maybe Tomorrow,* 1980.

WORK IN PROGRESS: A fictional portrayal of large public school systems, tentatively entitled, *System!,* 1981; *Bid Time Return* (novel); *Handful of Stars* (novel).

SIDELIGHTS: "My native state is Montana. I was born in Havre, but lived with my parents and an older sister on a wheat ranch many miles from town. Sometimes I think that my love for the out-of-doors must stem from those early years in the Northwest. Later we moved to Racine, Wisconsin, and I knew the joy of a big family of aunts and uncles and cousins of all ages, as well as a new brother. I went to school in Wisconsin, all the way from kindergarten through college, and I believe it is because of the excellent instruction I received in school that I am a writer today. One of the teachers who encouraged me a great deal was Ethel M. Holt, formerly of Washington Park High School in Racine. She shared her love of literature with me and encouraged me to write. Years afterward, she returned to me some early themes, poems, and short stories that I had done as homework in her English classes. They were marked: 'Save these—someday she'll be a writer.' It made me very happy to have Miss Holt as guest of honor at an autograph party

Sometimes flocks of waterfowl dotted the sky above the Colsterworth marshes. Isaac marveled at the sight. How great God was to have created so wonderful a world! ■ (From *Isaac Newton: Scientific Genius* by Pearle and Harry Schultz. Illustrated by Cary.)

held for me in a Racine bookshop shortly after the publication of my first book, *Sir Walter Scott: Wizard of the North.*

"All my life I have loved to read. I can recall with a chuckle that there were two contests I could always win: having the most freckles, and reading the most books in any one period of time. My parents had a summer home on a Wisconsin lake, and there I learned to swim and sail and play golf. In the afternoons a friend and I would take our canoes to a faraway spot on the lake and spend delightful hours reading the books that her librarian-cousin lent to us. During quiet winter evenings, books were my favorite companions. Although I did a good bit of writing of verse, it was as an instructor of English that I later earned my living. My first teaching assignment was in Franklin Junior High School, in Racine, and I can still remember all the children of my first homeroom— thirty-five wonderful seventh graders in a big, airy, old-fashioned classroom that I liked much better than the modern ones in a newer part of the school.

"I am married to a professor of chemistry in the University of Miami, here in Florida. He is someone that I first met in

PEARLE HENRIKSEN SCHULTZ

kindergarten. Once when I slid my dirty galoshes down the indoor slide, he helped me clean up the mess before our kindergarten teacher arrived to find it. We were good friends all the school years, sharing many similar interests. Our wartime wedding in my Racine Church was attended by a balcony full of very special guests—the bride's junior-high students.

"I was a teacher for a number of years, then became a guidance counselor, a principal (grades k-12), and a supervisor. Once I even had my own three children in the school where I was the principal. I rather enjoyed that, but years later they confided to me that *they* did not.

"In the books that I have written, Walter Scott will always remain my favorite character. Despite his crippled leg, he enjoyed hiking and horseback riding, and was a person of great courage. He was a splendid storyteller, even as a small lad. My book, *Generous Strangers*, is probably the one that I will always be most proud of, however. It tells the story of six foreign generals who came from Europe to aid us during the American Revolution. This book, written after some six years of research, is for readers age ten to ninety-nine. It was, in a way, a gift of myself to my country, and I expect that it will be a useful, interesting, worthwhile story for years to come.

"Once one begins to write, stories crowd their way into one's brain, begging to be written. I have done three novels lately, adult books written under the pen-name Marie Pershing, which is my middle name and that of my husband. During next year's school vacation, we hope to travel to Norway and Sweden and see the lands of our parents' roots. You can be sure that out of any trip like that will come more books!"

FOR MORE INFORMATION SEE: Science Books, September, 1972.

SCURO, Vincent 1951-

PERSONAL: Born September 28, 1951, in Jersey City, N.J.; son of Joseph E. (an executive) and Phyllis (Amato) Scuro; married Katherine Anne Krettecos, 1978. *Education:* St. Peter's College, A.B., 1973; Fairleigh Dickinson University, M.A., 1976. *Politics:* Independent. *Religion:* Roman Catholic. *Home:* Hillsdale, N.J.

CAREER: Writer, photographer, and musician. Has performed with five-piece rock music group, "Sweet Ensemble," playing trumpet, guitar, and bass guitar in night clubs and on cruise ships.

WRITINGS: (With own photographs) *Presenting the Marching Band*, Dodd, 1974; (with Sigmund A. Lavine) *Wonders of the Bison World*, Dodd, 1975; *Wonders of Donkeys*, Dodd, 1979; *Wonders of Elephants*, Dodd, 1979; (with Sigmund A. Lavine) *Wonders of Goats*, Dodd, 1980; *Wonders of Cattle*, Dodd, 1980. Contributor to *Twin-Boro News, Camera Life U.S.A., Woman's Coaching Clinic*, and *Pauw Wow* (of St. Peter's College).

Photographs published in: James C. Sparks, *Moon Landing: Project Apollo*, Dodd, 1970; Bernadine Bailey, *Wonders of Bears* (jacket photo), Dodd, 1975; Sigmund A. Lavine, *Wonders of Herbs*, Dodd, 1976; Bernadine Bailey, *Bells, Bells,* *Bells*, Dodd, 1977; Sigmund A. Lavine and Brigid Casey, *Wonders of Ponies*, Dodd, 1980.

WORK IN PROGRESS: With Sigmund A. Lavine, a book on pigs and other books in the "Wonder" series.

SIDELIGHTS: "It seems that everything I've done so far in my life has been geared toward writing—or perhaps I've been able to channel everything I've done into my writing.

"My first writing experience came as sports editor of the sixth grade newspaper in Lincoln Elementary School in Bergenfield, N.J. Since the school system placed more emphasis on music and sports than it did on journalism, I spent most of my early years practicing the trumpet and playing baseball.

"In high school I played first trumpet with the Bergenfield High School Marching Band and also belonged to the orchestra and concert band. During my junior year, I won a place in the McDonald's All-American High School Band (1967) and performed with them in the Macy's Thanksgiving Day Parade.

"After high school I began to redevelop my interest in writing and also pursue a college education. At Saint Peter's College in Jersey City, where I received a B.A. degree in political science, I played varsity baseball for three years, wrote a sports column for the college paper, and pinched-hit occasionally on trumpet for the Saint Peter's College Band. During my last year in college, I hooked up with a rock band called 'Sweet Ensemble.' By then, I had taught myself how to play the guitar and bass guitar, so I was performing on three instruments in night clubs, taverns, and on cruise ships.

"My big break came while I was employed as a free-lance publicity writer at Dodd, Mead. Since they had never published a book about marching bands before, my idea for *Presenting the Marching Band* was enthusiastically received. Photography is also a hobby of mine, so I put it to use taking the photos for my book. It has been economically rewarding, too, because I can keep the costs of my own books down and take pictures for other people's books.

"I started collaborating with Sigmund A. Lavine in May, 1974 when we both came up with the same idea for the same book, *Wonders of the Bison World*, at the same time. We've written four books together so far, and plan to finish a fifth soon."

HOBBIES AND OTHER INTERESTS: Baseball (played on varsity team in college), photography.

That place that does contain
My books, the best companion, is to me
A glorious court where hourly I converse
With the old sages and philosophers.

—John Fletcher and Francis Beaumont

FRANCOISE SEIGNOBOSC

SEIGNOBOSC, Francoise   1897-1961 (Francoise)

PERSONAL: Surname is pronounced se-nyo-*bo;* born November, 1897 (or 1900, according to some sources), in Lodève, Herault, France; daughter of Henri (an army officer) and Julie (Guerin) Seignobosc. *Education:* College Sévigné (Paris), Baccalaureat Latin-Langues, 1914; student, Monmouth College (Illinois), 1926.

CAREER: Author and illustrator of children's books. Began drawing as a child; illustrator for a publishing company in France, 1927-35, which led to an association with Scribner's in New York, beginning 1937. *Awards, honors:* New York Herald Tribune award, 1951, for *Jeanne-Marie Counts Her Sheep;* New York Times choice as one of the best illustrated children's books of the year, 1958, for *Chouchou.*

WRITINGS—All self-illustrated; all published by Scribner's, except as noted: *Fanchette and Jeannot,* Grosset, 1937; (editor with Alice Dalgliesh) *The Gay Mother Goose,* 1938; *Mr. and Mrs. So and So,* Oxford University Press, 1939; *The Gay ABC,* 1939; *The Story of Colette,* 1940; *The Thank-You Book,* 1947; *Jeanne-Marie Counts Her Sheep* (ALA Notable Book), 1951; *Small-Trot* (Junior Literary Guild selection), 1952; *Biquette: The White Goat,* 1953; *Noel for Jeanne-Marie,* 1953; *Springtime for Jeanne-Marie,* 1955; *Jeanne-Marie in Gay Paris* (ALA Notable Book), 1956; *What Do You Want to Be?,* 1957; *Chouchou,* 1958; *Jeanne-Marie at the Fair,* 1959; *The Things I Like,* 1960; *The Big Rain,* 1961; *Minou,* 1962; *What Time Is It, Jeanne-Marie?,* 1963.

SIDELIGHTS: "I was born in Lodève, in the southern part of France. When very young, I was already most talkative. I began to talk at the age of nine months. I liked to make up stories, too, and I used to tell them to my dolls, to my cats, or to anyone who was willing to listen to me.

"At age of five I received a box of colors and coloring books as a Christmas present. Ever since then, I have kept painting all the pictures that came my way. If I had no paper, I drew pictures on the wall. Then, of course, I was scolded. That made my cat Toupie very nervous. She loved me so much that she could not bear to have me scolded. She let me play with her all I wanted. I would dress her in my doll's clothes. I would put her to sleep in a small bed. But never did she protest.

"When I went to school, I liked to read stories about the Indians in America. Later, much later, I went to America and became a student at Monmouth College in Illinois. The first thing I looked for was an Indian, and I was quite disappointed to find that there were no Indians on the streets. I consoled myself then by eating ice cream—more and more ice cream.

"Before going to America, I attended Sévigné College in Paris. I also studied drawing, design, engraving, layout, and advertising.

"Be quiet," he says to Chouchou. "Don't switch your tail all the time, and everything will be all right."
■ (From *Chouchou* by Francoise. Illustrated by the author.)

(From *Jeanne-Marie at the Fair* by Francoise. Illustrated by the author.)

"When the war came and the Germans occupied Paris, I was able to escape with my best drawings. As a refugee in a small village in the southern part of France, without work, I nevertheless wanted to draw. And that is when I made the book, *Small-Trot*. Thanks to this little dancing mouse, I was able to forget the hunger and the cold. I worked continuously and thought: 'Someday the war will end. Then I will go to America and perhaps this little book will be published.' Now I am in America, and the book is published."

Seignobosc's works are included in the Kerlan Collection at the University of Minnesota.

FOR MORE INFORMATION SEE: Bertha E. Mahony and others, compilers, *Illustrators of Children's Books: 1744-1945,* Horn Book, 1947; B. M. Miller and others, compilers, *Illustrators of Children's Books: 1946-1956,* Horn Book, 1958; Muriel Fuller, editor, *More Junior Authors,* H. W. Wilson, 1963; Lee Kingman and others, *Illustrators of Children's Books: 1957-1966,* Horn Book, 1968.

SHAHN, Ben(jamin)   1898-1969

OBITUARY NOTICE: Born September 12, 1898, in Kovno, Lithuania; died March 21, 1969, in New York, N.Y. Painter, advertising designer, illustrator. Shahn, in his creation of paintings, murals, and posters, espoused liberal, political and social causes, and indeed first gained recognition in 1932 with twenty-three satirical paintings on the trial of Sacco and

Vanzetti. He was awarded many commissions for public buildings, one of his best known murals being in the main corridor of the Social Security Building in Washington, D.C. He also carried out commercial assignments for Container Corporation of America, CBS, *Time, Esquire, Harper's,* and *Fortune,* among others. Shahn was awarded the American Institute of Graphic Arts Gold Medal in 1958, and was selected by the Museum of Modern Art as one of two artists to represent America at the 1954 Venice, Italy Biennial Exhibition of International Art. Shahn's book illustrations have also earned honors. His *A Boy of Old Prague* became an ALA Notable Children's Book, and *Kay-Kay Comes Home* appeared on the list of the New York Times Choice of Best Illustrated Children's Books of the Year in 1962. *For More Information See: Current Biography,* Wilson, 1954; *Who's Who in Graphic Art,* Amstutz & Herdeg Graphis, 1962; *The Oxford Companion to American Literature,* 4th edition, Oxford University Press, 1965; *The Reader's Encyclopedia,* 2nd edition, Crowell, 1965; *Illustrators of Children's Books, 1957-1966,* Horn Book, 1968. *Obituaries: Current Biography,* Wilson, 1969; *New York Times,* March 15, 1969; *Time,* March 21, 1969; *Newsweek,* March 24, 1969; *Publishers Weekly,* April 7, 1969; *Kuntswerk,* April, 1969; *Art News,* May, 1969; *Progressive Architecture,* May, 1969.

Come, my best friends, my books, and lead me on.
—Abraham Cowley

SHANNON, Terry
(Jessie Mercer Knechtel Payzant)

PERSONAL: Born in Bellingham, Wash., real Christian name, Jessie; daughter of Frank Marshall and Abigail Ann (Jenkins) Mercer; married Charles Payzant (an illustrator); children: Ann Knechtel Broome. *Education:* Studied at Western Washington State College (now Western Washington University), University of Washington, Seattle, and University of California, Los Angeles. *Religion:* Episcopalian. *Home and office:* 609 Acacia Ave., Corona del Mar, Calif. 92625.

CAREER: Taught school briefly in Victor, Mont., and then a number of years elapsed before she took up a career again, this time as a movie columnist for several California newspapers and free-lance writer. Teamed with the artist, Charles Payzant, as illustrator, she has been a writer of children's books since 1952. *Awards, honors:* Boys' Clubs of America Junior Book Awards for *About Caves*, 1961, and *A Trip to Mexico*, 1962; University of California Friends of the Library Book and Author Award for *Zoo Safari*, 1972.

WRITINGS—All written under name, Terry Shannon, and illustrated by husband, Charles Payzant: *Jumper, Santa's Little Reindeer*, Jolly Books, 1952; *Today Is Story Day*, Al-ladin, 1954; *Wheels Across America*, 1954; *Little Wolf, the Rain Dancer*, Whitman, 1954; *Tyee's Totem Pole*, Whitman, 1955; *At Water's Edge*, Sterling, 1955; *Among the Rocks*, Sterling, 1956; *Come Summer, Come Winter*, Whitman, 1956; *Running Fox, the Eagle Hunter* (Junior Literary Guild selection), Whitman, 1957; *Where Animals Live*, Whitman, 1958; *Desert Dwellers*, Whitman, 1958; *Kidlik's Kayak* (Junior Literary Guild selection), Whitman, 1959; *A Trip to Paris*, Childrens, 1959.

About Caves, Melmont, 1960; *The Wonderland of Plants*, Whitman, 1960; *A Trip to Mexico*, Childrens, 1961; *And Juan* (Junior Literary Guild selection), Whitman, 1961; *About Ready-to-Wear Clothes*, Melmont, 1961; *About Food and Where It Comes From*, Melmont, 1961; *Stones, Bones, and Arrowheads*, Whitman, 1962; *A Dog Team for Ongluk*, Melmont, 1962; *Trail of the Wheel*, Golden Gate, 1962; *A Trip to Quebec*, Childrens, 1962; *Red Is for Luck*, Golden Gate, 1963; *Wakapoo and the Flying Arrows*, Whitman, 1963; *A Playmate for Puna*, Melmont, 1963; *Around the World with Gogo*, Golden Gate, 1964; *The Land, the Rain and Us*, Melmont, 1964; *Saucer in the Sea, the Cousteau Diving Saucer in Pacific Coast Waters*, Golden Gate, 1965; *Project Sealab*, Golden Gate, 1966; *The Sea Searchers*, Childrens, 1968; *Sentinels of Our Shores*, Childrens, 1969; *Smokejumpers and Fire Divers*, Childrens, 1969; *Ride the Ice Down*, Childrens,

Nearly half of all the people who live in teeming Hong Kong are girls and boys under the age of sixteen. ■ (From *Children of Hong Kong* by Terry Shannon. Photo by Charles Payzant.)

TERRY SHANNON

1970; *Zoo Safari*, Childrens, 1971; *New at the Zoo*, Childrens, 1972; *Windows in the Sea*, Childrens, 1973; *Antarctic Challenge*, Childrens, 1973; *Children of Hong Kong*, Childrens, 1975. Contributor to *Britannica Junior Encyclopaedia*.

SIDELIGHTS: "To gather material for *Children of Hong Kong* I spent considerable time in the Orient, especially, of course, in Hong Kong and the New Territories. I took many, many photographs in addition to obtaining information and pictorial material from Hong Kong government sources.

"In 1975 I spent several months in Iran gathering material and taking hundreds of photographs for a book about the children of Iran which was to be a follow-up to *Children of Hong Kong*. Unfortunately, however, due to a publishing policy change, the book is still unpublished. While in Iran, making my headquarters in Tehran, I traveled the country from the Caspian Sea to the Persian Gulf. I was entertained by the Empress (a private audience) at Niavaran Palace and visited the lowliest of villagers as well as the tribes people. It was an unforgettable experience. While there I spoke to a university class in children's literature and also attended a symposium on children's literature in which representatives of twenty-seven countries participated.

"In 1969 I wrote for the American Book Company, contributing to their then-new 'The Read System' series.

"Also, for several years I have produced film strips for Lyceum Productions, augmenting books such as the *Zoo* books, *Windows in the Sea* and *Antarctic Challenge*."

The books Shannon turned out in collaboration with Payzant were designed for the seven-to-twelve age group. In search

of authentic backgrounds (and "for pleasure," she added), she has traveled in Europe, Mexico, Alaska, and Canada, as well as the Middle and Far East.

Shannon's works are included in the Kerlan Collection at the University of Minnesota.

FOR MORE INFORMATION SEE: Seattle Post-Intelligencer, August 24, 1962; *Daily Pilot* (Newport Beach, Calif.), October 8, 1972.

SHINN, Everett 1876-1953

PERSONAL: Born November 7, 1876, in Woodstown, N.J.; died May 1, 1953; son of Isaiah Conklin and Josephine (Ransley) Shinn; married Florence Scovel (an author and illustrator), 1898; married second wife, Corrinne Baldwin; married third wife, Gertrude Chase, 1924; married fourth wife, Paula Downing; children: (second marriage) David and Janet. *Education:* Studied industrial design at Spring Garden Institute; attended Pennsylvania Academy of the Fine Arts; also studied art in Paris and London. *Home:* New York City.

EVERETT SHINN, 1949

(From *The Night Before Christmas* by Clement Clarke Moore. Illustrated by Everett Shinn.)

CAREER: Illustrator, painter, muralist. Began his career as a mechanical engineer at the Baldwin Locomotive Works and, later, at a lighting fixture company; became a highly acclaimed illustrator for many prominent newspapers and magazines in the 1890's; first one-man exhibition of his work, 1902; joint exhibition of "The Eight" at Macbeth Gallery, 1908; unveiling of his murals at the Trenton City Hall, N.J., 1911; several exhibitions of Shinn's work were held during the 1930's; illustrated biblical texts and books by various authors throughout the 1930's and 1940's; collected works shown at Ferargil Galleries, 1943; accorded exhibitions at American-British Art Center in 1945, 1946, and 1949; credited as art director for five motion pictures; wrote several vaudeville burlesques. *Member:* "The Eight Men of Rebellion" or the "ashcan" school of realists. *Awards, honors:* Elected associate of the National Academy, 1935; Watson F. Blair Prize, 1939; elected to the National Institute of Arts and Letters, 1951.

ILLUSTRATOR: Charles Dickens, *Christmas Carol: Being a Ghost Story of Christmas*, Winston, 1938; C. Dickens, *Life of Our Lord*, Garden City, 1939; Washington Irving, *Rip Van Winkle*, Garden City, 1939; Edward Everett Hale, *Man Without a Country*, Random House, 1940; Oscar Wilde, *Happy Prince: A Fairy Tale, and Other Tales*, Garden City, 1940; C. Dickens, *Christmas in Dickens*, Garden City, 1941; C. Dickens, *Mystery of Edwin Drood*, Heritage, 1941; Clement Clarke Moore, *Night Before Christmas*, Whitman, 1942; Maurois, *Frederic Chopin*, translated by Ruth Green Harris, Harper, 1942; *The Christ Story*, Winston, 1943; Claire Lee Stuart Purdy, *Victor Herbert, American Music Master*, Messner, 1944; *The Sermon on the Mount*, Winston, 1946; *Everett Shinn, 1873 [sic]-1953*, New Jersey State Museum, 1973.

SIDELIGHTS: **November 7, 1876.** Born in Woodstown, New Jersey, a sleepy little Quaker-dominated farm town. "I was born a Quaker, you see, so I always had to tell the truth." [*Art Digest*, November 15, 1952.[1]]

"True to the custom of the times, the little boy was dressed in long blond curls and a gingham pinafore. His mother pushed him forward toward one of the Misses Macaltioners and said fondly, 'This is little Everett.'

"Miss Macaltioner was delighted and leaned forward to coo words of confidence at the golden curls. Golden curls backed away from the loathsome cooing and threatened to be less of a Quaker than his mother.... The teacher gave him a piece of clay to work on ... I wish I could tell you at this point that the piece of clay electrified the little boy with its creative possibilities and that was the beginning, the awakening of a great American artist.

"My earliest remembrance is closely connected with acrobatics, squirming out of my teacher's strong and disapproving hands and turning somersaults backward in hilarious retreat ... climbing an iron column on my first day ... and hooking myself over a cross bar, refusing the succulent bribe of an apple and the inviting gobs of clay and blocks on the table below me." [Edith DeShazo, *Everett Shinn, 1876-1953, a Figure in His Time*, Crown, 1974.[2]]

His grandmother's death provided the bleakest moment in an otherwise agreeable childhood. "It was her utter quiet and serene placidity that shockingly thrust the word 'funeral' into my childish mind.... At the side of her coffin gripping

It was the night before the day fixed for his coronation, and the young King was sitting alone in his beautiful chamber. ■ (From *The Happy Prince and Other Tales* by Oscar Wilde. Illustrated by Everett Shinn.)

my mother's arm, I thought if grandma was dead then why this consideration for her hearing?

"Grandma would have liked the sunlight to stream in. She would have preferred cake and tea . . . and doughnuts and pie for the children, a party, a time of merriment and cheery words of remembrance for a guest that could not stay.

"Grandma Sayers' memory is part of my fiber as I am part of her blood and that part of my youth that could have trailed off to do small evil things, she checked, not by scolding or the switch but by her smile sitting at her table under the canary cage."[2]

1888. Built miniature submarine. Studied engineering and industrial design at the Spring Garden Institute, Philadelphia. "Its rise to the surface was a secret device. Four steel drums were released from the body of the ship that would rise to the surface on chains, where four sailors, inside the drums, would wind the submarine to the surface. Then again the four drums would fit neatly into the body of the ship. A hatch would close above the drums, and the sailors emerge from the bowels of the undersea craft, breathless, but having done their duty." [Bernard B. Perlman, *The Immortal Eight: American Painting from Eakins to the Armory Show (1870-1913)*, Exposition, 1962.[3]]

1890-1893. Worked for Thackeray Gas Fixture Works, Philadelphia.

1893-1897. Studied at the Pennsylvania Academy of Fine Arts. Shinn's employment as a staff artist for the *Philadelphia Press* led to an association with other artists who were to figure prominently in his life. "In the art department of the *Phila. Press* on wobbling ink-stained drawing boards . . . [we] . . . went to school, a school now lamentably extinct . . . a school that trained memory and quick perception. For in those days, there was not on any newspaper the handy use of the camera, that dependable box of mechanical memory which needed only the prodding of a finger to record all and sundry of the editor's wish. . . .

"The artists carried envelopes, menu cards, scraps of paper, laundry checks and rendered bills or frequently nothing to their work. Rigid requirements compelled them to observe, select and get the job done."[2]

1898. Married Florence Scovel, author/illustrator and member of Philadelphia's prestigious Biddle family.

1899. Decorated homes for celebrities; held first important one-man show in New York.

1900. Became well-known as an illustrator for *Harper's Weekly* and other magazines including *The Critic,* for which he illustrated Mark Twain. "Photographs of his lionlike head were plentiful, but I could not find anything of his body. The structure that must carry that head, I assumed in following my idolatry of genuis, must be so gigantic that no sheet of cardboard would be available to hold this literary colossus. To me he would be uncomfortable and cramped in the dimensions of a twelve-sheet poster."[3]

His glimpse of Twain in the flesh proved disappointing. "That man is Mark Twain, and he's coming aboard this ship. But how he has shrunk! I gazed down from the rail at that undersized figure shuffling toward the gangway while towering above him I saw an aura, a misty creation of my own—Mark Twain on stilts, peeking into the crow's nest."[3]

February, 1908. Participated in controversial exhibition of "The Eight" at Macbeth Gallery, New York. ". . . Art in America of that era was merely an adjunct of plush and cut glass.

"It [was in] a state of staggering decrepitude. . . . It was disciplined in an order of sameness, effete, delicate, and supinely refined. It revealed its pale countenance with the elegance of plush-lined shadow boxes in shrines and gilt grottos. Art galleries of that time were more like funeral parlors wherein the cadavers were displayed in their sumptuous coffins.

"One day an incredulous stare came into its imported plate-glass eye which had for a decade mirrored only lorgnettes and fawning patrons. For there on its velvet lawn stood a bedraggled group of invaders. The Eight had wandered in. The interlopers paused and removed their hats. The solemnity of death had caught at their scant respect. The Eight had journeyed out to see life and found themselves in a morgue."[2]

1912. Divorced by Florence on grounds of adultery. Wrote and produced plays with his friends at his studio.

1915. Theodore Dreiser's *The Genius* published. Main character of this publication was supposedly based on Shinn's character. "I have carefully read Theodore Dreiser's book, *The Genius,* and have ... made such marginal notes that touched on my art activities, incidents, and almost precise identification of some of my pictures that were fresh in the minds of Dreiser and in my own during a close office friendship where we both talked of our individual work. . . . We started at *Ainslee's* Magazine together.

"Beyond the actual art expression I am in no way related to Witla the artist in Dreiser's book, *The Genius.* His emotional side is far and away from mine. That side of Witla's character is presumably the emotional unrest of Dreiser himself.

"This boob, Witla, has no reserve, no doubts of his genius. . . . Idiot. My picture bought from Knoedler's Art Gallery produced at the time a particular elation but I didn't entertain a belief that I was in any way as good as Winslow Homer that hung on the right of my picture and one by Whistler on the left."[2]

1917. Art director for Sam Goldwyn.

1921. Divorced from Corrinne Baldwin, his second wife.

1923. Art director for William Randolph Hearst at Cosmopolitan Pictures. "The place of my meeting with Mr. Hearst was his temporary office in the Cosmopolitan Studios, a moving picture company of which he was president, owner, and producer. In this storage-loft-like room with its cluttered disarray of dusty props of chairs, pictures, mirrors, and ancient weapons our talk took place. He had asked me there to discuss 'Janice Meredith.'

"We had finished the preliminaries when Mr. Hearst was called on his private wire. This pause gave me more time to contemplate the picture's possibilities, particularly the need to keep fresh in the minds of our youth those events which had brought about our freedom. I saw ragged farmers holding the narrow bridge at Concord, the sudden erupting of bloody violence on the common at Lexington. I saw Bunker Hill and empty powder horns, Patrick Henry in the House of Burgesses. 'Give me liberty or give me death.' I heard the sound of gentle taps on the edge of a silver bowl that amplified into pounding hoof beats on Paul Revere's ride while far off tiny lanterns glow in a church belfry. I saw bales of tea hurtling over ships' rails in Boston harbor and the black waters and heaving ice floes of the Delaware River and the rigid figurehead of independence, General George Washington, inflexible, as if carved in oak at the prow of his barge, the leader determined against George III's Hessian mercenaries.

"I was thrilled with the prospect of seeing it all come to life again until Mr. Hearst placed the telephone on its cradle and turned to me. In one sentence he sunk my hopes for the picture's success under the ponderous weight of his final order.

"'I wish to spend a million dollars,' Mr. Hearst's thin voice was high pitched with desire. 'Yes, Janice Meredith should make a very inspiring picture and I wish to spend a million dollars on it.' How vastly different his mental picture must have been than mine. Where could a million dollars be spent? Mr. Hearst must not dare to gold plate the homely pewter.

"For the battle of Lexington, a long line of lumber laden trucks and a weaving trail of motor cars filled with carpenters,

Dogs, too, . . . barked at him as he passed.

(From *Rip Van Winkle* by Washington Irving. Illustrated by Everett Shinn.)

masons, mechanics, and their helpers from the Cosmopolitan Studios in New York drew in on a thousand acres of pastureland in Mount Kisco and deployed to dump their cargoes of building material at designated positions for houses that had been checked from a ground plan taken from ancient maps and old prints of the little hamlet of Lexington, Massachusetts.

"With the same precision that would mark the efficiency of a corps of Army engineers or the gangs that pitch a tented circus city there was to come out of their labor a mirroring duplicate of that historic spot on a stage in a Manhattan suburb, ready to echo again the surge of violence and the blast of guns which had wedged apart the colonies from their mother country.

"One other important scene was yet to be recorded, General Washington in his floating deep freeze crossing the Delaware River. This scene was filmed at Lake George as no snow was scheduled to fall about any waterway near New York. Mr. Hearst's millions held no lure for the custodians of cosmic forces. It was old stuff. Everybody had seen the Currier and Ives lithographs of the event. Everyone had seen the original or post cards of the world wide famous great dimensional painting hanging in the Congressional Library at Washington. Why fill the screen with such bleakness.

"The scene was admittedly historical but why repeat it when refreshing interest waited in the person of Janice Meredith on the opposite shore impatient to greet Washington with the

EVERETT SHINN

news that the whole damned British army was soused and the General would have a pushover with them when he and his men entered the Inn."[2]

1932. Divorced by Gertrude Chase, his third wife.

1939. Received Watson F. Blair Prize for watercolor.

1942. Divorced from his fourth wife, Paula Downing, a much younger woman. "In risking the precarious hazards on the slack wire of matrimony one needs the intrepidity of a Blondel who teetered out standing in a bucket over the roar and suctional pull of Niagara Falls. Four times above the whirlpools that were set in violent motion by so slight a stir I have had an imbecilic confidence in my success. Having, since a small child, a predilection for acrobatics, I have on each successive disaster followed the patterned coercion of a circus boss, who, having witnessed the precipitous drop of an aerial performer, demands, 'Get back up there while your leg is broken and try again . . . never mind your fractured wrist . . . get up there *now* understand *now*—*not tomorrow . . . now, now, now or you're fired*.['] The voice of the boss was the voice of experience for he knew that had the trapeze artist nursed his broken bones and convalesced with the mounting thought of the dangers in his act he would never perform again. Once you've lost your nerve, you're through.

"So bruised as I was I went up again. I looped and pinwheeled and hanging from toes I believed, as always, that I was giving my best performance. Look, no hands. I was even cheered by the doubters who had shown no faith in my

ability to stick. I swung higher. Still no hands. I just couldn't fall. Then both wires on the trapeze snapped and shot up to the top of the tent like released watch springs and I spun to earth. Ah, as usual, some woman had removed the net.

"Bruised again and in the same manner of warding off fright I allowed no time to gather timidity between my flops in matrimony. Because of desire that bolsters confidence and I had desire enough to be irked at being grounded, I tried again. A casual check on the apparatus and I was again swinging from my toes . . . de . . . da . . . de . . . da . . . airy as a bird . . . swinging from my toes . . . up . . . down . . . up . . . down . . . no hands . . . de . . . da . . . de . . . da . . . but fate had dipped the trapeze bar in a biting corrosive acid . . . snap . . . and as I fell I saw a cobweb substituted for the net . . . held at each end by two lawyers dressed as clowns."[2]

1950-1951. Inducted into American Academy of Arts and Letters.

May 1, 1953. Died in New York Hospital. "An artist's life . . . Lord, you can have an awful lot of fun, but it's hard too, awfully hard; you can never stop, you know."[1]

Shinn's works are included in the Kerlan Collection at the University of Minnesota and in the collections of the Metropolitan Museum of Art, Whitney Museum and Philips Memorial Gallery in Washington.

FOR MORE INFORMATION SEE: Bertha E. Mahony and others, *Illustrators of Children's Books: 1744-1945*, Horn Book, 1947; J. Fitzsimmons, "Everett Shinn: Lone Survivor of the Ashcan School," *Art Digest*, November 15, 1952; Bertha E. (Mahony) Miller and others, *Illustrators of Children's Books: 1946-1956*, Horn Book, 1958; Bernard B. Perlman, *The Immortal Eight: American Painting from Eakins to the Armory Show (1870-1913)*, Exposition, 1962; M. S. Young, "Everett Shinn: Out of the Ashcan," *Art News*, November, 1973; Edith DeShazo, *Everett Shinn, 1876-1953: A Figure in His Time*, Potter, 1974.

Obituaries: *Art Digest*, May 15, 1953; *Art News*, June, 1953; *Current Biography Yearbook*, 1953; *New York Times*, May 3, 1953; *Newsweek*, May 11, 1953; *Time*, May 11, 1953; *Americana Annual*, 1954.

SHOWERS, Paul C. 1910-

PERSONAL: Born April 12, 1910, in Sunnyside, Wash.; son of Frank L. and M. Ethelyn (Walker) Showers; married Kay M. Sperry, 1946 (divorced); children: Paul W., Kate B. (twins). *Education:* University of Michigan, A.B., 1931. *Home:* Palo Alto, Calif.

CAREER: Detroit Free Press, Detroit, Mich., copyreader, 1937-40; *New York Herald Tribune*, New York, N.Y., copy desk, 1940-42; *New York Times*, New York, N.Y., editorial staff of Sunday department, 1946-63, editorial staff of *Times* Sunday Magazine, 1963-76; freelance writer, 1976—. *Military service:* U.S. Army, 1942-45; became staff sergeant; on staff of *Yank*, Army weekly, one-time editor of Okinawa edition.

WRITINGS—All published by Crowell, except as noted: *Find Out By Touching*, 1961; *In the Night*, 1961; *The Listening Walk*, 1961; *How Many Teeth*, 1962; *Look at Your*

Eyes, 1962; *Follow Your Nose*, 1963; *Your Skin and Mine*, 1965; *Columbus Day*, 1965; *How You Talk*, 1967; *A Drop of Blood*, 1967; *Before You Were a Baby*, 1968; *Hear Your Heart*, 1968; *A Baby Starts to Grow*, 1969; *Indian Festivals*, 1969; *What Happens to a Hamburger?*, 1970; *Use Your Brain*, 1971; *Where Does the Garbage Go?*, 1974; *Sleep is for Everyone*, 1974; *The Moon Walker*, Doubleday, 1975; *The Bird and the Stars*, Doubleday, 1975; *A Book of Scary Things*,

Doubleday, 1977; *Me and My Family Tree*, 1978; *No Measles, No Mumps for Me*, 1980.

ADAPTATIONS—All published by Crowell: "Look at Your Eyes" (filmstrip with record; film with cassette), 1962; "How Many Teeth" (filmstrip with record; film with cassette), 1962; "Follow Your Nose" (filmstrip with record; film with cassette), 1963; "Your Skin and Mine" (filmstrip with record;

As the weeks go by, the baby becomes bigger and stronger. ■(From *A Baby Starts to Grow* by Paul Showers. Illustrated by Rosalind Fry.)

film with cassette), 1965; ''Drop of Blood'' (filmstrip with record; film with cassette), 1967; ''How You Talk'' (filmstrip with record; film with cassette), 1967; ''Hear Your Heart'' (filmstrip with record; film with cassette), 1968; ''Baby Starts to Grow'' (filmstrip with record; film with cassette), 1969; ''What Happens to a Hamburger?'' (filmstrip with record; film with cassette), 1970; ''Use Your Brain'' (filmstrip with record; film with cassette), 1971.

SIDELIGHTS: ''I write children's books sporadically, usually on topics suggested by the editors. These deal mainly with 'science' subjects, but I am less interested in writing about science than in putting together books that will appeal to kids who are still learning to read a new language (as kids in kindergarten and the first three grades are doing—even in high school, it seems.) It is important to have a lot of easy books that are also interesting. To paraphrase Dr. Johnson on writing, I think that unless we find it easy to read, we aren't likely to do much reading.

''When I have settled on a subject for a book, I do a lot of research, gathering as many facts as possible so I can decide which ones to throw out. When I finally get down to the typewriter, I work out all sorts of sentence sequences, trying to be clear and specific and, when possible, amusing. It takes a lot of tries to work out a simple text that develops a new idea in terms already familiar and also repeats word combinations and groupings to give the struggling reader occasional patches of familiar ground over which he/she can skim quickly to the harder parts. While working on a book, I try, whenever possible, to eavesdrop on the conversation of kids, paying attention to the kinds of sentences they use when talking among themselves. In 'science' primers you need a lot of familiar easy words and sentence structures to compensate for the inevitable terminology.''

Showers' works are included in the Kerlan Collection at the University of Minnesota.

FOR MORE INFORMATION SEE: Horn Book, April, 1969, April, 1975; *Redbook,* August, 1974; *Wilson Library Bulletin,* October, 1975.

PAUL C. SHOWERS

SIMON, Howard   1903-1979

OBITUARY NOTICE: Born July 22, 1903, in New York, N.Y.; died October 15, 1979, in White Plains, N.Y. Artist, illustrator, book designer, educator, and author. Simon illustrated more than fifty books, including a number of children's books written by his second wife, Mina Lewiton. He collaborated with Lewiton on *If You Were an Eel, How Would You Feel?* and *Who Knows Where Winter Goes?.* Among the other books he wrote were *500 Years of Art and Illustration, From Albrecht Duerer to Rockwell Kent; Primer of Drawing for Adults;* and *Cabin on a Ridge.* At the time of his death Simon was artist-in-residence at the Barlow School. *For More Information See: More Junior Authors,* Wilson, 1963; *Illustrators of Books for Young People,* 2nd edition, Scarecrow, 1975; *Who's Who in American Art,* Bowker, 1978; *Contemporary Authors,* Volume 33-36, revised, Gale, 1978. *Obituaries: New York Times,* October 17, 1979; *Contemporary Authors,* Volume 89-92, Gale, 1980.

Better to be driven out from among men than to be disliked of children.

—Richard Henry Dana

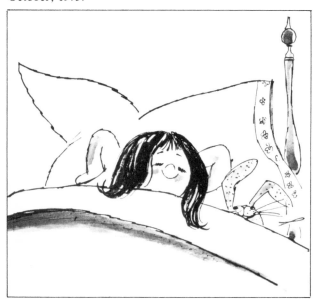

In the morning my nose tells me about breakfast.
■ (From *Follow Your Nose* by Paul Showers. Illustrated by Paul Galdone.)

SMITH, Jessie Willcox   1863-1935

PERSONAL: Born September, 1863, in Philadelphia, Pennsylvania; died May 3, 1935, in Philadelphia, Pennsylvania; buried in Woodland Cemetery, Philadelphia, Pennsylvania; daughter of Charles Henry (an investment broker) and Katherine DeWitt (Willcox) Smith. *Education:* Attended the School of Design for Women, the Pennsylvania Academy of the Fine Arts, 1885-1888, and studied under Howard Pyle at the Drexel Institute. *Home:* "Cogshill," Chestnut Hill, Philadelphia, Pennsylvania.

CAREER: Illustrator of books for children, artist. Began career teaching kindergarten for a year; after early training did several drawings for *St. Nicholas* magazine, but it was during her study with Pyle that she got first book commissions—illustrations for two books about Indians; went on to illustrate such classics as *Little Women* and *A Child's Garden of Verses.* Did advertisements and illustrations for periodicals, including the *Ladies' Home Journal, Collier's, Scribner's, Harper's* and *Good Housekeeping,* for which she did covers. *Member:* Plastic Club of Philadelphia; Philadelphia Water Color Club; Pennsylvania Academy of the Fine Arts; Society of Illustrators; New York Water Color Club; Philadelphia Art Alliance; American Federation of Arts. *Awards, honors:* Bronze medal, Charleston exposition, 1902, Mary Smith prize of the Pennsylvania Academy of the Fine Arts, 1903; silver medal, St. Louis exposition, 1904; the Beck prize of the Philadelphia Water Color Club, 1911, silver medal for water colors, Panama-Pacific exposition, 1915.

ILLUSTRATOR: Henry Wadsworth Longfellow, *Evangeline* (illustrated with Violet Oakley), Houghton, 1897; Mary P. Smith, *Young Puritans in Captivity,* Little, Brown, 1899; Louisa May Alcott, *An Old-Fashioned Girl,* Little, Brown, 1902; Mabel Humphrey, *The Book of the Child* (illustrated with Elizabeth Shippen Green), F. A. Stokes, 1903; Frances H. Burnett, *In the Closed Room,* McClure, Phillips, 1904; Robert Louis Stevenson, *A Child's Garden of Verses,* Scribner, 1905, reissued, 197?; Helen Whitney, *The Bed-Time Book,* Duffield, 1907; Aileen C. Higgins, *Dream Blocks,* Duffield, 1908; Carolyn Wells, *The Seven Ages of Childhood,* Moffat, Yard, 1909; Jessie Willcox Smith (compiler), *A Child's Book of Old Verses,* Duffield, 1910; Betty Sage, *Rhymes of Real Children,* Duffield, 1910.

Penrhyn Coussens (compiler), *A Child's Book of Stories,* Duffield, 1911; Angela M. Keyes, *The Five Senses,* Moffat, Yard; *Dicken's Children: Ten Drawings by Jessie Willcox Smith,* Scribner, 1912; Clement C. Moore, *'Twas the Night Before Christmas,* Houghton, 1912; *The Jessie Willcox Smith Mother Goose,* Dodd, 1914; Alcott, *Little Women,* Little, Brown, 1915, reissued, 1968; Priscilla Underwood, *When Christmas Comes Around,* Duffield, 1915; Charles Kingsley, *The Water-Babies,* Dodd, 1916; Mary Stewart, *The Way to Wonderland,* Dodd, 1917; *The Little Mother Goose,* Dodd, 1918; George MacDonald, *At the Back of the North Wind,* McKay, 1919; Ada and Eleanor Skinner (compilers), *A Child's Book of Modern Stories,* Duffield, 1920; MacDonald, *The Princess and the Goblin,* McKay, 1920.

Johanna Spyri, *Heidi,* McKay, 1922; Ada and Eleanor Skinner (compilers), *A Little Child's Book of Stories,* Duffield, 1922; Nora A. Smith, *Boys and Girls of Bookland,* Cosmopolitan, 1923; Ada and Eleanor Skinner (compilers), *A Very Little Child's Book of Stories,* Duffield, 1923; Samuel Crothers, *The Children of Dickens,* Scribner, 1925; Ada and Eleanor Skinner (compilers), *A Child's Book of Country Sto-*

JESSIE WILLCOX SMITH

ries, Duffield, 1925; Jessie Willcox Smith (compiler), *A Portfolio of Real Children,* Duffield.

Also illustrator of "Beauty and the Beast" and "Goldilocks," and with Elizabeth Shippen Green illustrated a calendar, "The Child," 1903.

SIDELIGHTS: **September, 1863.** Born in Philadelphia the youngest in a family of two sisters and two brothers. The Smiths, originally from New York, transplanted into the rigidly Victorian society of Philadelphia. "Everyone knows the Smiths are a large family but it's been brought to my attention that they're *very* large. I frequently get letters beginning something like this, 'Aren't you the little golden-haired Jessie Smith I used to go to school with?' And never yet *have* I been that little golden-haired Jessie Smith!" [An interview with Jessie Willcox Smith taken from a Personal Collection from The Archives of the Pennsylvania Academy of the Fine Arts.[1]]

During Smith's early school years, artistic abilities were not demonstrated—she never drew as a child. By her own admission: "The margins of my schoolbooks were perfectly

Meg, Jo, Beth and Amy. ■ (From *Little Women* by Louisa M. Alcott. Illustrated by Jessie Willcox Smith.)

clean and unsullied with any virgin attempts at drawing.'' [S. Michael Schnessel, *Jessie Willcox Smith*, Crowell, 1977.[2]]

1879. After a private elementary school education, Smith, intrigued with children, was sent to finish her education in Cincinnati to begin study for a career as a kindergarten teacher. ''I had always loved children and, since I was obliged to earn my own living, decided to be a kindergarten teacher. The friend with whom I lived while I was studying was an artist and had consented to give some lessons to a young chap who was anxious to learn to draw. I went along as chaperone—this was in the day of chaperones. . . .

''My friend looked around the room in which the lesson was about to begin. 'What do you want to draw?' she asked the boy, 'Here's a student lamp. Try that. Why don't you sketch it, too, Jessie, just for fun?' The boy grasped his crayon hard, screwed up his face and began laboriously to copy the lamp. I took a pencil, made a few swift lines and then went on with the book I had brought to read. When my friend saw the sketch exclaimed, 'Why, Jessie, you can *draw*—that's good! How do you do it?' She took the sketch to her mother who was an illustrator of some note and on the strength of that sketch of a student lamp I was actually persuaded to cut short my kindergarten course and study art.

''[So] . . . I decided to become a sculptor. The first thing I ever sold was a little colored boy eating a watermelon—I didn't know enough to have it cast and was peddling my model, fired. I took it to our biggest Philadelphia art store which was where the Benjamin Franklin Hotel now stands and was prepared to sell it for anything over five cents. I showed it to a clerk who told me they didn't often buy things of that kind and was turning disconsolately to go when he said he'd look at it again and then asked me how much I'd sell it for.

'''Would five dollars be too much?'

'''It's really worth more.'

'''Would ten be too much?'

'''I'll give you fifteen!'

''I walked home feeling a millionaire. I had made my first sale!

''My career as a sculptor, however, was brief, for my clay had bubbles in it and would burst when it was being fired. 'Heavens,' I decided, 'being a sculptor is too expensive! I'll be a painter!'

''I can't remember when I decided that children were my forte. I always wished there were children in the life classes— the men and women were so flabby and fat! The first picture I ever sold was an advertisement for Ivory soap—two children building block houses with Ivory cakes!''[1]

1885. Returned to Philadelphia after giving up teaching to enroll in the School of Design for Women.

Fall, 1885-1888. Transferred to the Pennsylvania Academy of the Fine Arts where she studied under Thomas Eakins. One critic concluded that 'only the most tenacious student could subject herself to the rigorous demands of Eakins' teaching, which made no allowances for the 'frailties' of women.''[2]

''The first work I sold was some place cards. . . . They had been ordered by some one who was having a performance of 'The Mikado.' I can remember distinctly painting the little Japanese figures on them.'' [*The Philadelphia Ledger*, July 16, 1922.[3]]

May, 1888. First illustration appeared in *St. Nicholas*, a magazine for children. Obtained a position with *Ladies' Home Journal* in Philadelphia illustrating advertisements and borders for editorials.

When asked to give her ideas on the coordination of women's interests, Smith responded: ''It's a subject on which I've squandered a good bit of thought. Of course my viewpoint is that of the childless and unmarried woman—and it is quite definite.

''A woman's sphere is as sharply defined as a man's. If she elects to be a housewife and mother—that is her sphere, and no other. Circumstance may, but volition should not, lead her from it.

''If on the other hand she elects to go into business or the arts, she must sacrifice motherhood in order to fill successfully her chosen sphere.

"What is the matter with the children of today? Why, their parents are *bored* by them. That's the explanation of the 'flapper' and the ungovernable youth. The bored parents have been seeking other interests and the neglected children have been shifting for themselves.

"To me this seems one of the greatest problems in the country—this neglect of children in the so-called 'better' homes. . . . I am very strongly *against* the coordination of a married woman's interests!"[1]

1894. Enrolled in an afternoon illustration class at Drexel Institute taught by Howard Pyle. "At the Academy we had to think about compositions as an abstract thing, whether we needed a spot here or a break over here to balance, and there was nothing to get hold of. With Mr. Pyle it was absolutely changed. There was your story, and you knew your characters, and you imagined what they were doing, and in consequence you were bound to get the right composition because you lived these things. . . . It was simply that he was always mentally projected into his subject."[2]

With Pyle as her mentor, Smith found her niche as an illustrator. "When, however, I came under the guidance of Howard Pyle I began to think of illustration in a light different from that of a pot-boiler'"[2]

"Mr. Pyle frequently made arrangements with publishers to have the illustrations for new editions done by pupils in his classes. He then had his pupils compete in making potential drawings for the story, and to the one he considered had done the best he turned over the work of illustrating the book.

"One time I, fortunately or unfortunately, got the illustrating of an Indian book. I hated to do Indians and I struggled and plodded through the task and was delighted at last to complete the commission and dispatch it to the publisher. You can imagine my surprise when, a few days later, the same publishers sent me another Indian story to illustrate. I received it with none too good grace, but in those days I was not declining any work, and I appreciated that my future hinged on how I fulfilled my early commissions. So, unpleasant though I found the work, I took infinite pains to make it both attractive and accurate in detail.

"When the third Indian story came in quick succession, I said to myself, 'This must cease.' And so, when I had finished the drawings for that one, I sent them back with a little note to the effect that if the publishers would send me some other children's stories I thought I could illustrate them satisfactorily. If I hadn't done that I might still be drawing Indians."[3]

Pyle was immediately impressed with three of his students—Smith, Violet Oakley and Elizabeth Shippen Green (the three women were to maintain a life-long friendship).

1898. Pyle recruited Oakley and Smith for the commission of illustrating Longfellow's *Evangeline*. In a preface to the text Pyle discussed his students' illustrations: "I do not know whether the world will find an equivalent pleasure to my own in the pictures that illustrate this book, for there is a singular delight in beholding the lucid thoughts of a pupil growing into form and color; the teacher enjoys a singular pleasure in beholding his instruction growing into a definite shape.

(From *Bugs and Wings and Other Things* by Annie W. Franchot. Illustrated by Jessie Willcox Smith.)

Nevertheless, I venture to think that the drawings possess both grace and beauty."[2]

After leaving Drexel, Smith was offered a teaching position. However, numerous commissions already undertaken caused her to decline the offer. "You have put your plea most temptingly and flatteringly in the face of what Howard Pyle is able to accomplish in his life. The excuse of being too busy is such a feeble one. However, he brings a man's strength and endeavour to it. I can duly judge for myself and realize that my woman's strength would be too severely taxed if I undertook a class in addition to all the rest."[2]

1901. Moved to the Red Rose Inn near Bryn Mawr with fellow artists Green and Oakley and was later joined by Henrietta Cozen who oversaw the management of both the household and the gardens.

1902. Won Bronze Medal at Charleston Exposition.

1903. *The Child* (later published as *The Book of the Child*), a calendar and collaborative effort between Smith and Green, brought both women national attention.

"Some days my doll-child is so bad." ■ (From *Dream Blocks* by Aileen C. Higgins. Illustrated by Jessie Willcox Smith.)

December 23, 1903. Commissioned by *Scribner's Magazine* to illustrate *The Child's Garden of Verse*. Scribner's proposal: ". . . I write to say that it is understood that you are to illustrate (in colors) *The Child's Garden of Verse* for the lump sum of $3600., we to own the originals and have exclusive publications rights.

"It is further understood that there are to be:

12	Full pages at 200	2400.
1	Cover design	75.
1	Lining design	75.
1	Title page	50.
100	Small drawings	1000.

"(Or whatever number is necessary to distribute properly throughout the book—when final dummy is arrived at it will probably be found that some of the drawings can be very slight.)

"We will appreciate it greatly if you will make an early selection of the twelve (12) full page subjects in order that *Collier's Weekly* may nominate from the list of twelve, the six (6) which they will reproduce. The six drawings which they are to publish will, of course, have to be done first as we must begin to deliver these drawings to them for reproduction as early as October or November, 1904. If we could have all six ready at that time it would be desirable.

"The cover, linings, etc., would be the next in importance.

"In making our arrangement with *Collier's* for the publication of the six drawings we have agreed to deliver to them the first of the drawings in the fall of 1904, the others to follow at short intervals. In view of what you told me, I judge that it will be entirely possible to live up to this arrangement. . . ." [Charles Scribner's Sons to Jessie Willcox Smith, New York, December 23, 1903. Taken from a Personal Collection from the Archives of the Pennsylvania Academy of the Fine Arts.[4]]

1904. Won Silver Medal for illustration at the St. Louis International Exposition.

1905. Moved into the newly refurbished Hill Farm, Chestnut Hill, Philadelphia, named COGSLEA—the first four letters of the name derived from the first initials of its occupants—*C*ozen, *O*akley, *G*reen, and *S*mith.

1905. *A Child's Garden of Verses* published. A letter from Scribner's expressed their satisfaction with Smith's illustrations. "I have used up all the adjectives that I believe in using, (there are certain ones which are ruled out) so I will simply say that the last two drawings which reached me today are delightful examples of the sort of thing of which you are master." [Charles Scribner's Sons to Jessie Willcox Smith, New York, April 26, 1905. Taken from a Personal Collection from the Archives of the Pennsylvania Academy of the Fine Arts.[5]]

A critic commented at the time of Smith's greatest popularity that "Miss Smith has created for us more of a type of childhood. There is no mistaking a drawing or painting by this artist: that charm in children that appeals to all pervades her work, and, although it is essentially illustrative in its rendering, a high order of craftsmanship is displayed. There is

(From *The Book of the Child* by Mabel Humphrey. Illustrated by Jessie Willcox Smith.)

no better nor significant way to describe the irresistible charm of Miss Smith's work than to say its spirit is akin to that which pervades Stevenson's *A Child's Garden of Verse*. . . . On the seashore, or in the fields, Miss Smith asks us to join her little army at play; but if we do, we must leave behind anything not distinctly of the child's world, for these little people will be intolerant of the artificial.''[2]

Maxfield Parrish was a recipient of one of Smith's paintings. He wrote her in his exuberance: ''She came today at last, and my! But we are glad to have her. We never knew of such a long water color exhibition, and had almost given up hope. She is a perfect wonder, and I am proud as can be. It's the first hand made picture I ever owned, and to have gotten it so dirt cheap, really doesn't seem right. I hope you don't regret the deal very much. I think she is worthy of a better frame than the one she is in, and as soon as our living room is built I am going to have her set in the wall. I thank you a thousand times for her.'' [Maxfield Parrish to Jessie Willcox Smith, New Hampshire, May 11, 1905. Taken from a Personal Collection from the Archives of the Pennsylvania Academy of the Fine Arts.[6]]

Of all her illustrations, Smith considered advertisements least desirable even though these commissions proved financially lucrative. Smith created advertisements for Ivory Soap, Cuticura Soap, Kodak, Campbell Soup, and Fleischmann's Yeast.

The Cream of Wheat Company commissioned Smith for advertisement services as well. ''We are in receipt of your esteemed favor of June 8th also of rough sketch mentioned, which we are returning to you today by express, for completion.

Must we to bed indeed? Well then,
Let us arise and go like men,
And face with an undaunted tread
The long black passage up to bed.
■ (From "North-West Passage," in *A Child's Garden of Verses* by Robert Louis Stevenson. Illustrated by Jessie Willcox Smith.)

(From *The Now-A-Days Fairy Book* by Anna Alice Chapin. Illustrated by Jessie Willcox Smith.)

''We wish to congratulate you very much indeed in this instance upon the happy way in which you have caught and reproduced our idea. We have had this idea in mind for several years and have had sketches from same made by many different artists, none of which, however, have seemed to catch the idea as you have in the present sketch.

''We would ask you to complete same at your earliest convenience and, in this connection, would request that you do not attempt to alter the present rough sketch, but to re-draw it and complete the re-drawing, sending us together with the present sketch for comparison. The beauty of this picture is in the intangible something which you have in the child's face and I appreciate that it is many times difficult for an artist, in a completed painting, to again catch the happy expression that they have in their rough drawing.

''As an illustration of this, I recollect a very pretty design that was drawn for us by Otto Schneider, the beauty of it, however, lying entirely in the arch expression of one of the children's faces. He attempted to finish this design and told me that he worked on it off and on for three months and absolutely had to give it up. We could never again catch the expression.

"The painting should be finished so that it would reproduce, if possible, equally well either in two, three or four colors. The color scheme which you have in this rough sketch strikes me as peculiarly adaptable to this class of work." [The Cream of Wheat Co. to Jessie Willcox Smith, Minneapolis, June 10, 1908. Taken from a Personal Collection from the Archives of the Pennsylvania Academy of the Fine Arts.[7]]

1914. With brother, aunt, and Cozen, Smith moved into her own sixteen-room house "Cogskill," adjacent to Cogslea to afford herself greater privacy and richly flowered gardens—inspirational setting in which her young models could behave naturally. ". . . And while they were playing at having a perfect time, I would watch and study them, and try to get them to take unconsciously the positions that I happened to be wanting for a picture. All the models I have ever had for my illustrations are just the adorable children of my kind friends, who would lend them to me for a little while."[2]

"Children are like flowers. It seems to me inappropriate to dress them in bizarre colors or to paint them in a bizarre manner." [Edith Emerson, "The Age of Innocence: Portraits by Jessie Willcox Smith," *The American Magazine of Art,* Volume XVI, No. 7, July, 1925.[8]]

It was indeed the natural movement which she encouraged in her young subjects. "Once during the war, when I was painting children's portraits while doing my bit for one of the Liberty Loan drives . . . many of the artists painted a portrait gratis for any one who would buy $10,000 worth of Liberty Bonds—I painted the portrait of three little brothers. They were just steps apart, little yellow-headed fellows, all dressed in canary-colored suits and as much alike as the proverbial peas. Their greatest distinction lay in the toys they carried. One had an elephant, one a camel and the smallest one a kiddie car. . . . He disported himself by riding it round and round my easel while I worked, and I could catch a glimpse of his face only as he looked this way for a second while turning a corner."[3]

Professional child models were to Smith distasteful. "Such a thing as a paid and trained child model is an abomination and a travesty on childhood—a poor little crushed and scared, unnatural atom, automatically taking the pose and keeping it in a spiritless, lifeless manner. The professional child model is usually a horribly self-conscious, overdressed child whose fond parents proudly insist that he or she is just what you want, and give a list of the people for whom he or she has posed."[2]

A way to hold a child's attention was "to tell fairy stories—tell them with great animation! A child will always look directly at anyone who is telling a story; so while I paint, I tell tales marvelous to hear. But to paint with half one's mind, and tell a thrilling, eye-opening tale with the other half is an art I have not fully conquered even yet. Alas the resplendent Cinderella sometimes stops halfway down the stairs, slipper

**The children were nestled all snug in their beds,
While visions of sugar-plums danced in their heads...**
■ (From *'Twas the Night Before Christmas* by Clement C. Moore. Illustrated by Jessie Willcox Smith.)

Little Miss Muffet. ■(From *The Little Mother Goose* by Jessie Willcox Smith. Illustrated by the author.)

and all, while I am considering the subtle curve in the outline of the listener's charming, enthralled little face.

"Many of my portraits are painted out-of-doors. Out-of-doors seems the natural background for childhood. Given leaves, and flowers and sunshine, which is theirs by right, their little faces glow in the full light as though illumed from within. Heavy draperies and dark shadows, with the strong concentrated studio light, are not expressive of childhood to me. I want children under the blue sky, in the shining radiance and joy which is their birthright, and with the flowers of God's earth, of which they are only a higher bloom at their feet."[2]

An ill-mannered child did not please her, yet she admitted that they "are often like this, poor little things, through no fault of their own."[2]

Smith never regretted the presence of children in her studio. "It has been one long joyous road along which troop delightful children, happy children, sad children, thoughtful children, and above all wondering, imaginative children, who give to their charmingly original thoughts a delicious quaintness of expression. I love to paint them all."[2]

Her illustrated children's books carried a tremendous appeal for adults as well. On one occasion, Smith making a gift of one of her works to a young child who posed for her included

the following note: "To Pierre—With the understanding that if he finds this book too young for his advanced years—he shall give [it] to his father. With love, Jessie Willcox Smith."[2]

1917. First *Good Housekeeping* cover appeared. Smith, receiving $1500 and $1800 per cover, was affectionately called "The Mint" by her friends.

1925. Devoted less time to book and magazine illustration to concentrate her efforts on portrait painting. ". . . Even as a young art student my ambition was to do portrait painting, and all other work seemed to me at first but a means by which I could make enough money to afford eventually to do the work I wanted. . . .

". . . I shall never do portrait work to the exclusion of everything else.

"My portrait work began as the result of using a neighbor's child to pose for an illustration. The picture proved so true to life that the parents wanted the original painting because of its portrait value. This incident has since been repeated several times, and so I kill two birds with one stone, the little model's family having the original and the public having its print either as a book illustration or as a cover design for *Good Housekeeping* Magazine. Of course, I frequently do pure portrait work."[3]

Smith at work, 1930.

"The ideals of Jessie Willcox Smith have been woven into the fabric of contemporary thought and impressed upon the consciousness of innumerable mothers who hope that their children will look like the children she paints. With unerring directness and sure instinct she has touched the heart of the people and it is there that we must look if we seek to find her special shrine." ["Memorial Exhibition of the Work of Jessie Willcox Smith: Pennsylvania Academy of the Fine Arts, March 14 through April 12, 1936." Taken from a Personal Collection from the Archives of the Pennsylvania Academy of the Fine Arts.[9]]

Art critic Rilla Evelyn Jackman summed up Smith's contribution to American illustration: "In the peculiar place which Miss Smith holds in the art world she is quite as worthy of our interest as are many of the artists who paint easel pictures for our great exhibitions or murals for our public buildings. In fact, she, more than most of them, is bringing art to the people. We are proud of the eagle, and fond of the warbler, but even for them we would not give up the robin and the bluebird."[2]

1933. Sailed for Europe. Suffered from various maladies—difficulty in walking and seeing.

May 3, 1935. Died in Cogshill, Philadelphia. Edith Emerson

offered a final tribute to her friend. "Nothing morbid or bitter ever came from her brush. This is not because the difficulties of life left her untouched. She had more than her full share, but when they came she met and conquered them. She demanded nothing for herself but obeyed the simple injunction on the poster she designed for the Welfare Federation—GIVE. She helped those in need, the aged, the helpless, the unfortunate. She gave honest and constructive advice to students who came to her for criticisms. She rejoiced in the success of others and was modest about her own. Tall, handsome and straightforward, she carried herself well, with no trace of self-assertion. She always spoke directly and to the point. She lived quietly, and loved natural unaffected things and people. Altogether hers was a brave and generous mind, comprehending life with a large simplicity, free from all pettiness, and unfailingly kind."[1]

FOR MORE INFORMATION SEE: Elinor Whitney and Bertha E. Mahony, *Contemporary Illustrators of Children's Books,* Women's Educational and Industrial Union, 1930, republished, Gale Research, 1978; Stanley Kunitz and Howard Haycraft, editors, *Junior Book of Authors,* second edition revised, H. W. Wilson, 1951; Edward T. James, editor, *Notable American Women, 1607-1950,* Harvard University Press, 1971; S. Michael Schnessel, *Jessie Willcox Smith,* Crowell, 1977.

SPENCE, Eleanor (Rachel) 1927-

PERSONAL: Born October 21, 1927, in Sydney, New South Wales, Australia; daughter of William Charles (a farmer) and Eleanor (Henderson) Kelly; married John A. Spence (a management consultant), June 17, 1952; children: Alister Martin, Nigel Henderson, Lisette Eleanor. *Education:* University of Sydney, B.A., 1949. *Religion:* Roman Catholic. *Home:* 11 Handley Ave., Turramurra, New South Wales 2074, Australia.

CAREER: Author of children's books. Commonwealth Public Service Board, Canberra, Australia, librarian, 1950-52; Coventry City Libraries, Coventry, England, children's librarian, 1952-54; Autistic Children's Association of New South Wales, Sydney, Australia, teaching assistant, 1974—. *Member:* Autistic Children's Association of New South Wales, Australian Society of Authors, Royal Australian Historical Society. *Awards, honors:* Australian Children's Book of the Year award, 1964, for *The Green Laurel,* and 1977, for *The October Child;* Hans Christian Andersen Honor List, 1979, for *A Candle for St. Antony.*

WRITINGS—Children's books; all published by Oxford University Press, except as noted: *Patterson's Track,* 1958; *Summer in Between,* 1959; *Lillipilly Hill,* 1961, Roy, 1963; *The Green Laurel,* 1963, Roy, 1965; *The Year of the Currawong,* Roy, 1965; *The Switherby Pilgrims,* Roy, 1967; *Jamberoo Road,* Roy, 1969; *The Nothing Place,* 1972, Harper, 1973; *Time to Go Home,* 1973; *The Travels of Hermann,* Collins, 1973; *The October Child,* 1976, published in the U.S. as *The Devil Hole,* Lothrop, 1977, *A Candle for St. Antony,* 1978.

WORK IN PROGRESS: The Symbols at Your Door.

SIDELIGHTS: "MYSELF—THE WRITER? I've added the question-mark because, as I often try to explain to children and adults alike during Children's Book Week activities, I'm always at a loss to separate the essential 'me' from the 'author' of a dozen or so novels. I don't believe it can be done; even works of fiction bear, written large or small, the imprint of the writer's personality, interests, and experience, though they are—and should be—in disguise.

"The disguise can often wear thin. When asked by young readers (who seem to come up with more subtle questions every year) if any character in my books is actually *me,* I usually start mumbling and dodging, because I recall with a kind of guilt the number of literary, well-read, sensitive and imaginative heroes and heroines who emerge in so many of my books, to say nothing of the independent and ambitious ones like Harriet in *Lillipilly Hill* and Cassie in *Switherby Pilgrims* and *Jamberoo Road.*

"I'm not saying I really *was* like that. Rather, these characters are romantic images of what I *sometimes* was. And they are the kinds of people I loved to read about in my own childhood. I think that as I grow older, becoming further removed in time from the days of my youth, I tend to recall some of the deeper, less obvious aspects of myself-as-child-and-teenager, and this has led to the creation of characters like Rowan, in *Time to Go Home,* and Rudi in *A Candle for St. Antony;* the fact that they are both boys, whereas earlier I tended to use girls as central figures, may have a significance in itself. To even things up, I've gone back to the female side in my latest book, *The Symbols at Your Door,* and make no apologies for calling my heroine 'Rachel,' which is my own

Shane liked to have his calculations properly worked out. It meant that he could make the most of the free time which seemed to be dwindling so alarmingly as he grew older. ■ (From *The Nothing Place* by Eleanor Spence. Illustrated by Geraldine Spence.)

second name. Names for characters are a source of preoccupation—I can never settle down to create a character in my mind without giving him or her a suitable, and sometimes distinctive, name. Similarly, I find it hard to see the story as a whole unless I have a title all ready for it.

"Thus, the answer to my young questioner, seeking to discover which person in my books is really me-in-disguise, would have to be: 'All the central characters have something of me in them, and not just me-as-a-child. They also contain me-as-writer—and storyteller.'

"(It is much easier if I'm asked: 'Which is my *favourite* character?' I can then say, without mumbling at all: 'Rudi!'— and hurry on to the next raised hand before the first child can add 'Why?' The reply would have to be too long-winded for a snappy 'Meet the Author' session.)

"To return to me-as-storyteller—I have always believed that every novel for young readers must have a story worth telling, on my side, and worth reading, on their side. The fact that many adults are dipping into children's fiction these days (either furtively or openly) suggests to me that they are as inevitably drawn to a 'good yarn' as their children. Yet it is this feature of the writer's task that has always given me the most trouble. My heart goes out to primary-school pupils who are expected to write a 'story' in the course of their 'Creative Language' lessons; I know exactly how hard it is to come up with a sound, believable, *original* plot. So often you think you have one, only to find that it breaks down miserably in the middle, or collapses before it reaches the

ELEANOR SPENCE

finish-line. I rather tend to create characters first and foremost, and then hope they will obligingly suggest their own 'story,' by doing things natural to their own personalities; this can be over-optimistic, and is by no means always successful. I would much prefer to be inspired right away by a brilliant plot-idea—or group of ideas—and build up my characters in the course of the action. I feel that must be the way a truly great storyteller works; he manipulates his 'people' according to his clearly thought-out plan, rather than letting the people manipulate *him.*

"The problems I have with plots no doubt reflects the real-life difficulties I have with organising my own thinking. I invariably see two sides to every question, and try to follow both at once. Or I start off to pursue a line of thought to its necessary conclusion, and become distracted by all kinds of fascinating little byways, and never get to the end at all. As a child, I spent hours day-dreaming; as an adult, I still do it, though I might appear to observers to be concentrating on the sheet of paper in my typewriter, boldly headed: 'Chapter Six.'

"How much attention do I pay to the needs and wants and abilities of my young readers? This is the most vexed question of all, and one being rightly asked by many librarians, teachers and parents, and sometimes the children themselves. I certainly don't work at my typewriter with, posed in the imagination in the middle distance, an 'average' boy or girl aged eleven and a half, with an IQ of 110 and a reading age of twelve; that kind of limitation would rapidly stifle even the brightest flame of inspiration. Yet we must work within a certain framework of rules, and it is just this that, to my mind, makes writing for the young a more demanding job than writing for adults, or for no definable age-group at all.

"I did not set out with the intention of being a 'writer for children.' I *did* set out to be a writer. As a nine-year-old, I

scribbled away at my own stories, unmoved by the fact that they were shamelessly derived from *Anne of Green Gables* or *Seven Little Australians.* (I loved to read and write about families, and I was especially fascinated by orphans. I yearned to adopt neglected infants; as there were none available in our neighbourhood of small farms and orchards, where parents, though often hard-pressed financially, did a great job of bringing up their children, I had to settle for adopting stray kittens, or turning my assortment of dolls into orphanage-waifs. Because another dearly-loved book was Noel Streatfeild's *Ballet Shoes,* the foundlings usually graduated to brilliant futures.)

"Quite early in my career, I discovered that no story of my own really satisfied me unless somebody else *read* it. It was my mother who filled the role of both reader and tactful critic. Perhaps I might have been better prepared for harsh reality if her criticism had been sterner, but I think not—I would probably have retired in floods of tears, and my literary career would have ended forthwith. (These days I am a little tougher in the face of criticism—I simply tell myself firmly that the critic must have got out of the wrong side of bed that morning. Or perhaps his bio-rhythms were upset.)

"Years later, when experience as a children's librarian gave me the idea of writing stories for children, I found it relatively easy to adopt style suited to the theme—in this case, a straightforward adventure in the bush, called *Patterson's Track.* I was *comfortable* using this means of expression, and time proved that young readers accepted and enjoyed it. I simply went on as I had begun.

"Twelve books have seen the light of day since then, and I still believe that what I want to say—or tell—and the way in which I can best say it, make these novels fit naturally into the category 'Young Peoples' Fiction.' If *A Candle for St. Antony* appeals to fourteen- or fifteen-year-olds rather than to their younger brothers and sisters, then it would seem to be because I had a particular story to tell whose protagonists could not have been, themselves, any younger than fifteen—otherwise, there would have been no story. And it was a story I very much wanted to tell, at that particular time in my own life.

"The writer, like any other person, grows and alters and develops with time and circumstances. His or her books will inevitably reflect this pattern of growth, separated from the reality by distance, imagination, and much embroidery. Even my 'historical' stories, like *Lillipilly Hill* and *Switherby Pilgrims,* have their roots in a certain period of my own life when I was especially interested in local history, and the theme of *The Nothing Place* reflects the beginning of my concern for the handicapped and the 'disadvantaged' in the community.

"This makes it all sound very serious and heavy, and indeed I have been accused of being too 'moral.' (I've also been called 'naive,' but sometimes, I suspect, this is because I use in my books only the more acceptable kinds of four-letter words.) I can only repeat that my first consideration is to tell a story, not to pass on messages. At the same time, however, I do hope that the occasional reader might gain something positive from one or two of my books; after all, I am trying to share a particular experience with that person, who happens to be young. The gain, as I recall from my own childhood reading, is a moment of recognition, a glow of feeling shared with a character in a certain situation—a very special kind of joy.

''I believe the young still find much joy in reading. And writers, in spite of all the struggling and disappointments and frustrations, still find much joy in writing.''

Spence became interested in writing Australian fiction for children as a result of her work as a librarian in Coventry, where there was a lack of reading matter for children of families intending to move to Australia. She is keeping journals of her work with autistic and handicapped children for possible literary use in the future.

FOR MORE INFORMATION SEE: Horn Book, April, 1964, April, 1970, August, 1977, October, 1979.

STEPHENS, William M(cLain)   1925-

PERSONAL: Born May 11, 1925, in Chattanooga, Tenn.; son of W. M. and Lela (Brown) Stephens; married Margaret McCurdy, January 5, 1945; children: Don C., Julia, Roger, Melani. *Education:* University of Tennessee, J.D., 1950; University of Miami, Coral Gables, LL.M., 1974. *Religion:* ''Loving the one God who is behind *all* religions.'' *Home:* 1401 Havens Dr., Crescent Beach, S.C. 29582.

CAREER: Attorney at law in Chattanooga, Tenn., 1950-53; *Florida Outdoors* (magazine), Sun City and Fort Myers, Fla., editor, 1954-59; *Underwater* (magazine), Homestead, Fla., editor, 1960-62; free-lance writer and photographer, 1962-63; University of Miami, Institute of Marine Science, Coral Gables, Fla., science writer and editor, 1963-66; *Oceanology International* (magazine), Beverly Shores, Ind., editor, 1966-68; Miami Seaquarium, Miami, Fla., director of education, 1968-70; University of Miami, associate director of publications, 1971-74; Gaston College, Dallas, N.C., professor of police science, 1974–76; Tennessee Commission on Aging, staff attorney, 1976-77; Legal Services of Upper East Tennessee, director, 1977-79; University of South Carolina, Coastal Carolina College, Conway, S.C., adjunct professor, 1979—. *Military service:* U.S. Marine Corps, 1942-45.

When disturbed or frightened, a ghost crab may remain absolutely still, as shown, until all danger has passed. ■ (From *Come With Me to the Edge of the Sea* by William M. Stephens. Photographs by the author.)

William Stephens prepares to make a research dive in the submersible, *Star II.*

MEMBER: International Oceanographic Foundation, American Museum of Natural History, Friends of the Earth, Audubon Society, Smithsonian Institution.

WRITINGS: *Our World Underwater,* Lantern Press, 1962; *Science Beneath the Sea*, Putnam, 1966; *Southern Seashores,* Holiday House, 1968.

For children: *Life in the Open Sea,* McGraw, 1971; *Come with Me to the Edge of the Sea,* Messner, 1972; *A Day in the Life of a Sandy Beach,* McGraw, 1973; *Islands,* Holiday House, 1974; *Life in a Tidepool,* McGraw, 1975.

Children's books, with wife, Peggy Stephens—All published by Holiday House: *Octopus,* 1968; *Sea Horse,* 1969; *Hermit Crab Lives in a Shell,* 1970; *Sea Turtle Swims the Ocean,* 1971; *Killer Whale*, 1972; *Flamingo,* 1972.

WORK IN PROGRESS: A novel about a spiritual search in India; a book for young people about saints and masters of the East; a book about teaching marine education (for elementary grade teachers).

SIDELIGHTS: "The major motivating influence on my life has been the teaching and guidance of a great spiritual master of India, Avatar Meher Baba (1894-1969). Everything else has been secondary."

SUTTLES, Shirley (Smith) 1922- (Lesley Conger)

PERSONAL: Born March 25, 1922, in Seattle, Wash.; daughter of Walker Conger and Marie (Beidel) Smith; married Wayne Suttles, 1941; children: seven. *Education:* University of California, B.A., 1944. *Home:* 5750 S.W. Hewett Blvd., Portland, Oregon. *Agent:* Howard Moorepark, 444 East 82nd St., New York, N.Y. 10028.

CAREER: Free-lance writer.

WRITINGS—All under pseudonym Lesley Conger: *Love and Peanut Butter,* Norton, 1961; *Adventures of an Ordinary Mind,* Norton, 1963; *Three Giant Stories,* Four Winds, 1968; *Tops and Bottoms: Adapted from a Folk Tale,* Four Winds, 1970; *To Writers, With Love,* Writer, Inc., 1971. Writer of radio and television scripts for Canadian Broadcasting Corp. Contributor to popular magazines, including *Redbook, Cosmopolitan, Good Housekeeping,* and *Ladies' Home Journal.* Author of monthly column "Off the Cuff," *The Writer,* 1965—.

WORK IN PROGRESS: "I am working on a novel which I suppose can best be described as a realistic fantasy. Its theme involves the moral question of the dominion of man over the other forms of life with whom he shares this planet."

SIDELIGHTS: "I always wanted to write, and I began when I was a very young girl. I wrote fairy stories in what were

SHIRLEY SUTTLES

But as soon as the plow dug into the good, black dirt, pop!—there in front of him stood a goblin.
"Fine!" cried the goblin. "And *I'll* take the crop, I will!"

(From *Tops and Bottoms*, adapted from *A Folk Tale* by Lesley Conger. Illustrated by Imero Gobbato.)

then called 'nickel notebooks' (imagine a notebook for only a nickel!), then read them aloud to whatever smaller children I could round up in the neighborhood. There weren't any smaller children in my own family—*I* was the smallest.

"I didn't have long to wait to become a published writer. My first story was published when I was eleven years old. However, since my uncle owned the little newspaper it was printed in, I can hardly claim to have broken into the world of print through talent alone.

"Because my husband and I have seven children, people I meet have always assumed that I write mainly for young people. But the truth is that I have written, so far, only two books for children—and that it took me eighteen years of my writing career to get around to those! It all began when Robin, the youngest of our seven, asked me to write a book for her. I'm sure the other children must have asked the same thing, one after the other, years before, but I had never done it. It wasn't that I didn't want to; I think I was afraid to try. But Robin was the last of seven, and that made a difference, for if I were ever going to try writing for children, I thought, it really had to be now or never. (It strikes me today, of course, how absurd this was. Anyone with seven children should have been able to look into the future and see grandchildren.)

"I wrote a lot of stories for children before I wrote the ones that were finally published in my two books. (I didn't have any soft-hearted uncle in the children's books business!) I found I liked retelling folktales, and I was especially pleased to discover the one I used in *Tops and Bottoms*—and then pleased all over again when I first saw the fine goblin the artist, Imero Gobbato, created for the illustrations.

"One of the best things about writing for children is reading the letters they write to me. My favorite of all time begins, 'Dear Mrs. Conger, I am writing to you because I have to do this for school.' When our county library asked some local writers to lend fan letters to be put on display with our books, that one was one of the two I sent.

"Now that I am expecting another grandchild—and that will make seven—and now that my grandchildren are beginning to be old enough to read, I am beginning to think about writing a book for one of *them*."

In an article for *The Writer*, Conger puts in a "good word for failure." "Thomas Huxley once said, 'There is the greatest practical benefit in making a few failures early in life.'

"Let's wrestle!" bellowed the giant. Poor Big-Mouth! Struggling in the giant's grasp, he began to sweat.
■ (From *Three Giant Stories,* as told by Lesley Conger. Illustrated by Rosalind Fry.)

"I suppose he meant that it's salutary and chastening, that it tempers the spirit—something of that sort. Good enough, and I agree; but I'm not sure about that 'early in life' part. I suspect that most of us go on making failures of one sort and another all the way through life, to the bottom of the final page. Of 'the greatest practical benefit?'—well, not all of them, surely; and yet, with Huxley's maxim in mind, I've been taking a less jaundiced view of failure, no matter when it comes.

"When I look back over my thirty-year writing career, I can see that my path, while marked by the milestones of various publications and productions—short stories, radio plays, books, . . . all the items that would appear in my bibliography—has also been determined by, directed by, and detoured by all sorts of other things which will never be listed anywhere because they were my failures and my mistakes.

"My first book is, of course, a milestone. But why did I write it? It was, you might say, a book written on the rebound from a literary affair that went sour. I was under contract

for a novel. I had submitted three chapters and an outline, had received an advance, and was writing along merrily when suggestions that came to me from New York made me wonder whose book it was, and my relationship with my editor eroded. Things began to come apart, and after several months of this, I had a terrible attack of psychosomatic eczema and began gobbling tranquilizers like salted peanuts. I quit the novel cold, shoved it into a box, stared at my empty typewriter, and thought I was, as a writer, done for. Then a friend wrote to me with the suggestion that I simply write an account of my daily life as I had been doing in letters to her. I had to be writing *something* (either that, or curl up and die on the spot), and it seemed an agreeable enough idea, so I did it.

"I don't think I would ever have conceived of such a book, nor would my friend, had she not been casting about for some help to give her rather miserable correspondent—who would not have been miserable had it not been for that failure of a novel. I cannot know what course my writing career would have taken had that novel-in-progress not fallen apart; nevertheless it was that first book that showed me what I could do—writing in the first person—and prepared me for the challenges and pleasures of [my] column.

"A second example: my two books for children. When we moved from Canada to Nevada some years ago, I left behind a promising career as a playwright for the Canadian Broadcasting Corporation. I could have gone on writing plays in Reno, but I discovered that I couldn't function effectively in the vacuum that resulted from not having good radio to listen to and not being close to the studios and the producers. Moreover, I also discovered that I could no longer write the kind of magazine fiction I had been doing very well with. I'm not sure why, except that I have a very strong sense of *place* when I write—and it took a me a long time to get accustomed to the new climate and the new landscape; I never *did* get accustomed to the new house. Again, I felt wiped out. I retreated into motherhood, spending all my time with our youngest, and it was she, who knew I wrote (and had on at least one occasion banished me from her room with an imperious 'Mommy, go work on your story!'), who played in time the role my friend had played a half-dozen years before. If I wrote stories, surely I could write for her, couldn't I? I didn't think I could. I certainly never had. But she insisted. So I relented, and wound up with two juveniles to my credit.

"Again, this was certainly not a well-thought-out decision of mine. Again, it was a direction determined by blank walls that suddenly rose up where I had been wont to go.

"Do you find this disillusioning? I hope not. And I hope you don't find it depressing, either, for it assuredly doesn't depress me. It is simply one of the ways in which I see myself being moved and motivated, and it is one of the ways in which I think all but the most efficient of us function, not progressing confidently from one project to the next, finishing each successfully in turn, but rather tending to stumble about, making false starts, messing things up, and constantly having to stop and get our bearings again. Early in life?—I'm still doing it; how about you?

"But look at it this way: 'If everything were to turn out just like I would want it to, just like I would plan for it too, then I would never experience anything new; my life would be an endless repetition of stale successes. When I make a mistake I experience something unexpected.' That's Hugh Prather, in *Notes to Myself* (Real People Press, Moab, Utah,

1970), a small book full of interesting insights. (He also says, 'If the desire to write is not accompanied by actual writing, then the desire is not to write,' a thought that all by itself may be worth the two-dollar purchase price.)

"Actually, failure isn't so bad. It seems to me that failure, like microbes, has suffered from bad PR. A lot of failures are completely benign. They do you more good than harm and may often teach you a lot more than your successes do. Sometimes they propel you into new and fruitful directions; they can at least show you where it is that you don't want to go again.

"We often tend to think of success as a place of arrival, a status achieved once and for all. As if that weren't wrong-headed enough, we do the same thing with failure. And then we begin using the words *success* and *failure* as labels—for people. He's a failure. She's a success.

"But failures and successes aren't people; failures and successes are events, things that happen during the processes of a life and a life's work. People who fail may go on to even fail again.

"And remember: the thing that happens to you if you fail is the same thing that happens to you if you succeed. You start over again. In *both* cases hoping to do better." [Lesley Conger, "Off the Cuff," *The Writer,* March, 1977.[1]]

SWAIN, Su Zan (Noguchi)   1916-

PERSONAL: Born March 8, 1916, in Iliff, Colo.; daughter of Minosuke and Tomi (Ogawa) Noguchi; married Ralph Brownlee Swain (an entomologist), died in 1953; married William K. Firmage, 1968; children: (first marriage) Tom Alfred, Ralph Adrian. *Education:* University of Colorado, B.F.A., 1938; attended Penn State College. *Home:* Berkshire Hills, Alford, Mass. and (winter) Sun City Center, Fla.

CAREER: School Nature League, New York, N.Y., staff artist, 1938-40; American School, Managua, Nicaragua, substitute teacher, 1951-53; free-lance illustrator of books besides her own. *Member:* American Association of University Women (chairman of art group, Summit, N.J., 1960-63), John Burroughs Association, Art Association (Gulfport, Miss.), Summit Nature Club, Sheffield Art League (Mass.), Southern Berkshire Community Art Council (Mass.; 1975-78), New York Entomological Society for "producing consistently accurate paintings of nature," (honorary life member), Delta Phi Delta (art fraternity; honorary life member).

WRITINGS—Self-illustrated: *Insects in Their World,* Garden City, 1955; *Plants of Woodland and Wayside,* Garden City, 1958; *First Guide to Insects,* Doubleday, 1964.

Illustrator: Ralph Brownlee Swain, *The Insect Guide,* Doubleday, 1948; Dorothy Shuttlesworth, *Story of Rocks,* Garden City, 1956; D. Shuttlesworth, *Story of Spiders,* Garden City, 1959; *Nature Guide: Rocky Mountains,* Golden Press, 1964; *The Story of Ants,* Garden City, 1964; E. Klots, *Field Guide to Fresh Water Life,* Putnam, 1966; D. Shuttlesworth, *All Kinds of Bees,* Random House, 1967; D. Shuttlesworth, *Natural Partnership,* Doubleday, 1969. Contributor to *Merit Students Encyclopedia* and *Crowell-Colliers Encyclopedia.*

SU ZAN SWAIN

WORK IN PROGRESS: Nature illustrations for Crowell's *Pictorial Junior Encyclopedia.*

SIDELIGHTS: "Being born to Japanese parents, much emphasis was put on appreciation of nature in our upbringing. My [four] sisters and I joined our parents in caring for the flowers and sapling trees on our farm in eastern Colorado. There was no running water, all the water for the house and yard and barnyard came from the pump run by windmill. After dinner the entire family formed a bucket brigade from the water tank to the house. Father had a large flower garden enclosed in a picket fence. By this method we watered the flower garden in front of the house and the kitchen garden in the back yard—both flourished with healthy plants in the sunny dry atmosphere.

"There were quite a few nights we got to stay up late to observe the lunar eclipse and meteor showers and even an aurora-borealis. Father would explain why and how these phenomenon occur. Later when some of us had learned to read, our parents bought a set of *Compton's Pictured Encyclopedia* so that we could look up almost anything we wanted to know."

(From *The Rocky Mountain* by Herbert S. Zim.
Illustrated by Su Zan Noguchi Swain.)

Swain reflects: "Our parents were a great influence on me.
In tragic crisis or overwhelming good experiences, I was able
to keep a more even keel because of things my mother used
to say—or better how she met all kinds of happenings, good
and bad." [Nell B. Propst, "The Wonderful Harvest of Minosuke Noguchi," *Empire* Magazine of the Denver Post,
April 22, 1979.[1]]

"Although I majored in fine arts at the University of Colorado, I took many biological sciences as electives. Since I
needed to work part of my way through school, I did drawings
for the biology department professors for their books and
papers. This experience led to a job at the American Museum
of Natural History, with the School Nature League in New
York City, immediately following graduation.

"My marriage to Dr. Ralph B. Swain, an entomologist, came
naturally after graduating. I did all the illustrations for his
scientific papers.

"In 1947 Doubleday and Company asked Dr. Swain if he
would write a guide to the insects for their Nature Series.
We worked as a team, he as author and I as illustrator. Our
two sons accompanied us on our field trips and they were
exposed to nature study. In 1948 *The Insect Guide* was published. Many other joint projects followed such as, preparing
huge biological charts, models of various human cells, etc.,
etc.

"No matter where my husband's work took us, we were able
to enjoy our surroundings and constantly learned new things.
Our sojourn in Nicaragua gave us the opportunity to become
familiar with tropical plants and animals.

"After Dr. Swain's untimely and sudden death, our children
and I returned to New Jersey to put together our shattered
life. I made a large studio in my home to return to illustrating
and writing in earnest.

"I always thought what better way can one share with others
the appreciation of nature and instill in youngsters the excitement of nature than through illustrated books. When planning a book I was influenced by things that would arouse the
curiosity and imagination of the reader. I also tried to make
the little readers reach higher than the standard average age
interests.

"Now in our semi-retirement, interest in nature and pleasant
environment gives us much joy. My husband, William Kenneth Firmage, born in Utah at the foothills of the Wachung
Range and as a youngster attended his family's kitchen garden
and learned at an early age the thrill of growing plants. Gardening as a hobby is a most rewarding activity at any age.

"My childhood ambition of seeing the entire planet Earth in
the fourth grade has been largely satisfied through travel. We
had a winter place in Ibiza, Spain in the Mediterranean Sea
and traveled annually to Europe for many years. We have
had two trips around the world, one for six months, the other
for eight and a half months. Altogether in our travels we have
covered fifty-six countries and European countries many
times. We add ethnic dances, music and arts and crafts to
the usual sight-seeing and museum and gallery visits and
trying foreign dishes. We have four languages between us
and I am unusually good in sign language with pantomime
and sound effects.

"Now that I have a little more time, I am trying new (for
me) crafts, such as weaving. Cooking has always been a
hobby and we have added many international dishes to my
repertoire."

Swain gives a modest assessment of her work: "If there is
one merit, it is accuracy."[1]

HOBBIES AND OTHER INTERESTS: Travel, study of
Spanish and Japanese; collecting records, especially classical
music; conservation, oil painting, Japanese Sumie, sculpture;
made a five month round-the world trip in 1965; numerous
trips to Europe, 1970-75; eight and a half month round-the-
world trip, 1973, with emphasis on ethnic music, dances, and
crafts; oil painting and weaving.

FOR MORE INFORMATION SEE: Diana Klemin, *The Art
of Art for Children's Books,* Clarkson Potter, 1966; Diana
Klemin, *The Illustrated Book,* Clarkson Potter, 1970.

SWEENEY, James B(artholomew) 1910-

PERSONAL: Born July 7, 1910, in Philadelphia, Pa.; son of
Anthony J. (a hotel owner) and Bertha (Collins) Sweeney;
married Helen Ver (a lieutenant in U.S. Navy), December
2, 1944; children: Dr. Frank James. *Education:* Villanova
University, B.S., 1932; attended University of Pennsylvania,
School of Industrial Art, Philadelphia, University of Okla-
homa, and University of Florida. *Home:* 7205 Burtonwood
Dr., Alexandria, Va. 22307.

CAREER: Served four years with U.S. Merchant Marine
before enlisting in Pennsylvania National Guard, 1940; U.S.
Army, 1941-50, became regimental sergeant major, 1941,
commissioned second lieutenant, 1942, later transferred to
staff of *Yank* (Army weekly); U.S. Air Force, officer, 1950-
65, with duty as a combat reporter during Korean War.
Served as a civilian public information officer with the Naval

JAMES B. SWEENEY

Oceanographic Office for nine years. *Member:* National Press Club, Children's Book Guild; Armed Forces Writers League. *Awards, honors*—Military: Bronze Star (received as combat reporter in Korea), and sixteen other military medals. Civilian: Various medals and awards from Japanese government, Georgia Sheriff's Association, and for organizing, coaching, and managing youth markmanship rifle teams.

WRITINGS: Pictorial History of Oceanographic Submersibles, Crown, 1970; *Pictorial History of Sea Monsters and Other Dangerous Marine Life,* Crown, 1972; (with Peter R. Limburg) *Vessels for Underwater Exploration,* Crown, 1973; (with Peter R. Limburg) *102 Questions and Answers About the Sea,* Messner, 1975; *Sea Monsters! A Collection of Eyewitness Accounts,* McKay, 1978; *Ghosts! A Collection of Eyewitness Accounts,* McKay, 1979; *Search and Rescue! A Collection of Eyewitness Accounts,* McKay, 1980; *A Combat Report's Report,* Watts, 1980; *Military Museum USA,* Crown, 1981; *Spies, Spooks and Undercover Agents,* Watts, 1981. Contributor of articles and stories to periodicals.

SIDELIGHTS: "When I was in grammar school, *Beau Geste,* by Percival Wren, was big on the book market, as was the first volume of Lowell Thomas' travels. Classics, such as Jack London's *Call of the Wild* and Robert Louis Stevenson's *Treasure Island,* then had the run of the first rate movie houses. While the exploits of men like Admiral Richard E. Byrd and Lawrence of Arabia were household topics.

"This was heady stuff for a boy. It was inducive to more daydreaming than studying. Which thereby earned a greater number of thumps alongside the ear, than pats on the back. One day, in a serious classroom probe of our likely futures, the teacher asked each what they would like to be. Most earned her nod of approval by dutifully saying they would like to be a parish priest, doctor, engineer, or banker. I shattered classroom decorum by stating I wanted to be, 'a professional adventurer.' As I discovered then, the road to adventure is paved with misadventure, for I wound up having to stand with my face in the corner.

"A high school degree brought about no change in outlook and at fifteen I overstated my age and went away to the army for military training. Being returned home in short order did not act as a deterrent, and neither did four years of college. By then I discovered two important facts that made life worthwhile. First, it was not against any law to stow away aboard an outgoing ship. Second, the pulps would buy my stories of adventure and daring-do. Wonderful magazines such as *Sea Stories, True, Mister, Blue Book* and *Argosy,* were thirsty markets for yarns hot off the deck of a tramp steamer plugging a passage through the China Seas. At one time I was selling a story a week for the fabulous sum of $125 each.

"However, my parents insisted that I should get married and settle down. Why it was that they always pointed out marriage as a pre-requisite to settling down, I could never figure. In any event, I tried settling down as prelim to marriage. Being a writer, I turned to advertising. After producing copy and publicity stories for numerous national accounts, I had money, a good future, and an absolute disgust for my way of life. The clouds of war were beginning to gather. The army advertised for men to be trained as 'combat reporters.' The idea, even at only $21 a month, sounded attractive. I enlisted. After much sweat and tears, the high rank of Regimental Sergeant Major was attained. Following which I was ordered to The Infantry School to be recycled into an officer. As a Second Lieutenant, I was assigned to the armed forces as a 'combat reporter.' Twenty-five years later I retired as a uniformed member of the armed forces and went with the navy as a civilian public information officer. Throughout this latter era I commenced to realize a lifelong ambition—writing adventure books for young adults. Crown Publishers saw things my way and published three of my books, two on submersibles and one on sea monsters.

"My greatest discovery in life is that a fellow neither has to settle down in order to marry, for I married a navy Lieutenant named Helen Ver, nor does he have to stop traveling to raise a family. In the course of our almost constant travels we have raised one son, Frank, who has earned his doctorate in nuclear engineering. Our only worry is that when asked what he'd like to do with his life, he'll shatter our hopes by saying he'd like to climb the Himalayas."

Sweeney lived in many countries during his career in the military, including Japan, Germany, North Africa, England, Greece, and Turkey.

SWENSON, Allan A(rmstrong)   1933-

PERSONAL: Born December 26, 1933, in Passaic, N.J.; son of Harold O. (an attorney) and Amy T. (Dugdale) Swenson; married Sheila Jane Kerr Haglund; children: Peter Jon, Drew Erik, Boyd Allan, Meade Christopher. *Education:* Rutgers University, B.A., 1955. *Religion:* Protestant. *Home address:* Windrows Farm, P.O. Box 94, Kennebunk, Maine 04043. *Agent:* Anita Diamant, Writer's Workshop, Inc., 52 East 42nd St., New York, N.Y. 10017.

CAREER: National Broadcasting Co., New York, N.Y., writer and producer of garden and farm programs for radio and television, 1955; Armstrong Associates, Inc. (nursery and house plant mail order business), Basking Ridge, N.J. and Kennebunk, Maine, owner and president, 1957—. Writer, 1955—. Host of "Gardener's Notebook" for Enterprise Broadcast Features, 1966; appears regularly on "Good Day," WCVB-TV; producer of syndicated radio programs and television specials. Lecturer and garden consultant. *Military service:* U.S. Army, 1955-57; became captain.

MEMBER: American Society of Authors and Journalists, American Federation of Radio and Television Artists, International Horticultural Fellowship of Rotarians, Garden Writers of America, Overseas Press Club, Deadline Club, Sigma Delta Chi.

WRITINGS: The Practical Book of Organic Gardening, Award Books, 1974; *Inflation Fighter's Victory Gardening,* Ballantine, 1975; *Terrariums: Your Complete Guide,* Fawcett, 1975; *My Own Herb Garden* (juvenile), Rodale Press, 1976; *Allan A. Swenson's Big Fun to Grow Book* (juvenile), McKay, 1977; *Cultivating Carnivorous Plants,* Doubleday, 1977; *Grow Better Tomatoes,* Green Thumb Publishing, 1977; *Happy Coloring Flowers,* Green Thumb Publishing, 1977; *Happy Coloring Vegetables,* Green Thumb Publishing, 1977; *World Beneath Your Feet,* McKay, 1978; *World Above Your Head,* McKay, 1978; *Starting Over,* A & W Publishing, 1978; *Plan Your Own Landscape,* Grosset & Dunlap, 1978; *Landscape You Can Eat,* McKay, 1978; *Gardener's Almanac,* Grosset & Dunlap, 1978; *Warm Yourself with Wood,* Fawcett, 1979; *World Beneath the Tidal Pool,* McKay, 1979; *Starting Over,* A & W Publishing, 1979.

Author of "Gardener's Notebook," a column syndicated by United Media to about three hundred fifty newspapers, 1958—. Contributor to outdoor and farm journals.

WORK IN PROGRESS: Nine books; "Good Growin'," television series.

SIDELIGHTS: Farm raised, Swenson has been active in gardening, agriculture and outdoor living since his first 4-H prize winning projects when ten years old. After heading the Passaic County 4-H Club Council and helping run the family farm he attended Rutgers University. Majoring in journalism, Swenson worked his way through college with various editorial jobs and was graduated Phi Beta Kappa in 1955. He began his career with NBC in New York writing and producing garden and farm radio and television shows as well as free-lancing for outdoor and farm publications.

Following service as an Army officer, Swenson returned to the Garden State to launch Armstrong Associates, Inc., a nursery and house plant mail order business. The firm specializes in unusual plants selling worldwide. Swenson continues his plant oddities activities privately in Kennebunk,

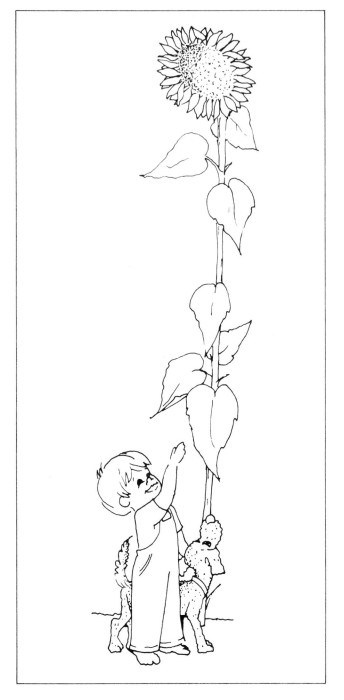

One of the unusual habits of this fun plant is an ability to turn its flowers to follow the sun. That, most likely, is why it was named sunflower by the earliest American pioneers. ■(From *Big Fun to Grow Book* by Allan A. Swenson. Illustrated by Donna R. Sabaka.)

Maine, with growing operations in North Carolina, Florida, Oregon, New Jersey and Maine.

Swenson has been the Newspaper Enterprise Association (now United Media) garden columnist since its inception twenty years ago. It is now carried by some 350 newspapers. In 1966 Swenson launched a "Gardener's Notebook" radio show, including outdoor and farm news on the Mutual Radio System and selected stations.

He has produced syndicated radio programs and television specials and continues his radio activities from his farm in Maine for stations nationwide. Swenson has appeared on the nationally syndicated "Good Day" television show as America's Green Thumb Gardener.

Swenson has lectured in many parts of the country and as garden expert on the Queen Elizabeth II at sea. He periodically serves as horticultural tour director to such exotic places as the Galapagos Islands, Peru, Fiji, Tahiti and elsewhere.

Swenson is married and lives with his family, including their garden active sons in Kennebunk, Maine. As a garden writer, broadcaster, lecturer and recognized authority, Swenson travels extensively each year. He interviews experts on all phases of gardening and outdoor activities, serving his millions of readers and viewers nationwide and abroad.

"I have a philosophy, if it's good news, dig it out and write about it, whether gardening books, children's books, nature books, columns or radio-tv shows. The world needs and wants good news, so I concentrate on it."

E. G. THORPE

THORPE, E(ustace) G(eorge) 1916-

PERSONAL: Born December 25, 1916, in Loscoe, Derbyshire, England; son of Walter Alfred (a coal miner and farmer) and Ivy (Burton) Thorpe; married Freda Davies (a schoolmistress), December 29, 1940; children: Judith Ann, Margaret Jane. *Education:* Borough Road College, B.A. (University of London). *Home:* 4, Boscawen Rd., Falmouth, Cornwall, England.

CAREER: Schoolmaster, Middlesex, England, 1938-39, 1946-54; Margaret Wix School, St. Albans, England, headmaster, 1954-76. *Military service:* British Army, Duke of Cornwall's Light Infantry, 1939-45.

WRITINGS: Chance Intruder (novel), R. Hale, 1952; *Out of Darkness* (novel), R. Hale, 1953; *Endless Road* (novel), R. Hale, 1954; *Sad Little Star* (juvenile), University of London Press, 1958; *Dobbo* (juvenile), University of London Press, 1958; *Young Ruffles* (juvenile), University of London Press, 1958; *Complete English* (introductory books, 1-6) Heinemann, 1962-76, *Junior Dictionary,* Heinemann, 1967; *Illustrated Junior Dictionary,* Heinemann, 1971; *Correct English,* Heinemann, 1972. Writer of seven short stories for British Broadcasting Corp. radio.

SIDELIGHTS: "Born in a southeast Derbyshire mining valley (father was a miner, his four brothers were miners, and five sisters married miners) during the First World War. Lived there through the depressed 20's and early 30's, escaping by means of the classic route of teaching (grammar school scholarship, college, university degree, etc.). Taught one year in West London (no return to the valley, thank you!). Then the six war years as an infantryman, culminating in the Normandy Beaches, Seine Crossing, Battle of Arnheim, Rhine Crossing, and the Baltic.

"Returned to teaching in West London in 1946. Was Headmaster at St. Albans, 1954-76, retiring to Cornwall to become full-time author. Most of the old comrades we did not leave behind from Normandy to the Baltic live in Cornwall (The Duke of Cornwall's Light Infantry) which is one reason for my retirement here."

HOBBIES AND OTHER INTERESTS: History, archaeology.

VALEN, Nanine 1950-

PERSONAL: Born November 7, 1950, in New York, N.Y.; daughter of Herbert (a writer) and Felice (a writer; maiden name, Holman) Valen. *Education:* Bryn Mawr College, B.A. (magna cum laude), 1971; Yale University, graduate study, 1971-73. *Home:* 158 Hillspoint Rd., Westport, Conn. 06880.

CAREER: Writer. Director of computer animation for "The Electric Co." for Children's Television Workshop, 1974-76.

WRITINGS—Juvenile: (With Felice Holman) *The Drac,* Scribner, 1975; *The Devil's Tail,* Scribner, 1978.

Anthologized in *The Scribner Anthology for Young People,* Scribner, 1976. Created animated films for "The Electric Co." and filmstrips for "Sesame Street," Children's Television Workshop.

And yet, instead of turning to flee as had all the other victims, Martha continued her steady approach until she was only a few lengths from the monster. ■ (From *The Drac* by Felice Holman and Nanine Valen. Illustrated by Stephen Walker.)

WORK IN PROGRESS: Another children's book.

SIDELIGHTS: "I spent the year preceding the publication of *The Drac* in the south of France researching the tales of these creatures of the 'fantastique' in libraries, archives, and attics. These tales make many trips across the Atlantic until Ms. Holman and I arrived at the completed manuscript, composed of five tales—five of the eeriest, most captivating creatures."

Valen spent 1980 in Bali, Indonesia researching future works.

FOR MORE INFORMATION SEE: Horn Book, December, 1975.

VANDIVERT, Rita (Andre) 1905-

PERSONAL: Born December 1, 1905, in London, England; daughter of Frank and Alice Frederica (Matthes) Andre; married William Vandivert (a photographer), June 7, 1940; children: Susan. *Education:* Attended Sydenham Secondary School for Girls, London, England; London School of Economics; Regent Street Polytechnic School of Commerce; Inter. B. Comm. *Home:* Lindsell House, Sheep St., Charlbury, Oxford OX7 3RR, England.

CAREER: R.K.O. Radio Pictures, London and Paris; Time, Inc., London, New York; British Information Service, New York; Time, Inc., war correspondent in England, France, and Germany; Magnum Photos, Inc., New York, N.Y., president, one year; free-lance writer, 1948—.

WRITINGS: Common Wild Animals and Their Young, Dell, 1957; *The Porcupine Known as J.R.,* Dodd, 1959; *Young Russia,* Dodd, 1960; *Barnaby,* Dodd, 1963; *Chicken as You Like It* (cookbook), Rand McNally, 1968; *Favorite Wild Animals of North America,* Scholastic, 1973; *Understanding Animals as Pets,* Warne, 1975; *Favorite Pets,* Scholastic, 1975. Contributor to *Saturday Evening Post.*

WORK IN PROGRESS: A book about endangered animals.

SIDELIGHTS: "I was born within sound of Bow Bells (provided the wind was in the right direction), which makes me a true Londoner. London has greatly changed since those days, but I still find it the most lovable of cities.

"I went to school there and at eighteen had no particular bent, except that I was keen on modern languages, loved English literature and was fairly fluent in French and German.

"I took a variety of jobs in London, ones that I thought interesting or challenging and using my knowledge of languages, but I believed in changing these jobs rather frequently to gain fresh experiences.

"Then with the Second World War came many changes. I married William Vandivert, an American photographer who had been sent to England to cover the London blitz and the activities of the Royal Navy and RAF for *Life* Magazine. I worked along with him, then he was ordered back to New York, and he took me too. Quite a transatlantic crossing, on a Norwegian oil tanker in convoy!

"A new world—a new life—and a new daughter. We headquartered in New York City and at that point we decided to earn our living as free-lancers, so that we could decide when and where we would go.

This is Bambi, the fawn that was abandoned, cared for, and returned to the wild. ■ (From *Understanding Animals as Pets* by Rita Vandivert. Photograph by William Vandivert.)

RITA VANDIVERT

"Somehow, with a small daughter in the house, the animals began to arrive. The first pet was a Siamese cat, Penelope, who lived with us for eighteen years, while many other pets came and went. During her lifetime she saw come and go wild cat kittens, flying squirrels, a baby porcupine, a pair of bush babies and of course, Barnaby, our kinkajou who lived with us for seven years. These were all animals that Bill photographed and about which we produced children's books. There were, of course, other animals that did not actually live with us, we just visited and studied them, but we have never been without an animal or two however much we travelled. Some animals can travel too, if you go about it the right way. Barnaby had a fine tall cage in our hallway complete with a tree inside it, but he also had a neat traveling cage into which he went when we took him in the car.

"We had many happy times with our animals, were sad to see any of them leave us, or die, but—apart from creatures like elephants or tortoises—animals have fairly short lives compared to the length of time people last. So one must be prepared for parting.

"Now we live most of the year in an old house in an English village with a walled garden round it, and at the moment our only animal is Honey Lass, but she makes up for a waggon-load of monkeys. She is a Burmese Tortie cat and a mighty climber, up over the walls, up and down the trees and even over the rooftops.

"We had a hedgehog who lived in the garden for two years, came out each night for his bread and milk and a wander around the garden during the summer months, and found himself a hidden spot to curl up in through the winter. But he too has left us.

"We are just beginning work on a new book, one about animals which are in danger of extinction. This means we are visiting special parks and other areas where birds and beasts are being protected and reared so that these beautiful creatures may not die out and leave us all the poorer."

HOBBIES AND OTHER INTERESTS: Her family, good cooking, animals, and travel.

VAN WOERKOM, Dorothy (O'Brien) 1924-

PERSONAL: Born June 26, 1924, in Buffalo, N.Y.; daughter of Peter S. (a refinery superintendent) and Helen (Miller) O'Brien; married John W. Van Woerkom (retired from the U.S. Army), Feburary 22, 1961. *Education:* Graduate of Mount Mercy Academy and Bryant and Stratton Business College. *Politics:* "I wish we could vote on issues rather than for individuals." *Religion:* Roman Catholic. *Home and office:* 8826 McAvoy Dr., Houston, Tex. 77034.

DOROTHY VAN WOERKOM

Harry did not wake up for a long time. ■(From *Harry and Shellburt* by Dorothy O. Van Woerkom. Illustrated by Erick Ingraham.)

CAREER: U.S. Army Corps of Engineers, Buffalo, N.Y., secretary, 1943-47, 1956-61; elementary school teacher in the parochial schools of Buffalo, N.Y., 1947-51; free-lance writer, 1968—. *Member:* Authors Guild, Mystery Writers of America, Council of Teachers of English, American Library Association, National Wilderness Society, National Audubon Society. *Awards, honors: Stepka and the Magic Fire* was named best religious children's book of 1974 by Catholic Press Association.

WRITINGS—Juveniles: *Stepka and the Magic Fire,* Concordia, 1974; *Journeys to Bethlehem,* Concordia, 1974; *The Queen Who Couldn't Bake Gingerbread* (Junior Literary Guild selection), Knopf, 1975; *Becky and the Bear* (Junior Literary Guild selection), Putnam, 1975; *The Dove and the Messiah,* Concordia, 1975; *Sea Frog, City Frog,* Macmillan, 1975; *Abu Ali: Three Tales of the Middle East,* Macmillan, 1976; *The Rat, the Ox, and the Zodiac,* Crown, 1976; *Meat Pies and Sausages,* Greenwillow, 1976; *Let Us Go to Bethlehem!,* Concordia, 1976; *Wake Up and Listen,* Concordia, 1976; *Hundred Angels Singing,* Concordia, 1976; *Tit for Tat,* Greenwillow, 1977; *Harry and Shellburt* (ALA Notable Book), Macmillan, 1977; *Donkey Ysabel,* Macmillan, 1978; *The Friends of Abu Ali: Three More Tales of the Middle East,*

Macmillan, 1978; *Alexandra the Rock-Eater,* Knopf, 1978; *Hidden Messages,* Crown, 1979; *When All the World Was Waiting,* Concordia, 1979; *Lands of Fire and Ice,* Concordia, 1980; *Try Again, Mendelssohn!,* Crown, 1980; *Pearl in the Egg,* Crowell, 1980; *A Mascot for the Team,* Garrard, 1980.

Series editor for Concordia's "Beginning Bible Readers," six volumes per year, the first was scheduled for publication in 1976. Contributor of book reviews to *Houston Chronicle;* contributor of articles and stories to adult and children's magazines.

WORK IN PROGRESS: Two untitled books for Concordia; a historical novel; several stories for beginning readers.

SIDELIGHTS: "Whenever I'm asked if I write every day I think of a little cartoon on my bulletin board. A man at his typewriter is being scolded by his wife for just sitting there, staring into space. The man is trying to explain: 'But even when I'm not writing, I'm *writing!*'

"Yes, I do write every day, but not always with typewriter or pen. I'm writing when I seem only to be staring at the wall, daydreaming. I'm daydreaming, of course, but I'm not really staring at the wall! I'm looking into my mind, trying to work out an idea, which for me generally starts after a character has popped into my thoughts.

"So I 'write' while I drive or fly to a school to speak. I write while standing in line at the supermarket, preparing dinner, doing the laundry.

"Days go by while I think, trying to see this character more clearly. As he or she becomes more familiar to me—like a new friend getting acquainted—I ask questions. What is your problem? How did it start? What are you going to do about it? Who are your friends? Are they helping you with your problem or just making it worse? Are your friends your problem?

"When my character and I have found answers to some of these questions, I'm ready to begin the story. I'll start it with *the day that is different* in the life of this character, with the day when things begin to happen that will bring on the problem. I write a few sentences down in my notebook, scratch them out, and go back to staring at the wall again. This is the most difficult time of all for me, trying to write that first sentence, and trying to write the last sentence later on. The first and last sentences are probably the most important ones in a story, and they are the hardest of all for me to write.

"After a while I'll have a dozen pages of scratched-out sentences, and perhaps half a page of sentences that sound worth saving. I study these, select one, and write it carefully on a fresh page in my notebook. From this point on, I'll write each part of the story in my head while I'm running errands in the car, sorting the laundry, getting dinner, or waiting in the checkout line at the supermarket. People will speak to me and I won't hear them. Sometimes they will think I'm staring at them and I won't even see them. I'll drive to the library when I really mean to go to the dry cleaners. But the story keeps growing in my mind, and later I will write it down in my notebook.

"These strange daydreaming times in the life of a creative person are often difficult for more active people to understand. They think that all a writer need do is sit down at a desk and write!

"One morning I was invited to a coffee at a neighbor's house. 'No,' I said. 'Today I must finish my new book.' I was finally getting *Donkey Ysabel* written in my notebook. I did not yet have the right last sentence, but I hoped it would come to me that day as I wrote. It didn't. I put down my pen and closed the notebook. The story was finished. Donkey Ysabel's problem was solved. But where was that exactly right last sentence which the story needed? Ysabel's friend, Pig Pedro, had been a know-all throughout the story, and now I wanted Ysabel to have the last line, directed at Pedro, and it had to be funny.

"I decided to take a walk around my yard and think. I pulled weeds, cleaned out the bird bath and filled it with fresh water. I found a stick and coaxed my cat to play. I took my dog for a walk and met a neighbor coming home from the coffee. She stopped in surprise and said accusingly, 'You told me you were going to write today.' I tried to explain that even when I wasn't writing, I was *writing*. But she didn't understand.

"Very few adults do understand, probably because most of them have forgotten what writers remember and what children have always known—the importance of daydreaming."

HOBBIES AND OTHER INTERESTS: Needlework, travel to historic places.

FOR MORE INFORMATION SEE: The Houston Chronicle, October 14, 1973, November 10, 1974, July 20, 1975, April 13, 1978, October 29, 1979; *Junior Literary Guild,* March, 1975; *The Alvin Sun,* March 10, 1975, March 18, 1975, April 8, 1976, March 13, 1977, March 21, 1977, March 22, 1979; *Horn Book,* October, 1975, February, 1977; *The Houstonian,* February 3, 1976; *Buffalo Evening News,* May 20, 1976; *Dispatch,* November 18, 1976; *The Tomball News,* January 26, 1977; *The Woodlands Sun,* August 17, 1977.

Jules Verne, age 25. Photo by Nadar.

VERNE, Jules   1828-1905

PERSONAL: Born February 8, 1828, in Nantes, France; died March 24, 1905, in Amiens, France; son of a magistrate; married Honorine (de Viane) Morel; children: Michel (son), two stepdaughters—Valentine and Suzanne. *Education:* Attended local schools; studied law in Paris. *Home:* Amiens, France.

CAREER: Novelist, regarded by many as the father of science fiction. Early jobs included stockbrocker and secretary of the Theatre Lyrique. Began literary career by writing plays, some with Alexandre Dumas, the younger; one of those, "Les Pailles Rompues," was performed in 1850 and was quite successful. In his later life, Verne traveled extensively on boats that he purchased, and also served on the municipal council in Amiens. Many of his novels were serialized in the *Boy's Own Paper. Awards, honors:* Chevalier of the Legion of Honor (France); acclaimed by the French Academy.

WRITINGS—Novels, except as noted; *Cinq Semaines en Ballon: Voyage de Decouvertes en Afrique par Trois Anglais,* J. Hetzel, 1863, translation by William Lackland published as *Five Weeks in a Balloon; or, Journeys and Discoveries in Africa by Three Englishmen,* Appleton, 1869, reissued, Arco, 1964; *Voyage au Centre de la Terre,* J. Hetzel, 1864, translation published as *A Journey to the Center of the Earth* (illustrated by Edouard Riou), H. L. Shepard, 1874, reissued,

Pendulum Press, 1974 [other English editions illustrated by Ralph Ray, Jr., Didier, 1950; Alan E. Cober, Collier, 1962; Edward A. Wilson (with an introduction by Isaac Asimov), Heritage Press, 1966]; *De la Terre a la Lune: Trajet Direct en 97 Heures 20 Minutes,* J. Hetzel, 1865, translation by Louis Mercier and Eleanor E. King published as *From the Earth to the Moon Direct in Ninety-Seven Hours and Twenty Minutes,* Scribner, 1874, reprinted, Aeonian Press, 1974 [other English editions illustrated by John C. Wonsetler, Didier, 1947; Robert Shore, Limited Editions, 1970].

Voyages et Aventures du Capitaine Hatteras: Les Anglais au Pole Nord [et] Le Desert de Glace, J. Hetzel, 1866, translations published separately as *At the North Pole* (illustrated by E. Riou), Porter & Coates, 1874, and *The Field of Ice* (illustrated by Riou), Routledge, 1876 [another translation published as *The Voyages and Adventures of Captain Hatteras* (illustrated by Riou), J. R. Osgood, 1874, portions of the above reissued separately as *At the North Pole: The Adventures of Captain Hatteras,* Aeonian Press, 1976, and *The Desert of Ice,* Aeonian Press, 1976]; *Geographie Illustree de la France et de ses Colonies* (description and travel), Hetzel, 1867; *Les Enfants du Capitaine Grant: Voyage autour du Monde,* Hetzel, 1868, translation published as *A Voyage round the World,* Lippincott, 1873 [another edition published as *Captain Grant's Children*, Associated Book-sellers, 1964, portions of the above published separately as *Among the Cannibals*, Arco, 1964, and *The Mysterious Document*, Arco, 1964].

L'Ile Mysterieuse, Hetzel, 1870, translations by W. H. G. Kingston published separately as *Abandoned*, Scribner, 1875, *Dropped from the Clouds*, Scribner, 1875, and *The Secret of the Island*, S. Low, 1875, reissued together as *The Mysterious Island* (illustrated by Edward A. Wilson), Heritage Press, 1959 [other editions published as *The Mysterious Island* illustrated by N. C. Wyeth, Scribner, 1918; Lloyd Osborne, J. H. Sears, 1927; Henry C. Pitz (with an introduction by May Lamberton Becker), World Publishing, 1957]; *Vingt Mille Lieues sous les Mers*, J. Hetzel, 1870, translation published as *Twenty Thousand Leagues under the Sea*, Douglas & Myers, 1874 [another edition translated by Anthony Bonner, with a special introduction by Ray Bradbury, Bantam books, 1964, reissued, Transworld, 1975; other English editions illustrated by Henry Austin, Ward, Lock, 1899; Milo Winter, Rand, McNally, 1922; W. J. Aylward, Scribner, 1925, reissued, 1960; Anton O. Fischer, J. C. Winston, 1932; George Lawson, Saalfield, 1935; Kurt Wiese, World Publishing, 1946; Guy Fraumeni, Globe Books, 1955; H. C. Pitz, Junior Deluxe Editions, 1956; E. A. Wilson, Heritage Press, 1957; Raoul Auger, Grosset, 1958; Charles Molinn, Macmillan, 1962; Walter Brooks, Washington Square Press, 1965; Don Irwin, Childrens Press, 1968; David Knight, Heron, 1969].

Autour de la Lune, J. Hetzel, 1870, translation by Edward Roth published as *All Around the Moon*, Catholic Publication Society, 1876 [other translations published as *Round the Moon* (translated by L. Mercier and E. E. King), S. Low, 1876, reissued, Associated Booksellers, 1963, and *Around the Moon* (translated by Jacqueline and Robert Baldick; illustrated by W. F. Phillipps), Dutton, 1970]; *Une Ville Flottante* (includes *Les Forceurs de Blocus*), J. Hetzel, 1871, translation published as *A Floating City [and] The Blockade Runners*, Scribner, 1875, reissued, Arco, 1960; *Aventures de Trois Russes et de Trois Anglais dans l'Afrique Australe*, J. Hetzel, 1872, translation published as *Meridiana: The Adventures of Three Englishmen and Three Russians in South Africa*, Scribner, 1873 [other translations published as *Adventures in the Land of the Behemoth*, H. L. Shepard, 1874; *The Adventures of Three Englishmen and Three Russians in South Africa* (translated by Ellen E. Frewer), S. Low, 1876; *Measuring a Meridian*, Associated Booksellers, 1964].

Le Tour du Monde en Quatre-Vingts Jours, J. Hetzel, 1872, translation published as *The Tour of the World in Eighty Days*, J. R. Osgood, 1873 [another translation by George M. Towle published as *Around the World in Eighty Days*, J. R. Osgood, 1874; other editions under that title illustrated by Fran Foley, Scott, Foresman, 1952; Tom Gill, Simon & Schuster, 1957; E. A. Wilson (with an introduction by R. Bradbury), Limited Editions, 1962; Libico Maraja, Golden Press, 1962; Robin Jacques, Junior Deluxe Editions, 1964; Adolf Hoffmeister, P. Hamlyn, 1965; Quentin Blake, Chatto, 1966; Don Irwin, Childrens Press, 1969; also translated by Henry Frith as *Round the World in Eighty Days*, Routledge, 1885; other editions under that title illustrated by Arthur Harper, Didier, 1949; Justin Todd, Longmans, 1967]; *Le Pays des Fourrures*, [Paris], 1873, translation by N. D'Anvers published as *The Fur Country; or, Seventy Degrees North Latitude*, W. L. Allison, 1873, reissued, Arco, 1966; *The Baltimore Gun Club* (translated from the French by E. Roth), King & Baird, 1874.

Second Empire Interior: the salon of the Nautilus.

Le Docteur Ox, Maitre Zacharius, Un Hivernage dans les Glaces, [et] Un Drame dans les Airs (stories), J. Hetzel, 1874, translation by G. M. Towle published as *Doctor Ox, and Other Stories*, J. R. Osgood, 1874, reissued, Arco, 1964 [another translation by A. L. Alger published as *From the Clouds to the Mountains, Comprising Narratives of Strange Adventures by Air, Land, and Water*, W. F. Gill, 1874; also translated as *A Winter amid the Ice, and Other Thrilling Stories*, World Publishing, 1877]; *Le Chancellor*, J. Hetzel, 1875, translated by G. M. Towle published as *The Wreck of the Chancellor*, J. R. Osgood, 1875 [another edition translated by E. Frewer as *The Survivors of the Chancellor*, G. Munro, 1880; also published as *The Chancellor*, Associated Booksellers, 1965]; *Michel Strogoff*, [Paris], 1876, translation by W. H. G. Kingston published as *Michael Strogoff: The Courier of the Czar*, Scribner, 1877 [another English edition illustrated by N. C. Wyeth, Scribner, 1927.].

Hector Servadac: Voyages et Aventures a Travers le Monde Solaire, [Paris], 1877, translation published as *Hector Servadac*, G. Munro, 1877 [other translations by E. Roth published as *Off on a Comet: A Journey through Planetary Space*, Claxton, 1878, reissued, Ace books, 1957, and *To the Sun: A Journey through Planetary Space*, Claxton, 1878, reissued, Dover, 1960; also published separately as *The Anomalous Phenomena*, Arco, 1965, and *Homeward Bound*, Arco, 1965]; *Les Indes-Noires*, J. Hetzel, 1877, translation by W. H. G. Kingston published as *The Child of the Cavern;*

Passepartout wandered for some hours among this motley crowd and then found himself in the immense paddy fields. ■ (From *Around the World in Eighty Days* by Jules Verne. Illustrated by Quentin Blake.)

or, Strange Doings Underground, S. Low, 1877 [other editions published as *The Black-Indies,* G. Munro, 1879; *Black Diamonds,* Associated Booksellers, 1961]; *Un Capitaine de Quinze Ans,* J. Hetzel, 1878, translation published as *A Captain at Fifteen,* G. Munro, 1878, reissued, Abelard-Schuman, 1976 [another edition published as *Dick Sand; or, A Captain at Fifteen,* G. Munro, 1878].

Les Tribulations d'un Chinois en Chine, J. Hetzel, 1879, translation published as *The Tribulations of a Chinaman in China,* G. Munro, 1879, reissued, Associated Booksellers, 1963; *Les Cinq Cents Millions de la Begum [et] Les Revoltes de la Bounty,* J. Hetzel, 1879, translation published as *The 500 Millions of the Begum,* G. Munro, 1879 [another translation by W. H. G. Kingston published as *The Begum's Fortune, with an Account of the Mutineers of the Bounty,* S. Low, 1887; also published as *The Begum's Fortune,* Associated Booksellers, 1958]; *Histoire des Grandes Voyages et des Grandes Voyageurs,* [Paris], circa 1879, translation by J. Cottrell published as *Great Voyages and Great Navigators,* G. Munro, 1879 [also published as *Celebrated Travels and Travellers,* S. Low, 1880-82; portions of the above published separately as *The Exploration of the World* (illustrated by L. Bennett and P. Philippoteaux), S. Low, 1882, *The Great Navigators of the Eighteenth Century,* S. Low, 1880, and

The Great Explorers of the Nineteenth Century, Scribner, 1881].

La Maison a Vapeur: Voyage a Travers l'Inde Septentrionale, J. Hetzel, 1880, translation by J. Cottrell published as *The Steamhouse; or, A Trip across Northern India,* G. Munro, 1880-81 [also published separately as *The Demon of Cawnpore,* Arco, 1959, reissued, Aeonian Press, 1976, and *Tigers and Traitors,* Arco, 1959, reissued, Aeonian Press, 1976]; *La Jangada: Huit Cents Lieues sur l'Amazone,* J. Hetzel, 1881, translation by J. Cottrell published as *The Jangada; or, Eight Hundred Leagues over the Amazon,* G. Munro, 1881-82 [another translation by W. J. Gordon published as *The Giant Raft,* Scribner, 1881-82, reissued, Associated Booksellers, 1967; portions of the above published separately as *Down the Amazon,* Arco, 1967, and *The Cryptogram,* Arco, 1967]; *Le Rayon-Vert,* J. Hetzel, 1882, translation by J. Cottrell published as *The Green Ray,* G. Munro, 1883 [another edition under the same title published with *The Blockade Runners,* Associated Booksellers, 1965].

L'Ecole des Robinsons, J. Hetzel, 1882, translation published as *Robinsons' School,* G. Munro, 1883 [another translation by W. J. Gordon published as *Godfrey Morgan: A Californian Mystery,* S. Low, 1883; also published as *The School for Crusoes,* Arco, 1966]; *Keraban-le-Tetu,* J. Hetzel, 1883, translation published as *Keraban the Inflexible,* S. Low, 1884-85; *L'Etoile du Sud: Le Pays des Diamants,* J. Hetzel, 1884, translation published as *The Southern Star; or, The Diamond Land,* G. Munro, 1885 [another edition published as *The Southern Star Mystery,* Associated Booksellers, 1966]; *L'Archipel en Feu,* J. Hetzel, 1884, translation published as *The Archipelago on Fire,* G. Munro, 1885; *Mathias Sandorf,* J. Hetzel, 1885, translation published under the same title, G. Munro, 1885; (with Paschal Grousset) *L'Epave du Cynthia,* [Paris], circa 1885, translation published as *The Waif of the Cynthia,* G. Munro, 1886 [another translation by I. O. Evans published as *Salvage from the Cynthia; or, The Boy on the Buoy,* Associated Booksellers, 1964].

Robur-le-Conquerant, J. Hetzel, 1886, translation published as *Robur the Conqueror; or, A Trip Round the World in a Flying Machine,* G. Munro, 1887 [another edition published as *Clipper of the Clouds,* S. Low, 1908, reissued, Associated Booksellers, 1962]; *Un Billet de Loterie,* [Paris], 1886, translation published as *The Lottery Ticket: A Tale of Tellemarken,* S. Low, 1887; *Le Chemin de France,* J. Hetzel, 1887, translation published as *The Flight to France; or, The Memoirs of a Dragoon,* G. Munro, 1889, reissued, Arco, 1966; *Nord Contre Sud,* J. Hetzel, 1887, translation by Laura E. Kendall published as *Texar's Vengeance; or, North Versus South,* G. Munro, 1887, [another edition published as *North against South,* Associated Booksellers, 1963; portions of the above published separately as *Burbank the Northerner,* Arco, 1963, and *Texar the Southerner,* Arco, 1963].

Deux Ans de Vacances, J. Hetzel, 1888, translation published as *A Two Years' Vacation,* G. Munro, 1889 [another edition published as *Two Years' Holiday,* Associated Booksellers, 1964; portions of the above published separately as *Adrift in the Pacific,* Arco, 1964, and *Second Year Ashore,* Arco, 1964; another translation by Olga Marx published as *A Long Vacation,* Holt, 1967]; *Famille-sans-Nom,* [Paris], 1889, translation published as *A Family without a Name,* J. W. Lovell, 1889, reissued, Associated Booksellers, 1963 [portions of the above published separately as *Leader of the Resistance,* Arco, 1963, and *Into the Abyss,* Arco, 1963]; *Sans Dessus Dessous,* J. Hetzel, 1889, translation published as *The Purchase of the North Pole*, S. Low, 1891, reissued, Associated Booksellers, 1966; *Topsy-Turvy* (children's stories translated from the French), J. S. Ogilvie, 1890.

Cesar Cascabel, J. Hetzel, 1890, translated by A. Estoclet published as *Caesar Cascabel* (illustrated by George Roux), Cassell, 1890, reissued, Associated Booksellers, 1966 [portions of the above translation published separately as *The Travelling Circus*, Arco, 1966, and *The Show on Ice*, Arco, 1966]; *Mistress Branican*, [Paris], 1891, translation by A. Estoclet published under the same title (illustrated by L. Benett), Cassell, 1891, reissued, Sun Books, 1970; *Le Chateau des Carpathes*, J. Hertzel, 1892, translation published as *The Castle of the Carpathians*, Merriam, 1892 [another edition published as *Carpathian Castle*, Associated Booksellers, 1963]; *Claudius Bombarnac*, J. Hetzel, 1892, translation published under the same title, Hurst, 1894; *P'tit Bonhomme*, [Paris], 1893, translation published as *Foundling Mick*, S. Low, 1895; *Mirifiques Aventures de Maitre Antifer*, [Paris], 1894, translation published as *Captain Antifer*, R. F. Fenno, 1895.

L'Ile a Helice, [Paris], 1895, translation published as *Floating Island; or, The Pearl of the Pacific*, S. Low, 1897 [another edition published as *Propeller Island*, Associated Booksellers, 1961]; *Face au Drapeau*, [Paris], 1896, translation published as *Facing the Flag*, F. T. Neely, 1897 [another edition published as *For the Flag*, Associated Booksellers, 1961]; *Clovis Dardentor*, J. Hetzel, 1896, translation published as *Clovis Dardentor*, S. Low, 1897; *Le Sphinx des Glaces*, J. Hetzel, 1897, translation by Mrs. Cashel Hoey published as *An Antarctic Mystery*, Lippincott, 1900, reissued, Gregg, 1975; *Le Testament d'un Excentrique*, [Paris], 1899, translation published as *The Will of an Eccentric*, S. Low, 1902; *Le Village Aerien*, J. Hetzel, 1902, translation by I. O. Evans published as *The Village in the Tree Tops*, Associated Booksellers, 1964; *Les Histoires de Jean-Marie Cabidoulin* (stories), J. Hetzel, 1902, translation by I. O. Evans published as *The Sea Serpent: The Yarns of Jean Marie Cabidoulin*, Associated Booksellers, 1967; *Les Freres Kip*, [Paris], 1902.

Maitre du Monde, [Paris], 1904, translation published as *The Master of the World: A Tale of Mystery and Marvel*, S. Low, 1914, reissued, Airmont, 1965; *Un Drame en Livonie*, Hachette, 1904, translation by I. O. Evans published as *A Drama in Livonia*, Associated Booksellers, 1970; *Le Phare de Bout de Monde*, J. Hetzel, 1905, translation by Cranstoun Metcalfe published as *The Lighthouse at the End of the World*, G. H. Watt, 1924; *L'Invasion de la Mer*, J. Hetzel, 1905; *Le Volcan d'Or*, J. Hetzel, 1906, translation by I. O. Evans published as *The Golden Volcano*, Associated Booksellers, 1963 [portions of the above published separately as *The Claim on Forty Mile Creek*, Arco, 1962, and *Flood and Flame*, Arco, 1962]; *L'Agence Thompson*, J. Hetzel, 1907, translation by I. O. Evans published as *The Thompson Travel Agency*, Arco, 1965 [portions of the above published separately as *Package Holiday*, Arco, 1965, and *End of the Journey*, Associated Booksellers, 1965].

La Chasse au Meteore, J. Hetzel, 1908, translation by Frederick Lawton published as *The Chase of the Golden Meteor*, G. Richards, 1909 [another edition published as *The Hunt for the Meteor*, Ace Books, 1965]; *Le Pilote du Danube*, J. Hetzel, 1908, translation by I. O. Evans published as *The Danube Pilot*, Associated Booksellers, 1970; *Les Naufrages du Jonathan*, J. Hetzel, 1909, translation by I. O. Evans published as *The Survivors of the Jonathan*, Associated Booksellers, 1962 [portions of the above published separately as *The Masterless Man*, Arco, 1962, and *The Unwilling Dic-*

The beast's jaws opened wide, like a pair of factory shears, and in another instant all would have been over for our host. ■ (From *Twenty Thousand Leagues Under the Sea* by Jules Verne. Illustrated by Milo Winter.)

tator, Arco, 1962]; *Hier et Demain* (stories), J. Hetzel, 1910, translation by I. O. Evans published as *Yesterday and Tomorrow*, Associated Booksellers, 1965; *Le Secret de Wilhelm Storitz*, J. Hetzel, 1910, translation by I. O. Evans published as *The Secret of Wilhelm Storitz*, Associated Booksellers, 1963; *L'Etonnante Aventure de la Mission Barsac*, Hachette, 1920, translation by I. O. Evans published as *The Barsac Mission*, Associated Booksellers, 1960 [portions of the above published separately as *Into the Niger Bend*, Arco, 1960, reissued, Aeonian Press, 1976, and *The City in the Sahara*, Arco, 1960, reissued, Aeonian Press, 1976]; *Their Island Home: The Later Adventures of the Swiss Family Robinson* (translated from the French by C. Metcalfe; takes up the adventures of the Swiss family Robinson where the original narrative by Johann Wyss ended), G. H. Watt, 1924; *The Castaways of the Flag: The Final Adventures of the Swiss Family Robinson* (translation from the French by Metcalfe; sequel of *Their Island Home*), G. H. Watt, 1924.

Collections and selections: *Works of Jules Verne*, 15 volumes (edited by Charles F. Horne), V. Parke, 1911; *The Omnibus Jules Verne* (illustrated by Helene Carter), Lippincott, 1931; *The Fitzroy Edition of Jules Verne* (edited by I. O. Evans), B. Hanison, 1958; *Space Novels*, Dover, 1960.

Contributor to *Musee des Familles*.

ADAPTATIONS—Movies and filmstrips: "In Search of the Castaways" (motion pictures), adaptations of *The Children of Captain Grant,* Societe Francaise des Films et Cinematographes Eclair, 1914, Walt Disney Productions, starring Hayley Mills and Maurice Chevalier, 1962; "In Search of the Castaways" (filmstrip; available in both phonodisc and phonotape, with a teacher's guide), Walt Disney Productions, 1975; "Around the World in Eighty Days" (motion pictures), Lewis Pennant Features, 1914, United Artists, starring David Niven and Cantinflas, 1956; "Twenty Thousand Leagues under the Sea" (motion pictures), Universal Films, 1916, Walt Disney Productions, starring James Mason, Kirk Douglas, and Peter Lorre, 1954, Argyle Enterprises/Telemated Motion Pictures (10 minutes, color, with a teacher's guide), 1967; "Twenty Thousand Leagues under the Sea" (filmstrips), Eye Gate House (color, with a teacher's manual), 1958, Encyclopaedia Britannica Films (color, with filmstrip facts), 1961, Brunswick Productions, 1971, Walt Disney Educational Materials (available in both phonodisc and phonotape, color, with a teacher's guide), 1974.

"Michael Strogoff; or, The Courier of the Czar," Universal Pictures, 1926; "The Mysterious Island" (motion pictures), Metro-Goldwyn-Mayer, starring Lionel Barrymore, 1929, Ameran Films, starring Michael Craig and Michael Callan, 1961; "The Soldier and the Lady" (motion picture), adaptation of *Michael Strogoff,* RKO Radio Pictures, 1937; "From the Earth to the Moon" (motion picture), starring Joseph Cotton and George Sanders, Warner Brothers, 1958; "Journey to the Center of the Earth" (motion picture), starring James Mason, Pat Boone, and Arlene Dahl, Twentieth Century-Fox, 1959; "The Fabulous World of Jules Verne" (motion picture), adaptation of *Face au Drapeau,* Warner Brothers, 1960; "Master of the World" (motion picture), starring Vincent Price and Charles Bronson, Alta Vista Productions, 1961; "Valley of the Dragons" (motion picture), adaptation of *Hector Servadac,* Columbia Pictures, 1961; "Five Weeks in a Balloon" (motion picture), starring Red Buttons, Cedric Hardwicke, Fabian, Peter Lorre, and Barbara Eden, Twentieth Century-Fox, 1962.

"Adventures in Search of the Castaways" and "The End of the Search for the Castaways" (filmstrips), adaptations of *The Castaways; or, A Voyage round the World* and Walt Disney's movie, "In Search of the Castaways," Encyclopaedia Britannica Films, 1964; "Up to His Ears" (motion picture), adaptation of *Chinese Adventures in China,* starring Ursula Andress, Lopert Pictures Corp., 1965; "Those Fantastic Flying Fools" (motion picture; inspired by the writings of Verne), American International Pictures, 1967; "Monster from under the Sea" (motion picture; excerpts from the 1954 Walt Disney motion picture, "Twenty Thousand Leagues under the Sea"; 12 minute and four minute versions available in both black and white and color, and in several foreign languages), Walt Disney Home Movies, 1968; "The Southern Star" (motion picture), starring George Segal, Ursula Andress, and Orson Welles, Columbia Pictures, 1968; "Strange Holiday" (motion picture), adaptation of *Deux Ans en Vacances,* Mass-Brown Pictures, 1969.

"Captain Nemo and the Underwater City" (motion picture), starring Robert Ryan and Chuck Connors, Metro-Goldwyn-Mayer, 1970; "Indian Fantasy" (animated motion picture), adaptation of a part of *Around the World in Eighty Days,* Films Incorporated, 1971; "The Light at the Edge of the World" (motion picture), starring Kirk Douglas, Yul Brynner, and Samantha Eggar, National General, 1971.

Play: Rodney Dawes, *Around the World in Eighty Days* (three-act), Dramatic Publishing, 1957.

Television: "The Mysterious Island" (animated film special), presented on CBS, November 15, 1975; "The Return of Captain Nemo" (three pilot episodes), starring Jose Ferrer and Burgess Meredith, presented on CBS, beginning March 8, 1978.

SIDELIGHTS: **February 8, 1828.** Born at Nantes, France. "When I run up the scale of my ancestors, I come across military men, magistrates, barristers and sailors." [Kenneth Allott, *Jules Verne,* Macmillan, 1941.[1]]

1834. Attended boarding school.

1837. With younger brother, Paul, entered St. Stanislas, a secondary school.

1844-1845. Studied at the Royal Lycée.

1847. Sent to Paris to take his first year law exams. As the eldest son, Verne was expected to assume his father's law profession. He, however, already demonstrated a preference for literature over law. He returned home after passing his first exams.

1848. Persuaded his father to allow him to return to Paris for his third year of law studies rather than study in Nantes.

January 24, 1849. When his father voiced concern over his obvious interest in literature, Verne reassured him. "I'm due to sit for my examination next Tuesday and I can assure you I'm losing my wits over it. I think I can promise that I will pass, though I wouldn't swear to anything; I've been working a lot and still am, and that's why I wish it were done with. But that doesn't mean that afterwards I'm going to sit back and drop law altogether . . . I *know* that a third of my qualifying exam depends on the *Institutes.* I *know* that I have to submit this thesis around August in order to qualify. . . . If I had some other career in view, would I have come this far only to drop out of school or delay my qualifying? Surely that would be utter madness. . . .

"You know how irresistibly appealing Paris is to everybody, young people in particular. I would much sooner live in Paris than in Nantes. . . . But there would only be one difference between the two life styles: in Paris, I don't miss Nantes, but in Nantes, I will miss Paris a little—but that won't stop me from living there peacefully. . . .

"You're absolutely right in saying that literary studies are useful in every position in life. If my studies in this field led me to envisage an attempt in this direction, it would merely be an adjunct, as I have frequently repeated, and would not divert me from that aim we have set. . . . Yet, you say this: 'Do you mean that you will be an Academician, a poet, a renowned novelist?' If I were fated to become any of those, my dear father, you would be the first to urge me towards this career. And you'd be the first to be proud of it, because it's the finest position any man can hold! And if I were fated to become such a man, my vocation would urge me towards it irresistibly. But that is not the case." [Jean Jules-Verne, *Jules Verne* (translation from the French by Roger Greaves), Taplinger, 1976.[2]]

Met "the elder" Alexandre Dumas and the two became close. Verne sought Dumas' advice about the plays he wrote while working on his law thesis.

(From *The Mysterious Island* by Jules Verne. Illustrated by N. C. Wyeth.)

(From the movie "Mysterious Island," starring Lionel Barrymore. Copyright 1929 by Metro-Goldwyn-Mayer.)

1850. Passed his final law examination, but refused his father's offer to assume his legal practice. "The only career for which I am really suited is the one I am already pursuing: literature. I am deeply moved by your suggestions, but surely I must trust to my own judgment in this matter. If I took it over, your practice would only wither away. Please forgive your respectful and loving son." [Marguerite Allotte de la Fuÿe, *Jules Verne* (translated from the French by Erik de Mauny), Coward, 1956.³]

1850. Passed his final law examination, but refused his father's offer to assume his legal practice. "The only career for which I am really suited is the one I am already pursuing: literature. I am deeply moved by your suggestions, but surely I must trust to my own judgment in this matter. If I took it over, your practice would only wither away. Please forgive your respectful and loving son." [Marguerite Allotte de la Fuÿe *Jules Verne* (translated from the French by Erik de Mauny), Coward, 1956.³]

March, 1851. Gave private law lessons and continued to write plays. In response to his father's objections he wrote: "As for my working as a barrister, remember your own dictum about not trying to do too many things at once; a job in a law practice means starting at seven-thirty in the morning and finishing at nine at night. How much time do I have left for myself?

"With respect, you're quite wrong about why I'm acting as I am. To begin with, literature matters more to me than anything else, because that is all I can succeed at, since my mind is made up on this point. . . . If I practised law for a couple of years at the same time as my writing, one of these two careers would stifle the other; and the stronger of the two would not be law!

"To leave Paris for two years would mean losing all my contacts and allowing the enemy to dig himself in all over again. You just can't work an eight-hour day as a law clerk in Paris. When you're a clerk, you're a clerk and that's it."²

1851. Became secretary of the Theatre Lyrique in Paris. Wrote his mother: "I assure you, my dear mama, that I don't look in the least like a lyric poet, on the contrary, I cut quite a dash on the Paris boulevards. I don't know who can have given you such a disastrous notion of me. Of course, I am fully aware that there are thoroughbred horses and pedigree dogs which present a better-groomed appearance, but it isn't everyone's luck to trot daintily in front of a carriage, or snuggle down on a duchess's eiderdown. Nevertheless, for a mere man, I am reasonably well turned out, almost as well as a lackey from the Faubourg Saint-Germain.

On a more practical note, he added: "It is true that I must still send you a pattern for some shirts, with full corpographical details, since I am badly off in this respect. When I take my coat off, my shirt sleeve sometimes comes away with it; and others have frayed into delicate patterns that would make an excellent lacy edging for a shawl. I have one of which only the upper part remains. In fact, I don't know why I still call it a shirt, it's really no more than a collar!

"And then, there's the question of socks, dear mama! My woollen ones to begin with. They are dead, and have been buried with fitting honours. As for the ones I shall wear next winter, *they* are still grazing on the green fields of the Berry region. The cotton socks that I am wearing at present are like a spider's web in which a hippopotamus has been in

residence. Uncle Prudent, who is truly remarkable in this same respect, hasn't a single pair that can touch mine for holes. Never, in fact, have holes multiplied with such astonishing fecundity. The reality still clings about my calves, but my feet tread the void, etc. . . ."³

October 14, 1852. Content to live meagerly and to pursue writing, he wrote his mother in characteristic good humor: "So my shirts are giving you nightmares, are they? You advise me to buy a false front but, dearest mother, they haven't even got a real back. But I know what your reply to that will be: Her Ladyship will never notice. Catch me saying she will! But I, too, lie awake at nights worrying about this lack of clobber. I'm not pursued by ghosts any more, but I *am* pursued by shirts. Only pretty women are fit to be seen, *I am told,* in such undress. Anyway, I've decided to end my suffering by having a shirt made to measure here in Paris and sending it to you to be copied. That *is* the best thing to do, isn't it?

"Anyway, I must have shirts. I'm even out of handkerchiefs as well. Just think, dearest mother, what a mess I'm in: I can't even blow my nose on my shirt tails! In the words of Shakespeare: how sad, how sad!

"How exceedingly happy I would be if you came up to Paris to furnish your drawing-room! It would be so much more fine and artistic. You would really save by making the trip; as you know, I've seen lots of fine furnishings in the best of taste, and I'd be able to give you first-rate advice. On Saturday we shall be regaled by the Solemn Entrance into Paris of His Imperial Majesty Napoleon III. I find the whole thing most entertaining. We shall see what happens.

"The weather is beginning to get cold. Now's the time when fires are lit in honest homes, and when poor devils like me do without. But I've put on my woollies and am keeping as warm as I can. I expect you will soon be moving back to town; the trees are beginning to lose their hair. . . ."²

May, 1856. Visited the town of Amiens, where he was best man at the wedding of a college friend and house guest of the de Viane family. "I am still in Amines, the charming solicitations of the Viane family having forced me to make a much longer stay than I had intended. I shall, in fact, have spent eight days here in all, in the midst of galas and gallantries, protestations of friendship, tears of joy and pleasure, wedding feasts, conjugal effusions, nuptial emotions, Amiens *pâtés,* stuffed chitterlings, *truculent* hams, breakfasts lasting an hour and luncheons lasting three, dinners that begin at six and end at eleven in the evening. Ah! I shall be lucky if I don't die of indigestion! But that's not true, for I'm in the best of health, I sleep, I eat, I laugh, and more than ever, I have very distinct views on marriage. I want to get married, I must get married, and it just isn't possible that the woman who is to marry me hasn't yet been born.

"The Vianes are a charming family, made up of a delightful young widow (Mme Morel, *née* Honorine de Viane, the sister of the bride), and of a young man of about my age, who is a stock-broker in Amiens, making a lot of money at it, too, and who is certainly the most charming fellow one could hope to meet. The father is an old retired military man, but much more pleasant than the usual run of crusty characters retired from service, and the mother is a woman of great intelligence.

"You are not used to see me indulging in such praise of the human race . . . and your natural perspicacity will tell you that there is more here than meets the eye. And indeed, I believe I have fallen in love with the young widow of twenty-six. Oh, why does she have to have two children? I always run up against impossibilities of one sort or another."³

Returned to Paris, where he wrote his father: "Auguste's marriage and the family that he has married into gave me much food for thought. . . . In this Devianne [*sic*] family there is a brother of my own age who is the most charming fellow on earth. He has gone into partnership with one of his friends as an intermediary between shareholders . . . and the stockbrokers in Paris. . . . This is a good position for a young man, and it is absolutely safe. The point is that what he can do in Amiens, one could do even more easily in Paris on a smaller scale. . . . M. Devianne is very well in with financiers and brokers; he could easily get a friend of his involved in a large firm in Paris, even for a small amount. . . . So what I need to know, father, is whether (if the need arose) you would be prepared to buy me a share in a firm like this, which is just as official as a law firm. I need to change my way of life, because this precarious existence of mine cannot go on. . . . When I go for a year without earning anything, my allowance is only half enough to keep me, what with prices going up the way they are. . . ."²

November, 1856. Became engaged to Honorine de Viane. "After being presented to the family, I made the usual round of visits just as any other man would have done, and didn't jib at a thing. The father, for an ex-cuirassier, is quite human in his sentiments—indeed, he must have found his cuirasse a nuisance more than once in the past. Honorine and I have agreed that we should have as little ceremony and as little fuss as possible. She has a few simple pieces of furniture: a sofa, four armchairs, four ordinary chairs. . . . I will buy the silver and other things. As soon as I have finished my apprenticeship with Giblain [the stockbroker] I shall be in a very good position. Yesterday evening, I lost a wonderful opportunity to run off to Brussels with Honorine, and set myself up in magnificent style. I was carrying 500,000 francs in bonds in my despatch case, and 95,000 francs in notes, which de Viane had given me for Giblain. However, I decided to be patient. . . . truly, without illusions or wild fancies, I believe I have really found happiness."³

January 10, 1857. Married in a small ceremony in Paris. "I was the groom and I had a white suit and black gloves! I didn't know where I was, and I handed out money to everyone; Town Hall clerks, beadle, sacristan, errand boy. Someone shouted for the bridegroom. They meant me! Thank heavens there were only a dozen people watching the spectacle!"³

Summer, 1859. Visited Scotland with his brother, Paul. "Alfred Hignard, who is the Saint-Nazaire agent for a shipping line, has asked my brother and myself if we would like to make a free trip to Scotland and back. I quickly seized the chance of making such a voyage. . . . Peace has come at last! But people take a very unfavourable view of Napoleon III's proclamation. It was certainly not worth while spending five hundred millions to arrive at such a result. As far as Italian independence is concerned, it is of little importance whether Lombardy belongs to Piedmont or not. Austria will be more powerful than ever, thanks to this Italian confederation. It is quite clear that what is in Napoleon's mind is war with Prussia in the near future, and then with England. He divides in order to rule: he beats Russia in the Crimea, makes her the enemy of Austria, and then allies himself with

her. And so it will go on with all the signatory Powers of 1815. In the meanwhile, all my clients have been speculating on a rising market, and I have had every reason to be thankful for the return of peace."³ The trip to Scotland impressed Verne greatly as he later used it as a source for one of his novels.

August 3, 1861. Only child, Michel, born.

1863. First novel accepted by the publisher, Jules Hetzel, with whom Verne began a lifelong affiliation. Verne's book, *Five Weeks in a Balloon* was an immediate best-seller in both adult and children's markets.

April, 1864. At work on the second part of *The Voyages and Adventures of Captain Hatteras,* Verne wrote to Hetzel: "I do not particularly want to be an arranger of facts. Consequently, I will always be willing to change things for the good of all concerned. What I want to become more than anything is a writer, an honest ambition that I think you will endorse. You say some very nice and flattering things about my style improving. You must be referring to the descriptive passages, which I really worked hard at. Nothing could have touched me or pleased me more than such approval coming from you. I admit as much, but in my heart of hearts I wonder whether you didn't intend to sugar the pill slightly for me. I assure you, good and kind editor that you are, that there was no need to do so. I swallow any pill without fuss and without persuasion. I can't help wondering, then, whether you were really as pleased with me as a writer as you claim—and whether you didn't prefer my writing to my novel!

"If I told you that to your face, you would hit the roof!

"What I am saying is silly, but sincere. All I am trying to say is that I very much want to become a stylist, a serious one. This is my one aim in life. And when you, of all people, write as you do at the start of your letter, I could jump for joy."²

January, 1866. Wrote his father: "I am working like a galley-slave on an *Illustrated Geography of France,* which is coming out in ten-centime parts. Théophile Lavallée, who had started the work for Hetzel, is dying, and I have taken it over. It will mean an advance on my contract, which Hetzel is going to alter further to my advantage as soon as he has arranged his capital. I hope, at the same time, to be able to write the first volume of the *Voyage Under the Oceans,* the outline of which is completely finished, and which will be really marvellous, but I mustn't lose a minute."³

March, 1867. Sailed with his brother to America. "I'm ashamed to admit that I spent only one week in your country. But it couldn't be helped: my round-trip ticket did not allow a longer stay. All the same, I can say that I have seen New York. I stayed at the Fifth Avenue Hotel, travelled up the Hudson to Albany, visited Buffalo and Lake Erie, marvelled at the Niagara Falls from the top of Terrapin Tower with a lunar rainbow showing in the spray of the falls, and crossed the Suspension Bridge into Canada. And then I came home! It is one of deepest regrets to think that I shall never see your country again. I love America; and every Frenchman can love her as a sister of France."²

March, 1869. Moved to the seaside town of Le Crotoy. "Though I have settled at Le Crotoy, I have not abandoned Paris. Yet, in the situation that I was going to find myself in, needing a bigger apartment and all my expenses increasing, I would have been unavoidably hard-up because my

(From the movie "In Search of the Castaways," adapted from *The Children of Captain Grant,*
starring Maurice Chevalier and Hayley Mills. Copyright © 1962 by Walt Disney Productions.)

income was insufficient. Here, we can get by easily and still live well. Since my family seem to like it, why hesitate? Remember that I have three children, and though the future holds no fears for me, the present can be hard."[2]

August, 1870. Only days before the Franco-Prussian war Verne was awarded the Legion of Honor. Wrote to Hetzel: "Your letter says that you were happy to be able to do something for me in this respect. Rest assured that you did everything, absolutely everything, and that I owe it to you and you alone. . . . I am certain that at this moment my father and mother are very happy and very proud. You are sufficiently broadminded to accept in others the little weaknesses that you do not share. . . . Your office must be disorganized at present owing to the conscription. . . . How serious it all is. In all the towns I visited, the feeling against Napoleon was very great. This must be the end of the dynasty, but we are likely to pay a high price for it."[2]

February, 1871. During the months of war, continued to work as usual. "Yes, I have been doing a lot of work. That much I was capable of. I was alone here, anyway. . . .

"One of the volumes . . . is *terrifyingly realistic*. It is entitled *Les Naufragés du Chancelor*. I believe it outdoes the *Medusa* for sheer horror, but above all I think it will ring true if I am not mistaken.

"The other volume has no title, but might be described as the adventures of six scientists in South Africa. It's about an Anglo-Russian commission sent to measure a meridian; it's scientific, but not too scientific. I got the idea from the writings of Arago.

"Finally, I am just starting a new book, *Le Pays des Fourrures*."[2]

1872. Moved to Amiens. "At my wife's behest, I am fixing my home in Amiens—a quiet town, well-governed and level-headed; its inhabitants are cordial and literate. It's near to Paris—near enough to feel a reflection of Paris but without its insufferable noise and sterile agitation. And when all is said and done my *Saint-Michel* [Verne's sail boat] will continue to be berthed at Le Crotoy."[2]

March, 1872. Elected to the local learned society, the Académie d'Amiens.

Verne's biggest success in fiction during his lifetime, *Around the World in Eighty Days,* was published. "I have dreams about it! I hope our readers enjoy it as much as I. You know, I must be a bit crazy: I fall for all the extravagant things my heroes get up to. There's only one thing I regret: not to be able to get up to those things with them."[2]

(From the movie "Twenty Thousand Leagues Under the Sea," starring Kirk Douglas and Peter Lorre. Copyright 1954 by Walt Disney Productions Inc.)

(From the movie "From the Earth to the Moon," starring Joseph Cotten and George Sanders. Copyright © 1958 by Warner Brothers Pictures.)

(From the movie "Journey to the Center of the Earth," starring Pat Boone and Diane Baker. Released by Warner Brothers-Seven Arts, 1960.)

(From the movie "Valley of the Dragons," adapted from the novel *Hector Servadac*, starring Cesare Danova. Copyright © 1961 by Columbia Pictures.)

1876. After the success of *The Mysterious Island* and the novels and plays of *Around the World* and *Michael Strogoff,* Verne's situation was quite prosperous. Bought a sailing yacht, which he called the *Saint-Michel II.*

1877. Replaced the *Saint-Michel II* with a steam yacht, which he christened *Saint-Michel III.* "What madness! 55,000 francs! I'm paying half cash down and the rest in a year's time! But what a boat, too, and what trips in store! The Mediterranean, the Baltic, the northern seas, Constantinople, St Petersburg, Norway, Iceland, and more besides! And what a reservoir of impressions and ideas for my books! I'm sure that I will get back every penny—and in any case the boat will still be worth what I'm paying two years from now: she cost over 100,000 francs to build. . . . I can foresee a few more good books ahead. . . ."[2]

October, 1879. Son, Michel, was increasingly disobedient and delinquent. Verne, unable to discipline him, had at one time committed him to prison. "Although his professor has told him that he can take the baccalauréat examinations in April, Michel has already stopped working. It has all started all over again: dissipation, debts beyond all reason, theories that are horrifying to hear come from a boy of his age, avowed intentions to get money by all possible means, threats and so on—the whole scene as before. The wretched boy is revoltingly cynical. You would not believe how bad it is. Even allowing for what is undeniably a small dose of madness, he is a thorough delinquent. So long as he was working, I put up with everything. But now that he has stopped working entirely, I must act. But how? Show him the door. Of course. Then at seventeen and a half [he was eighteen and a quarter] he will go wandering around Paris on his own. The future is terribly worrying; once he is gone I shall never see him again. Ah . . . I am very unhappy, it can't go on! What would you do in my place? Throw him out and never see him again. Yes, I will be forced into it eventually. I am unbelievably unhappy."[2]

December, 1879. Michel was thrown out of his home.

March, 1880. Michel ran away with an actress to live with her in Le Havre. "Now that she is certainly his mistress, I do not think that he will go and get married in England, although he had the church banns published in Amiens. Debts and grievances on all sides, and there is nothing I can do. He is heading straight for the madhouse along the road of poverty and shame."[2]

1885. Dedicated *Mathias Sandorf* to "the young" Alexandre Dumas.

"TO ALEXANDRE DUMAS

"I dedicate this book to you as I also dedicate it to the memory of that great story teller, your father, Alexandre Dumas. I have tried to make *Mathias Sandorf* the Monte Cristo of the extraordinary Journeys. I beg you to accept the dedication as a token of my deep friendship."[1]

Dumas replied with all the civilities.

"MY DEAR FRIEND,

"I am touched by the kind thought you have had in dedicating *Mathias Sandorf* to me . . . you are right in your dedication to associate the father's memory with son's friendship. Nobody would have been more delighted than the author of *Monte Cristo* to read your brilliant, original and interest-

ing compelling fantasies. There is between you and him so evident a literary parenthood that in terms of literature you are more his son than I am. . . .

"A. DUMAS."[1]

March, 1886. Shot in the foot by his nephew, Gaston, which caused Verne to walk with a permanent limp. His brother and the father of Gaston, Paul, recounted the tragedy: "What a frightful misfortune! I have just returned from Amiens where I saw poor Gaston, who had been taken to the hospital infirmary at the request of his uncle. The poor dear child has no consciousness of the act that he has committed. He says that he wanted to attract attention to his uncle in order to gain him a seat in the Académie—that is the only explanation that anyone has been able to get from him. The public attorney and the doctors with whom I talked have declared him totaly *irresponsible;* he is going to be put in a home.

"Nothing could have made us foresee such a misfortune. It was on his arrival in Paris that he disappeared. (He was returning from *Blois* with his aunt to attend his cousin's wedding.) He stopped the carriage, saying that he wanted to get to the hairdresser's, and was not seen again. We searched for him for twenty-four hours, but the first news was Jules's telegram calling me to Amiens. What a misfortune! It has driven me to distraction; and we are all as upset as you will be.

"Jules is hurt in the foot—but the doctors hope that the wound will not have serious consequences; the bullet has not been extracted yet and probably won't be. He is not in pain. They are going to fit an appliance to immobilize the foot until it recovers."[2]

March 17, 1886. Hetzel died.

February, 1887. Mother died. "My father was the first to go, my mother surviving him by fifteen years: but now, she too has gone. These two deaths have caused me much sorrow, but that is fate. One must lose those one loves just as one loses those one doesn't love. All the same, let us try to be among those who have been loved when our own time comes to depart."[3]

November, 1887. First and last public reading tour.

Recognized his son's second marriage, which helped cement a reconciliation between the two. "We have just had Michel and family here for a month. His wife is charming, and so are his children. But the Lefèvres [husband of Honorine's daughter, Suzanne] refused to see them and persuaded our false friends to do likewise. Our only true friends were the Labbés and the Pinsards. Mind you, we didn't try to force the couple on any one. You know me better than that. But if the Lefèvres and the rest believe they did their duty, we are convinced we did ours. One of the children was ill, he needed a change of air, he came here: every liberal mind and every true heart is with us and to blazes with fools."[2]

May, 1888. Elected on Amiens' town council. "My sole aim is to make myself useful, and to see that certain urban reforms are properly carried out. Why must one always mix politics and Christianity with administrative matters?. . . In sociology, my taste is for order; in politics, my ambition is: to create, within the present administration, a party guided by reason and a sense of proportion, having a respect for justice and higher beliefs, a friend of men, of the arts, and of life. Believe me, I have made no secret of my feelings concerning

(From the movie "Around the World in Eighty Days," starring David Niven and Cantinflas. Released by United Artists Corp., 1956.)

the proscription laws, and in the same way, I am determined to defend, whenever necessary, the individual's freedom of conscience. . . . I may add that, since my infirmity obliges me to lead a more sedentary life, this is a useful way of keeping in contact with affairs, and with my fellow men. It's a professional matter. A number of my colleagues are extremists, but they will moderate their ways. Others among them are eminently sensible men—so much the better! And a few are fools—better still! Their remarks will provide me with entertainment. I need it."[3]

1892. Made an officer of the Legion of Honor.

June, 1893. Suffered attacks of dizziness, eye trouble, and leg pains, which severely limited his activity.

June, 1894. Wrote his brother, Paul, a sailor who often helped Verne with the technical aspects of his novels: "I shall soon have need of you, my dear Paul, to help me finish *The Floating Island*. The first volume is already written. The second will be ready in three months' time. Do you think that, theoretically and ideally speaking, it would be possible to steer the island without a rudder, but with a system of propellors on starboard and port sides, driven by dynamos generating a million horsepower? Can one do away with the need for a rudder by sailing slowly, in short, by regulating the speed of the propellors? Let me know when you have a moment. I am sending you the ending of *The Wonderful Adventures of Captain Antifer*. I am utterly done in; I shall melt. Tonight we had a storm and a torrential downpour, but the heat persists. . . ."[3]

September, 1894. "Dear old Paul, I'm sending you the first volume, in galley-proof, of *The Floating Island*. Jules Hetzel [the younger], who comes to Amiens once a fortnight to talk about books and business, said to me: 'It's extremely original, and you've dealt with the subject from the most daring aspect, in fact, it would be too daring in any other hands but yours.' You will see for yourself whether that's true. In the second volume, which is thick with incident, you will see the consequences of the state of affairs described in the first. Correct the hydrographic errors, if there are any. If you notice other errors concerning the displacement of the island in the water, its tonnage, or its motive power, tell me what the correct figures should be.

". . . In the book which is to follow *The Floating Island (Clovis Dardentor)*, I shall bring the Balearic Islands in, and that will give me a chance to speak of his magnificent enterprise in the archipelago.

"As I said before, my own view is that the second volume of *The Floating Island* will be much more interesting than the first, because of its humorous character. It will all be based on manners and events of the day, but I am still a novelist first and foremost, and my books will always be fictions to outward view."[3]

In a letter to Paul, Verne again asked his advice for the proper design for his latest literary creation, the seaplane. The actual invention of the seaplane occurred twenty years later. "Tell me everything that comes into your head concerning our fantastic ship, apart from actual absurdities. My volumes for 1895, 1896 and 1897 are ready. I am actively at work on the one for 1898. Thus, I have plenty of time ahead of me, and it amuses me to try and find the formula for this vessel. The most original idea would be to have a ship capable of sailing under the water, on the surface, and in the air as well. Shall

I go as far as that? As to the theme, it must be both extremely romantic and extremely elevated. It will be no good merely rewriting *Twenty Thousand Leagues* and creating a second Nemo. I have always been moved by the story of the Rorique brothers, but I don't want to use it in this book. Failing them, I will put an inventor in charge of the ship, although he will not be confined to it, but will have dealings with the Land as well, appearing sometimes as a noble figure and sometimes as a vulgar adventurer. The ship would have to be a double one, perhaps after the Goubet model, so that at night, a schooner or brig could be detached from it, which would be found there in its place. This inventor would close the Mediterranean, across the Straits of Gilbratar, with nets, and after that, I don't know yet how the story would end. Perhaps a spy could find his way abroad the ship. Anyway, you can see all the crazy ideas that are passing through my head. If you have any yourself, do tell me.

"I have had further letters from the Archduke Louis Salvador of Austria, who has sent me his latest works on the Lipari Islands. He also sent me details of how the *Nixe* was wrecked, near Cape Matifou; in the ordinary way, he himself was in charge of the vessel, but this time, he had engaged an experienced captain, who ran her on the rocks."[3]

1895. "I have great difficulty with writing what with my writer's cramp, but that does not prevent me from labouring over *The Eccentric's Will*. . . . Michel has come to stay a week here with his wife and has decided to work at a book for which I gave him the idea. It is a continuation of my vein and he has a remarkable facility in writing. We'll see what will come of it.

"I hardly budge from my chair and am now as sedentary as I used to be fond of wandering. Age, infirmity and worries make me as heavy as lead. Oh! my dear Paul, the good times we have spent sailing together. They will not come again."[2]

September, 1896. Sent young Hetzel part one of *The Sphinx des Glaces* which was dedicated to Edgar Allan Poe, who had influenced Verne greatly. "It will be a kind of counterpart to *Captain Hatteras*, although there is nothing in the two books—plot or characters—to make them alike. It will come at the right time, since people are talking about voyages and discoveries at the South Pole. My point of departure is one of Edgar Poe's strangest novels, *The Narrative of Arthur Gordon Pym*, but it will not be necessary to have read Poe's novel to understand mine. I have used everything that Poe left in suspense and have developed the mystery surrounding certain of the characters. I have one particularly good *trouvaille*: one of my heroes who, like everyone else, thought that Poe's novel was entirely fictitious, comes face to face with a matching reality. Needless to say, I go much further than Poe did. Let me know what you think; I hope that my readers will be very interested.

"I am so taken with the extraordinary side of a work like this that I wish to dedicate it to the memory of Edgar Poe and to our friends in America. I'm very excited about this novel; we shall see whether it gets the public excited too. . . . In my opinion, it's another *Gordon Pym*, but more true to life and I think more interesting. Tomorrow I'm going sailing to get myself shaken around a little."[2]

August, 1897. Brother, Paul, died.

1898. Destroyed all his personal files.

1900. Continued to work and to fight age and illness. "It won't stop me from working. It won't stop me from slaving. What could I do without my work? What would become of me?"[2]

March 24, 1905. Died at his home in Amiens as a result of diabetes. His grandson recalled his death: "When he saw that we were all there, he gave us one fond look that clearly meant: 'Good, you are all here. Now I can die'; then he turned to the wall to await death bravely. His serenity impressed us greatly and we wished that we might have as fine a death ourselves when our time came. According to Marie Guillon, his beloved little sister, who sat with him for five days until the end, he remarked to the priest who came to see him every day: 'You have done me good. I feel regenerated.' More significantly, it seems to me, he asked that any disagreements that might have arisen among the family should be forgotten."[2]

March 28, 1905. Buried in the cemetery of La Madeleine in Amiens. "Everything that I invent, everything that I imagine, will always fall short of the truth, because there will come a time when the creations of science will outstrip those of the imagination."[3]

Proclaimed the father of science-fiction, Verne predicted such twentieth century inventions as television (he called it phono-tele-photo), helicopters, dirigibles, neon lights, air conditioning, skyscrapers, guided missiles, tanks, submarines, and airplanes. Those who later created these wonders gladly gave Verne credit—France's famous Marshal Lyautey once told the Chamber of Deputies in Paris that modern science was simply a process of working out in practice what Jules Verne had envisioned in words.

FOR MORE INFORMATION SEE: Kenneth Allott, *Jules Verne,* Cresset, 1940, Macmillan, 1941, reprinted, Kennikat, 1970; George H. Waltz, *Jules Verne: The Biography of an Imagination,* Holt, 1943; H. G. Tompkins, "Jules Verne: Uncanny Prophet," *Coronet,* January, 1950; Marguerite Allotte de la Fuÿe, *Jules Verne* (translated from the French by Erik de Mauny), Staples Press, 1954, Coward, 1956; G. Kent, "Mister Imagination," *Saturday Review,* June 5, 1954; Ray Bradbury, "Marvels and Miracles—Pass It On!" *New York Times Magazine,* March 20, 1955; Idrisyn O. Evans, *Jules Verne: Master of Science Fiction,* Sidgwick, 1956; V. Cohen, "Jules Verne," *Contemporary Review,* October, 1956; Frank Magill, editor, *Cyclopedia of World Authors,* Harper, 1958; H. Forman, "Verne: His Visions and Voyages," *Saturday Review,* March 14, 1959.

Sam Moskowitz, *Explorers of the Infinite,* World Publishing, 1963; Franz Born, *Jules Verne: The Man Who Invented the Future* (translated from the German by Juliana Biro), Prentice-Hall, 1964, reissued, Scholastic Book Services, 1973; Russell Freedman, *Jules Verne: Portrait of a Prophet,* Holiday House, 1965; Beril Becker, *Jules Verne,* Putnam, 1966; I. O. Evans, *Jules Verne and His Work,* Twayne, 1966; Stanley J. Kunitz and Vineta Colby, editors, *European Authors, 1000-1900,* H. W. Wilson, 1967; Brian Doyle, editor, *Who's Who of Children's Literature,* Schocken Books, 1968; Jean Chesneaux, *Political and Social Ideas of Jules Verne* (translated from the French by Thomas Wikeley), Thames, 1972; Arty Pereira, *They Won Fame and Fortune,* Hind Pocket Books, 1973; Jean Jules-Verne, *Jules Verne* (translated from the French by Roger Greaves), Taplinger, 1976.

For children: Elizabeth R. Montgomery, *Story behind Great Books,* McBride, 1946; S. J. Kunitz and Howard Haycraft,

Verne at 49. Photo by Nadar.

editors, *Junior Book of Authors,* second edition revised, H. W. Wilson, 1951; Beryl Williams and Samuel Epstein, *Rocket Pioneers on the Road to Space,* Messner, 1955; G. Kent, "Mister Imagination," in *Great Adventures in Science,* edited by Helen Wright and S. B. Rapport, Harper, 1956; Catherine O. Peare, *Jules Verne: His Life,* Holt, 1956; Nora Stirling, *Who Wrote the Classics?,* Day, 1965.

VINSON, Kathryn   1911-

PERSONAL: Born March 23, 1911, in Cordele, Ga.; daughter of Edward Augustus (a banker, owner of Crisp County Lumber Co. and rancher) and Cordelia (Scott) Vinson; married Blenus Williams (retired owner of an insurance agency), April 16, 1933; children: Edward Vinson, Melissa Jane (Mrs. Arthur Sanford Kirkindall). *Education:* Woman's College of Georgia, A.B., 1932; Rollins College, M.A.T., 1966. *Religion:* Protestant. *Home:* 844 Kenilworth Terrace, Orlando, Fla. 32803.

CAREER: Chandler County High School, Metter, Ga., English and French teacher, 1932-33; Orlando Junior College, Orlando, Fla., instructor in English, 1966-69, assistant professor of English, 1969-71; Florida Technological University, Orlando, Fla., adjunct instructor in English, 1970-71; Valencia Community College, Orlando, Fla., adjunct instructor in humanities, 1971-72. *Member:* National Council of Teachers of English, Delta Kappa Gamma (honorary member),

KATHRYN VINSON

Antiquarian Society of Orange County (secretary and vice-president), Orange County Historical Society, Friends of the Orlando Public Library. *Awards, honors:* Numerous awards, Central Florida art shows for landscapes in watercolors and oils; *The Luck of the Golden Cross* was a Catholic Children's Book Club choice for May, 1961; *The Luck of the Golden Cross* and *Run With the Ring* were transcribed into Braille and made into talking books.

WRITINGS: The Luck of the Golden Cross, Lippincott, 1960; *Run With the Ring,* Harcourt, 1965. Contributed feature stories in Sunday magazines of newspapers during college years.

WORK IN PROGRESS: Untitled novel for young adults.

SIDELIGHTS: "Unlike most people who wish to write, I did not have a lonely childhood. I grew up in a little town, the eldest of five children, and I also had a succession of pets, several cousins and a number of children living in the neighborhood with whom to play. Oh, how we played in those days! We invented most of our own games. We dug trenches all over the vacant lots and there made last ditch stands against the Indians, unmindful of the fact that Indian fighters did not entrench themselves. We had heard about trench warfare from our uncles who had fought in World War I, and that's the way we wanted to win the West. We held fairs and circuses, building merry-go-rounds and roller coasters out of scrap lumber, of which we always seemed to have a plentiful supply. It's a wonder that any of us survived. On rainy days, we resorted to experimenting with chemistry and elec-

tricity, or we repaired to the kitchen where we boiled down syrup and pulled candy into long sticky ropes that gummed up our hands, hair and clothes. We had a glorious time!

"Yet those unhurried days were long enough for both activity and solitude. Often on a drowsy summer's day, I climbed with a book to the top of a chinaberry tree, where I read for hours. Then all the far-off places of the world became my playground and all the people in the books materialized into playmates.

"For some reason that I have never been able to explain, a deep and abiding love for the sea possessed me, an inland child living hundreds of miles from the ocean. There was not even a lake nearby to solace me. The best that I could do until I visited Florida when I was nine was to stare at the goldfish flashing in the fountain on the back lawn of our Carnegie library ever time I went to change my books. I read the bookshelves through twice, adult shelves included.

"When I wasn't reading I was drawing, hoping someday to write my own books and to illustrate them.

"About the time I entered junior high school, I developed a trait that separated me from my peers. I wanted to learn. In my pursuit of knowledge, I adopted as my credo the lines from *Ulysses* in which the far-faring wanderer vowed 'To strive, to seek, to find, and not to yield.' After that, I was lonely a great deal.

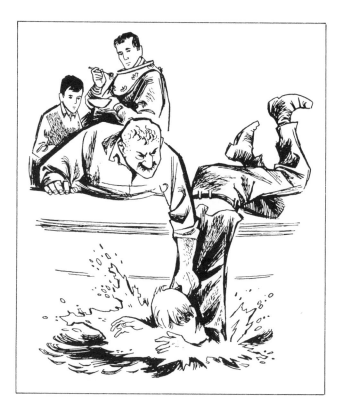

"Then I'll wash you, myself." Captain Volos set aside his plate, rose, and with one powerful hand caught Joe by the back of his greasy collar, swept him over the rail, and dipped him into the sea. ■ (From *The Luck of the Golden Cross* by Kathryn Vinson. Illustrated by Allan Eitzen.)

"Perhaps that early unsatisfied longing for the sea had something to do with my writing my first novel for children about the Greek sponge divers who live on the west coast of Florida. (I had married and come to live in Florida by the time that I wrote it.) But it is probable that my love for the Greek myths had more to do with the writing of it. For, when, as a child, I was obliged to endure mustard plasters when suffering from bouts of so-called bronchial pneumonia, my parents kept me quiet by spelling each other in reading me the Greek myths. My imagination would take flight along with the wonderful winged horse, and then I would forget all about the fiery sting of the mustard while I hobnobbed with gods and goddesses up on Mount Olympus.

"Soon after I married and came to Orlando to live, my husband took me to Tarpon Springs to show me some early paintings of George Innes, who used to winter there. But before that visit was over, I had seen a great deal more than the Innes paintings, and I had fallen completely under the spell of the picturesque colony of Greek sponge divers, who daily practiced old world customs two and three thousand years old. I was hooked! Year after year we returned to witness the beautiful ceremonies celebrated in the Greek Orthodox Church and on the waterfront. In this way, I gathered the material for my first book, *The Luck of the Golden Cross.*

"My second book was inspired by an item in the Orlando Sentinel. It concerned a track meet that was to be held between the boys from the state school for the blind and the sighted athletes of a local high school. 'What courage it must take to dash into the dark!' I exclaimed to my husband. My working title for the book was *Dash in the Dark,* as I attempted to express in fiction my admiration for the boys who could run the hundred yard dash without eyesight. After extensive research in libraries and at the school for the blind in St. Augustine, I learned that the blind do not like to be thought of as 'living in darkness.' The word *dark* is anathema to them. So in deference to their feelings, I changed my title to *Run with the Ring,* which is descriptive of the way they push a steel ring along a taut wire to keep them in the proper lane as they run.

"My writing came to a halt as I began teaching in the junior college just across the street from my home when my daughter went away to college. As soon as she came home for the summer, I extracted from her a promise to take good care of our ever-cooperative daddy/husband, tossed her the frying pan and boarded a plane for Greece to visit our son who had an apartment in Athens. Subsequent summers were spent in exploring other wonderful places with which I first had become acquainted in the chinaberry tree. And now that I have left off teaching, I am returning to my typewriter to take up my writing where I left off nearly ten years ago. I have reams of material crying to become stories."

HOBBIES AND OTHER INTERESTS: Antiques, painting, travel.

FOR MORE INFORMATION SEE: The Orlando Sentinel Florida Magazine, Ocotber 31, 1960, October 10, 1965; *The Orlando Evening Star,* April 17, 1964; *New York Times Book Review,* November 7, 1965; *Chicago Tribune Books Today,* November 7, 1965; *The Horn Book,* December, 1960, February, 1966; *Tampa Tribune,* October 15, 1966.

Wearing No. 3 for the last time during ceremonies marking the twenty-fifth anniversary of Yankee Stadium. ■(From *Babe Ruth: His Life and Legend* by Kal Wagenheim. Photograph courtesy of the National Baseball Hall of Fame.)

WAGENHEIM, Kal 1935-

PERSONAL: Born April 21, 1935, in Newark, N.J.; son of Harold and Rozlon (Heller) Wagenheim; married Olga Jimenez, June 10, 1961; children: David, Maria-Dolores. *Education:* Rutgers-Newark University, 1953-56, 1959; State University of New York at Buffalo, M.A., 1975. *Religion:* Jewish. *Home:* 52 Maple Ave., Maplewood, N.J. 07040.

CAREER: Free-lance writer, teacher, consultant. *Newark Star-Ledger,* Newark, N.J., part-time sports reporter, 1953-54, 1956-58; Prudential Insurance Co., Newark, N.J., copywriter, 1956-60; Keuffel & Esser Engineering Products, Hoboken, N.J., technical writer, 1960-61; reporter for weekly periodicals and radio announcer for WKYN, San Juan, Puerto Rico, 1961-63; free-lance writer on Caribbean affairs, also translator and reseacher, Puerto Rico, 1967-70; University of Puerto Rico, Rio Piedras, editor of scientific publications for Nuclear Center, 1968-70; *Buffalo Evening News,* Buffalo, N.Y., reporter, 1970-71; Columbia University, New York, N.Y., lecturer, 1978-80. Co-founder and co-editor of *San Juan Review* (monthly), 1964-66, and *Caribbean Review* (quarterly), 1969-70; part-time correspondent for *New York Times,* 1967-70; editorial and research consultant, U.S. Atomic Energy Commission, 1968-70, U.S. Commission on Civil Rights, 1975, U.S. Information Agency, 1977; public relations and advertising, U.S. Environmental Protection Agency, 1973, Puerto Rican government's Tourism Bureau, 1976. *Military service:* U.S. Army, 1954-56.

MEMBER: Authors Guild, American Newspaper Guild, Overseas Press Club of Puerto Rico (member of board of directors, 1968-70). *Awards, honors:* Overseas Press Club of Puerto Rico Award, 1969, for best story published off-island (in *New York Times*); recipient with Barry Bernard Levine of grant from the Plumstock Foundation to support publication of *Caribbean Review,* 1969.

WRITINGS; Puerto Rico: A Profile, Praeger, 1971, 1975; (editor) *Puerto Rican Short Stories,* Institute of Puerto Rican Culture, 1971; (translator) Ricardo Alegria, *Discovery, Conquest and Colonization of Puerto Rico,* Institute of Puerto Rican Culture, 1971; *Clemente!,* Praeger, 1973; *Babe Ruth: His Life and Legend,* Praeger, 1974; (editor with Olga Jimenez de Wagenheim) *The Puerto Ricans: A Documentary History,* Praeger, 1975; *A Survey of Puerto Ricans on the U.S. Mainland in the 1970's,* Praeger Special Studies, 1975; *Paper Gold,* McKay, 1976; (editor) *Short Stories from Puerto Rico,* Schocken, 1979. Contributor of more than one hundred news articles to *New York Times* and other articles to *Nation, New Leader, New Republic,* and *Liberation.* Has sold cartoon ideas to *New Yorker, Playboy,* and other magazines.

SIDELIGHTS: "I fully subscribe to the old saying that 'variety is the spice of life.' A writer's life can sometimes be precarious, in the financial sense, but it is one of never-ending surprises and fascination."

WATTS, Franklin (Mowry) 1904-1978

OBITUARY NOTICE: Born June 11, 1904, in Sioux City, Iowa; died May 21, 1978, in New York, N.Y. Publisher and author. Watts was a bookseller, department store book buyer, and sales representative for a group of publishers before he established the publishing firm of Franklin Watts, Inc. in 1942. The firm specialized in books for children and young people. Watts—with his wife and business associate, Helen Hoke—developed several successful series of children's books, including the "First Books" series that was launched with *The First Book of Airplanes* and grew to 100 books by 1959. Watts also developed a series of over 50 books for Doubleday under the Real Books name, as well as a series of adult books published by Pocket Books. He was also affiliated with Vanguard Press, Julian Messner, and Heritage Press. In addition to his work as a publisher, Watts was the author of a number of children's books and several books for adults. *For More Information See: Contemporary Authors,* Gale, Volume 25-28, 1971, Permanent Series, Volume 2, 1978; *Author's and Writer's Who's Who,* 6th edition, Burke's Peerage, 1973; *Who's Who in America,* 40th edition, Marquis, 1978. *Obituaries: New York Times,* May 23, 1978; *Publishers Weekly,* June 5, 1978.

WEIR, Rosemary (Green) 1905-

PERSONAL: Born July 22, 1905, in Kimberley, South Africa; daughter of George Alfred Lawrence (editor of *Cape Argus*) and Katherine (Bell) Green; widowed; children: Alison. *Education:* Educated privately and at schools in England. *Politics:* Conservative. *Religion:* Church of England. *Home:* 12A Bath Place, Taunton, Somerset, Devonshire, England. *Agent:* Charles Lavell Ltd., 176 Wardour St., London W.I.U. 3AA, England.

CAREER: Trained for stage in England and then became partner in a touring theatrical company, playing one-night stands in rural districts of England and Wales for three years; joined First Aid Nursing Yeomanry when World War II began (invalided out); after that, in partnership with a friend, Lelia Downes-Martin, farmed in North Wales and Devonshire, taught elocution and sewing in a school, ran a furniture renovating business, and worked as a domestic and cook, privately and in hotels and lodges; began writing short stories and articles "in sheer desperation, to dig myself out of tiring and boring jobs with my pen"; now full-time writer for children and young people.

WRITINGS—All youth books: *The Secret Journey,* Parrish, 1957; *The Secret of Cobbet's Farm,* Parrish, 1957; *No. 10 Green Street,* Parrish, 1958; *The Island of Birds,* Parrish, 1959; *The Honeysuckle Line,* Parrish, 1959, published as *Robert's Rescued Railway,* F. Watts, 1959.

The Hunt for Harry, Parrish, 1960; *Great Days in Green Street,* Parrish, 1960; *Pineapple Farm* (school reader), Parrish, 1960; *Little Lion's Real Island,* Harrap, 1960; *A Dog of Your Own* (nonfiction), Harrap, 1960; *The House in the Middle of the Road,* Parrish, 1961; *Albert the Dragon,* Abelard, 1961; *What a Lark,* Brockhampton Press, 1961; *Tania Takes the Stage,* Hutchinson, 1961; *Top Secret,* Parrish, 1962; *Soap Box Derby,* Brockhampton Press, 1962, Van Nostrand, 1965; *Black Sheep,* Criterion, 1963; *The Young David Garrick* (nonfiction), Parrish, 1963; *The Smallest Dog on Earth,* Abelard, 1963; *The Further Adventures of Albert the Dragon,* Abelard, 1964; *The Star and the Flame,* Farrar, Straus, 1964; *Mike's Gang,* Abelard, 1964; *A Patch of Green,* Parrish, 1965; *The Real Game,* Van Nostrand, 1965; *Soap-Box Derby,* Van Nostrand, 1965; *The Boy From Nowhere,* Abelard, 1966; *High Courage,* Farrar, Straus, 1967; *Pyewacket,* Abelard, 1967; *Albert and the Centaur,* Abelard, 1968; *No Sleep for Angus,* Abelard, 1969; *Summer of the Silent Hands,* Brockhampton Press, 1969.

Lion and the Rose, Farrar, Straus, 1970; *The Man Who Built a City: A Life of Sir Christopher Wren,* Farrar, Straus, 1971; *Boy on a Brown Horse,* Hawthorn, 1971; *Three Red Herrings,* T. Nelson, 1972; *Blood Royal,* Farrar, Straus, 1973; *Uncle Barney and the Sleep Destroyer,* British Book Center, 1976; *Uncle Barney and the Shrink-Drink,* British Book Center, 1977; *Albert and the Dragonettes,* British Book Center, 1977.

Scripts for British Broadcasting Corp. include serialization of *The Secret Journey* and a series, "Strange Tales."

WORK IN PROGRESS: A sequel to Pyewacket.

SIDELIGHTS: "What I would like to stress is that it is never too late to start writing. I never particularly wanted to be a writer. Writing was something everyone else in the family did and I wanted to be different. However, economic necessity finally forced me into it and I was lucky enough to hit it off right from the start. I began with a talk for radio and went on to short stories, both for radio and various magazines. I never had anything returned so was unable to paper the walls of my study with rejection slips in the orthodox way! In any case, in the early days I didn't have a study. I wrote on the kitchen table in the hotel where I was at that time working as a waitress. I was then in my middle forties.

"I wrote my first book for children as an experiment. I can remember vividly my own happy childhood and this is the most important thing for a children's author. The book was accepted at once and the B.B.C. asked me to script it into a four part play for radio. After that there was no holding me and I wrote so much and so rapidly that I soon found I had six London publishers and three in New York. This is not a good way to work, nor is it a good thing to write, as I did, for all age groups. But it brings in ready money in advances, which was my objective at that time. Later I was able to work more slowly and, I considered, better, but it

The lion closed his eyes in an ecstasy of pleasure as the strong fingers caressed his head. ■ (From *The Lion and the Rose* by Rosemary Weir. Illustrated by Richard Cuffari.)

is an odd fact that it is the books I wrote during the 'crowded years' which are now being re-issued as paperbacks. There must be a reason for this, but I don't know what it is!

"Finally, to encourage those older people who would like to start a new career but feel it is too late, I would like to quote from a biography of my brother, Lawrence G. Green, himself a very successful author of travel books. He told his biographer, 'Even with my newspaper experience it took me years to reach the top and independence as an author and I started at a youngish age (eighteen) and yet my sister, Rosemary Weir, only started to write when she was nearly fifty and immediately hit the jackpot in England and America with her childen's books without any training at all. She has done nearly as well as I have and in half the time.'"

Weir's books for children have appeared in Holland, France, Switzerland, Germany, Norway, Finland, Denmark, as well as in the United States.

HOBBIES AND OTHER INTERESTS: Theater, classical music, animals, gardening, and country life.

FOR MORE INFORMATION SEE: Trade News, September 23, 1961; *Horn Book,* December 1964, February, 1972, June, 1973.

ROSEMARY WEIR

WEISBERGER, Bernard A(llen) 1922-

PERSONAL: Born August 15, 1922, in Hudson, N.Y.; son of Joseph H. (a dentist) and Anne (Eckstein) Weisberger; married June Miller (an attorney), September 9, 1951 (divorced, 1970); children: Jonathan, Lise, Beth. *Education:* Columbia University, A.B., 1943; University of Chicago, A.M., 1947, Ph.D., 1950. *Politics:* Independent. *Religion:* Jewish. *Home:* 55 W. 55th St., New York, N.Y. 10019.

CAREER: Swarthmore College, Swarthmore, Pa., instructor, 1950-51; Antioch College, Yellow Springs, Ohio, assistant professor, 1952-54; Wayne State University, Detroit, Mich., assistant professor, 1954-59; University of Chicago, associate professor of history, 1959-63; University of Rochester, Rochester, N.Y., professor of history, 1963-67, chairman, 1964-65; *American Heritage,* associate editor, 1970-72; Vassar College, Poughkeepsie, N.Y., visiting professor,

1972-80; *Readers Digest Encyclopedia of American History,* chief consultant, 1975; *Story of America,* Readers Digest Books, general consultant, 1975; NBC Radio Network, bicentennial programming, consultant, 1975-76; *City Out of Wilderness* (film), consultant, 1975; advisory committee, NEH Feasibility Study of a New Journal in Humanities, member, 1975. *Military service:* U.S. Army, Signal Corps, 1942-46; served in China-Burma-India theater; became second lieutenant; Historical Section, Joint Chiefs of Staff, 1951-52; became first lieutenant.

MEMBER: Authors League of America, Phi Beta Kappa. *Awards, honors:* Social Science Research Council grant, 1956; fellow, American Council of Learned Societies, 1959-60; program chairman, American Historical Association, 1962; Ramsdell prize, Southern Historical Association, 1962; honorary member, Phi Beta Kappa (Iota of N.Y.), 1964; Ford Foundation lecturer, Atlanta University Center, 1965; Na-

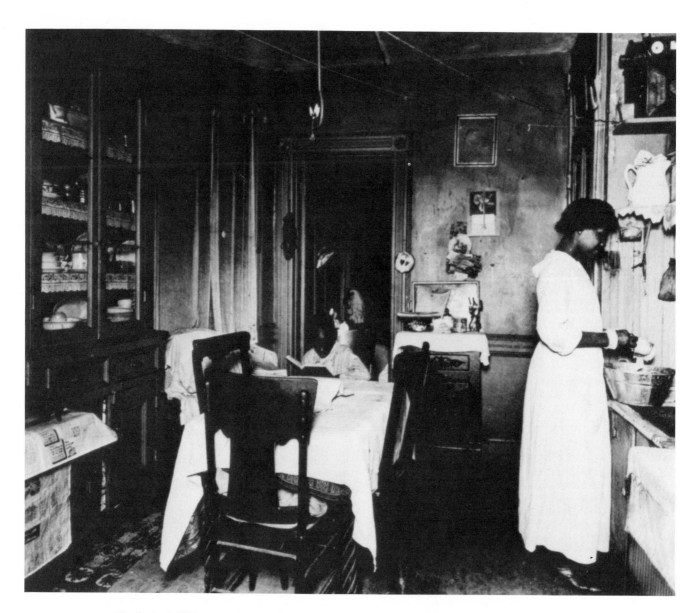

The "colorful" Negro slum, a profit maker for writer, painter, and real-estate owner, was for its residents a sink of disillusionment and despair. Many blacks found the only lasting joy of their existence in religion. ∎ (From *The American Heritage History of the American People* by Bernard A. Weisberger. Photograph by Brown Brothers.)

BERNARD A. WEISBERGER

tional Humanities Faculty, 1969; elected member, Society of American Historians, 1972; board of judges, Francis Parkman Prize, Society of American Historians, 1973.

WRITINGS: Reporters for the Union, Little, Brown, 1953; *The Gathered at the River,* Little, Brown, 1958; *The American Newspaperman,* University of Chicago Press, 1961; (contributor) *The Life History of the United States,* Time-Life Books, 1964; *The Age of Steam and Steel,* Time-Life Books, 1964; *Reaching for Empire,* Time-Life Books, 1964; (with Allan Nevins) *Captains of Industry,* American Heritage Junior Library, 1966; (with the editors of Silver Burdett) *Samuel Gompers,* Silver Burdett, 1966; (with the editors of Time-Life) *The District of Columbia,* Time, Inc., 1968; *The New Industrial Society,* Wiley, 1969; *The American Heritage History of the American People,* American Heritage, 1971; *The Impact of Our Past,* McGraw, 1972, reissued, 1976; *Booker T. Washington,* New American Library, 1973; *Pathways to the Present,* Harper, 1976; *The Dream Maker: William C. Durant, Founder of General Motors,* Little, Brown, 1979. Articles in *American Heritage,* and professional journals; reviews in newspapers.

SIDELIGHTS: "I always squirm a bit when asked to talk about how and why I write. It makes a self-conscious process out of something that I just started doing naturally around age fourteen, and haven't found myself able to stop. I grew up mostly in New York City, with long stretches in Hudson, N.Y. (pop. 12,000), and had no more than the usual share of childhood mishaps, so far as I know. I always loved reading and being read to—so did my three children, I'm happy to say. I enjoyed composition classes from the earliest years, and published my first story in the Stuyvesant High School magazine, *The Caliper,* in 1937. I quickly discovered I had no gift for fiction, but went into history in college and graduate school in search of drama, character, irony, and all the other things writers are supposed to create. I've found it in abundance. Writing is my vehicle for whatever inchoate philosophy I have, and I suppose, for exorcising various neuroses. Whether I write for children or adults, scholars or the general public, my goals are the same—to tell a good story, to stimulate curiosity, to entertain—I'm not ashamed of the word. All that differs is the vocabulary and the amount of back-ground information that I assume. Whatever else I do is more or less adjunct to writing."

HOBBIES AND OTHER INTERESTS: Fishing, long distance running.

WESTON, John (Harrison)   1932-

PERSONAL: Born May 17, 1932, in Prescott, Ariz.; son of Omer Austin (a miner) and Eloine (Osment) Weston; married Catherine Jane Storms, February 6, 1954 (divorced); children: Tracy Cathlin, Jennifer Ann. *Education:* Arizona State University, B.A., 1954; University of Arizona, M.A., 1961; Yale University, graduate study, 1964-65. *Home:* 22152 Paso del Sur, South Laguna, Calif. 92677. *Agent:* Harold Matson Co., Inc., 22 East 40th St., New York, N.Y. 10016.

CAREER: Teacher of English, music, and humanities at Needles High School, Needles, Calif., 1954-57, Yuma High School, Yuma, Ariz., 1957-60, Rincon High School, Tucson, Ariz., 1960-67, The University of Arizona, 1957-71, California State University, 1971—. John Hay Fellow in Humanities at Williams College, summer, 1959, and Yale University, 1964-65; fellow, Bread Loaf Writers Conference, 1965; consultant to Humanities Institute, Eugene, Ore., summer, 1966; director of the Poetry Center, The University of Arizona, 1967-70; teacher, University of Indiana Writers Workshop, summer, 1967. *Member:* Authors Guild, National Public Radio (fiction reviewer). *Awards, honors:* Silver medal of the Commonwealth Club of California for *The Boy Who Sang the Birds,* 1967.

WRITINGS: Jolly (novel), McKay, 1965; *The Telling* (novel), McKay, 1966; *Hail, Hero!* (novel), McKay, 1968; *Goat Songs* (three novellas), Atheneum, 1971; *The Walled Parrot* (novel), McGraw, 1975; *The Boy Who Sang the Birds* (novel), Scribner, 1976. Author of short stories, essays, reviews, and poetry in U.S. journals.

WORK IN PROGRESS: Two novellas, *The Drinking Stone* and *The Taste of Ashes;* two full-length books; a filmstrip.

SIDELIGHTS: "I grew up on a meager ranch far out in the country—which is a good place for a writer to start, I think, because if he is forced to be alone a great part of the time, he is also forced to find his own amusements, and that is good for developing creativity. Besides—or while—wandering all over the countryside studying the complex ways of nature (although I wouldn't have called it 'studying'), I made up stories in my head with many fantastic characters and I spoke all the parts. Sometimes a story would continue from day to day, like a serial. Because I lived in the West, cowboys and train robbers played heavy roles in my stories, but by the time I actually began writing, in junior high, they had been replaced, generally, by ghouls and bloody sorts in creaking old mansions, due, I guess, to my avid reading-affair with Edgar Allan Poe.

"The setting of *The Boy Who Sang the Birds* is very much like the country in which I lived as a child, although not so cold and wintry as that. I have never been able—nor wanted—to forget the place; it is called Skull Valley, so named because of the many Indian bones dug up as the railroad was being put through, late in the 19th century. The Indians had died in battles between tribes, apparently, not in fights with white people. Anyway, that geographic location

Dorkle lived with Tobe beyond the great creek and farther. ■ (From *The Boy Who Sang the Birds* by John Weston. Illustrated by Donna Diamond.)

is so imprinted on my mind that it hangs around, waiting to be pressed into service again and again.

"When I wrote *The Boy Who Sang the Birds,* I did not intend it for children, especially, rather, it was for anyone with a simple heart who liked to read or be read to. The plot is entirely made up. That is, unlike some stories of mine, I didn't get the idea from ever having observed or heard of such a series of events but, as I've said above, the *place* was there; all I had to do was invent something to put in it.

"Writing is not my whole life, however, I'm usually happily working on a new story. It's important to me to be able to do, at least passably well, many things; therefore, I paint, sing, play the piano, teach, cook, travel, read and attend as many plays, concerts, and operas as possible. Of all these, reading is the most important."

WILSON, Joyce M(uriel Judson) (Joyce Stranger)

PERSONAL: Born in London, England; daughter of Ralph (an advertising manager) and Beryl Judson; married Kenneth Wilson (patents manager with Imperial Chemicals Industry), February 28, 1944; children: Andrew Bruce, Anne Patricia and Nicholas David (twins). *Education:* University College, London, B.Sc., 1942. *Religion:* Church of England. *Agent:* Hughes Massie Ltd., 31 Southampton Row, London, WC1B 5HL, England.

CAREER: Imperial Chemicals Industry, Manchester, England, research chemist, 1942-46. *Member:* Society of Authors, Society of Women Journalists and Writers, British Mammal Society, British Deer Society, Council for Wild Life, Institute of Journalists.

WRITINGS—All under pseudonym Joyce Stranger: *Wild Cat Island* (juvenile), Methuen, 1961; *Circus All Alone* (juvenile), Harrap, 1965; *The Running Foxes,* Hammond, Hammond, 1965, Viking, 1966; *Breed of Giants,* Hammond, Hammond, 1967; *Rex,* Harvill Press, 1967, Viking, 1968; *Jason* (juvenile), Dent, 1967; *Casey,* Harvill Press, 1968, published as *Born to Trouble,* Viking, 1969; *Rusty,* Harvill Press, 1969, published as *The Wind on the Dragon,* Viking, 1970; *The Honeywell Badger* (juvenile), Dent, 1969.

Zara, Harvill Press, 1970, Viking, 1971; *Chia: The Wildcat,* Harvill Press, 1971; *One for Sorrow,* Transworld Publishers, 1971; *Paddy Joe* (juvenile), Collins, 1972; *The Hare at Dark Hollow* (juvenile), Dent, 1972; (contributor) Noel Streatfeild, editor, *Summer Holiday Book,* Dent, 1972; *Lakeland Vet,* Harvill Press, 1972, Viking, 1973; (contributor) Noel Streatfeild, editor, *Christmas Holiday Book,* Dent, 1973; *Walk a Lonely Road,* Harvill Press, 1973; *Never Count Apples,* Harvill Press, 1974; *Trouble for Paddy Joe* (juvenile), Collins, 1974; *A Dog Called Gelert,* Dent, 1974; *The Secret Herds,* Dent, 1974; *Paddy Joe at Deep Hollow Farm* (juvenile), Collins, 1975; *Never Tell a Secret,* Harvill Press, 1975; *Joyce Stranger's Book of Hanak Animals,* Dent, 1976; *The Fox at Drummers' Darkness,* Farrar, Straus, 1977; *Flash,* Collins, 1977; *Kym,* Michael Joseph, 1977; *Two's Company,* Michael Joseph, 1978; *A Walk in the Dark,* Michael Joseph, 1978; *The January Queen,* Michael Joseph, 1979; *Paddy Joe and Thomson's Folly. . . .,* Pelham, 1979; *The Curse of Seal Valley,* Dent, 1979; *All About Your Puppy,* Pelham, 1980; *Vet on Call,* Transworld, in press; *Double Trouble,* Transworld, in press.

JOYCE M. WILSON

Former writer of "The World About Us" column in *Annabel.* Contributor of short stories to *Woman's Journal, Woman's Own,* and other periodicals and of occasional articles to *Gamekeeper and Countryside, Dog World, Alsatian League Magazine, Off Lead,* and *Dog Training Weekly.*

WORK IN PROGRESS: "*Three's a Pact,* the true story about my German Shepherd; a sequel to *Walk a Lonely Road,* tentatively titled, *The Stallion.*"

SIDELIGHTS: "All the animal material in my books is in fact autobiographical, except for *Chia: The Wildcat.* I write about animals I have known. They may be a mixture of some—*Zara* is based on the mare I used to ride, though she wasn't a racehorse. Friends who trained racehorses for many years gave the background information for *Zara.*

"The horses in *Breed of Giants* were in fact the Lymm Shires, belonging to James Gould, another friend, now deceased, who owned one of the best Shires in Britain (Lymm Sovereign) and also some of the best past Shire horses, among them His Exellency. He gave me all his press cuttings back to 1900 and the story is that of his horses. He did not want a biography, so, as always, the people are invented; I never base them on anyone I know, except, perhaps, very roughly.

The fox avoided the cats. His first encounter had been with the oldest son of the black-and-white tom, and he had no wish to risk another. ■(From *The Fox at Drummers' Darkness* by Joyce Stranger. Illustrated by William Geldart.)

"Places come from the places I know. *In Casey,* the farm is the stables where I used to ride, Holly Tree Farm, at Plomley, in Cheshire. The *Running Foxes* was based on fox stories told to me over the years or seen for myself.... I saw the Huntsman but never in fact, spoke to him. He is an invention as are all the men and dogs in this book. The hounds are based on dogs I knew, but turned into a different breed.

"*One for Sorrow* we lived through. The epidemic struck Cheshire and closed the farm. Jim Gould used to ring me on Saturday evenings and just talk about his week and his cattle and asked me to write the book. It is based on his conversation with me all through that period. . . .

"The *Hare at Dark Hollow* came from a hare that lived near us in the middle of a housing estate. She reared her family on a tiny playing field and fed in the gardens. There were hares there until we moved to Anglesey, yet the field was only about an acre in size. Another hare was on our caravan site and used to lurk and watch stock car racing. There are hares all over Manchester airport (Ringway).

"*Lakeland Vet* was based on experiences of friends and my son who is a veterinarian as is his wife. They have a practice in Yorkshire. . . .

"Dogs now proliferate in my life . . . [especially] helping others with all kinds of dogs of all breeds. Gardens are also important since we have a two-acre wilderness.

"I work closely with my artist, William Geldart. Bill has now illustrated a number of children's books besides mine. He has created the illustrations for *Kym* and the *Fox at Drummer's Darkness.*

"I write sitting at a desk facing out over fields that rise to the horizon; fantastic skyscapes; hedges and trees; a mixed herd of cattle, often a cow calving; and in the next field are sheep which lamb in spring and are very noisy. Herons fly by and there are magpies, sometimes a hare. We have partridges nesting near Chita's jumps. She is being trained on police dog lines, except that she is not trained to attack. She has to jump, scale, retrieve, search, track. Her story is told in *Three's a Pact.*

"My next book will be a sequel to *Walk a Lonely Road* with a great deal more experience of the way a police dog does track."

WINTER, Milo (Kendall)   1888-1956

PERSONAL: Born August 7, 1888, in Princeton, Ill.; died August 15, 1956; married Mary Adams, 1912; children: Milo, Jr., Monroe Adams. *Education:* Studied art at the Chicago Art Institute and also abroad.

MILO WINTER

CAREER: Illustrator of books for children. Employed as chief illustrator for the Silver Burdett Co., and as art director for the Field Enterprises.

WRITINGS: Billy Popgun (illustrated by the author), Houghton, 1912.

Illustrator: Jonathan Swift, *Gulliver's Travels,* Rand McNally, 1912; Aesop, *Aesop for Children,* Rand McNally, 1912; Nathaniel Hawthorne, *Wonder Book,* Rand McNally, 1913; *Thousand and One Nights,* Rand McNally, 1914; Robert L. Stevenson, *Treasure Island,* Rand McNally, 1915; Mary M. Dodge, *Hans Brinker,* Rand McNally, 1916; Lewis Carroll, pseudonym of Charles Lutwidge Dodgson, *Alice's Adventures in Wonderland and Through the Looking Glass and What Alice Found There,* Rand McNally, 1916; Hans Christian Andersen, *Fairy Tales,* Rand McNally, 1916, reissued, 1972; Frances Jenkins Olcott, *Book of Elves and Fairies,* Houghton, 1918; Mary Hunter Austin, *Trail Book,* Houghton, 1918; F. J. Olcott, editor, *Wonder Garden,* Houghton, 1919.

Jules Verne, *Twenty Thousand Leagues under the Sea,* Rand McNally, 1922; Alexandre Dumas, *The Three Musketeers,* Rand McNally, 1923; Edith H. Berrien, *Siegfried,* T. S. Rockwell, 1930; Marjorie Barrows, *Who's Who in the Zoo,* Reilly

He then turned the head of Pegasus towards the east, and set out for Lycia. ■ (From *A Wonder Book for Girls and Boys* by Nathaniel Hawthorne. Illustrated by Milo Winter.)

A human skeleton lay on the ground. ■ (From *Treasure Island* by Robert Louis Stevenson. Illustrated by Milo Winter.)

& Lee, 1932; Hector H. Malot, *Adventures of Perrine,* Rand McNally, 1932; Zoe S. Loveland, *Illustrated Bible Story Book,* Rand McNally, 1935; Joel Chandler Harris, *Tales from Uncle Remus,* Houghton, 1935; (with Margaret E. Price) *Treasure Chest of Nursery Favorites,* Rand McNally, 1936; Aesop, *Favorite Fables,* Rand McNally, 1939, a large print version published as *Aesop's Fables,* Aeonian Press, 1976; Virginia Moe, *Animal Inn,* Houghton, 1946.

SIDELIGHTS: "I have always lived in the Middle West, my home now being in Lake Forest, Illinois. My art training was started at the Chicago Art Institute and finished abroad." [Bertha E. Mahony, and other, compilers, *Illustrators of Children's Books, 1745-1945,* Horn Book, 1947.]

"The whimsical and imaginative side of juvenile illustration has been the type of work that I feel I do best, and for the obvious reason that I like it most. The introduction of natural material such as animals and plant life into my compositions with care in the detail I believe lends value to the work from the child's standpoint. They see much in a drawing that one would scarcely give them credit for. My own two boys are severe critics and fiends for details. Nothing escapes them."[1]

(From *Twenty Thousand Leagues Under the Sea* by Jules Verne. Illustrated by Milo Winter.)

The Ghost of Christmas Present. ■(From *A Christmas Carol* by Charles Dickens. Illustrated by Milo Winter.)

FOR MORE INFORMATION SEE: Bertha E. Mahony and others, compilers, *Illustrators of Children's Books, 1744-1945*, Horn Book, 1947; B. E. Miller and others, compilers, *Illustrators of Children's Books: 1946-1956*, Horn Book, 1958; Obituaries—*New York Times,* August 17, 1956; *Publishers Weekly,* September 3, 1956.

WRIGHT, Dare 1926(?)-

PERSONAL: Born about 1926, in Ontario, Canada. *Education:* Attended the American Academy of Dramatic Arts and the Art Students League. *Home:* 11 E. 80th St., New York, New York, 10021.

CAREER: Children's author, illustrator, photographer. Began career as a photographer's fashion model; became a professional photographer; has worked in advertising and has done editorial photography, which has appeared in national magazines. Her fashion photography has appeared in *Harper's Bazaar* and *Vogue.* Has been writing books for children since 1957, and over the past twenty-two years has had eighteen books published. *Awards, honors: Look at a Calf* named an Outstanding Science Trade Book for Children, 1974.

DARE WRIGHT

They waited and waited. ■ (From *Edith and Midnight* by Dare Wright. Photograph by the author.)

WRITINGS:—All for children: *The Lonely Doll* (Junior Literary Guild selection; photographs by Dare Wright), Doubleday, 1957; *Holiday for Edith and the Bears* (photographs by D. Wright), Doubleday, 1958; *The Little One* (illustrated by D. Wright), Doubleday, 1959; *The Doll and the Kitten* (illustrated by D. Wright), Doubleday, 1960; *The Lonely Doll Learns a Lesson,* Random House, 1961; *Lona: A Fairy Tale,* Random House, 1963; *Edith and Mr. Bear,* Random House, 1964; *A Gift from the Lonely Doll,* (photographs by D. Wright), Random House, 1966; *Look at a Gull,* (photographs by D. Wright) Random House, 1967; *Edith and Big Bad Bill,* Random House, 1968; *Look at a Colt,* Random House, 1969; *The Kitten's Little Boy,* Four Winds, 1971; *Edith and Little Bear Lend a Hand,* Random House, 1972; *Look at a Calf* (photographs by D. Wright), Random House, 1974; *Look at a Kitten* (photographs by D. Wright), Random House, 1975; *Edith and Midnight,* Doubleday, 1978.

Other: *Date with London*, Random House, 1962; *Take Me Home*, Random House, 1965.

SIDELIGHTS: An early Dare Wright book, *Holiday for Edith and the Bears*, one in a series of "Edith" books, was well-received by the critics. The *Christian Science Monitor's* opinion was that, "Those who love islands, those who value skillful photographs, and little girls who cherish dolls will revel in *Holiday for Edith and the Bears*. . . . The toys have a wonderfully animated look and the island background is a delight, with real horses, a lighthouse and a wobbling baby gull."

Gulls are the subject of a later book, *Look at a Gull*. The *Library Journal* feels, "The photographs are excellent and well reproduced; the gull's simple account of his life is accurate in fact, and the photographs convey a sense of the grace and freedom of gulls in flight. The text describes dangers they face, their endless search for food, and their adaptability to extremes of climate."

Later books in this same vein include *Look at a Colt, Look at a Calf* and *Look at a Kitten*, about which *Booklist* has written, "A straightforward informative text combined with large unsentimental black-and-white photographs makes this an excellent introduction to cats. Observations are backed up by unobtrusive explanation. . . . There is respect for and insight into the animal's independent nature and a direct acknowledgement of its hunting instincts. The text proceeds smoothly through points on birth, development, eating, grooming, and muscular coordination."

FOR MORE INFORMATION SEE: Christian Science Monitor, November 6, 1958; Martha E. Ward and D. A. Marquardt, *Authors of Books for Young People*, Scarecrow, 1964; *Library Journal*, May 15, 1967; *Booklist*, November 1, 1975.

MARJORY HALL YEAKLEY

YEAKLEY, Marjory Hall　1908-
(Marjory Hall, Carol Morse)

PERSONAL: Born May 16, 1908, in Pittsfield, Mass.; daughter of Walter Atwood and Lucile Carol (Reynolds) Hall; married Taylor Blair Yeakley, 1937. *Education:* Wellesley College, A.B., 1930; studied at Columbia Univeristy, 1934-35, Harvard University, 1938-39. *Home:* 572 Commonwealth Ln., Sarasota, Fla. 33581.

CAREER: Curtis Publishing Co., Philadelphia, Pa., 1931-42, started as clerk in advertising department, became an associate editor, also worked in Boston office in retail publicity; H. B. Humphrey Advertising Agency, Boston, Mass., vice president and account executive, 1942-56; *Yankee* Magazine, Dublin, N.H., travel editor, 1946–72. *Member:* The Authors Guild.

WRITINGS: Success in Reserve, Houghton, 1941; *Bread and Butter* (Junior Literary Guild selection), Houghton, 1942; *After a Fashion*, Houghton, 1944; *Model Child*, Houghton, 1945; *Copy Kate*, Houghton, 1947; *Your Young Life*, Houghton, 1947; *Linda Clayton*, Sloane, 1951; *Saralee's Silver Spoon*, Sloane, 1952; *A Year From Now*, Sloane, 1952; *Greetings from Glenna*, Funk, 1953; *Star Island*, Funk, 1953; *Orchids for Anita*, Funk, 1954; *Paper Moon*, Funk, 1954; *Picnic for Judy*, Funk, 1955; *Star Island Again*, Funk, 1955.

Morning Glory, Funk, 1956; *Mirror, Mirror*, Westminster, 1956; *Cathy and Her Castle*, Funk, 1957; *Straw Hat Summer*, Westminster, 1957; *Three Stars for Star Island*, Funk, 1958; *The Glass House*, Washburn, 1958; *Carnival Cruise*, Washburn, 1958; *Roundabout Robin*, Washburn, 1959; *White Collar Girl*, Funk, 1959; *Romance at Courtesy Bend* (Junior Literary Guild selection), Westminster, 1959; *Magic Word*, Westminster, 1959.

Hatbox for Mimi (Junior Literary Guild selection), Funk, 1960; *Tomorrow is Another Day*, Westminster, 1960; *Bright Red Ribbon*, Funk, 1961; *Whirl of Fashion*, Westminster, 1961; *Green Light for Sandy*, Doubleday, 1961; *Rita Rings a Bell*, Funk, 1962; *To Paris and Love*, Westminster, 1962; *Fanfare for Two*, Funk, 1963; *See The Red Sky* (Junior Literary Guild selection), Westminster, 1963; *Judy North: Drum Majorette*, Doubleday, 1963; *One Perfect Rose* (Junior Literary Guild selection), Funk, 1964; *Double Trouble*, Doubleday, 1964; *A Hatful of Gold*, Westminster, 1964; *A Valentine for Vinnie*, Funk, 1965; *Drumbeat on the Shore*, Westminster, 1965.

Clotheshorse (Junior Literary Guild selection), Funk, 1966; *Treasure Tree* (Junior Literary Guild selection), Westminster, 1966; *Three Cheers for Polly*, Doubleday, 1966; *Look at Me!*, Funk, 1967; *Mystery at Lion's Gate*, Funk, 1967; *Another Kind of Courage*, Westminster, 1967; *The Gold-Lined*

Box (Junior Literary Guild selection), Westminster, 1968; *The Whistle Stop Mystery,* Funk, 1969; *The Seventh Star,* Westminster, 1969.

Quite Contrary, Funk, 1970; *Beneath Another Sun,* Westminster, 1970; *The Carved Wooden Ring,* Westminster, 1972; *Rosamunda,* Dell, 1974; *The Other Girl,* Westminster, 1974; *The April Ghost,* Westminster, 1975; *Mystery at October House,* Westminster, 1977.

SIDELIGHTS: "Like every other writer, I suppose, I pointed myself right at the business from early childhood. The question of what or for whom to write did not, at the age of six or whatever, concern me, and the fact that I turned out to be primarily an author of teen-aged novels was pure happenstance.

"First I tumbled into a job (with *Ladies' Home Journal*) that involved teen-age-advice-giving. Then I fell into another job (related, to be sure) that put me in charge of running a teen-age promotion in department stores across the country. At the same time, I wrote a column in a Boston newspaper called 'Talking to Teens.' From the department store experience and the twice-a-week column, it was (to me) a natural step into trying my hand at a book of teen-age advice. A publisher coldly informed me that such works were a dime a dozen, but how about a novel ('vocational' was the big thing in those days) for the age group. They were, he told me, written by old ladies (I was *much* younger then!) who had forgotten what it was like to be a girl. 'Read one,' he said, 'and you'll see I'm right.'

"I did, and he was. So I tried it—and never stopped. By that time I was in an advertising agency, and all around me were fascinating jobs and wonderful businesses to use for backgrounds. I couldn't write it all fast enough. Then came the day when I was fired with the desire to write a historical novel. The publisher said girls don't like them, won't read them, librarians hate them, you're wasting your time, but you apparently must get it out of your system. And while I was writing *See the Red Sky,* guess what! Historical novels suddenly came into vogue. I loved it all—the research, the writing, the drama of history, the inevitable coping with dates that *must* be used accurately, no matter how inconvenient to the author and her carefully constructed story.

"A while ago, fashion moved again, into what an editor called 'period pieces.' Hence, *The April Ghost* and *Mystery at October House,* giving more scope to the imagination and less restricting than the building of a book around an actual charracter. Then, somehow, fiction became unfashionable. What next? Whatever it is, I welcome it.

"What surprises me most, I think, is that I'm still getting letters from girls who write me about books published as long as twenty years ago, asking what finally happened to Melissa, and why don't I write a sequel. (This, of course, sends me scurrying to my book shelves. Who was this Melissa anyway, and what was *her* problem?) But there is a certain satisfaction for anyone who writes, who tries to make her characters honest and her situations real, to find, after all these years, someone who cares. It's the best reward I know, and would keep me going even if I wanted to stop—which I don't. Besides, I still retain the wistful hope that my simple prose and contemporary characters may have encouraged a girl who would have put down Jane Austen or Dickens at the end of the second sentence to take that first step into the vital world of reading. What more could you ask?"

Descended from a long line of teachers and preachers, all New England, Yeakley was born May, 1908, in Pittsfield, Mass., in the heart of the Berkshires. Her mother had taught algebra and Latin at Cambridge Latin School; her father was an engineer. The family moved to Swampscott where she graduated from the local high school and then two years at Drew Seminary, Carmel, New York. At Wellesley, where she majored in English composition, she went out for athletics, was house president and member of the local TZE Society, and took her A.B. degree in 1930. She also won third prize of $25 in an *Atlantic Monthly* contest, her first earning as a writer.

YERIAN, Cameron John

PERSONAL: Born in Michigan; married wife, Margaret A. (a writer); children: Phoebe A., C. Scot, *Education:* Earned degree from University of Michigan. *Residence:* Ann Arbor, Mich. *Office:* Y4 Design Ltd., P.O. Box 1101, Ann Arbor, Mich. 48106.

CAREER: Writer. President of Y4 Design Ltd., Ann Arbor, Mich.

WRITINGS—All children's books; all with wife, Margaret A. Yerian: *ABC's of Aerospace,* Elk Grove Press, 1971; *ABC's of Hydrospace,* Elk Grove Press, 1971; *Rainbows and Jolly Beans: A Look at Drugs,* Elk Grove Press, 1971; *The Yawn Book,* Steck, 1971; *Actor's Workshop,* Childrens Press, 1974.

Editor; all children's books; all with M. A. Yerian; all published by Grolier; all 1974: *Creative Activities,* Volume 1: *Making,* Volume 2: *Playing,* Volume 3: *Discovering,* Volume 4: *Performing,* Volume 5: *Creating,* Volume 6: *Collecting,* Volume 7: *Communicating,* Volume 8: *Producing,* Volume 9: *Fooling,* Volume 10: *Organizing,* Volume 11: *Growing,* Volume 12: *Caring,* Volume 13: *Building,* Volume 14: *Searching,* Volume 15: *Foraging,* Volume 16: *Traveling,* Volume 17: *Exploring,* Volume 18: *Sewing,* Volume 19: *Cooking,* Volume 20: *Finding.*

Editor; all children's books; all with M. A. Yerian; all published by Childrens Press: *Batik and Tie Dyeing,* 1974; *Competitive Games,* 1974; *Games for One, Two, or More,* 1974; *Group Games,* 1974; *Jewelry, Candles, and Papercraft,* 1974; *Macrame, Knitting, and Weaving,* 1974; *Actors' Workshop,* 1974; *Projects: Earth and Sky,* 1974; *Puppets and Shadow Plays,* 1974; *Showtime,* 1974; *Magnificent Magic,* 1975; *Make-Up and Costumes,* 1975; *Stages, Scenery, and Props,* 1975; *Plays and Special Effects,* 1975; *Easy Tricks and Spooky Games,* 1975; *Codes and Mystery Messages,* 1975; *Money-Making Ideas,* 1975; *Doodling, Drawing, and Creating,* 1975; *Radio and Movie Productions,* 1975; *Community Projects,* 1975; *Easy Sewing Projects,* 1975; *For Campers Only: Sewing and Cooking,* 1975; *Gifts for Everybody,* 1975; *Handmade Toys and Games,* 1975; *Indoor Gardening,* 1975; *Outdoor Gardening,* 1975; *Party Foods,* 1975; *Sew It! Wear It!,* 1975; *Weird Gardens,* 1975; *Working with Wood,* 1975.

WORK IN PROGRESS: (With wife Margaret A. Yerian) series of preschool coping books, and work in the area of affective education.

YERIAN, Margaret A.

PERSONAL: Born in Ohio; married Cameron John Yerian (a writer); children: Phoebe A., C. Scot. *Education:* Earned degree from University of Michigan. *Residence:* Ann Arbor, Mich. *Office:* Y4 Design Ltd., P.O. Box 1101, Ann Arbor, Mich. 48106.

CAREER: Writer. Vice-president of Y4 Design Ltd., Ann Arbor, Mich.

WRITINGS—All children's books; all with husband, Cameron John Yerian: *ABC's of Aerospace*, Elk Grove Press, 1971; *ABC's of Hydrospace*, Elk Grove Press, 1971; *Rainbows and Jolly Beans: A Look at Drugs*, Elk Grove Press, 1971; *The Yawn Book*, Steck, 1971; *Actor's Workshop*, Childrens Press, 1974.

Editor; all children's books; all with C. J. Yerian; all published by Grolier; all 1974: *Creative Activities*, Volume 1: *Making*, Volume 2: *Playing*, Volume 3: *Discovering*, Volume 4: *Performing*, Volume 5: *Creating*, Volume 6: *Collecting*, Volume 7: *Communicating*, Volume 8: *Producing*, Volume 9: *Fooling*, Volume 10: *Organizing*, Volume 11: *Growing*, Volume 12: *Caring*, Volume 13: *Building*, Volume 14: *Searching*, Volume 15: *Foraging*, Volume 16: *Traveling*, Volume 17: *Exploring*, Volume 18: *Sewing*, Volume 19: *Cooking*, Volume 20: *Finding*.

Editor; all children's books; all with C. J. Yerian; all published by Childrens Press: *Batik and Tie Dyeing*, 1974; *Competitive Games*, 1974; *Games for One, Two, or More*, 1974; *Group Games*, 1974; *Jewelry, Candles, and Papercraft*, 1974; *Macrame, Knitting, and Weaving*, 1974; *Actors' Workshop*, 1974; *Projects: Earth and Sky*, 1974; *Puppets and Shadow Plays*, 1974; *Showtime*, 1974; *Magnificent Magic*, 1975; *Make-Up and Costumes*, 1975; *Stages, Scenery, and Props*, 1975; *Plays and Special Effects*, 1975; *Easy Tricks and Spooky Games*, 1975; *Codes and Mystery Messages*, 1975; *Money-Making Ideas*, 1975; *Doodling, Drawing, and Creating*, 1975; *Radio and Movie Productions*, 1975; *Community Projects*, 1975; *Easy Sewing Projects*, 1975; *For Campers Only: Sewing and Cooking*, 1975; *Gifts for Everybody*, 1975; *Handmade Toys and Games*, 1975; *Indoor Gardening*, 1975; *Outdoor Gardening*, 1975; *Party Foods*, 1975; *Sew It! Wear It!*, 1975; *Weird Gardens*, 1975; *Working with Wood*, 1975.

WORK IN PROGRESS: (With husband, Cameron John Yerian) series of preschool coping books, and work in the area of affective education.

SIDELIGHTS: "We write for children because we feel that they are our most important natural resource."

Eat no green apples or you'll droop,
Be careful not to get the croup,
Avoid the chicken-pox and such,
And don't fall out of windows much.

— Edward Anthony

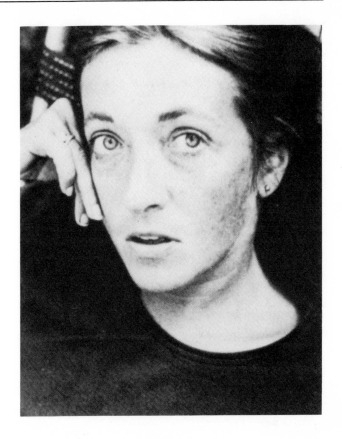

MARGOT ZEMACH

ZEMACH, Margot   1931-

PERSONAL: Born November 30, 1931, in Los Angeles, Calif.; daughter of Benjamin (a theatre director) and Elizabeth (an actress; maiden name Dailey) Zemach; married Ralph Novak, 1953 (died, 1954); married Harvey Fischtrom (an author under pseudonym, Harve Zemach), January 29, 1957 (died November, 1974); children: (second marriage) Kaethe (Mrs. Raymond Bird), Heidi, Rachel, Rebecca. *Education:* Attended Los Angeles County Art Institute, Jepson Institute of Art, Otis Art Institute, Los Angeles, Kahn Art Institute, Los Angeles, Chouinard Art Institute, Los Angeles; studied at Vienna Academy of Fine Arts under a Fulbright scholarship, 1955-56. *Home and office:* 2421 Oregon St., Berkeley, Calif. 94705.

CAREER: Illustrator and author. *Exhibitions:* Gropper Gallery, Cambridge, Mass., 1957. *Awards and honors: Salt, A Russian Tale* received first prize at the *Herald Tribune* Spring Book Festival, 1965; *Mommy, Buy Me a China Doll* was an ALA Notable Children's Book, 1966; *Too Much Nose: An Italian Tale* was an honor book at the *Herald Tribune* Spring Book Festival, 1967; *Mazel and Shlimazel: or, The Milk of a Lioness* was an ALA Notable Children's Book, 1967; *When Shliemiel Went to Warsaw, and Other Stories* was an ALA Notable Children's Book, 1968; *The Judge: An Untrue Tale* was a Caldecott Honor Book and an ALA Notable Children's Book, 1970; *A Penny a Look: An Old Story* was an ALA Notable Children's Book, 1971; *Simon Boom Gives a Wedding* was named to the list of the *New York Times* Best Illustrated Books, 1972, and received the Lewis Carrol Bookshelf Award; *Duffy and the Devil: A Cornish Tale* was an honor book at *Book World* Children's Spring Book Festival,

(From *Self-Portrait: Margot Zemach* by Margot Zemach. Illustrated by the author.)

1973, received the Caldecott Award, 1974, and received the Lewis Carroll Bookshelf Award; *Hush Little Baby* was chosen to represent the United States on the International Board on Books for Young People, 1978; *It Could Always be Worse: A Yiddish Folktale* was named to the list of the *New York Times* Best Illustrated Books, 1978, and was a Caldecott Honor Book; *Self-Portrait: Margot Zemach* was an honor book for the Golden Globe *Horn Book* Award, 1979; United States nominee for the Hans Christian Andersen Medal, 1980.

WRITINGS—All self-illustrated: (adaptor) *The Three Sillies,* Holt, 1963; (editor) *The Little Tiny Woman, a Folktale,* Bobbs-Merrill, 1965; (adaptor) *Hush Little Baby* (Junior Literary Guild selection), Dutton, 1976; (adaptor) *It Always be Worse: A Yiddish Folktale,* (Caldcott Honor Book), Farrar, 1976; *To Hilda for Helping,* Farrar, 1977; *Self-Portrait: Margot Zemach,* Addison-Wesley, 1978; *Jake and Honeybunch go to Heaven,* Farrar, 1981.

Illustrator: Harve Zemach, *A Small Boy is Listening,* Houghton, 1959; Hannelore Hahn, *Take a Giant Step,* Little, Brown, 1960; Harve Zemach, *A Hat with a Rose,* Dutton, 1961; Fleming Lee Blitch, *The Last Dragon,* Lippincott, 1964; Harve Zemach (adaptor), *Nail Soup: A Swedish Folktale Retold,* Follett, 1964; Alexei Afansev (adapted by Harve Zemach), *Salt, A Russian Tale,* translated by Benjamin Zemach, Follett, 1965, Farrar, 1976; Jay Williams, *The Question Box,* Norton, 1965; Harve Zemach, *The Tricks of Master Dabble,* Holt, 1965; Brothers Grimm, *The Fisherman and His Wife,* Norton, 1966, revised edition translated by Randall Jarrell, Farrar, 1980; Harve Zemach (adaptor), *Mommy, Buy Me a China Doll* (ALA Notable Children's Book), Follett, 1966, Farrar, 1975; Jack Sendak, *The King of the Hermits and Other Stories,* Farrar, 1966; Harve Zemach (adaptor), *The Speckled Hen, a Russian Nursery Rhyme,* Holt, 1966; Harve Zemach (adaptor), *Too Much Nose: An Italian Tale,* Holt, 1967; Isaac B. Singer, *Mazel and Shlimazel; or, The Milk of a Lioness* (ALA Notable Children's Book), translated by the author and Elizabeth Shub, Farrar, 1967; Rose L. Minciel, *Harlequin,* Knopf, 1968; Isaac B. Singer, *When Shliemiel Went to Warsaw and Other Stories* (ALA Notable Children's Book), Farrar, 1968; Harve Zemach, *The Judge: An Untrue Tale* (ALA Notable Children's Book; Caldecott Honor Book), Farrar, 1969.

Harve Zemach, *Awake and Dreaming,* Farrar, 1970; Harve Zemach, *A Penny a Look: An Old Story,* Farrar, 1971; Virginia Haviland, *Favorite Fairy Tales Told in Denmark,* Little, Brown, 1971; Isaac B. Singer, *Alone in the Wild Forest,* Farrar, 1971; Yuri Suhl, *Simon Boom Gives a Wedding,* Four Winds, 1972; Harve Zemach (adaptor) *Duffy and the Devil: A Cornish Tale* (Caldecott Award Book), Farrar, 1973; Lloyd Alexander, *The Foundling and Other Tales of Prydain,* Holt, 1973; Harve and Kaethe Zemach, *The Princess and Froggie,* Farrar, 1975; Isaac Bashevis Singer, *Naftali the Storyteller and His Horse, Sus and Other Stories,* Farrar, 1976; Edward Smith (collector), *The Frogs Who Wanted a King,* Four Winds, 1977.

ADAPTATIONS—Filmstrips: "Famous Author/Illustrator Filmstrips" includes "The Judge," "Duffy and the Devil,"

"Mazel and Shlimazel," "It Could Always be Worse," and "A Penny a Look," produced and distributed by Miller-Brody Productions; "The Princess and Froggie" is included in "Plan A Language Arts-Stories for Children," distributed by Doubleday Multimedia; "Salt," "Nail Soup," and "Mommy, Buy Me a China Doll," produced by Weston Woods.

SIDELIGHTS: "Humor is the most important thing to me—it's what I'm thinking about. If I can make it beautiful, too—so much the better!

"I use colored inks (Pelican) almost exclusively or pen and ink. I was strongly influenced by Francoise-Gropper, Goya, Rowalandson, and Hogarth."

Zemach has definite opinions about good illustrations for children's books. "The modern trend of oversimplification is impossible; it's merely foisting designers' ideas on children. Children are fascinated by detail. Take a child to the zoo and you may well find that amid all the exotic beasts, it's the pigeon walking around the child's feet that catches the attention. In the most eleaborate picture, the chances are that what gives special delight is a little fly or a dropped glove. Children need detail, color, excellence—the best a person can do. I always think, when I'm drawing the view of a town or the inside of a hut: 'Would I have liked to live there?' One doesn't need meticulous authenticity of costume or architecture; to a certain extent, one can invent one's own styles of dress and house shapes. But things have to be made real. The food has to be what you'd want to eat, the bed has to be what you'd want to get into right away. But, all in all, I'm not sure that one should consciously bear in mind that the drawings are meant for the gaze of children. If I make a book for children, I draw it the same as I'd draw for grownups." [A. L. Lloyd, "Margot Zemach," *Horn Book* Magazine, August, 1974.[1]]

Zemach's works are included in the Kerlan Collection at the University of Minnesota.

FOR MORE INFORMATION SEE: Horn Book, October, 1963, October, 1965, June, 1973, October, 1973, August, 1974, October, 1974, February, 1977, April, 1977, June,1977, June, 1979, October, 1979; Lee Kingman and others, compilers, *Illustrators of Children's Books: 1957-1966,* Horn Book, 1968; Selma G. Lanes, *Down the Rabbit Hole,* Atheneum, 1971; *Top of the News,* April, 1971, April, 1974; *Graphis 155,* Volume 27, The Graphis Press, 1971-72; Doris de Montreville and Donna Hill, editors, *Third Book of Junior Authors,* H. W. Wilson Co., 1972; *Publishers Weekly,* June 4, 1973, February 23, 1976, February 28, 1978; *Contemporary American Illustrators of Children's Books,* Rutgers University Art Gallery, 1974; Martha E. Ward and Dorothy A. Marquardt, *Illustrators of Books for Young People,* second edition, Scarecrow Press, 1975; Lee Kingman, editor, *Newbery and Caldecott Medal Books: 1966-1975,* Horn Book, 1975; Margery Fisher, *Who's Who in Children's Books,* Holt, 1975; Margot Zemach, *Self-Portrait: Margot Zemach,* Addison-Wesley, 1978.

CUMULATIVE INDEX TO
ILLUSTRATIONS AND AUTHORS

Illustrations Index

(In the following index, the number of the volume in which an illustrator's work appears is given *before* the colon, and the page on which it appears is given *after* the colon. For example, a drawing by Adams, Adrienne appears in Volume 2 on page 6, another drawing by her appears in Volume 3 on page 80, another drawing in Volume 8 on page 1, and another drawing in Volume 15 on page 107.)

YABC

Index citations including this abbreviation refer to listings appearing in *Yesterday's Authors of Books for Children,* also published by the Gale Research Company, which covers authors who died prior to 1960.

Author Index

(In the following index, the number of the volume in which an author's sketch appears is given *before* the colon, and the page on which it appears is given *after* the colon. For example, the sketch of Aardema, Verna, appears in Volume 4 on page 1).

YABC

Index citations including this abbreviation refer to listings appearing in *Yesterday's Authors of Books for Children,* also published by the Gale Research Company, which covers authors who died prior to 1960.

Amoss, Berthe, *5:* 4
Anckarsvard, Karin, *6:* 2
Ancona, George, *12:* 10
Andersen, Hans Christian,
 YABC 1: 23
Andersen, Ted. *See* Boyd, Waldo
 T., *18:* 35
Anderson, C(larence) W(illiam),
 11: 9
Anderson, Ella. *See* MacLeod,
 Ellen Jane (Anderson), *14:* 129
Anderson, Eloise Adell, *9:* 9
Anderson, George. *See* Groom,
 Arthur William, *10:* 53
Anderson, J(ohn) R(ichard) L(ane),
 15: 3
Anderson, Joy, *1:* 8
Anderson, (John) Lonzo, *2:* 6
Anderson, Lucia (Lewis), *10:* 4
Anderson, Mary, *7:* 4
Andrews, J(ames) S(ydney), *4:* 7
Andrews, Julie, *7:* 6
Andrews, Roy Chapman, *19:* 1
Angell, Madeline, *18:* 3
Angelo, Valenti, *14:* 7
Angier, Bradford, *12:* 12
Angle, Paul M(cClelland), *20:* 1
 (Obituary)
Anglund, Joan Walsh, *2:* 7
Angrist, Stanley W(olff), *4:* 9
Annett, Cora. *See* Scott, Cora
 Annett, *11:* 207
Annixter, Jane. *See* Sturtzel, Jane
 Levington, *1:* 212
Annixter, Paul. *See* Sturtzel,
 Howard A., *1:* 210
Anno, Mitsumasa, *5:* 6
Anrooy, Frans van. *See* Van
 Anrooy, Francine, *2:* 252
Anthony, C. L. *See* Smith, Dodie,
 4: 194
Anthony, Edward, *21:* 1
Anticaglia, Elizabeth, *12:* 13
Anton, Michael (James), *12:* 13
Appel, Benjamin, *21:* 5 (Obituary)
Appiah, Peggy, *15:* 3
Appleton, Victor [Collective
 pseudonym], *1:* 9
Appleton, Victor II [Collective
 pseudonym], *1:* 9
Apsler, Alfred, *10:* 4
Aquillo, Don. *See* Prince, J(ack)
 H(arvey), *17:* 155
Arbuthnot, May Hill, *2:* 9
Archer, Frank. *See* O'Connor,
 Richard, *21:* 111
Archer, Jules, *4:* 9
Archer, Marion Fuller, *11:* 12
Archibald, Joseph S. *3:* 12
Arden, Barbie. *See* Stoutenburg,
 Adrien, *3:* 217
Ardizzone, Edward, *1:* 10; *21:* 5
 (Obituary)
Arenella, Roy, *14:* 9
Armer, Alberta (Roller), *9:* 11
Armer, Laura Adams, *13:* 2

Armour, Richard, *14:* 10
Armstrong, George D., *10:* 5
Armstrong, Gerry (Breen), *10:* 6
Armstrong, Richard, *11:* 14
Armstrong, William H., *4:* 11
Arnett, Carolyn. *See* Cole, Lois
 Dwight, *10:* 26
Arnold, Elliott, *5:* 7
Arnold, Oren, *4:* 13
Arnoldy, Julie. *See* Bischoff, Julia
 Bristol, *12:* 52
Arnott, Kathleen, *20:* 1
Arnov, Boris, Jr., *12:* 14
Arnstein, Helene S(olomon), *12:* 15
Arntson, Herbert E(dward), *12:* 16
Arora, Shirley (Lease), *2:* 10
Arquette, Lois S(teinmetz), *1:* 13
Arrowood, (McKendrick Lee)
 Clinton, *19:* 10
Arthur, Ruth M., *7:* 6
Artis, Vicki Kimmel, *12:* 17
Artzybasheff, Boris (Miklailovich),
 14: 14
Aruego, Ariane. *See* Dewey,
 Ariane, *7:* 63
Aruego, Jose, *6:* 3
Arundel, Honor, *4:* 15
Asbjörnsen, Peter Christen, *15:* 5
Asch, Frank, *5:* 9
Ashabranner, Brent (Kenneth),
 1: 14
Ashe, Geoffrey (Thomas), *17:* 14
Ashey, Bella. *See* Breinburg,
 Petronella, *11:* 36
Ashford, Daisy. *See* Ashford,
 Margaret Mary, *10:* 6
Ashford, Margaret Mary, *10:* 6
Ashley, Elizabeth. *See* Salmon,
 Annie Elizabeth, *13:* 188
Asimov, Isaac, *1:* 15
Asinof, Eliot, *6:* 5
Aston, James. *See* White,
 T(erence) H(anbury), *12:* 229
Atene, Ann. *See* Atene, (Rita)
 Anna, *12:* 18
Atene, (Rita) Anna, *12:* 18
Atkinson, M. E. *See* Frankau,
 Mary Evelyn, *4:* 90
Atkinson, Margaret Fleming, *14:* 15
Atticus. *See* Fleming, Ian
 (Lancaster), *9:* 67
Atwater, Florence (Hasseltine
 Carroll), *16:* 11
Atwater, Montgomery Meigs,
 15: 10
Atwood, Ann, *7:* 8
Aung, (Maung) Htin, *21:* 5
Aung, U. Htin. *See* Aung, (Maung)
 Htin, *21:* 5
Austin, Elizabeth S., *5:* 10
Austin, Margot, *11:* 15
Austin, Oliver L. Jr., *7:* 10
Austin, Tom. *See* Jacobs, Linda C.,
 21: 78
Averill, Esther, *1:* 16

Austin, Tom. *See* Jacobs, Linda C.,
 21: 78
Avery, Al. *See* Montgomery,
 Rutherford, *3:* 134
Avery, Gillian, *7:* 10
Avery, Kay, *5:* 11
Avery, Lynn. *See* Cole, Lois
 Dwight, *10:* 26
Avi. *See* Wortis, Avi, *14:* 269
Ayars, James S(terling), *4:* 17
Ayer, Jacqueline, *13:* 7
Ayer, Margaret, *15:* 11
Aylesworth, Thomas G(ibbons),
 4: 18

Baastad, Babbis Friis. *See* Friis-
 Baastad, Babbis, *7:* 95
Babbis, Eleanor. *See* Friis-Baastad,
 Babbis, *7:* 95
Babbitt, Natalie, *6:* 6
Bach, Richard David, *13:* 7
Bachman, Fred, *12:* 19
Bacmeister, Rhoda W(arner), *11:* 18
Bacon, Elizabeth, *3:* 14
Bacon, Margaret Hope, *6:* 7
Bacon, Martha Sherman, *18:* 4
Bacon, Peggy, *2:* 11
Baden-Powell, Robert (Stephenson
 Smyth), *16:* 12
Baerg, Harry J(ohn), *12:* 20
Bagnold, Enid, *1:* 17
Bailey, Alice Cooper, *12:* 22
Bailey, Bernadine Freeman, *14:* 16
Bailey, Carolyn Sherwin, *14:* 18
Bailey, Jane H(orton), *12:* 22
Bailey, Maralyn Collins (Harrison),
 12: 24
Bailey, Matilda. *See* Radford, Ruby
 L., *6:* 186
Bailey, Maurice Charles, *12:* 25
Bailey, Ralph Edgar, *11:* 18
Baity, Elizabeth Chesley, *1:* 18
Bakeless, John (Edwin), *9:* 12
Bakeless, Katherine Little, *9:* 13
Baker, Augusta, *3:* 16
Baker, Betty (Lou), *5:* 12
Baker, Charlotte, *2:* 12
Baker, Elizabeth, *7:* 12
Baker, Jeffrey J(ohn) W(heeler),
 5: 13
Baker, Laura Nelson, *3:* 17
Baker, Margaret, *4:* 19
Baker, Margaret J(oyce), *12:* 25
Baker, Mary Gladys Steel, *12:* 27
Baker, (Robert) Michael, *4:* 20
Baker, Nina (Brown), *15:* 12
Baker, Rachel, *2:* 13
Baker, Samm Sinclair, *12:* 27
Balaam. *See* Lamb, G(eoffrey)
 F(rederick), *10:* 74
Balch, Glenn, *3:* 18
Balducci, Carolyn Feleppa, *5:* 13
Baldwin, Anne Norris, *5:* 14
Baldwin, Clara, *11:* 20

Author Index

Carpenter, Allan, *3:* 35
Carpenter, Frances, *3:* 36
Carpenter, Patricia (Healy Evans),
    11: 43
Carr, Glyn. *See* Styles, Frank
    Showell, *10:* 167
Carr, Harriett Helen, *3:* 37
Carr, Mary Jane, *2:* 50
Carrick, Carol, *7:* 39
Carrick, Donald, *7:* 40
Carroll, Curt. *See* Bishop, Curtis,
    6: 24
Carroll, Latrobe, *7:* 40
Carroll, Laura. *See* Parr, Lucy,
    10: 115
Carroll, Lewis. *See* Dodgson,
    Charles Lutwidge,
    YABC 2: 297
Carse, Robert, *5:* 41
Carson, Captain James. *See*
    Stratemeyer, Edward L.,
    1: 208
Carson, John F., *1:* 46
Carter, Bruce. *See* Hough, Richard
    (Alexander), *17:* 83
Carter, Dorothy Sharp, *8:* 21
Carter, Helene, *15:* 37
Carter, (William) Hodding, *2:* 51
Carter, Katharine J(ones), *2:* 52
Carter, Phyllis Ann. *See* Eberle,
    Irmengarde, *2:* 97
Carter, William E., *1:* 47
Cartner, William Carruthers, *11:* 44
Cartwright, Sally, *9:* 30
Cary. *See* Cary, Louis F(avreau),
    9: 31
Cary, Louis F(avreau), *9:* 31
Caryl, Jean. *See* Kaplan, Jean
    Caryl Korn, *10:* 62
Case, Marshal T(aylor), *9:* 33
Case, Michael. *See* Howard,
    Robert West, *5:* 85
Casewit, Curtis, *4:* 43
Casey, Brigid, *9:* 33
Casey, Winifred Rosen. *See* Rosen,
    Winifred, *8:* 169
Cason, Mabel Earp, *10:* 19
Cass, Joan E(velyn), *1:* 47
Cassel, Lili. *See* Wronker, Lili
    Cassell, *10:* 204
Cassel-Wronker, Lili. *See*
    Wronker, Lili Cassell, *10:* 204
Castellanos, Jane Mollie
    (Robinson), *9:* 34
Castillo, Edmund L., *1:* 50
Castle, Lee. [Joint pseudonym].
    See Ogan, George F. and
    Margaret E. (Nettles), *13:* 171
Caswell, Helen (Rayburn), *12:* 67
Catherall, Arthur, *3:* 38
Catlin, Wynelle, *13:* 19
Catton, (Charles) Bruce, *2:* 54
Catz, Max. *See* Glaser, Milton,
    11: 106
Caudill, Rebecca, *1:* 50
Causley, Charles, *3:* 39

Cavallo, Diana, *7:* 43
Cavanah, Frances, *1:* 52
Cavanna, Betty, *1:* 54
Cawley, Winifred, *13:* 20
Cebulash, Mel, *10:* 19
Ceder, Georgiana Dorcas, *10:* 21
Cerf, Bennett, *7:* 43
Cerf, Christopher (Bennett), *2:* 55
Cetin, Frank (Stanley), *2:* 55
Chadwick, Lester [Collective
    pseudonym], *1:* 55
Chaffee, Allen, *3:* 41
Chaffin, Lillie D(orton), *4:* 44
Chalmers, Mary, *6:* 41
Chambers, Aidan, *1:* 55
Chambers, Margaret Ada
    Eastwood, *2:* 56
Chambers, Peggy. *See* Chambers,
    Margaret, *2:* 56
Chandler, Edna Walker, *11:* 45
Chandler, Ruth Forbes, *2:* 56
Channel, A. R. *See* Catherall,
    Arthur, *3:* 38
Chapman, Allen [Collective
    pseudonym], *1:* 55
Chapman, (Constance) Elizabeth
    (Mann), *10:* 21
Chapman, Walker. *See* Silverberg,
    Robert, *13:* 206
Chappell, Warren, *6:* 42
Charles, Louis. *See* Stratemeyer,
    Edward L., *1:* 208
Charlip, Remy, *4:* 46
Charlot, Jean, *8:* 22
Charmatz, Bill, *7:* 45
Charosh, Mannis, *5:* 42
Chase, Alice. *See* McHargue,
    Georgess, *4:* 152
Chase, Mary (Coyle), *17:* 39
Chase, Mary Ellen, *10:* 22
Chastain, Madye Lee, *4:* 48
Chauncy, Nan, *6:* 43
Chaundler, Christine, *1:* 56
Chen, Tony *6:* 44
Chenault, Nell. *See* Smith, Linell
    Nash, *2:* 227
Cheney, Cora, *3:* 41
Cheney, Ted. *See* Cheney,
    Theodore Albert, *11:* 46
Cheney, Theodore Albert, *11:* 46
Chernoff, Goldie Taub, *10:* 23
Cherryholmes, Anne, *See* Price,
    Olive, *8:* 157
Chetin, Helen, *6:* 46
Chew, Ruth, *7:* 45
Chidsey, Donald Barr, *3:* 42
Childress, Alice, *7:* 46
Childs, (Halla) Fay (Cochrane),
    1: 56
Chimaera, *See* Farjeon, Eleanor,
    2: 103
Chipperfield, Joseph E(ugene),
    2: 57
Chittenden, Elizabeth F., *9:* 35
Chittum, Ida, *7:* 47

Chorao, (Ann Mc)Kay (Sproat),
    8: 24
Chrisman, Arthur Bowie,
    YABC 1: 94
Christensen, Gardell Dano, *1:* 57
Christgau, Alice Erickson, *13:* 21
Christian, Mary Blount, *9:* 35
Christopher, Matt(hew F.), *2:* 58
Christy, Howard Chandler, *21:* 22
Chu, Daniel, *11:* 47
Chukovsky, Kornei (Ivanovich),
    5: 43
Church, Richard, *3:* 43
Churchill, E. Richard, *11:* 48
Chute, B(eatrice) J(oy), *2:* 59
Chute, Marchette (Gaylord), *1:* 58
Chwast, Jacqueline, *6:* 46
Chwast, Seymour, *18:* 42
Ciardi, John (Anthony), *1:* 59
Clair, Andrée, *19:* 61
Clapp, Patricia, *4:* 50
Clare, Helen, *See* Hunter Blair,
    Pauline, *3:* 87
Clark, Ann Nolan, *4:* 51
Clark, Frank J(ames), *18:* 43
Clark, Garel [Joint pseudonym].
    See Garelick, May, *19:* 130
Clark, Margaret Goff, *8:* 26
Clark, Mavis Thorpe, *8:* 27
Clark, Merle. *See* Gessner, Lynne,
    16: 119
Clark, Patricia (Finrow), *11:* 48
Clark, Ronald William, *2:* 60
Clark, Van D(eusen), *2:* 61
Clark, Virginia. *See* Gray, Patricia,
    7: 110
Clark, Walter Van Tilburg, *8:* 28
Clarke, Arthur C(harles), *13:* 22
Clarke, Clorinda, *7:* 48
Clarke, John. *See* Laklan, Carli,
    5: 100
Clarke, Mary Stetson, *5:* 46
Clarke, Michael. *See* Newlon,
    Clarke, *6:* 174
Clarke, Pauline. *See* Hunter Blair,
    Pauline, *3:* 87
Clarkson, Ewan, *9:* 36
Cleary, Beverly (Bunn), *2:* 62
Cleaver, Carole, *6:* 48
Cleishbotham, Jebediah. *See* Scott,
    Sir Walter, *YABC 2:* 280
Cleland, Mabel. *See* Widdemer,
    Mabel Cleland, *5:* 200
Clemens, Samuel Langhorne,
    YABC 2: 51
Clemons, Elizabeth. *See* Nowell,
    Elizabeth Cameron, *12:* 160
Clerk, N. W. *See* Lewis, C. S.,
    13: 129
Cleven, Cathrine. *See* Cleven,
    Kathryn Seward, *2:* 64
Cleven, Kathryn Seward, *2:* 64
Clevin, Jörgen, *7:* 49
Clewes, Dorothy (Mary), *1:* 61
Clifford, Eth. *See* Rosenberg,
    Ethel, *3:* 176

Author Index

Dobell, I(sabel) M(arian) B(arclay), _11:_ 77

Dobler, Lavinia G., _6:_ 63

Dobrin, Arnold, _4:_ 67

"Dr. A." _See_ Silverstein, Alvin, _8:_ 188

Dodd, Ed(ward) Benton, _4:_ 68

Dodge, Bertha S(anford), _8:_ 42

Dodge, Mary (Elizabeth) Mapes, _21:_ 27

Dodgson, Charles Lutwidge, _YABC 2:_ 97

Dodson, Kenneth M(acKenzie), _11:_ 77

Doherty, C. H., _6:_ 65

Dolson, Hildegarde, _5:_ 56

Domanska, Janina, _6:_ 65

Donalds, Gordon. _See_ Shirreffs, Gordon D., _11:_ 207

Donna, Natalie, _9:_ 52

Doob, Leonard W(illiam), _8:_ 44

Dor, Ana. _See_ Ceder, Georgiana Dorcas, _10:_ 21

Doré, (Louis Christophe Paul) Gustave, _19:_ 92

Dorian, Edith M(cEwen) _5:_ 58

Dorian, Harry. _See_ Hamilton, Charles Harold St. John, _13:_ 77

Dorian, Marguerite, _7:_ 68

Dorman, Michael, _7:_ 68

Doss, Helen (Grigsby), _20:_ 37

Doss, Margot Patterson, _6:_ 68

Dougherty, Charles, _18:_ 74

Douglas, James McM. _See_ Butterworth, W. E., _5:_ 40

Douglas, Kathryn. _See_ Ewing, Kathryn, _20:_ 42

Douglas, Marjory Stoneman, _10:_ 33

Douty, Esther M(orris), _8:_ 44

Dow, Emily R., _10:_ 33

Dowdell, Dorothy (Florence) Karns, _12:_ 75

Dowden, Anne Ophelia, _7:_ 69

Dowdey, Landon Gerald, _11:_ 80

Downey, Fairfax, _3:_ 61

Downie, Mary Alice, _13:_ 32

Doyle, Richard, _21:_ 31

Draco, F. _See_ Davis, Julia, _6:_ 58

Dragonwagon, Crescent, _11:_ 81

Drake, Frank. _See_ Hamilton, Charles Harold St. John, _13:_ 77

Drapier, M. B.. _See_ Swift, Jonathan, _19:_ 244

Drawson, Blair, _17:_ 52

Dresang, Eliza (Carolyn Timberlake), _19:_ 106

Drew, Patricia (Mary), _15:_ 100

Drewery, Mary, _6:_ 69

Drummond, V(iolet) H., _6:_ 71

Drummond, Walter. _See_ Silverberg, Robert, _13:_ 206

Drury, Roger W(olcott), _15:_ 101

du Blanc, Daphne. _See_ Groom, Arthur William, _10:_ 53

du Bois, William Pene, _4:_ 69

DuBose, LaRocque (Russ), _2:_ 93

Ducornet, Erica, _7:_ 72

Dudley, Nancy. _See_ Cole, Lois Dwight, _10:_ 26

Dudley, Ruth H(ubbell), _11:_ 82

Dugan, Michael (Gray), _15:_ 101

du Jardin, Rosamond (Neal), _2:_ 94

Dulac, Edmund, _19:_ 107

Dumas, Alexandre (the elder), _18:_ 74

Duncan, Gregory. _See_ McClintock, Marshall, _3:_ 119

Duncan, Julia K. [Collective pseudonym], _1:_ 81

Duncan, Lois. _See_ Arquette, Lois S., _1:_ 13

Duncan, Norman, _YABC 1:_ 108

Dunlop, Agnes M. R., _3:_ 62

Dunn, Judy. _See_ Spangenberg, Judith Dunn, _5:_ 175

Dunn, Mary Lois, _6:_ 72

Dunnahoo, Terry, _7:_ 73

Dunne, Mary Collins, _11:_ 83

Dupuy, T(revor) N(evitt), _4:_ 71

Durrell, Gerald (Malcolm), _8:_ 46

Du Soe, Robert C., _YABC 2:_ 121

Dutz. _See_ Davis, Mary Octavia, _6:_ 59

Duvall, Evelyn Millis, _9:_ 52

Duvoisin, Roger (Antoine), _2:_ 95

Dwiggins, Don, _4:_ 72

Dwight, Allan. _See_ Cole, Lois Dwight, _10:_ 26

Eagar, Frances, _11:_ 85

Eager, Edward (McMaken), _17:_ 54

Eagle, Mike, _11:_ 86

Earle, Olive L., _7:_ 75

Earnshaw, Brian, _17:_ 57

Eastman, Charles A(lexander), _YABC 1:_ 110

Eastwick, Ivy O., _3:_ 64

Eaton, George L. _See_ Verral, Charles Spain, _11:_ 255

Ebel, Alex, _11:_ 88

Eberle, Irmengarde, _2:_ 97

Eckert, Horst, _8:_ 47

Edell, Celeste, _12:_ 77

Edgeworth, Maria, _21:_ 33

Edmonds, I(vy) G(ordon), _8:_ 48

Edmonds, Walter D(umaux), _1:_ 81

Edmund, Sean. _See_ Pringle, Laurence, _4:_ 171

Edsall, Marian S(tickney), _8:_ 50

Edwards, Bertram. _See_ Edwards, Herbert Charles, _12:_ 77

Edwards, Bronwen Elizabeth. _See_ Rose, Wendy, _12:_ 180

Edwards, Dorothy, _4:_ 73

Edwards, Harvey, _5:_ 59

Edwards, Herbert Charles, _12:_ 77

Edwards, Jane Campbell, _10:_ 34

Edwards, Julie. _See_ Andrews, Julie, _7:_ 6

Edwards, Julie. _See_ Stratemeyer, Edward L., _1:_ 208

Edwards, Monica le Doux Newton, _12:_ 78

Edwards, Sally, _7:_ 75

Eggenberger, David, _6:_ 72

Egielski, Richard, _11:_ 89

Egypt, Ophelia Settle, _16:_ 88

Ehrlich, Bettina (Bauer), _1:_ 82

Eichberg, James Bandman. _See_ Garfield, James B., _6:_ 85

Eichenberg, Fritz, _9:_ 53

Eichner, James A., _4:_ 73

Eifert, Virginia S(nider), _2:_ 99

Einsel, Naiad, _10:_ 34

Einsel, Walter, _10:_ 37

Eiseman, Alberta, _15:_ 102

Eisenberg, Azriel, _12:_ 79

Eitzen, Allan, _9:_ 57

Eitzen, Ruth (Carper), _9:_ 57

Elam, Richard M(ace, Jr.), _9:_ 57

Elfman, Blossom, _8:_ 51

Elia. _See_ Lamb, Charles, _17:_ 101

Eliot, Anne. _See_ Cole, Lois Dwight, _10:_ 26

Elisofon, Eliot, _21:_ 38 (Obituary)

Elkin, Benjamin, _3:_ 65

Elkins, Dov Peretz, _5:_ 61

Ellacott, S(amuel) E(rnest), _19:_ 117

Elliott, Sarah M(cCarn), _14:_ 57

Ellis, Edward S(ylvester), _YABC 1:_ 116

Ellis, Ella Thorp, _7:_ 76

Ellis, Harry Bearse, _9:_ 58

Ellis, Mel, _7:_ 77

Ellison, Virginia Howell, _4:_ 74

Ellsberg, Edward, _7:_ 78

Elspeth. _See_ Bragdon, Elspeth, _6:_ 30

Elting, Mary, _2:_ 100

Elwart, Joan Potter, _2:_ 101

Emberley, Barbara A(nne), _8:_ 51

Emberley, Ed(ward Randolph), _8:_ 52

Embry, Margaret (Jacob), _5:_ 61

Emerson, Alice B. [Collective pseudonym], _1:_ 84

Emery, Anne (McGuigan), _1:_ 84

Emrich, Duncan (Black Macdonald), _11:_ 90

Emslie, M. L. _See_ Simpson, Myrtle L(illias), _14:_ 181

Engdahl, Sylvia Louise, _4:_ 75

Engle, Eloise Katherine, _9:_ 60

Englebert, Victor, _8:_ 54

Enright, Elizabeth, _9:_ 61

Epp, Margaret A(gnes), _20:_ 38

Epple, Anne Orth, _20:_ 40

Epstein, Anne Merrick, _20:_ 41

Epstein, Beryl (Williams), _1:_ 85

Epstein, Samuel, _1:_ 87

Erdman, Loula Grace, _1:_ 88

Ericson, Walter. _See_ Fast, Howard, _7:_ 80

Erlich, Lillian (Feldman), _10:_ 38

Ervin, Janet Halliday, _4:_ 77

Estep, Irene (Compton), _5:_ 62

Estes, Eleanor, _7:_ 79

Franchere, Ruth, *18:* 111
Francis, Dorothy Brenner, *10:* 46
Francis, Pamela (Mary), *11:* 97
Francoise. *See* Seignobosc,
    Francoise, *21:* 145
Frank, Josette, *10:* 47
Frankau, Mary Evelyn, *4:* 90
Frankel, Bernice, *9:* 72
Franklin, Harold, *13:* 53
Franklin, Steve. *See* Stevens,
    Franklin, *6:* 206
Franzén, Nils-Olof, *10:* 47
Frasconi, Antonio, *6:* 79
Frazier, Neta Lohnes, *7:* 94
Freedman, Russell (Bruce), *16:* 115
Freeman, Don, *17:* 60
Freeman, Ira M(aximilian), *21:* 43
French, Allen, *YABC 1:* 133
French, Dorothy Kayser, *5:* 69
French, Fiona, *6:* 81
French, Paul. *See* Asimov, Isaac,
    1: 15
Frewer, Glyn, *11:* 98
Frick, C. H. *See* Irwin, Constance
    Frick, *6:* 119
Frick, Constance. *See* Irwin,
    Constance Frick, *6:* 119
Friedlander, Joanne K(ohn), *9:* 73
Friedman, Estelle, *7:* 95
Friendlich, Dick. *See* Friendlich,
    Richard, *11:* 99
Friendlich, Richard J., *11:* 99
Friermood, Elisabeth Hamilton,
    5: 69
Friis, Babbis. *See* Friis-Baastad,
    Babbis, *7:* 95
Friis-Baastad, Babbis, *7:* 95
Friskey, Margaret Richards, *5:* 72
Fritz, Jean (Guttery), *1:* 98
Froman, Elizabeth Hull, *10:* 49
Froman, Robert (Winslow), *8:* 67
Frost, A(rthur) B(urdett), *19:* 122
Frost, Erica. *See* Supraner, Robyn,
    20: 182
Frost, Lesley, *14:* 61
Frost, Robert (Lee), *14:* 63
Fry, Rosalie, *3:* 71
Fuchs, Erich, *6:* 84
Fujita, Tamao, *7:* 98
Fujiwara, Michiko, *15:* 120
Fuller, Catherine L(euthold), *9:* 73
Fuller, Edmund (Maybank), *21:* 45
Fuller, Iola. *See* McCoy, Iola
    Fuller, *3:* 120
Fuller, Lois Hamilton, *11:* 99
Funk, Thompson. *See* Funk, Tom,
    7: 98
Funk, Tom, *7:* 98
Funke, Lewis, *11:* 100
Fyleman, Rose, *21:* 46

Gaeddert, Lou Ann (Bigge), *20:* 58
Gág, Wanda (Hazel), *YABC 1:* 135
Gage, Wilson. *See* Steele, Mary Q.,
    3: 211

Galdone, Paul, *17:* 69
Gallant, Roy (Arthur), *4:* 91
Gallico, Paul, *13:* 53
Galt, Thomas Franklin, Jr., *5:* 72
Galt, Tom. *See* Galt, Thomas
    Franklin, Jr., *5:* 72
Gamerman, Martha, *15:* 121
Gannett, Ruth Stiles, *3:* 73
Gannon, Robert (Haines), *8:* 68
Gantos, Jack. *See* Gantos, John
    (Bryan), Jr., *20:* 59
Gantos, John (Bryan), Jr., *20:* 59
Gard, Joyce. *See* Reeves, Joyce,
    17: 158
Gard, Robert Edward, *18:* 113
Garden, Nancy, *12:* 85
Gardner, Jeanne LeMonnier, *5:* 73
Gardner, Martin, *16:* 117
Gardner, Richard A., *13:* 64
Garelick, May, *19:* 130
Garfield, James B., *6:* 85
Garfield, Leon, *1:* 99
Garis, Howard R(oger), *13:* 67
Garner, Alan, *18:* 114
Garnett, Eve C. R., *3:* 75
Garrett, Helen, *21:* 48
Garrigue, Sheila, *21:* 49
Garrison, Barbara, *19:* 132
Garrison, Frederick. *See* Sinclair,
    Upton (Beall), *9:* 168
Garst, Doris Shannon, *1:* 100
Garst, Shannon. *See* Garst, Doris
    Shannon, *1:* 100
Garthwaite, Marion H., *7:* 100
Gates, Doris, *1:* 102
Gatty, Juliana Horatia. *See* Ewing,
    Juliana (Horatia Gatty), *16:* 90
Gault, William Campbell, *8:* 69
Gaver, Becky. *See* Gaver,
    Rebecca, *20:* 60
Gaver, Rebecca, *20:* 60
Gay, Kathlyn, *9:* 74
Gay, Zhenya, *19:* 134
Geis, Darlene, *7:* 101
Geisel, Theodor Seuss, *1:* 104
Geldart, William, *15:* 121
Gelinas, Paul J., *10:* 49
Gelman, Steve, *3:* 75
Gemming, Elizabeth, *11:* 104
Gentleman, David, *7:* 102
George, Jean Craighead, *2:* 112
George, John L(othar), *2:* 114
George, S(idney) C(harles), *11:* 104
Georgiou, Constantine, *7:* 102
Gergely, Tibor, *20:* 61 (Obituary)
Gessner, Lynne, *16:* 119
Gibbs, Alonzo (Lawrence), *5:* 74
Gibson, Josephine. *See* Joslin,
    Sesyle, *2:* 158
Gidal, Sonia, *2:* 115
Gidal, Tim N(ahum), *2:* 116
Giegling, John A(llan), *17:* 75
Gilbert, (Agnes) Joan (Sewell),
    10: 50
Gilbert, Nan. *See* Gilbertson,
    Mildred, *2:* 116

Gilbert, Sara (Dulaney), *11:* 105
Gilbertson, Mildred Geiger, *2:* 116
Gilbreath, Alice (Thompson), *12:* 87
Gilbreth, Frank B., Jr., *2:* 117
Gilfond, Henry, *2:* 118
Gill, Derek L(ewis) T(heodore),
    9: 75
Gillett, Mary, *7:* 103
Gillette, Henry Sampson, *14:* 71
Gilman, Dorothy. *See* Dorothy
    Gilman Butters, *5:* 39
Gilman, Esther, *15:* 123
Gilson, Barbara. *See* Gilson,
    Charles James Louis,
    YABC 2: 124
Gilson, Charles James Louis,
    YABC 2: 124
Ginsburg, Mirra, *6:* 86
Giovanopoulos, Paul, *7:* 104
Gipson, Frederick B., *2:* 118
Gittings, Jo Manton, *3:* 76
Gittings, Robert, *6:* 88
Gladstone, Gary, *12:* 88
Glaser, Milton, *11:* 106
Glaspell, Susan, *YABC 2:* 125
Glauber, Uta (Heil), *17:* 75
Glazer, Tom, *9:* 76
Glick, Carl (Cannon), *14:* 72
Gliewe, Unada, *3:* 77
Glines, Carroll V(ane), Jr., *19:* 137
Glovach, Linda, *7:* 105
Glubok, Shirley, *6:* 89
Glynne-Jones, William, *11:* 107
Godden, Rumer, *3:* 79
Gode, Alexander. *See* Gode von
    Aesch, Alexander (Gottfried
    Friedrich), *14:* 74
Gode von Aesch, Alexander
    (Gottfried Friedrich), *14:* 74
Goettel, Elinor, *12:* 89
Goffstein, M(arilyn) B(rooke), *8:* 70
Golann, Cecil Paige, *11:* 109
Golbin, Andrée, *15:* 124
Gold, Phyllis, *21:* 50
Gold, Sharlya, *9:* 77
Goldfeder, Cheryl. *See* Pahz,
    Cheryl Suzanne, *11:* 189
Goldfeder, Jim. *See* Pahz, James
    Alon, *11:* 190
Goldfrank, Helen Colodny, *6:* 89
Goldin, Augusta, *13:* 72
Goldsborough, June, *19:* 138
Goldston, Robert (Conroy), *6:* 90
Goodall, John S(trickland), *4:* 92
Goode, Diane, *15:* 125
Goodman, Elaine, *9:* 78
Goodman, Walter, *9:* 78
Goodwin, Hal. *See* Goodwin,
    Harold Leland, *13:* 73
Goodwin, Harold Leland, *13:* 73
Goossen, Agnes. *See* Epp,
    Margaret A(gnes), *20:* 38
Gordon, Colonel H. R. *See* Ellis,
    Edward S(ylvester),
    YABC 1: 116
Gordon, Dorothy, *20:* 61

Hirsh, Marilyn, 7: 126
Hiser, Iona Seibert, 4: 118
Hitte, Kathryn, 16: 158
Hitz, Demi, 11: 134
Ho, Minfong, 15: 131
Hoban, Russell C(onwell), 1: 113
Hobart, Lois, 7: 127
Hoberman, Mary Ann, 5: 82
Hochschild, Arlie Russell, 11: 135
Hodge, P(aul) W(illiam), 12: 99
Hodges, C(yril) Walter, 2: 138
Hodges, Carl G., 10: 56
Hodges, Elizabeth Jamison, 1: 114
Hodges, Margaret Moore, 1: 116
Hoexter, Corinne K., 6: 115
Hoff, Carol, 11: 136
Hoff, Syd(ney), 9: 106
Hoffman, Phyllis M., 4: 120
Hoffman, Rosekrans, 15: 133
Hoffmann, Felix, 9: 108
Hofsinde, Robert, 21: 69
Hogan, Inez, 2: 140
Hogan, Bernice Harris, 12: 99
Hogarth, Jr. See Kent, Rockwell, 6: 128
Hogg, Garry, 2: 142
Hogner, Dorothy Childs, 4: 121
Hogrogian, Nonny, 7: 128
Hoke, Helen (L.), 15: 133
Hoke, John, 7: 129
Holbeach, Henry. See Rands, William Brighty, 17: 156
Holberg, Ruth Langland, 1: 117
Holbrook, Peter. See Glick, Carl (Cannon), 14: 72
Holbrook, Stewart Hall, 2: 143
Holding, James, 3: 85
Holisher, Desider, 6: 115
Holl, Adelaide (Hinkle), 8: 84
Holland, Isabelle, 8: 86
Holland, Janice, 18: 117
Holland, John L(ewis), 20: 87
Holland, Marion, 6: 116
Hollander, John, 13: 99
Holliday, Joe. See Holliday, Joseph, 11: 137
Holliday, Joseph, 11: 137
Holling, Holling C(lancy), 15: 135
Holm, (Else) Anne (Lise), 1: 118
Holman, Felice, 7: 131
Holmes, Rick. See Hardwick, Richard Holmes Jr., 12: 94
Holmquist, Eve, 11: 138
Holt, Margaret, 4: 122
Holt, Michael (Paul), 13: 100
Holt, Stephen. See Thompson, Harlan H., 10: 177
Holt, Victoria. See Hibbert, Eleanor, 2: 134
Holton, Leonard. See Wibberley, Leonard, 2: 271
Holz, Loretta (Marie), 17: 81
Homze, Alma C., 17: 82
Honig, Donald, 18: 119
Honness, Elizabeth H., 2: 145
Hood, Joseph F., 4: 123

Hood, Robert E., 21: 70
Hooker, Ruth, 21: 71
Hooks, William H(arris), 16: 159
Hoopes, Ned E(dward), 21: 73
Hoopes, Roy, 11: 140
Hoover, Helen (Drusilla Blackburn), 12: 100
Hope, Laura Lee [Collective pseudonym], 1: 119
Hope Simpson, Jacynth, 12: 102
Hopf, Alice L(ightner) 5: 82
Hopkins, Joseph G(erard) E(dward), 11: 141
Hopkins, Lee Bennett, 3: 85
Hopkins, Lyman. See Folsom, Franklin, 5: 67
Hopkins, Marjorie, 9: 110
Horgan, Paul, 13: 102
Hornblow, Arthur, (Jr.), 15: 138
Hornblow, Leonora (Schinasi), 18: 120
Horner, Dave, 12: 104
Hornos, Axel, 20: 88
Horvath, Betty, 4: 125
Horwich, Frances R(appaport), 11: 142
Hosford, Jessie, 5: 83
Hoskyns-Abrahall, Clare, 13: 105
Hough, (Helen) Charlotte, 9: 110
Hough, Richard (Alexander), 17: 83
Houghton, Eric, 7: 132
Houlehen, Robert J., 18: 121
Household, Geoffrey (Edward West), 14: 81
Houston, James A(rchibald), 13: 106
Howard, Prosper. See Hamilton, Charles Harold St. John, 13: 77
Howard, Robert West, 5: 85
Howarth, David, 6: 117
Howell, Pat, 15: 139
Howell, S. See Styles, Frank Showell, 10: 167
Howell, Virginia Tier. See Ellison, Virginia Howell, 4: 74
Howes, Barbara, 5: 87
Hoyle, Geoffrey, 18: 121
Hoyt, Olga (Gruhzit), 16: 161
Hubbell, Patricia, 8: 86
Hudson, Jeffrey. See Crichton, (J.) Michael, 9: 44
Huffaker, Sandy, 10: 56
Hughes, Langston, 4: 125
Hughes, Monica, 15: 140
Hughes, Richard (Arthur Warren), 8: 87
Hughes, Shirley, 16: 162
Hull, Eleanor (Means), 21: 74
Hull, Eric Traviss. See Harnan, Terry, 12: 94
Hull, H. Braxton. See Jacobs, Helen Hull, 12: 112
Hülsmann, Eva, 16: 165
Hults, Dorothy Niebrugge, 6: 117
Hume, Lotta Carswell, 7: 133
Humphrey, Henry (III), 16: 167

Hungerford, Pixie. See Brinsmead, H(esba) F(ay), 18: 36
Hunt, Francis. See Stratemeyer, Edward L., 1: 208
Hunt, Irene, 2: 146
Hunt, Mabel Leigh, 1: 120
Hunter, Dawe. See Downie, Mary Alice, 13: 32
Hunter, Hilda, 7: 135
Hunter, Kristin (Eggleston), 12: 105
Hunter, Mollie. See McIllwraith, Maureen, 2: 193
Hunter Blair, Pauline, 3: 87
Huntington, Harriet E(lizabeth), 1: 121
Huntsberry, William E(mery), 5: 87
Hurd, Clement, 2: 147
Hurd, Edith Thacher, 2: 150
Hurwitz, Johanna, 20: 88
Hurwood, Bernhardt J., 12: 107
Hutchins, Carleen Maley, 9: 112
Hutchins, Pat, 15: 141
Hutchins, Ross E(lliott), 4: 127
Hutchmacher, J. Joseph, 5: 88
Hutto, Nelson (Allen), 20: 90
Hutton, Warwick, 20: 90
Hyde, Dayton O(gden), 9: 113
Hyde, Hawk. See Hyde, Dayton O(gden), 9: 113
Hyde, Margaret Oldroyd, 1: 122
Hyde, Wayne F., 7: 135
Hylander, Clarence J., 7: 137
Hyman, Robin P(hilip), 12: 108
Hyman, Trina Schart, 7: 137
Hymes, Lucia M., 7: 139
Hyndman, Jane Andrews, 1: 122
Hyndman, Robert Utley, 18: 123

Iannone, Jeanne, 7: 139
Ibbotson, Eva, 13: 108
Ibbotson, M. C(hristine), 5: 89
Ilsley, Velma (Elizabeth), 12: 109
Ingham, Colonel Frederic. See Hale, Edward Everett, 16: 143
Ingraham, Leonard W(illiam), 4: 129
Ingrams, Doreen, 20: 92
Inyart, Gene, 6: 119
Ionesco, Eugene, 7: 140
Ipcar, Dahlov (Zorach), 1: 125
Irvin, Fred, 15: 143
Irving, Robert. See Adler, Irving, 1: 2
Irving, Washington, YABC 2: 164
Irwin, Constance Frick, 6: 119
Irwin, Keith Gordon, 11: 143
Isaac, Joanne, 21: 75
Isham, Charlotte H(ickox), 21: 76
Ish-Kishor, Judith, 11: 144
Ish-Kishor, Sulamith, 17: 84
Israel, Elaine, 12: 110
Iwamatsu, Jun Atsushi, 14: 83

Jackson, C. Paul, 6: 120

Landau, Elaine, *10:* 75
Landeck, Beatrice, *15:* 175
Landin, Les(lie), *2:* 171
Landshoff, Ursula, *13:* 124
Lane, Carolyn, *10:* 76
Lane, John, *15:* 175
Lanes, Selma G., *3:* 96
Lang, Andrew, *16:* 178
Lange, John. *See* Crichton, (J.)
    Michael, *9:*
Lange, Suzanne, *5:* 103
Langner, Nola, *8:* 110
Langstaff, John, *6:* 135
Langstaff, Launcelot. *See* Irving,
    Washington, *YABC 2:* 164
Langton, Jane, *3:* 97
Lanier, Sidney, *18:* 176
Larrick, Nancy G., *4:* 141
Larsen, Egon, *14:* 115
Larson, Eve. *See* St. John, Wylly
    Folk, *10:* 132
Larson, William H., *10:* 77
Lasell, Elinor H., *19:* 178
Lasell, Fen H. *See* Lasell, Elinor
    H., *19:* 178
Lasher, Faith B., *12:* 129
Lasker, Joe, *9:* 131
Lasky, Kathryn, *13:* 124
Lassalle, C. E. *See* Ellis, Edward
    S(ylvester), *YABC 1:* 116
Latham, Barbara, *16:* 187
Latham, Frank B., *6:* 137
Latham, Jean Lee, *2:* 171
Latham, Mavis. *See* Clark, Mavis
    Thorpe, *8:* 27
Latham, Philip. *See* Richardson,
    Robert S(hirley), *8:* 164
Lathrop, Dorothy P(ulis), *14:* 116
Lattimore, Eleanor Frances, *7:* 155
Lauber, Patricia (Grace), *1:* 138
Laugesen, Mary E(akin), *5:* 104
Laughbaum, Steve, *12:* 131
Laughlin, Florence, *3:* 98
Laurence, Ester Hauser, *7:* 156
Lauritzen, Jonreed, *13:* 125
Lavine, Sigmund A., *3:* 100
Lawrence, Louise de Kiriline,
    13: 126
Lawrence, Mildred, *3:* 101
Lawson, Don(ald Elmer), *9:* 132
Lawson, Robert, *YABC 2:* 222
Laycock, George (Edwin) *5:* 105
Lazarevich, Mila, *17:* 118
Lazarus, Keo Felker, *21:* 94
Lea, Alec, *19:* 179
Lea, Richard. *See* Lea, Alec,
    19: 179
Leacroft, Helen, *6:* 139
Leacroft, Richard, *6:* 139
Leaf, (Wilbur) Munro, *20:* 99
Lear, Edward, *18:* 182
LeCain, Errol, *6:* 141
Lee, Carol. *See* Fletcher, Helen
    Jill, *13:* 36
Lee, Dennis (Beynon), *14:* 120
Lee, (Nelle) Harper, *11:* 154

Lee, Mary Price, *8:* 111
Lee, Mildred, *6:* 142
Lee, Robert C., *20:* 104
Lee, Robert J., *10:* 77
Lee, Tanith, *8:* 112
Lefler, Irene (Whitney), *12:* 131
Le Gallienne, Eva, *9:* 133
LeGrand. *See* Henderson,
    LeGrand, *9:* 104
Le Guin, Ursula K(roeber), *4:* 142
Legum, Colin, *10:* 78
Lehr, Delores, *10:* 79
Leichman, Seymour, *5:* 106
Leighton, Margaret, *1:* 140
Leipold, L. Edmond, *16:* 189
Leisk, David Johnson, *1:* 141
Leitch, Patricia, *11:* 155
Lenard, Alexander, *21:* 95
    (Obituary)
L'Engle, Madeleine, *1:* 141
Lengyel, Emil, *3:* 102
Lens, Sidney, *13:* 127
Lenski, Lois, *1:* 142
Lent, Blair, *2:* 172
Lent, Henry Bolles, *17:* 119
Leodhas, Sorche Nic. *See* Alger,
    Leclaire (Gowans), *15:* 1
Leong Gor Yun. *See* Ellison,
    Virginia Howell, *4:* 74
Lerner, Marguerite Rush, *11:* 156
Lerner, Sharon (Ruth), *11:* 157
LeShan, Eda J(oan), *21:* 95
LeSieg, Theo. *See* Geisel, Theodor
    Seuss, *1:* 104
Leslie, Robert Franklin, *7:* 158
Lester, Julius B., *12:* 132
Le Sueur, Meridel, *6:* 143
Levin, Betty, *19:* 179
Levin, Marcia Obrasky, *13:* 128
Levin, Meyer, *21:* 96
Levine, I(srael) E., *12:* 134
Levine, Joan Goldman, *11:* 157
Levine, Rhoda, *14:* 122
Levitin, Sonia, *4:* 144
Lewin, Ted, *21:* 98
Lewis, C(live) S(taples), *13:* 129
Lewis, Claudia (Louise), *5:* 107
Lewis, E. M., *20:* 105
Lewis, Elizabeth Foreman,
    YABC 2: 243
Lewis, Francine. *See* Wells, Helen,
    2: 266
Lewis, Hilda (Winifred), *20:* 105
    (Obituary)
Lewis, Lucia Z. *See* Anderson,
    Lucia (Lewis), *10:* 4
Lewis, Richard, *3:* 104
Lewiton, Mina, *2:* 174
Lexau, Joan M., *1:* 144
Ley, Willy, *2:* 175
Leydon, Rita (Flodén), *21:* 100
Libby, Bill. *See* Libby, William M.,
    5: 109
Libby, William M., *5:* 109
Liberty, Gene, *3:* 106
Liebers, Arthur, *12:* 134

Lietz, Gerald S., *11:* 159
Lifton, Betty Jean, *6:* 143
Lightner, A. M. *See* Hopf, Alice L.
    5: 82
Limburg, Peter R(ichard), *13:* 147
Lincoln, C(harles) Eric, *5:* 111
Linde, Gunnel, *5:* 112
Lindgren, Astrid, *2:* 177
Lindop, Edmund, *5:* 113
Lindquist, Jennie Dorothea, *13:* 148
Lindquist, Willis, *20:* 105
Lingard, Joan, *8:* 113
Lionni, Leo, *8:* 114
Lipkind, William, *15:* 178
Lipman, David, *21:* 101
Lipman, Matthew, *14:* 122
Lippincott, Joseph Wharton,
    17: 120
Lipsyte, Robert, *5:* 114
Lisle, Seward D. *See* Ellis, Edward
    S(ylvester), *YABC 1:* 116
Liss, Howard, *4:* 145
List, Ilka Katherine, *6:* 145
Liston, Robert A., *5:* 114
Litchfield, Ada B(assett), *5:* 115
Little, (Flora) Jean, *2:* 178
Littledale, Freya (Lota), *2:* 179
Lively, Penelope, *7:* 159
Liversidge, (Henry) Douglas, *8:* 116
Livingston, Myra Cohn, *5:* 116
Livingston, Richard R(oland),
    8: 118
Llerena-Aguirre, Carlos Antonio,
    19: 180
Llewellyn Lloyd, Richard Dafydd
    Vyvyan, *11:* 160
Llewellyn, Richard. *See* Llewellyn
    Lloyd, Richard Dafydd
    Vyvyan, *11:* 160
Llewellyn, T. Harcourt. *See*
    Hamilton, Charles Harold St.
    John, *13:* 77
Lloyd, (Mary) Norris, *10:* 79
Lobel, Anita, *6:* 146
Lobel, Arnold, *6:* 147
Lobsenz, Amelia, *12:* 135
Lobsenz, Norman M., *6:* 148
Lochlons, Colin. *See* Jackson, C.
    Paul, *6:* 120
Locke, Clinton W. [Collective
    pseudonym], *1:* 145
Locke, Lucie, *10:* 81
Loeb, Robert H., Jr., *21:* 102
Loescher, Ann Dull, *20:* 107
Loescher, Gil(burt Damian),
    20: 107
Löfgren, Ulf, *3:* 106
Loeper, John J(oseph), *10:* 81
Lofting, Hugh, *15:* 180
Lofts, Norah (Robinson), *8:* 119
Lomas, Steve. *See* Brennan,
    Joseph L., *6:* 33
Lomask, Milton, *20:* 109
London, Jack, *18:* 195
London, Jane. *See* Geis, Darlene,
    7: 101

Martin, J(ohn) P(ercival), *15:* 190

Martin, Jeremy. *See* Levin, Marcia Obransky, *13:* 128

Martin, Lynne, *21:* 109

Martin, Marcia. *See* Levin, Marcia Obransky, *13:* 128

Martin, Nancy. *See* Salmon, Annie Elizabeth, *13:* 188

Martin, Patricia Miles, *1:* 146

Martin, Peter. *See* Chaundler, Christine, *1:* 56

Martin, Rene, *20:* 123 (Obituary)

Martin, Vicky. *See* Storey, Victoria Carolyn, *16:* 248

Martineau, Harriet, *YABC 2:* 247

Martini, Teri, *3:* 116

Marzani, Carl (Aldo), *12:* 140

Masefield, John, *19:* 204

Mason, F. van Wyck, *3:* 117

Mason, Frank W. *See* Mason, F. van Wyck, *3:* 117

Mason, George Frederick, *14:* 138

Mason, Miriam E(vangeline), *2:* 183

Mason, Tally. *See* Derleth, August (William), *5:* 54

Mason, Van Wyck. *See* Mason, F. van Wyck, *3:* 117

Masselman, George, *19:* 214

Massie, Diane Redfield, *16:* 193

Masters, Kelly R., *3:* 118

Masters, William. *See* Cousins, Margaret, *2:* 79

Mathis, Sharon Bell, *7:* 162

Matson, Emerson N(els), *12:* 141

Matsui, Tadashi, *8:* 126

Matsuno, Masako, *6:* 161

Matus, Greta, *12:* 142

Maves, Mary Carolyn, *10:* 88

Maves, Paul B(enjamin), *10:* 88

Mawicke, Tran, *15:* 190

Maxon, Anne. *See* Best, Allena Champlin, *2:* 25

Maxwell, Arthur S., *11:* 173

Maxwell, Edith, *7:* 164

May, Charles Paul, *4:* 151

May, Julian, *11:* 175

Mayberry, Florence V(irginia Wilson), *10:* 89

Mayer, Ann M(argaret), *14:* 140

Mayer, Mercer, *16:* 195

Mayne, William, *6:* 162

Mays, (Lewis) Victor, (Jr.), *5:* 126

Mazza, Adriana, *19:* 215

McCaffrey, Anne, *8:* 127

McCain, Murray, *7:* 165

McCall, Edith S., *6:* 163

McCall, Virginia Nielsen, *13:* 151

McCallum, Phyllis, *10:* 90

McCarthy, Agnes, *4:* 152

McCarty, Rega Kramer, *10:* 91

McCaslin, Nellie, *12:* 143

McClintock, Marshall, *3:* 119

McClintock, Mike. *See* McClintock, Marshall, *3:* 119

McClintock, Theodore, *14:* 140

McClinton, Leon, *11:* 178

McCloskey, Robert, *2:* 185

McClung, Robert M., *2:* 188

McCord, David (Thompson Watson), *18:* 217

McCormick, Dell J., *19:* 216

McCormick, (George) Donald (King), *14:* 141

McCoy, Iola Fuller, *3:* 120

McCoy, J(oseph) J(erome), *8:* 127

McCrady, Lady, *16:* 197

McCrea, James, *3:* 121

McCrea, Ruth, *3:* 121

McCullough, Frances Monson, *8:* 129

McCully, Emily Arnold, *5:* 128

McCurdy, Michael, *13:* 153

McDearmon, Kay, *20:* 123

McDermott, Beverly Brodsky, *11:* 179

McDermott, Gerald, *16:* 199

McDole, Carol. *See* Farley, Carol, *4:* 81

McDonald, Gerald D., *3:* 123

McDonald, Jill (Masefield), *13:* 154

McDonald, Lucile Saunders, *10:* 92

McDonnell, Lois Eddy, *10:* 94

McFall, Christie, *12:* 144

McFarland, Kenton D(ean), *11:* 180

McGaw, Jessie Brewer, *10:* 95

McGee, Barbara, *6:* 165

McGiffin, (Lewis) Lee (Shaffer), *1:* 148

McGinley, Phyllis, *2:* 190

McGovern, Ann, *8:* 130

McGowen, Thomas E., *2:* 192

McGowen, Tom. *See* McGowen, Thomas, *2:* 192

McGrady, Mike, *6:* 166

McGraw, Eloise Jarvis, *1:* 149

McGraw, William Corbin, *3:* 124

McGregor, Craig, *8:* 131

McGuire, Edna, *13:* 155

McHargue, Georgess, *4:* 152

McIlwraith, Maureen, *2:* 193

McKay, Robert W., *15:* 192

McKown, Robin, *6:* 166

McLean, Kathryn (Anderson), *9:* 140

McMeekin, Clark. *See* McMeekin, Isable McLennan, *3:* 126

McMeekin, Clark. *See* McMeekin, Isabel McLennan, *3:* 126

McMeekin, Isabel McLennan, *3:* 126

McMullen, Catherine. *See* Cookson, Catherine (McMullen), *9:* 42

McMurtrey, Martin A(loysius), *21:* 110

McNair, Kate, *3:* 127

McNeer, May, *1:* 150

McNeill, Janet, *1:* 151

McNulty, Faith, *12:* 144

McPherson, James M., *16:* 202

McQueen, Mildred Hark, *12:* 145

Mead, Margaret, *20:* 123 (Obituary)

Mead, Russell (M., Jr.), *10:* 96

Meade, Ellen (Roddick), *5:* 130

Meader, Stephen W(arren), *1:* 153

Meadowcroft, Enid LaMonte. *See* Wright, Enid Meadowcroft, *3:* 267

Meaker, M. J. *See* Meaker, Marijane, *20:* 124

Meaker, Marijane, *20:* 124

Means, Florence Crannell, *1:* 154

Medary, Marjorie, *14:* 143

Medearis, Mary, *5:* 130

Mee, Charles L., Jr., *8:* 132

Meeker, Oden, *14:* 144

Meeks, Esther MacBain, *1:* 155

Mehdevi, Alexander, *7:* 166

Mehdevi, Anne (Marie) Sinclair, *8:* 132

Meigs, Cornelia Lynde, *6:* 167

Melcher, Marguerite Fellows, *10:* 96

Melin, Grace Hathaway, *10:* 96

Mellersh, H(arold) E(dward) L(eslie), *10:* 97

Meltzer, Milton, *1:* 156

Melville, Anne. *See* Potter, Margaret (Newman), *21:* 119

Melwood, Mary. *See* Lewis, E. M., *20:* 105

Melzack, Ronald, *5:* 130

Memling, Carl, *6:* 169

Mendel, Jo. [House pseudonym]. *See* Bond, Gladys Baker, *14:* 41

Meng, Heinz (Karl), *13:* 157

Mercer, Charles (Edward), *16:* 203

Meredith, David William. *See* Miers, Earl Schenck, *1:* 160

Merriam, Eve, *3:* 128

Merrill, Jean (Fairbanks), *1:* 158

Metcalf, Suzanne. *See* Baum, L(yman) Frank, *18:* 7

Meyer, Carolyn, *9:* 140

Meyer, Edith Patterson, *5:* 131

Meyer, F(ranklyn) E(dward), *9:* 142

Meyer, Jean Shepherd, *11:* 181

Meyer, Jerome Sydney, *3:* 129

Meyer, June. *See* Jordan, June, *4:* 131

Meyer, Louis A(lbert), *12:* 147

Meyer, Renate, *6:* 170

Meyers, Susan, *19:* 216

Meynier, Yvonne (Pollet), *14:* 146

Micklish, Rita, *12:* 147

Miers, Earl Schenck, *1:* 160

Miklowitz, Gloria D., *4:* 154

Mikolaycak, Charles, *9:* 143

Miles, Betty, *8:* 132

Miles, Miska. *See* Martin, Patricia Miles, *1:* 146

Milhous, Katherine, *15:* 192

Militant. *See* Sandburg, Carl (August), *8:* 177

Millar, Barbara F., *12:* 149

Miller, Albert G(riffith), *12:* 150

Miller, Don, *15:* 194

Author Index

Author Index

Watkins-Pitchford, D. J., *6:* 214
Watson, Clyde, *5:* 196
Watson, James, *10:* 192
Watson, Jane Werner, *3:* 244
Watson, Pauline, *14:* 235
Watson, Sally, *3:* 245
Watson, Wendy (McLeod), *5:* 198
Watt, Thomas, *4:* 226
Watts, Bernadette, *4:* 226
Watts, Franklin (Mowry), *21:* 196
   (Obituary)
Watts, Mabel Pizzey, *11:* 227
Waugh, Dorothy, *11:* 228
Wayland, Patrick. *See* O'Connor,
   Richard, *21:* 111
Wayne, Kyra Petrovskaya, *8:* 213
Wayne, Richard. *See* Decker,
   Duane, *5:* 53
Waystaff, Simon. *See* Swift,
   Jonathan, *19:* 244
Weales, Gerald (Clifford), *11:* 229
Weaver, Ward. *See* Mason, F. van
   Wyck, *3:* 117
Webb, Christopher. *See* Wibberley,
   Leonard, *2:* 271
Webber, Irma E(leanor Schmidt),
   14: 237
Weber, Alfons, *8:* 215
Weber, Lenora Mattingly, *2:* 260
Weber, William John, *14:* 239
Webster, Alice (Jane Chandler),
   17: 241
Webster, David, *11:* 230
Webster, Frank V. [Collective
   pseudonym], *1:* 222
Webster, James, *17:* 242
Webster, Jean. *See* Webster, Alice
   (Jane Chandler), *17:* 241
Wechsler, Herman, *20:* 189
   (Obituary)
Weddle, Ethel H(arshbarger),
   11: 231
Wegner, Fritz, *20:* 189
Weihs, Erika, *15:* 297
Weik, Mary Hays, *3:* 247
Weil, Ann Yezner, *9:* 197
Weil, Lisl, *7:* 202
Weilerstein, Sadie Rose, *3:* 248
Weiner, Sandra, *14:* 240
Weingarten, Violet, *3:* 250
Weingartner, Charles, *5:* 199
Weir, LaVada, *2:* 261
Weir, Rosemary (Green), *21:* 196
Weisberger, Bernard A(llen),
   21: 198
Weisgard, Leonard (Joseph), *2:* 263
Weiss, Adelle, *18:* 296
Weiss, Harvey, *1:* 222
Weiss, Malcolm E., *3:* 251
Weiss, Miriam. *See* Schlein,
   Miriam, *2:* 222
Weiss, Renee Karol, *5:* 199
Welch, Jean-Louise. *See* Kempton,
   Jean Welch, *10:* 67
Welch, Pauline. *See* Bodenham,
   Hilda Esther, *13:* 16

Welch, Ronald. *See* Felton, Ronald
   Oliver, *3:* 67
Wellman, Manly Wade, *6:* 217
Wellman, Paul I., *3:* 251
Wells, H(erbert) G(eorge), *20:* 190
Wells, Helen, *2:* 266
Wells, J. Wellington. *See* DeCamp,
   L(yon) Sprague, *9:* 49
Wells, Rosemary, *18:* 296
Wels, Byron G(erald), *9:* 197
Welty, S. F. *See* Welty, Susan F.,
   9: 198
Welty, Susan F., *9:* 198
Werner, Jane. *See* Watson, Jane
   Werner, *3:* 244
Werner, K. *See* Casewit, Curtis,
   4: 43
Wersba, Barbara, *1:* 224
Werstein, Irving, *14:* 240
Werth, Kurt, *20:* 213
West, Barbara. *See* Price, Olive,
   8: 157
West, Betty, *11:* 233
West, James. *See* Withers, Carl A.,
   14: 261
West, Jerry. *See* Stratemeyer,
   Edward L., *1:* 208
West, Jerry. *See* Svenson, Andrew
   E., *2:* 238
West, Ward. *See* Borland, Hal,
   5: 22
Westervelt, Virginia (Veeder),
   10: 193
Westheimer, David, *14:* 242
Weston, John (Harrison), *21:* 199
Westwood, Jennifer, *10:* 194
Wexler, Jerome (LeRoy), *14:* 243
Wheatley, Arabelle, *16:* 275
Wheeler, Captain. *See* Ellis,
   Edward S(ylvester),
   YABC 1: 116
Wheeler, Janet D. [Collective
   pseudonym], *1:* 225
Whelan, Elizabeth M(urphy),
   14: 244
Whitcomb, Jon, *10:* 195
White, Anne Terry, *2:* 267
White, Dale. *See* Place, Marian T.,
   3: 160
White, Dori, *10:* 195
White, E(lwyn) B(rooks), *2:* 268
White, Eliza Orne, *YABC 2:* 333
White, Florence M(eiman), *14:* 244
White, Laurence B., Jr., *10:* 196
White, Ramy Allison [Collective
   pseudonym], *1:* 225
White, Robb, *1:* 225
White, T(erence) H(anbury),
   12: 229
White, William, Jr., *16:* 276
Whitehead, Don(ald) F., *4:* 227
Whitehouse, Arch. *See*
   Whitehouse, Arthur George,
   14: 246
Whitehouse, Arthur George,
   14: 246

Whitinger, R. D. *See* Place, Marian
   T., *3:* 160
Whitman, Walt(er), *20:* 215
Whitney, Alex(andra), *14:* 249
Whitney, Phyllis A(yame), *1:* 226
Wibberley, Leonard, *2:* 271
Widdemer, Mabel Cleland, *5:* 200
Widenberg, Siv, *10:* 197
Wier, Ester, *3:* 252
Wiese, Kurt, *3:* 254
Wiesner, Portia. *See* Takakjian,
   Portia, *15:* 273
Wiesner, William, *5:* 200
Wiggin, Kate Douglas (Smith),
   YABC 1: 258
Wilbur, Richard (Purdy), *9:* 200
Wilde, Gunther. *See* Hurwood,
   Bernhardt, J., *12:* 107
Wilder, Laura Ingalls, *15:* 300
Wildsmith, Brian, *16:* 277
Wilkins, Frances, *14:* 249
Wilkinson, Brenda, *14:* 250
Wilkinson, Burke, *4:* 229
Will. *See* Lipkind, William, *15:* 178
Willard, Barbara (Mary), *17:* 243
Willard, Mildred Wilds, *14:* 252
Willey, Robert. *See* Ley, Willy,
   2: 175
Williams, Barbara, *11:* 233
Williams, Beryl. *See* Epstein,
   Beryl, *1:* 85
Williams, Charles. *See* Collier,
   James Lincoln, *8:* 33
Williams, Clyde C., *8:* 216
Williams, Eric (Ernest), *14:* 253
Williams, Frances B. *See* Browin,
   Frances Williams, *5:* 30
Williams, Garth (Montgomery),
   18: 298
Williams, Guy R., *11:* 235
Williams, Hawley. *See* Heyliger,
   William, *YABC 1:* 163
Williams, J. R. *See* Williams,
   Jeanne, *5:* 202
Williams, Jay, *3:* 256
Williams, Jeanne, *5:* 202
Williams, Maureen, *12:* 238
Williams, Michael. *See* St. John,
   Wylly Folk, *10:* 132
Williams, Patrick J. *See*
   Butterworth, W. E., *5:* 40
Williams, Selma R(uth), *14:* 256
Williams, Slim. *See* Williams,
   Clyde C., *8:* 216
Williams, Ursula Moray, *3:* 257
Williamson, Joanne Small, *3:* 259
Wilma, Dana. *See* Faralla, Dana,
   9: 62
Wilson, Beth P(ierre), *8:* 218
Wilson, Carter, *6:* 218
Wilson, Dorothy Clarke, *16:* 283
Wilson, Ellen (Janet Cameron),
   9: 200
Wilson, (Leslie) Granville, *14:* 257
Wilson, Hazel, *3:* 260